PERSONALITIES OF THE COUNCIL OF FLORENCE

and other Essays

by

Joseph Gill, S.J.

(Professor of the Pontifical Oriental Institute, Rome)

BARNES & NOBLE, INC. · NEW YORK

PUBLISHERS · BOOKSELLERS · SINCE 1873

PRINTED IN GREAT BRITAIN

PREFACE

A general history of the Council of Florence was provided by my *The Council of Florence*,[1] which, if I may believe my critics (and I must admit that I am very pleased to do so), was an excellent account, fully documented and well balanced. But one book does not exhaust a subject. A history rests on a foundation of documents which need careful examination and comparison before the author can assess their worth, and his judgement of their value will decide his choice of sources and govern the story he will tell. The actors in the historical drama, even the leading characters, tend to be seen only piecemeal in a lengthy narrative. Others do not occupy the stage long enough to make themselves really known. Yet all were men whose lives helped to shape the destinies of nations and who merit to be studied for their own sakes. Questions raised in debate are spread out over many pages or involve consequences that the documents do not record but which interest the student. They all deserve a closer examination either to trace more concisely a line of argument or to define more exactly the extent of agreement or disagreement between the contending parties.

Each of these topics can form the subject of an interesting essay, and in the course of the last fifteen years or so I have written on many of them. My object in some of those studies was to explore the ground before embarking on the edition of the Greek Acts of the Council of Florence that I published in 1953, and to assess the historical value of that primary source of knowledge by comparing it with other similar documents of the same period. My judgement on that question determined which should be my chief instrument for the general history of the council that I wrote later. Others of the essays had the purpose of bringing into relief certain theological or historical questions that are subjects of controversy to-day. The rest are 'lives' of eight of the chief 'personalities of the Council of Florence', written without much parade of learning, because most of them were first printed in a periodical of a popular, rather than of a highly scholarly, appeal, but neglecting none of the latest findings of scholarship, supplemented by some little research of my own.

[1] Cambridge University Press, 1959: second impression 1961.

These studies, historical and theological, are presented to the reader in this volume. Most of them have appeared in print before. Three of them are new, written for this occasion, but on topics that would sooner or later have called forth an article, since they needed comment or elucidation. Inevitably, since these studies and *The Council of Florence* deal largely with the same facts, there will be a certain amount of repetition between them and the book, but the minimum repetition of events only, not of treatment; or perhaps the history contains in a paragraph or two the conclusions arrived at in a reasoned and documented essay of fifteen or twenty pages (e.g. *The Cost of the Council of Florence*, in O.C.P. XXII (1956), pp. 299–318, provided the conclusions summarized in one and a half pages (pp. 174–6) of the history). A similar kind of repetition will be found between some of the studies, but rarely, because these for the most part deal with separate and distinct subjects.

I wish to express my sincere thanks to the editors of the various periodicals who have so generously given me permission to reproduce articles that they had published—of *The Month* for no. 1; of *Orientalia Christiana Periodica* for nos. 2, 10, 11, 12, 14 and 18; of *Unitas* (English edition) for nos. 3, 4, 5, 6, 7 and 8; of *Studi bizantini e neoellenici* for no. 9; of *The Journal of Ecclesiastical History* for no. 15; of *Byzantinische Zeitschrift* for no. 17; of *The Heythrop Journal* for no. 20; and to the general editor of the volume of essays, *Le Concile et les Conciles* (Chevetogne-Paris, 1960) for no. 19. Nos. 13, 16, 21 and the appendix added to no. 20 are new and appear for the first time here.

Joseph Gill, S.J.

CONTENTS

ABBREVIATIONS

A.C.A.   *Acta camerae apostolicae et civitatum Venetiarum, Ferrariae, Florentiae, Ianuae, de Concilio Florentino,* ed. G. HOFMANN (Romae, 1950)

A.G.   *Quae supersunt actorum graecorum Concilii Florentini,* ed. J. GILL (Romae, 1953)

A.L.   *Andreas de Santacroce, advocatus consistorialis: Acta latina Concilii Florentini,* ed. G. HOFMANN (Romae, 1955)

CECCONI   E. CECCONI, *Studi storici sul Concilio di Firenze,* vol. I (Firenze, 1896)

E.O.   *Échos d'Orient*

E.P.   *Epistolae pontificiae ad Concilium Florentinum spectantes,* 3 vols., ed. G. HOFMANN (Romae, 1940–6)

JORGA   N. Jorga, *Notes et extraits pour servir à l'histoire des Croisades au XVe siècle,* vols. I–III (Paris, 1899–1902)

LAMBROS   S. LAMBROS, Παλαιολόγεια καὶ Πελοποννησιακά, 4 vols. (Athens, 1912–30)

MANSI   *Sacrorum Conciliorum nova et amplissima collectio,* ed. G. D. MANSI

M.C.   *Monumenta Conciliorum generalium saec. XV,* (Vindobonae, 1857–86)

MURATORI   *Raccolta degli storici italiani,* ed. L. A. MURATORI (2nd edit.)

O.C.   *Orientalia Christiana*

O.C.P.   *Orientalia Christiana Periodica*

PETIT, *Docs.*   *Documents relatifs au Concile de Florence.* I: *La question du Purgatoire à Ferrare;* II: *Oeuvres anticonciliaires de Marc d'Éphèse,* ed. L. PETIT, published in one volume from *Patrologia orientalis,* XV, pp. 1–168; XVII, pp. 309–524

P.G.	Migne, *Patrologia graeca*
Phrantzes	G. Phrantzes, *Chronicon*, ed. I. B. Papadopoulos, vol. I (Lipsiae, 1935)
P.L.	Migne, *Patrologia latina*
Raynaldus	*Annales ecclesiasticae*, ed. O. Raynaldus
R.E.B.	*Revue des Études Byzantines*
Schol.	*Oeuvres complètes de Gennade Scholarios*. 8 vols. ed. L. Petit, X. A. Sidéridès, M. Jugie (Paris, 1928–36)
Syr.	S. Syropoulus, *Memoirs*, ed. R. Creyghton under the title *Vera historia unionis non verae*, (Hagae-Comitis, 1660)
Trav.	A. Traversari, *Ambrosii Traversari . . . latinae epistolae* etc. ed. L. Mehus (Firenze, 1759)

CHAPTER ONE

THE COUNCIL OF FLORENCE (1438-9)

A Success That Failed

The Council of Florence is memorable chiefly for the fact that it brought to an end—unfortunately only for a short time—the division that for several centuries had reigned between eastern and western Christendom. Even in the earlier period of Church history relations between the ecclesiastically-superior Old Rome and the politically-superior New Rome (Constantinople) had often been strained. In the latter half of the ninth century there occurred the Photian Schism, which did not indeed last for long, but which was a severe blow to the peace of the Church and was never forgotten. The Cerularean Schism of the middle of the eleventh century was another, but not yet final, shock to ecclesiastical unity. The break between East and West, the Great Schism, drifted into being in the course of the next hundred years or so, due more than anything else to mutual ignorance, contempt and a lack of means of communication—mental more than physical. The crusaders might have knit the two Churches together. In fact they widened the breach, for Constantinople viewed with alarm masses of undisciplined soldiers and hangers-on at large in the neighbourhood and was loth to sacrifice the understanding it had with its immediate enemy, the Turk, for the prospect of a problematical victory of western arms. Besides, the crusading knights had more motives than devotion to the Holy Places. They had, too, territorial ambitions, which did not respect the areas that Constantinople claimed as traditionally its own. Challenged by the emperors and without the help that they believed they could reasonably expect from the eastern Christians, the crusaders spread abroad in the Latin world the idea that Byzantium was both treacherous and hostile. The climax came with the fourth crusade that, instead of attacking the infidel, attacked Constantinople to replace on his throne the deposed emperor, Angelus Comnenus, and when he could not fulfil the conditions previously agreed to, the crusaders captured and cruelly ravaged the city and set up a Latin empire with a Latin emperor (1204).

B

The Latin Empire ended its troubled existence in 1261, and once more a Greek, Michael VIII of Nicaea, sat on the throne. But his empire was not the same as before. The Venetians were in possession of most of the strategic positions for trade. Latins still held large tracts of Greece. Epirus and Trebizond were independent States. Michael for many years to come had always to be prepared to counteract the diplomatic and military moves of the princes of Sicily who, ostensibly defending the claims of the Latin Emperor to recover his eastern throne, coveted the crown for themselves.

Yet in the meantime there was developing a still more serious threat, that ultimately would bring the Christian empire of the East to an end. The Turkish masses in Asia Minor, disunited among themselves, were nevertheless pushing inexorably towards the West. While the Latins held Constantinople (1204–61), the north-western area of Asia Minor, of which Nicaea was the centre, was the chief of the three regions that still remained in Greek hands. Yet by 1331 Nicaea had fallen to the Ottoman Turks, who soon had possession of all the area right up to the Bosphorus. Within thirty years the infidel, invited into Europe in the first place by a Greek Emperor to help him against a more legitimate rival to the throne, had moved his capital from Asia Minor to Adrianople in Thrace and dominated all the territory that, at a little distance, encircled Constantinople. The Greek Emperor became the tribute-paying vassal of the Sultan. The crescent had come to stay where once there had been only the cross.

When the Greek usurper, John Cantacuzenus, realised the criminal folly of his action in bringing the Turk into Europe, he appealed to the pope for western help. But the Latins were slow to appreciate the danger threatening the fringe of Europe (which was Thrace and Constantinople), and, not unnaturally, even slower to evaluate the menace to Central Europe, that the presence of the Turk portended. Besides, western Christendom was itself sadly divided. English and French were at war. The German States and the rulers of Hungary and Austria were for ever at loggerheads. The Italian city-states were always fighting each other, and in particular Venice and Genoa, rivals for predominance in the commerce of the Black Sea and the eastern Mediterranean, could not be brought to combine in a common movement, especially in one that might damage trade. The pope was resident in Avignon and not in Rome, and no longer commanded the same respect from the nations, for he seemed to be too much under the influence of one of them, France.

But he was still the natural head of the West, and the Byzantine emperors addressed their appeals to him. Both requests and answers were influenced by the fact that at the second Council of Lyons in 1274 a Greek delegation, in the name of the Emperor and (so it was said) in that too of the Greek Church, had accepted Latin faith and union of the Churches. The Greeks, therefore, usually held out hopes of that union being finally implemented, but by means of a new general council; the popes usually urged that once the union was accomplished they could more effectively prevail on the Latin princes to combine in a common effort for brethren. So not much was done, because the emperors were powerless to persuade the Greek Church to union on Latin conditions, especially in the mid-fourteenth century when Constantinople was itself the scene of an intense doctrinal conflict; and the popes were unable to unite the Latin West for any unselfish purpose. Crusades on a small scale did take place. One captured Smyrna in 1334. Another released the Greek Emperor, John V, from captivity in Bulgaria. Gregory XI, the only European of that age to measure the Turkish menace accurately, tried in vain to stimulate the necessary action. Urban VI sent ships. The biggest western effort was crushed at Nicopolis (1396), but the Frenchman, Boucicaut, the only leader to respond to the appeal of Boniface IX, was largely instrumental in preserving Constantinople from capture when it was besieged by the Sultan, Bajezid, from 1397-1402. The eastern capital thereafter enjoyed a relative peace for two decades. But it was besieged again in 1422, and the pressure of Turkish power round it was always increasing. It was a question only of time before it would fall to Turkish arms, unless the West would help. That was for the Greeks the only hope—the West—and that still meant the pope.

Meantime, however, the situation in the Latin Church had changed. From 1378 till 1417—really till 1429, but the antipope, Clement VIII, was nearly isolated—there were two or three rival 'popes', and the Western Church was unable to heal its own schism. Unity came at last through a council, the Council of Constance, 1414-1418, and in consequence the Latins began to set an exalted value on general councils and to consider that what had solved their own internal problems of division might solve also the problem of the eastern-western division. There were Greek representatives at Constance who immediately introduced the subject of union to the new Pope, Martin V. He became enthusiastic for it and began a series of negotiations, first for a council to heal the breach between the Churches to be held in Constantinople; then, when he realised that that might be too imprudent, for one in Italy. He had just concluded arrangements for the Greeks to come to Italy when he died (20 February 1431). He had also convoked a general council to meet in Basel. He left the Greeks and the council of Basel as a legacy to his successor, Eugenius IV.

But the Greeks, who had so nearly made the journey to Italy in 1431, did not actually arrive till the beginning of 1438. In the meantime the Council of Basel and Eugenius had quarrelled sadly on a question of principle. The Council, heir to the ideas that had taken root during the Latin schism, was convinced that it was the highest authority in the Church and superior to the pope. Eugenius, defending the traditional teaching of the Church, but becoming more and more isolated as princes and cardinals acceded to the Council, seemed crushed and defeated. Both he and Basel had been negotiating with Constantinople about a council of union. But the Baseler, arrogant with the pride of success, alienated not a few of their more influential supporters and refused to implement the agreement they had solemnly made with the Greeks. Eugenius undertook to fulfil its conditions himself. The Greeks accepted. The Pope thereupon declared the Council of Basel translated to Ferrara, to reopen there on 8 January 1438.

The Greeks arrived in Venice on 8 February and in Ferrara on 4 March. There were the Emperor and his brother, the octogenarian Patriarch, eighteen metropolitans—some of them acting also as procurators of the Patriarchs of Alexandria, Antioch and Jerusalem, various ecclesiastical dignitaries, monks, courtiers, servants, etc., in all to the number of about seven hundred. The combined Council in Ferrara was solemnly inaugurated on 9 April. But the Emperor had stipulated that an interval of four months should elapse before formal doctrinal discussions were begun, as he wanted time to be left for the arrival of the western princes or their representatives, in whom he had set his hopes of getting military aid for his empire. The weeks passed. No western princes arrived. The Latins in the Council became more and more irritated at the delay. The Pope's treasury was fast being emptied trying to pay for the upkeep of the Greeks and for mercenary armies to protect papal territory. In June and July, to satisfy Latin impatience, conversations between ten Latins and as many Greeks were held on the subject of Purgatory, but they ended without any agreement being reached. In July, France officially adopted an attitude of neutrality—which in effect meant independence—as between the Council of Basel, which had resisted the Pope's decision to transfer it elsewhere, and Eugenius; but with a bias in favour of Basel. A few months earlier the German Electors had done the same. With the summer, a pestilence descended on Ferrara and caused great mortality in the city, though none of the Greeks fell victim to it.

By this time the Greeks too were anxious to get on with the Council. Ten months had passed since they had left Constantinople, seven of which they had spent in Ferrara, with nothing worth while to show for them. Idle and bored for lack of employment, sometimes in financial straits owing to the irregularity of the Pope's payments (for he could give them money only when he could borrow it), and always anxious about the safety of their homeland and their kin, most of the Greeks became very restive and desirous of hastening the return home. So there was no difficulty in arranging for the start of the formal discussions of the Council, which began on 8 October and continued in Ferrara till 13 December.

The Greeks had been given the choice of subject and they chose to talk about the legitimacy of the addition of the *Filioque* to the Creed. The original Creed had stated about the relation of the Holy Spirit within the Blessed Trinity, 'who proceeds from the Father'. That was changed in Spain in the seventh century into, 'who proceeds from the Father and the Son'. Rome did not introduce the addition *Filioque* (of the Son) till the beginning of the eleventh century, not that it doubted about the orthodoxy of the doctrine, but that it hesitated about the advisability of altering the traditional form of words. By the time of the Council of Florence the Eastern Church had no doubt whatever both that the doctrine was erroneous and that the act of introducing it into the Creed was illegitimate. It was this second point that was the sole subject of discussion in the public sessions in Ferrara.

Except for one speech of Bessarion which lasted through two sessions, the Greek arguments were exposed by Mark Eugenicus. Their case rested on a regulation of the Council of Ephesus of the year 431: 'To no one is it allowed to recite, write or compose a faith other than that defined by the holy Fathers in Nicaea.' Mark and Bessarion argued that that prohibition was absolute and forbade the change of a word or the addition or subtraction of even a syllable, and that it applied not only to the individual Churches but to the universal Church even when gathered together in a general council—much more so, then, to the Church of Rome, which had countenanced the addition of the *Filioque* without the sanction of any general council and without as much as consultation with the other patriarchates of the universal Church. For the Latins the Dominican, Andrew Chrysoberges, the Friar Minor, Aloysius de Perano, and Cardinal Cesarini were the speakers. At first they tried to show, not very successfully, that the *Filioque*-clause was not really an addition but only a clarification, and they asserted that the Church of Rome had full right to clarify. But their main argument, in the mouth of Cesarini, was that the famous prohibition of Ephesus neither did nor could intend to forbid merely verbal change; it forbade change in the faith of Nicaea, not just in its form; in point of fact, neither the Greek Church nor the Latin in its Liturgy and sacraments used the simple Nicene Creed, but the Nicene Creed as it was modified into the Constantinopolitan-Nicene Creed—indeed not even that, for both Churches had added words to it. But Mark Eugenicus blandly brushed the argument aside, saying that the Nicene and the Constantinopolitan-Nicene Creeds were accepted by the Council of Ephesus as equivalents, and so the prohibition still stood; and no Latin arguments could prevail to make him budge from that position.

So the sessions ceased in Ferrara on 13 December with agreement as far off as ever it was. The Greeks, however, were more miserable than before. Now there was added to their other griefs a sense of frustration and dejection—if they were to stop in Italy till union was achieved, at this rate they would be there for ever. Besides, the Pope was some five months in arrears with his payments. His enemies had captured two papal cities in the neighbourhood of Ferrara. There were rumours of the Council being moved.

The rumours were well founded. Florence had offered to accept responsibility for the upkeep of the Greeks against future repayment by the Pope; it was a healthy city and sufficiently far removed from Milanese mercenaries to be safe. The Council moved to Florence, therefore, in January 1439. With borrowed money Eugenius had paid off what he owed to the Greeks, who for their part had yielded to their Emperor's persuasions to move and to discuss in Florence no longer the question of the addition of the *Filioque* but the doctrine it implied.

There were eight sessions in Florence in the month of March about the Procession of the Holy Spirit. For the Greeks Mark of Ephesus was again the speaker, and for the Latins it was John of Montenero, O.P. Five of the eight sessions were spent largely in bickering over which party had the more accurate text of certain passages of St. Basil and St. Epiphanius. In the sixth, Mark expounded his arguments from Holy Scripture, the Councils and the Fathers to prove that the Holy Spirit proceeds from the Father only. In the seventh and eighth, John of Montenero set forth the Latin arguments drawn from the same general sources. He ended by roundly asserting that the Western Church knows 'but one cause of the Son and the Spirit, the Father. . . . Therefore it believes that there are not two principles or two causes, but one principle and one cause, and condemns those who affirm two principles or two causes'. That was the one gleam of hope that the Greeks got from all the discussions, and even that did not suffice to produce agreement and union immediately.

In fact, at the end of the sessions of March the Greeks were more dejected than ever. Public discussions in both Ferrara and Florence had widened the division between the Churches rather than closed it. They went on interminably. The Latins showed no signs of being exhausted for words; for every word the Greeks uttered they answered a dozen. The Greeks were thoroughly tired of public disputations. They would put up with no more. When the Pope urged them either to accept the Latin arguments and conclusions or to answer them in public session, they twice replied:

> We are having no more public disputations, because disputation produces nothing except irritation. If we say anything, you are never at a loss for an answer and that at great length. Hearing the endless things you say—who can go on

listening and answering for ever? So, do you take counsel to see if there is some other way leading towards union and tell us of it. If there is no such way, we have said as much as we can. What we hold to is the faith our fathers taught us, the faith of the seven councils, and for us that is enough.

With that answer the Latins had to be satisfied. So they did try other methods to discover a ground of agreement. Four or five meetings—there should have been eight—between ten delegates from either side were held to propose and to discuss possible approaches to union, but nothing came of them. Then at the request of the Greeks the Latins produced a carefully and accurately worded exposition, drawn up in the form of an agreed statement, of the theology of the Procession of the Holy Spirit from the Father and the Son. The Greeks amended it in such a way as to make it ambiguous and returned it to the Latins, who demanded explanations of its ambiguities, which the Greeks would not give.

By this time it was near the end of May 1439. The Latins urged the Greeks either to meet them in public session or at least to clarify their statement of trinitarian theology. The answer they got was: 'We do not write or say anything else, except this: "If you accept what we have given you, we will join you in union; if not, we shall go off home".' The Pope was in despair. As a last resort, he asked the Emperor to arrange for him to address the Greeks. On 27 May, therefore, he spoke to Greeks and Latins gathered together, recalling his earlier joy when he had welcomed them who had braved so arduous a journey in the cause of union, his later disappointment as time passed without action, his sadness at the failure to reach unity, and he warmly exhorted them by the charity of God not to let the opportunity be lost of achieving so great a good.

The evident sincerity of his words made a deep impression. The Greeks met together to study the Fathers anew and the pro-union party among them, which by now included all the theologians of merit among the metropolitans except for Mark Eugenicus, urged union. For the Greeks the question had been reduced to the simple demand: 'Were the quotations in favour of the doctrine of the *Filioque* made by the Latins from their own Latin Fathers genuine or spurious?' The reason for this simplification was that Bessarion, Isidore of Kiev and the other unionists were arguing in this fashion. All saints are inspired by the one Holy Spirit and therefore cannot differ about the faith. Greeks say that the Holy Spirit proceeds, bursts forth, issues, from the Father, from the Father through the Son, from both, etc.; Latin saints say that He proceeds from the Father and the Son. So, as the faith of both Greek and Latin saints must be the same, their expressions, though sounding different, must mean the same thing, which is another way of saying that the doctrine of the Latin Church and of the Greek Church is the same in substance though expressed differently. Union, therefore, was not only possible but obligatory. No Greek in Florence would have denied the axiom, which they all accepted, that all saints agree in the faith. All of those in Florence had heard *ad nauseam* quotations from Greek Doctors and Latin Doctors read by Montenero, by Bessarion and by others. The only way, then, of avoiding the conclusion of parity of doctrine, since the Greek codices were open for all the Greeks to read, was to accuse the Latins of falsifying their quotations from the Latin Fathers—and that Mark Eugenicus did. And so great was his prestige, for he was a man of learning and of austere life, that his denial had to be taken seriously. Only when his assertion was shown to be totally gratuitous—he did not attempt to prove it and he knew no Latin—did the majority of the Greeks ignore it and accept the inevitable conclusion of the argument and, with it, the orthodoxy of the Latin faith. But Mark remained obdurate in his opinion, and his steadfastness in what had hitherto been the general Greek view was disconcerting to the less intellectual among the prelates, for they could not rid themselves of the feeling that he was, after all, being more faithful to their ancestral faith than they were. The last steps to complete the agreement about the Procession of the Holy Spirit were taken on 8 June. On 10 June the Patriarch suddenly died.

So by the beginning of June there had been settled the difference between the Churches that in the mind of the Greeks was the most serious, peacefully, fully, freely. Other difficulties remained, about papal privileges, the Eucharist and Purgatory. These also were settled, though knowledge of the details of the process is wanting to us, for lack of authentic documents. On 16 June two of these subjects, the primacy of the pope and the Eucharist, were explained to the Greeks in a public session, and two days later in another public session difficulties that they had raised were answered. The Greeks spent the next two days studying the question of the primacy and late on Sunday evening, 21 June, they agreed to the Latin doctrine except that they made reservations in respect of the convocation of councils and appeals against the judgement of a Patriarch. Eugenius refused to entertain any curtailment of papal rights. Thereupon there was much coming and going between Latins and Greeks and a meeting of delegates in committee. Finally on Friday, 26 June, the Greeks accepted the Latin formula with the addition of a general clause to protect the rights of the patriarchs and with the inclusion of the traditional order of precedence of the five patriarchates. The decree of union, which consisted, after an introduction, of the statements about the Procession of the Holy Spirit, Purgatory, the Eucharist and the primacy as these had been separately presented and agreed upon by both Greeks and Latins, should have been solemnly promulgated on 29 June 1439, the feast of the apostles Peter and Paul, but owing to difficulties that arose about the wording of the decree the Bull was not ready in time. It was signed on 5 July by Pope Eugenius: 'I, Eugenius, bishop of the universal Church, thus defining, subscribe,' eight cardinals, two patriarchs, eight archbishops, fifty-two bishops, four heads of Religious Orders, forty-one abbots and the Archdeacon of Troyes as envoy of the Duke of Burgundy, on the Latin side: on the Greek side by the Emperor John VIII, eighteen metropolitans (three of them also as procurators of the three eastern patriarchs), Gregory the Emperor's confessor as procurator of the Patriarch of Alexandria, the Russian bishop, three procurators of absent bishops, five stauro-phoroi-deacons and six heads or representatives of monasteries. Of the Greek prelates in Italy only Mark Eugenicus, Metropolitan of Ephesus, and Isaias, Metropolitan of Stauropolis, did not sign. On 6 July 1439 the Bull *Laetentur caeli* was jubilantly read out in Latin by Cardinal Cesarini and in Greek by Archbishop Bessarion at the end of the solemn papal Mass in the cathedral of Florence, and acclaimed in both tongues by the Fathers present. The Eastern and the Western Churches were united in one faith and with equality of rite. The schism was ended.

But the Council was not yet over. In 1443 it was translated to the Lateran basilica in Rome and before it ceased to exist (there is no document extant that officially closed it, nor any record of when or how it ended) it had received into union with Rome Armenians of the Black Sea area, Copts of Egypt, Syrians of Mesopotamia, Nestorians of Cyprus. But for the Greeks the Council terminated with the promulgation of the decree of union of 6 July and they soon moved off to Venice to take ship for home, arriving in Constantinople on 1 February 1440, rather more than two years and two months after their departure.

Ducas, the Greek chronicler, described their return in these words:

As the metropolitans disembarked from the ships the citizens, as was customary, saluted them, asking: 'How about our business? How about the synod? Did we manage to prevail?' They answered: 'We have sold our faith; we have exchanged true piety for impiety; we have betrayed the pure sacrifice and become upholders of unleavened bread.' These, and even more disgraceful things, they said. And who were they that said them? The very ones that had signed the decree, Antony of Heraclea and all of them. If anyone asked them: 'Why then did you sign?', they said: 'For fear of the Franks'; and if any demanded further whether the Franks had tortured anyone, scourged anyone, imprisoned anyone, 'No,' they said. 'Well then?' 'This hand has signed,' they repeated, 'off with it. My tongue professed, let it be torn out.' They had nothing else to say, yet some of the metropolitans said in the act of signing: 'We do not sign, unless you provide us with a goodly sum of money.' They gave it: the pen was dipped into the ink. The money expended on them, counted out into the hand of each, was beyond calculation. Later, when they repented, they did not return the money. On their own confession, then, that they had sold their faith, they sinned far more than Judas, for he at any rate restored the pieces of silver.

Ducas wrote his chronicle about the year 1462 in the island of Lesbos, and his description is a gross exaggeration, if not a travesty, of the facts. But it gives, nevertheless, a fair idea of what was later being rumoured in Constantinople about the Council and indicates that a number of prelates who had signed the decree in Italy repudiated their signatures in Constantinople, and it suggests one of the reasons why they did so. There is no evidence whatsoever that the Greek signatures were sold for money. There is indeed positive testimony to the contrary from the pen of Syropoulus, who was one of the most active opponents of the union in Constantinople. But the Greek metropolitans did not come home poor and the malicious drew their own conclusions.

Syropoulus has his own explanation of the signing and the repentance: in Italy the Greeks were miserable, because largely idle for lack of work; reduced by hunger, because the Pope deliberately withheld his payments; browbeaten by the Emperor into submission, because he wanted military help for his capital. Syropoulus's version of the events is widely accepted as true, even to-day. It would take up too much time to make a detailed examination of each of the accusations contained in this assertion, to show that the Greeks were at times idle because they themselves were largely responsible for the long delays, that Eugenius was often late in his payments because his treasury was exhausted paying for the expenses of the Greeks over eighteen months instead of over the three or four that he had expected, and that the Emperor did not check freedom of speech. It must suffice to propose here two general considerations that answer fairly effectively such criticisms of the Council.

First, however, a word must be said about the situation of the Greeks in Italy. It must be admitted that the Greeks did suffer hardship. The Pope was often in arrears in his payments, which must have created difficulties and perhaps caused hunger among the lower ranks of the court, the soldiers and servants (yet these were the responsibility of their immediate masters), and of the clerics. The Council did go on for a much longer time than the Greeks (and the Latins) had expected, and separation from home and from kindred, especially when rumours were current of imminent Turkish attacks, meant nostalgia and mental anguish. Besides, the Greeks did not have the consolation of feeling either that they were attaining the object for which they had undertaken so perilous a journey or that they were showing themselves superior to the Latins, for Montenero and his colleagues had a reply to all their arguments and the Latins answered 'ten thousand words for ten of theirs'. That they suffered, then, psychological, rather than physical, duress can be admitted. But was it so great that it should be said to have deprived them of their free will in a matter which to them was of primary importance—their faith? Two considerations suggest a negative answer.

The history of events recounted above shows that till the end of May 1439, i.e., for fifteen months after their arrival in Ferrara, the Greeks were complete masters of their fate, for they still refused point-blank to take part in any more public disputations or to clarify the profession of faith that they had made. Instead, they bluntly told the Latins that it was for them to find some other way of union, because they (the Greeks) had done all that they intended to do. That attitude does not suggest that they were cowed, oppressed or browbeaten by anyone. It was an attitude of defiance. It is true that shortly afterwards the whole scene changed, and between 27 May and 8 June that most thorny of all subjects, the Procession of the Holy Spirit, was disposed of. Not, however, by illicit means. Fortunately the documents of the Council that are extant recount at length and in detail the stages by which that agreement was reached and they do not tell a tale of force or hardship, but one of conviction on the grounds of patristic arguments. So that, though the Greeks were most anxious to go home as quickly as possible, they refused the easy and sure means of a facile assent to Latin demands for fifteen months and accepted agreement and union only when their own learned theologians put before them arguments they could understand and could not reject.

The other general consideration that tells for freedom on the part of the Greeks is this. There was one, and only one, thorough-going, consistent and most bitter opponent of union from the beginning of the Council in Ferrara till its end for the Greeks in Florence—Mark Eugenicus, the Metropolitan of Ephesus. Yet it was he, elected by the Greeks themselves and confirmed by the Emperor as one of the spokesmen, who in the name of the Greeks spoke during all the debates about Purgatory of June–July 1438 except one, during all the public sessions in Ferrara about the 'addition' except for one speech of Bessarion covering two sessions, and in all without exception of the public sessions in Florence about the *Filioque*-doctrine. If John VIII had been as determined as Syropoulus makes out on achieving unity so as to get help for his country, to such a degree indeed that he suppressed all freedom of speech, surely he would have begun with Mark Eugenicus. In the eyes of his subjects, the Emperor's quasi-sacramental coronation had made him 'defender of the Church' and had given him a certain right to control at least the public exposition of its doctrines and its relations with others. He had at hand other theologians of note, more favourable to union, who could have put the Greek case ably enough. Instead, he did nothing either to remove or to repress Mark during the period of the public sessions or afterwards, and when Mark, seeing union coming, began to fear for his own safety, John promised him immunity and a return to Constantinople in his own royal ship. And he fulfilled his promise.

No. The Greek prelates in Florence were free and freely accepted the doctrine of the *Filioque* and the other doctrines, and freely united with the Latins. To say that they betrayed their faith because of some not very terrible inconveniences is to condemn them as cowards and to cast an aspersion on the whole of the Greek Church of that day whose highest ecclesiastics, except for two, would have to be said to have accepted what to them was heresy, because the alternative was, not martyrdom or even exile, but a rather protracted absence from home. That is a condemnation that is too scathing, and it is not true. The historical sources give a different picture. They portray a group of men of different intellectual capabilities. There was a minority of able theologians, all of whom except one were convinced of the orthodoxy of the Latin faith and the soundness of the union— and not one of these changed his opinion later. The rest, less capable theologians and so more liable to be influenced by circumstances, acclaimed Latin doctrine and union in Florence, when their own theologians produced convincing reasons and the atmosphere of the Council fostered unity, and in Constantinople began to doubt and to repent of their previous action, when the monks and mob assailed them and the atmosphere of the city was hostile to unity. These were not dishonest men. They were men whose sentiment was stronger than their intellects and they were, perhaps, not cast in an heroic mould.

CHAPTER TWO

JOSEPH II, PATRIARCH OF CONSTANTINOPLE

Ambrogio Traversari, in a letter of 20 February 1438, from Venice to Eugenius IV, described the Patriarch in these words: 'Assuredly in my judgement he is very prudent and very alert and, though in a decrepit old age (for he is thought to be almost an octogenarian), he is endowed with an active keenness of intellect and a most lively perception'[1]. He was, therefore, born round about the year 1360, 'a Bulgarian by nationality and of my own tongue', as John of Ragusa wrote to Cardinal Cesarini. Of the other chief events of his life little more is known except that he was Metropolitan of Ephesus before becoming Patriarch of Constantinople on 21 May 1416, and that he died in Florence on 10 June 1439.

The section of the letter of Ragusa from which the above quotation is taken deserves to be quoted at length, because it gives an idea of Joseph's character. 'The Father is old, and, like his age, his grey hair, long beard and face make him a venerable figure to all who see him; so too his common sense, experience in affairs and gravity of manner call forth the admiration of all who are brought into close contact with him and, to tell the truth, I should never have believed that such a Father could be found in Greece in our day. He was ready to resign from the patriarchate because of ill-health. I have been in touch with him, and still am, as much as I can, both personally and by means of others, secretly, because all are agreed that there has never been found in Greece any one like him and who was more favourable to union than he. This Father has, too, profound understanding in the spiritual life and assuredly, when I meet him privately (with, however, as interpreter[2] the monk Bathomius who was at the Council with Isidore) for four or five hours, I cannot bear to leave him. In fact, the question of the division between the Churches apart, I should

---

[1] Trav., No. 30.
[2] This is curious, since Joseph was 'of Ragusa's own tongue'. 'Tongue' presumably means no more than 'race'. Cf. V. Laurent, *Les origines princières du patriarche de Constantinople Joseph II (†1439)* in *R.E.B. XIII* (1955), pp. 131–4.

judge him to be a most complete and perfect old man and almost one of those holy Fathers whose lives we read with so much admiration and devotion'.[3] Traversari was equally attracted by the Patriarch's character: 'I have met the Patriarch and had a long talk with him, and was greatly delighted by his appearance and conversation, because his grey hair, his manner and deportment make him venerable and he is extremely sweet in conversation'.[4]

In this same letter Traversari again refers to the Patriarch's prudence—'from his extremely cautious and prudent words'—a quality of his noted also by the author of the descriptive part of the *Acta graeca*: 'The Patriarch, as was usual with him, spoke with moderation and great circumspection',[5] and hints at a weakness, common (so thinks Traversari) to all Greeks, for external honours: 'I gathered from the many and long familiar conversations which I have had with the Patriarch that my view is not far from the truth, for I have always held that that race is to be won by courtesy and the showing of respect and evidences of particular good will.' But neither Ragusa nor Traversari makes any mention of the Patriarch as a man of learning, even though he brought with him to Italy a codex of the works of St. Basil.[6] It would seem that he was not such, though it must be admitted that positive evidence to that effect is forthcoming only from the opponents of union. Syropoulus notes as exceptional the one occasion when the Patriarch showed an interest in the theological discussion that usually took place when a few of the Greek clerics found themselves together in his apartments,[7] and Scholarius in a letter of 1451 to the Grand Duke Notaras wrote scathingly of his scholarship in these words: '. . . as if "dia" meant, as the late futile Patriarch said, "cause," and having said it without further ado he died. For he had no right to go on living after philosophizing so brilliantly about the preposition and cause, and arrogating to himself pre-eminence in three sciences, namely grammar, philosophy and this quintessence of theology, about which even in his dreams he never hoped to have the courage to make any pronouncement.'[8]

[3] Letter of Ragusa to Card. Cesarini of 9 Feb., 1436, in Cecconi, doc. LXXVIII.
[4] Trav., no. 140.   [5] *A.G.*, p. 419.
[6] Bessarion, *Epistola ad Al. Lascarin de Processione Spiritus Sancti*, in *P.G.* 161, 325b
[7] Syr., p. 258.   [8] Schol. III, p. 142.

Syropoulus, apropos of the incident cited above, suggests that
the Patriarch escaped from the interminable theological bickerings
going on around him by retiring to his bedroom as if he were ill.
Usually at any rate there would be no pretence in that for he was
unquestionably a very sick man. Both the Emperor and the
Patriarch repeatedly alleged his age and infirmity as reasons why
the journey from Constantinople to Europe should be as short as
possible. Ragusa in the letter to Cesarini quoted earlier stated:
'. . . and notwithstanding the heart disease which afflicts him
almost weekly he would be prepared to-day, if things allowed it,
to board ship and come here'. In another letter to Cesarini of 10
March 1436 he narrates how, during a very long service of intercession for the happy issue of the negotiations about union and for
deliverance from the plague that then infested Constantinople, in
which the Emperor, the royal family, the court, and innumerable
clerics and layfolk took part standing all the time, the Patriarch,
because of his age and infirmity, remained seated, and that when
at the end he had prostrated himself in prayer for an hour he had
to be lifted to his feet by four of his clerics to give the final bene-
diction.[9] That a man in such a state would face the dangers and
fatigues of a sea-voyage in winter argues to his great courage and
his intense zeal for union.

Of that voyage the Bishop of Digne, who made it with them,
reported to the Council in Ferrara on 1 March 1438: 'And indeed
in this navigation and throughout the whole journey one reason
was abundantly clear why there was unwillingness to cross the
Tyrrhenian sea towards Avignon, for the Patriarch and the other
aged prelates, and sometimes the Emperor too, neither ate nor
drank nor slept, except in port. So, if there had not been numerous
islands with harbours under the domination of the Venetians or
of the Greeks themselves, assuredly they would not have been
able to reach the port of Venice.'[10] Though he made the journey
from Venice to Ferrara and later from Ferrara to Florence, the
Patriarch was rarely well during his stay in Italy and in consequence was unable to attend the Council on various important
occasions—the session of 9 April 1438 when the solemn proclamation of the opening was made, that of 28 November when the
Burgundian envoys presented their credentials, the session of 10
January 1439 when the Council was transferred. From 10 August

[9] CECCONI, doc. LXXXI.   [10] *Frag.*, p. 60.

C

1438 onwards Syropoulus says that he suffered from a quartan ague.[11] For sixteen days at the end of December 1438 he was too ill to be visited, 'unable to speak or hear',[12] and during January 1439 frequently confined to bed.[13] On Holy Saturday, 4 April 1439, he was so ill that he was thought to be dying and the last rites were administered to him.[14] Thereafter he was almost continuously confined to his room. His death came suddenly on 10 June, about which Syropoulus rather callously wrote: 'A detailed exposition of his long and many illnesses and of how from the journey by horseback from Ferrara to Florence there supervened dropsy, and of the way in which death overtook him, I leave to others who have a keener relish in retailing such things.'[15]

What buoyed him up to face the rigours of the journey was his hope for union and his great desire to meet the Pope. Both he and the Emperor insisted through their letters and embassies to Basel on the presence of the Pope at the future common council, because they were convinced that a council separated from the Pope was incomplete and would prove ineffective. He was very friendly disposed to Garatoni, the papal envoy, and to the Pope, even when the ambassadors of Basel were in Constantinople in 1435[16]; he would not let the interpreter, acting for the envoys of Basel at Constantinople in October 1437, read in his presence the Council's Monitorium against Eugenius[17]; it was the prospect of the Pope's presence at a council that finally made him overcome his repugnance to leaving Constantinople.[18]

He was, however, a little naive in his anticipations. He told his clerics in Constantinople that if the Pope were older than he, he would regard him as his father; if of equal age, as his brother; if younger, as his son; and that he hoped to be lodged so near the Pope that there might be easy mutual access for common counsel.[19] In Venice he scandalized some of the Latins by referring to Eugenius as his brother[20] (though why, it is hard to see, since the Pope in his official letters usually used that term with respect to him), and Traversari delicately prepared the Pope for this and advised a gentle tolerance.[21] Joseph thought that union would be

[11] SYR., p. 186.   [12] A.G., p. 218.
[13] Ibid., pp. 221, 224.   [14] Ibid., p. 403.
[15] SYR., p. 276.   [16] Ibid., p. 22.
[17] Report of the Bishop of Digne at Ferrara; Frag., p. 58.
[18] SYR., p. 41.   [19] Ibid., p. 92.
[20] TRAV., no. 140.   [21] Ibid., no. 30.

a much simpler business than it turned out to be—an affair of friendly arrangement between himself and Eugenius IV: 'He seeks nothing more than to meet Your Holiness, openly asserting that from your physical proximity and mutual speech peace will be brought to the situation'[22]: 'He desires wondrously to meet the Pope, hoping that everything will easily be arranged, if they both come together in charity. . . . I gathered from his extremely cautious and prudent words that in his judgement the whole thing should be concluded by love and peace rather than by discussion, since he said that the whole business lay in this—if both come together in body, mind and opinion; and all this he hopes will occur if there shall first be the meeting in body.'[23]

This conviction that union would prove to be an easy business was founded on his assurance that the Greek Church was right in the questions under dispute and the Latin Church wrong, and that it would need little to persuade the Latins of this. Syropoulus reports him as saying: 'When we go off there with God's help, they will welcome us all with great honour and affection and will take a marvellous care of us and we shall have full freedom and liberty to say whatever we like. And we shall prove, by the grace of Christ, that our doctrine is most pure and resplendent, and as regards the points of dogma ours will show themselves to be their teachers and they will be convinced and will embrace our doctrine, and so we shall be united . . . and even if they do not accept our position, we shall return again famous, having with the grace of God brilliantly proclaimed the true faith and strengthened our own Church and deviated from the truth in no point at all.'[24] Joseph's anticipations of the honours awaiting himself and the Greeks must have been rudely shaken by his reception at Ferrara, when the Pope insisted, though vainly, that the Patriarch conform to Latin custom by kissing his foot; but he did meet the Pope privately and have with him long conversations[25]; the Greeks had indeed full freedom to say whatever they wished, though they did not find the Latins easy to persuade: but exactly two weeks before he died, when he gave his *votum* for the equivalence of 'Dia' and 'Ek' and the truth, therefore, of both the Greek and the Latin doctrines, he could still confidently claim that his faith in his Church was unshaken: 'I will never change or surrender our traditional doctrine, but will abide in it to my last breath'.[26]

[22] Ibid.   [23] Ibid., no. 140.   [24] SYR., p. 60.
[25] Ibid., p. 99; 143.   [26] *A.G.*, p. 438.

When Ragusa wrote describing the Patriarch to Caesarini he always referred to him as 'Father', an unconscious disclosure of the chief impression that the venerable old man had made on him. Syropoulus, on whom unfortunately we have to depend for most of our information about Joseph, makes him out to have been on occasions rather a silly old man, easily beguiled by Garatoni[27] and Ragusa,[28] who was not above trying to persuade some of the Greek bishops[29] and the recalcitrant three of the Staurophoroi[30] to accept union from motives of loyalty to himself. Not everything that Syropoulus wrote should be taken literally, for his *Memoirs* were his defence of himself against the charge of having betrayed his faith and so he lets slip no opportunity of heightening the impression of his own steady resistance to persuasion, guile and force. He inveighs also against the Patriarch for not having insisted on having his Staurophoroi, 'his five senses', located near him in the public sessions,[31] but there was not much that the Patriarch could have done about that, as the arrangement of seats for those occasions was arrived at only after acrimonious dispute between Greeks and Latins, when every inch of distance or height was measured to assure equality of dignity. He further accuses the Patriarch of having been responsible why the superiors of the monasteries were deprived of their votes in the private Greek meetings of the summer of 1439, as being 'unordained'.[32]

If, however, one leaves aside the occasional complaints of Syropoulus against Joseph, the general impression one gets from reading the *Memoirs* is that the Patriarch was a father to his clerics, patient, long-suffering and occasionally, when tried beyond measure by their reiterated complaints, not above passing on the burden to the Emperor. And it must be borne in mind that throughout he was very ill. The truth is that his clerics used his apartments as a kind of club. When they had nothing else to do (and from April to October 1438, from mid-December to March 1439 apart from the journey to Florence, and from April to July of the same year they had abundance of leisure), they drifted to his rooms to talk, discuss, quarrel, complain. Phrases like 'A few days later when we were all sitting about in the Patriarch's lodgings, the question of maintenance came up'[33] or 'On another

[27] Syr., p. 22.
[28] Ibid., p. 44.
[29] Ibid., p. 260.
[30] Ibid., p. 271.
[31] Ibid., p. 108.
[32] Ibid., pp. 263–4.
[33] Ibid., p. 250.

occasion we gathered together at the Patriarch's apartments as usual'[34] are of frequent occurrence in the *Memoirs*. It was apparently the same in Constantinople for the earlier pages as much as the later report incidents of the kind. Joseph regarded himself as a father to them all, and they looked upon him as such. That is why, in spite of his sufferings and illnesses, they carried all their difficulties and complaints to him. For his part, he corrected, sympathised, encouraged and explained as far as he could. He was capable of quick action, as when, learning of the departure for Venice with imperial permission of Heraclea and Ephesus, two of the delegates of the eastern Patriarchates, he wasted no time in representing to the Emperor the necessity of their presence in the Council, despatched with all speed horsemen to reach them before their river-boat cast off, and had them, all unwilling, fetched back.[35] He was equally capable of a tactful biding of his time. Syropoulus with Lacedaimon appealed to him to intervene between Ephesus and Nicaea to patch up a quarrel that was developing (Bessarion had somewhat ostentatiously seated himself apart from Ephesus) and blamed him for doing nothing. But Joseph's way was the wiser. Some little time later when it was arranged that Nicaea and Mark should be the chief speakers of the Greeks, he quietly remarked: 'Nicaea then should sit alongside of Ephesus' and so he settled their quarrel without ever having made an issue out of it.[36]

In all the business of union, Joseph was closely associated with the Emperor, but he took second place. The ambassadors from the West were always furnished with letters and credentials to both. They were first received by the Emperor, then they visited the Patriarch who received them usually with great state. Ragusa and his two companions found him awaiting them in the church of St. Sophia vested in a cope, with burning candles before him and surrounded by a multitude of clerics, so Menger recounted at Basel in February 1436.[37] The report of the Basel envoys of 1438 states: 'As we entered the church several of the Greek cardinals came to meet us and receiving us graciously accompanied and led us to the presence of the lord Patriarch who was seated on a kind of ornate throne in the church, attended by cardinals, archbishops, bishops, priests and monks to the number of about 80 or

---

[34] Ibid., pp. 255, 256.   [35] Ibid., pp. 151–3.
[36] Ibid., pp. 137–9, 150.   [37] *M.C.*, II, p. 843.

100'.[38] The letters that went from Constantinople to the West were in duplicate, the one from the Emperor, the other from the Patriarch, couched in identical terms as far as the business-content was concerned. The Byzantine ambassadors who visited Rome and Basel were accredited by both Emperor and Patriarch and represented both. But the partnership between the head of the State and the head of the Church was not an equal partnership—the Emperor was the dominating figure. Syropoulus asserts that sometimes at any rate it was sorely against his will that Joseph wrote in conformity with the Emperor's views.[39] The envoys of Basel in 1437 noted that the Patriarch seemed to change his attitude towards their proposals on learning his sovereign's opinion.[40]

For his part the Emperor always consulted the Patriarch on ecclesiastical matters and would not act without his consent, even though that consent might on occasion have been rather grudgingly given. The reason may have been in part because he wanted to make sure that, whatever might be the final issue of all the negotiations and discussions, the Church would not in the end disown the results as having had no part in them (and so he very often called in representative clerics to the meetings), partly no doubt because he really did respect the authority of the Church in its own domain, even while he considered himself as in some respects over it. That is how he acted in Constantinople during the preliminary arrangements: such too was his habit in Ferrara and Florence. Examples of this are to be found throughout the *Acta* and the *Memoirs* of Syropoulus. At Venice when both he and the Patriarch were ill he would come to no decision about whether to go Ferrara or not till the Patriarch was well enough to visit him and discuss the matter.[41] At the end of December 1438 both again were ill and so it was not till after the Patriarch had managed to visit him, carried in a litter, that he proposed to the rest of the Greek clerics the necessity of discussing the doctrine of the *Filioque* with the Latins.[42] When Joseph was so frequently ill and unable to leave his apartments, particularly during the few months preceding his death, the Emperor might reasonably have considered himself excused from consulting him always, had he

[38] J. HALLER, *Concilium Basiliense* V (ed. BECKMANN, WACKER-NAGEL, COGGIOLA) (Basel, 1904), p. 316.
[39] SYR., p. 13.   [40] HALLER, V., p. 325.
[41] SYR., pp. 85–6.   [42] *A.G.*, p. 218.

thought it only a matter of courtesy and not of principle. What we find, however, in fact is an almost monotonous repetition of: 'The Emperor summoned the Greeks to a meeting in the apartments of the Patriarch who was ill,' so much so that nearly all the many Greek conferences of April and May 1439 took place there, the conferences where the decisions were taken that the Latin Saints affirming the doctrine of the *Filioque* were to be accepted as much as the Greek Fathers who did not use that phrase and so that there was basic agreement of East and West on the doctrine of the Holy Spirit.[43]

Here and there in the documents there are to be found indications that Joseph resented his imposed subservience to the Emperor. Syropoulus' *Memoirs* open with a fragmentary record of an incident that happened under Manuel, John's father, on the eve of Joseph's election to the patriarchal throne and while that throne was still vacant. It was a question of rights between the crown and the Church. The prelates were unwilling to concede what Manuel claimed, but yielded under pressure and were made to commit their assent to writing.[44] The new Patriarch, so Syropoulus declares, chafed under the restrictions so imposed on the Church and 'thought that by means of the Pope he would free the Church from the slavery imposed on it by the Emperor'.[45] His resentment showed itself when the other oriental patriarchs nominated their proxies for the Council without consulting him, for he thought that it was the Emperor who had in fact proposed the names for their acceptance, and it needed much explanation on John's part to mollify him.[46] Similarly when the Greek convoy was nearing Venice on its way to Italy the Emperor sent on ahead a messenger to acquaint the Doge of his approach: the Patriarch, hearing of this, also despatched his messenger.[47] He took it in very bad part that the Emperor departed from Venice first, leaving him behind for lack of ships, and entered Ferrara first—'Either both Emperor and Patriarch ought to have entered together or the Church have precedence and not follow along behind'.[48] So when the Council was transferred to Florence he urged and obtained that he should be the first to make his entry into that city.[49] He had a little, perhaps mildly spiteful, revenge over the incident of

[43] Ibid., pp. 428, 437.   [44] Syr., pp. 2–3.
[45] Ibid., p. 92.   [46] Ibid., pp. 45–6.
[47] Ibid., p. 80.   [48] Ibid., p. 90.
[49] Ibid., p. 212.

the Emperor's entry to the first full session in Ferrara on 8 October 1438. The Emperor, wishing to follow Byzantine court etiquette, had wanted to ride on horseback up to his throne. The papal attendants would not allow that, so perforce he had to dismount. To preserve his dignity as much as possible he would be carried through certain rooms and so arrive unseen and without (apparently) setting foot to ground till he was seated on his throne. But the Patriarch and his attendants occupied the rooms in question and Joseph flatly refused to leave himself or let his bishops and Staurophoroi leave them, though bidden to do so by several imperial messengers including Demetrius, the Emperor's brother. In the end John was half-carried, half-dragged through the midst of the clerics to the hall.[50]

That Joseph on a few occasions might stand out for his rights against the Emperor only emphasises the fact that the initiative on the Greek side lay throughout with the Emperor. But that does not mean that the Patriarch was in any respect less keen than John on bringing about union even at the cost of the long and fatiguing journey to the West. The Greek ambassadors to the Council of Basel declared (15 May 1435) that he had said that, if there were no other way, he would make the journey carried on men's shoulders.[51] Ragusa and Fréron reported (9 February 1436) that the 'Most Reverend Patriarch, a most devoted and fervent prosecutor of this holy union' was ordering 'fasts, supplications, devotions and other works of piety' for the happy outcome of the project.[52] About a month later Fréron wrote to Cesarini (5 March 1436): ' TheMost Reverend Patriarch also, like the old man Simeon, sighs in his heart from his longing to see peace and union of the two Churches.'[53] Even in the disturbed days of October 1437 when legations from the Pope and from Basel were both in Constantinople, each claiming the right to transport the Greeks to Europe, the Patriarch, though he might then have hesitated at such manifest division in the western Church, still was firm in his resolve to prosecute the work of union—and with the Pope: 'For this reason we (i.e. the papal representatives) went to the Patriarch and remained with him for the space of three hours and then he related to us everything which he had heard from the other (i.e. Baseler) envoys. He ended by asserting that he would

[50] Ibid., pp. 163–4.   [51] HALLER, I, p. 361.
[52] CECCONI, doc. LXXVII.   [53] Ibid., doc. LXXIX.

not depart even a fingernail's breadth from the agreement made with our lord the Pope, and that, even if France and Spain and Germany were to go together to Avignon, neither he nor the Emperor would go there. But he said: "Harmony is a good thing, and you others must strive, and I and the Emperor will strive, for the union of all to the very limit of our power".'[54]

When they left Constantinople, Emperor and Patriarch did not yet know where the Pope intended to hold his council: that it was to be in Ferrara they learnt shortly before their arrival in Venice. For a time they still hesitated whether to choose Ferrara or Basel. Ill-health which prevented mutual consultation and letters from Basel made them defer a decision for a time and, meanwhile, Joseph privately asked the Doge his opinion on the question. The Doge strongly advised Ferrara.[55] Two days before Cesarini's arrival in Venice (20 February 1438),[56] at a meeting of a committee of counsellors, prelates and Staurophoroi it was decided, the Emperor and the Patriarch both being emphatically in favour, to choose Ferrara.[57] Traversari, writing from Ferrara some weeks later (11 March), told a monk: 'There are among them (i.e. the Greeks) many learned men, excellently disposed towards us. But the Emperor and the Patriarch surpass them all in such disposition.'[58]

Syropoulus[59] makes out that Joseph was very opposed to the transference of the Council to Florence. Yet earlier in the *Memoirs*[60] he had stated that the idea of the removal to Florence was a plot hatched between the Emperor and the Patriarch to lure the Greeks deeper into the heart of Italy and further from home, an accusation repeated also later.[61] He says too that Joseph was against discussion of the doctrine of the *Filioque*,[62] but that when he did assent he advised his clerics to send most of their gear straight to Venice and to take little with them to Florence, though that little should include their sacred vestments as 'union will soon take place there', a statement which Syropoulus says disturbed the prelates considerably, as if union were a foregone conclusion

[54] Letter of Rodrigo, Dean of Braga, written from Constantinople, 13 Oct. 1437, published by G. HOFMANN, in *O.C.P.* IX (1943), pp. 178–84.
[55] Letter of 17 Feb. 1438 from Venice to Marco Dandolo, Venetian ambassador to the Holy See, in JORGA, III, p. 30.
[56] From a letter of Traversari from Venice, 21 Feb.; TRAV., no. 140.
[57] SYR., pp. 88–9.   [58] TRAV., no. 510.
[59] SYR., pp. 181 seq.   [60] Ibid., p. 153.
[61] Ibid., p. 184.   [62] Ibid., p. 202.

before any discussion at all, seeing that there was little likelihood that the Latins would relent.[63] These assertions of Syropoulus do not hang together, and the fact that later at Florence the Patriarch was decidedly in favour of union does not prove any one of them.

All the authorities are agreed that at Florence the Patriarch gave his *votum* to accept the genuineness of the passages of the western Fathers adduced by the Latins in favour of the doctrine of the *Filioque*, and the equivalence of 'Dia' and 'Ek' in the expressions of Greeks and Latins about the Procession of the Holy Spirit. There is, however, still debate about the authenticity of the so-called 'Last Profession' of the Patriarch, the note that was found on his desk after his death, wherein he professed his acceptance of the full faith of the Roman Church, specifying in particular the primacy of the pope and the doctrine of Purgatory. It is textually recorded in the descriptive part of the *Acta*[64] and in the *Libellus de ordine generalium Conciliorum et unione Florentina* of Fantinus Vallaresso composed in Crete in 1442.[65] None of the Greek anti-unionists—Syropoulus, Scholarius, Mark of Ephesus —refers to it at all, and Scholarius even wrote in a note on the signatories of the Decree of Union: 'The Patriarch Joseph: he died before the union and the composition of the decree, having proffered only a *votum* when there was discussion about the writings of the Europeans, whether they should be accepted as genuine, as proposed by the Latins, or not accepted. The *votum* is preserved and it is not without malice, but it is generally said it was amended afterwards.'[66] But, on Scholarius' own showing, as was mentioned earlier, the Patriarch also gave a public decision on the values of 'Dia' and 'Ek', so this statement of his is not wholly accurate. All the same it is hard to believe that Scholarius knew anything of a 'Last Profession'.

Among the Latins there was general belief that Joseph before his death had signified his acceptance of union and that that was the reason why, whereas Sardis in April 1438 had been buried outside the walls of the small church of St. Julian,[67] Joseph was accompanied to the grave by a cortège of most eminent Latins and interred within one of Florence's largest churches, S. Maria

---

[63] Ibid., p. 208. [64] *A.G.*, p. 444.
[65] Ed. B. SCHULTZE (Rome, 1944), pp. 105–6, which omits the phrase referring to Purgatory.
[66] SCHOL., III, p. 194. [67] SYR., p. 112.

Novella, where the Pope actually had his residence.[68] But they
nearly all refer the Patriarch's assent to a particular occasion, the
sending by the Latins of a draft-agreement on the Procession of
the Holy Spirit in the last days of April 1439. Andrea da S.
Croce in the so-called *Latin Acts* marks the connection most
distinctly. He affirms that the Greeks, having seen the truth,
summoned the Latin Fathers of the Council and with them concurred in the draft-agreement. There follows the text of the
agreement, and then he continues: 'Immediately all were filled with
joy, asserting that the affair already despaired of and shipwrecked
had miraculously been brought to the safe port of the truth; and
indeed it was no work of man, but of Truth itself. That ancient
Father, venerable in appearance and burdened with ill-health, the
Patriarch of Constantinople, longed for a session to be held, but
there were many of ours who averred that the dogmas of the
primacy of the pope, of the Consecration, and of Purgatory should
be first admitted by the Greek Fathers before they proceeded to
union with the Roman Church. So with this obstacle still in the
way he died that night. But before his death he signed with his
own hand the above-mentioned draft on the Procession of the
Holy Spirit and, submitting himself humbly to the rule of holy
mother Church, breathed his last'.[69] The same Andrea in his
Diary merely notes: '11 June there dies the Patriarch of the
Greeks who before his death had agreed with us in the faith . . .
he was, however, received by the Latins into the communion of
the Church whose faith he had recognised before his death.'[70]
Fantinus Vallaresso in the body of his work wrote: 'Joseph, the
Patriarch of Constantinople, who, after the agreement on the
article about the Holy Spirit had been made, to which he sub-
scribed with his own hand . . . died towards the end of the
Florentine Synod'[71]: and as a title to the 'Last Profession', which
he gives as a kind of appendix to the signatures of the Decree of
Union: 'The following profession is that of the Oecumenical
Patriarch of Constantinople which he uttered before his death and
left in writing in Florence for the holy work of the union of the
Churches of Christ.'[72] Finally there is the evidence of John of
Torquemada who wrote in 1441: 'Of whom the first, viz. the

[68] *A.L.*, pp. 224–5.   [69] Ibid.
[70] *Frag.*, p. 47.
[71] Fantinus VALLARESSO, ed. SCHULTZE, p. 20.
[72] Ibid., p. 105.

Patriarch of Constantinople, Joseph by name, was personally present (i.e. at the Council) and gave his assent to what followed; for although he ended his days before the synodal definition and the proclamation of the union, nevertheless he protested in the city of Florence that he died in that same faith that the universal oecumenical synod, congregated together, should define.[73]

From these quotations there arise two questions to be answered —do these references of the Latin writers to Joseph's acceptance of the western doctrine refer to the Patriarch's 'Last Profession' or to some other; and secondly, if they do not, is that Profession to be accepted as genuine, in view of the silence of all the later Greek polemics. To reply to the first question one must go back to the history of the events of late April and May 1439, which is recounted at length in the *Acta* and the *Memoirs* of Syropoulus. As usual, the *Acta* furnish more detail with exact dates, though much more briefly, than the corresponding account of the *Memoirs*.

According, then, to the Greek sources a Latin draft-agreement about the Procession of the Holy Spirit was delivered to the Greeks towards the end of April[74] and caused some consternation. Thereupon the Greeks formulated a draft of their own,[75] but it only occasioned a long reply from the Latins proposing twelve points which, they said, needed clarification.[76] There followed a succession of conferences among the Greeks and of messengers to the Pope, the discussions among the Greeks on the genuinity of the Latin Fathers equally with the Greek as enlightened by the same Holy Spirit, and the meanings of 'Dia' and 'Ek', which resulted in the almost unanimous admission on the part of the Greeks that the Latin and the Greek doctrines were identical. On these points the Emperor insisted on written *vota* from all the Greeks. The upshot was the composition of a *tomos* that recorded the Greek acceptance of the Procession of the Holy Spirit also from the Son, of which three copies were made, one for the Pope, one for the Emperor and the third for the Patriarch. That was on 4 June. On 5 June the *tomos* was sent to the Pope and read before the Cardinals. Thereupon a committee of ten members of each side was constituted which discussed the document and agreed on certain alterations. On 8 June a translation of the emended *tomos*

---

[73] IOANNES DE TORQUEMADA, O.P., *Apparatus super decretum Florentinum unionis Graecorum*, ed. E. CANDAL (Romae, 1942), pp. 12–13.
[74] *A.G.*, p. 413; *A.L.*, pp. 224–5; SYR., pp. 236–7.
[75] *A.G.*, p. 415; SYR., pp. 243–4.   [76] *A.G.*, p. 416; SYR., pp. 245–7.

in Latin was read in the presence of the Pope and the Greeks, and occasioned great joy.[77] On 10 June the Patriarch died.

There seems to be no question but that the two references to the Patriarch's union with the Latin Church in Andrea da S. Croce, and at least the first of those quoted above from Fantinus Vallaresso, refer not to Joseph's 'Last Profession' but to this *tomos* delivered shortly before his death. There is no record of the wording of the *tomos* in the *Acta*, and Syropoulus does not even mention it, but it is not unlikely that it was couched almost exactly in the terms of the Latin draft-agreement, firstly because Andrea da S. Croce asserts that that was what the Greeks accepted, and secondly because a comparison of that draft as it is given by Andrea with the final Decree of Union shows that it was incorporated into the latter almost word for word, the changes being nearly all a mere altering of first person plurals to the third—'We, Latins, etc.,' giving place to 'The Latins, etc'.

So, with some of the seeming evidence for its genuinity now removed, there comes the second question: Is the 'Last Profession' of the Patriarch authentic? The words of John of Torquemada written so shortly after the Patriarch's death are not decisive, for they are very general—'He protested in the city of Florence that he died in that same faith that the universal oecumenical Synod, congregated together, should define'—and they do not correspond exactly to what it is alleged the Patriarch wrote: 'Since I have come to the end of my life and am to pay the debt common to all, by God's grace I write openly and sign my profession for my children. Everything, therefore, that the Catholic and Apostolic Church of Our Lord Jesus Christ of the elder Rome understands and proclaims, I too understand and I declare myself as submitting in common on these points; further the most blessed Father of Fathers and supreme Pontiff and vicar of Our Lord Jesus Christ, the pope of elder Rome, I confess for the security of all: further the Purgatory of souls.' In this there is no reference to a future decision of the Council, as Torquemada wrote. But on the other hand Torquemada associates the profession with the Patriarch's death and not with the question only of the *Filioque*, and so, allowing that he learnt of the profession only by hearsay and did not himself see it (which is most likely) his evidence favours the authenticity.

[77] *A.G.*, pp. 438–40.

The most telling arguments for the genuineness of this 'Last Profession' are the fact that the text of it could be adduced in the Greek milieu of Crete as early as 1442 as proof of Joseph's adherence to the Decree of Union—and indeed in lieu of his autograph signature—by Vallaresso without fear of contradiction, with the assertion in its title that the Patriarch 'left it in writing in Florence'; and that the same is to be read in the descriptive part of the *Acta* which was written probably while the Council was still in progress.[78]

Another consideration that favours its authenticity is its curious content. It says nothing about the Procession of the Holy Spirit. There was no need. The Patriarch had already signified his agreement on that in the *tomos*. After the comprehensive declaration of the Patriarch's general submission to Roman doctrine, the profession specifies two points, the doctrine of the papal prerogatives and of Purgatory. The mention of just these two points fits in with the course of events in the Council. After the acceptance on 8 June of the mutually-agreed formula on the Procession of the Holy Spirit, on the two successive days the Latins brought up the three questions that Andrea da S. Croce says prevented them from concluding a general union on the spot, the primacy, the liturgy, and Purgatory and, according to the *Acta*, also a fourth, namely the palamistic question of essence and operation in God. The four prelates who represented the Greeks at these conferences with the Latins showed no enthusiasm about the Latin theory of the primacy, were amenable over the liturgical question and Purgatory, and would not touch the palamistic problem. They replied that they could not answer without consulting the Emperor, the Patriarch and their colleagues. So they 'recounted everything to the Emperor *viva voce* and did as much for the Patriarch'. That was within a few hours of the Patriarch's death.[79]

In the alleged 'Last Profession' two of these still outstanding points are particularised; two are not mentioned. Of the two points specified in the Profession one was especially controversial, the primacy; and the other, Purgatory, though at the moment it seemed to arouse no opposition, yet earlier, in the preliminary conferences of June and July 1438, it had been the subject of lively

[78] Ibid., pp. LXX sq.   [79] Ibid., pp. 440–4.

debate between Latins and Greeks and a question on which the Greeks were not altogether agreed among themselves.[80] Both of these questions were later accepted generally by the Greeks and written into the Decree of Union. But of the two points not mentioned in the Profession, one, namely the question of essence and operation in God, does not figure again in the negotiations and does not appear in the final Decree at all; the other was discussed several times under two aspects, namely the legitimate use of either fermented or unfermented bread in the Eucharist and the precise point in the liturgy where the consecration is effected, at the dominical words: 'This is my Body, etc.' or at the epiclesis. On the first of these aspects there was mutual agreement and it is included in the Decree. On the second of them the Greeks themselves were uncertain,[81] and so there was a compromise that on this they should make only a vocal declaration[82] (done by Bessarion on 5 July) and it was not introduced into the Decree.

So the Patriarch's 'Last Profession' harmonises with the general situation as this is known to us. But it can hardly be said to have influenced the course of events, otherwise it would have been well-known, one might even say notorious, also among the anti-unionists. Indeed the main argument against its authenticity, and it is no light one, is the fact that there is no reference to it at all in the later anti-unionist polemics. Had it been generally known that he had left behind him such a document, it is difficult to understand the silence of a Syropoulus, for example, who retails such a multitude of small facts in his *Memoirs* and who would not willingly have foregone the possibility of painting the Patriarch's iniquities in still darker colours. The only other consideration that militates against its authenticity is of less weight. The date of the signature of the Profession in the *Acta* is given as 9 June (Vallaresso assigns no day of the month), whereas the Patriarch died on 10 June—a manifest error of a bungling interpolator, it is said. A bungler, indeed, if he inserted into the midst of the short account of the Patriarch's death on the tenth and his burial on the eleventh a Profession dated the ninth. It is just as possible that the Patriarch himself was in error about the date. That does happen even to the best of us.[83]

[80] Ibid., pp. 19–26.
[81] Ibid., p. 447.   [82] Ibid.
[83] This discussion of the 'Last Profession' of Joseph II is fuller than that of the Introduction to the *A.G.* (pp. LXXXV–LXXXVII), which it also modifies.

But, whatever may be thought of the 'Last Profession' of the Patriarch Joseph, there was no doubt in the minds of the Greek anti-unionists about his attitude at Florence. Mark of Ephesus in his short account of the Council wrote: 'But those who did not shrink from the impiety and as many as had followed them from the beginning, suborned by specious promises and gifts, with bared heads declared the Son to be the cause of the Holy Spirit, a statement that is clearly to be found nowhere even in the writings of the Latins. With these the Patriarch also voted, he, too, the wretched man already corrupted and at the same time yearning for departure from that place, even though destiny was driving him to his death.'[84] Scholarius, as we have already seen, sneered at his daring to give his opinion on the equivalence of 'Dia' and 'Ek'. Syropoulus records his positive vote in the Greek conferences that led up to agreement on the *Filioque*, and in his brief notice of the Patriarch's death related: 'All the same, the Patriarch after giving the *votum* mentioned above began to make preparations for his return and sent the greater part of his baggage to Venice. For he kept saying that he would remain for a few days until he had signed the decree what was to be made and straightway then would leave Florence. He achieved neither, for he did not survive to sign it, but died and was buried there.'[85] At any rate he died with the satisfaction of feeling that what he had longed for so much for the benefit of both Churches was as good as accomplished.

Joseph II, for all his age and his fatherly benevolence to his flock, was not a man of weak will, otherwise at the hazard of his life from his chronic illness and the dangers likely to be encountered in a winter sea voyage, he would never have left Constantinople at all for the unionist council in the West. His strength of character showed itself also in incidents like those recounted above where he stood out for the dignity of the patriarchal office. It was even more strikingly demonstrated by episodes that occurred on his journey to Ferrara.

When the ornate barge that carried him reached the frontiers of the Duchy of Ferrara, it was found that the other boat that was bringing some of the lower clergy and his baggage had been delayed on the way. The Patriarch insisted on waiting till it arrived, and neither the persuasions and guarantees of Garatoni

---

[84] MARK EUGENICUS, *Relatio de rebus a se gestis*, in PETIT, *Docs.*, p. 448 (310).
[85] SYR., p. 276.

nor an incipient revolt of the boatmen made him change his mind. When the boatmen, in spite of his orders, made ready to start towing again, he would have disembarked there and then, had they not desisted. So the best part of a day was lost, but he had his way and was not separated from his baggage which in all probability contained a large part of the sacred ornaments of the church of St. Sophia and the robes he wanted to wear at his entry into Ferrara.[86]

But that entry into Ferrara was not the magnificent spectacle that he hoped it would be. At the frontier he was met by a courier of the Emperor to tell him that Eugenius IV expected that he would conform to the Latin custom of kissing the Pope's foot and that the Emperor, who had so far tried for three days in vain to dissuade the Pontiff from insisting on this, urged him to be firm and not to accede. Joseph was shocked and disappointed. So when on arrival at the port of Ferrara he was met by six bishops who pressed him to conform, he flatly refused. A council of his prelates and Boullotes with another message from the Emperor confirmed him in his decision. Towards evening the bishops came back and urged him again, only to be told that he would rather return straight to Constantinople. Later that evening they were back again with the same demand, but Joseph said that he would not even disembark from the boat unless the Pope would agree to forgo the ceremony of the foot-kissing both for himself and for his prelates and Staurophoroi. Late that night the Pope's messengers acquainted him that Eugenius had yielded, but that the reception would in consequence not be public and solemn but private—the Pope would receive the Patriarch and his clerics in a private room in groups of six. So the next day Joseph rode into Ferrara between two cardinals (all the cardinals had accompanied the Emperor on his entry) with an escort of bishops, court officials and courtiers of Ferrara and, without his accustomed head-dress and staff, was received by the Pope.[87]

This incident of the foot-kissing was not just a trial of strength between Pope and Patriarch. It was rather a manifestation of the attitude to each other of the two Churches, and the heads of those Churches were both acting on principle. The question at issue

[86] Ibid., 91, 62.
[87] Ibid., pp. 93–8; *A.L.*, pp. 27–8; GEMINIANUS INGHIRAMI, *Diarium*, in *Frag.*, p. 34.

D

was whether the two Churches were in all respects equal or whether the Western Church, personified by the Pope, was superior to the Eastern, in the person of the Patriarch. In the event neither gave way on the principle, the more meagre reception accorded by Eugenius to Joseph being, not the result of pique and mortified pride, but a way of showing that, though he yielded the point of etiquette so as not to impede the possibility of gaining the greater good of harmony between the Churches, he did not accept the grounds on which the Patriarch had objected. The relations between the Churches were still to be discussed and decided by the Council: neither side was willing to prejudice the decision by premature action.

Syropoulus recounts this incident in great detail. Whatever else he may have written about the Patriarch, he had no doubts about his strength of character. Sphrantzes, because Joseph was opposed to one of his friends, characterised the Patriarch as 'proud and insatiable'.[88] Syropoulus did not make the mistake of interpreting strength as pride, and so, when at the end of his *Memoirs* he lists the causes that had favoured the anti-unionist opposition in Constantinople, he puts in the first place: 'And first [God] delivered to death in Italy the Patriarch, Kyr Joseph, who had approved and declared his opinion in favour of the union, but who shortly after was snatched away without having survived to append his signature and take part in the ceremony. He was a man of profound mind who inspired great reverence and awe. Had he survived he would have added great support to the union also in Italy, and here, if he had returned, very few indeed would have managed to remain outside his communion.'[89]

[88] PHRANTZES, p. 158. The chronicler's name was Sphrantzes, but his chronicle is published always under the name Phrantzes.
[89] SYR., p. 347.

CHAPTER THREE

POPE EUGENIUS IV

The person most responsible for the success of the Council of Florence was the Pope, Eugenius IV. Gabriele Condulmaro, born in Venice about the year 1383 of a rich family, while still young gave all his heritage to the poor to enter the newly-founded monastery of St. Giorgio in Alga. There he lived an exact and laborious life. In 1407 he was made Bishop of Siena by his uncle Gregory XII and the next year he was created cardinal. He took part in the Council of Constance after the abdication of Gregory and assisted at the election of Martin V (Nov. 1417), by whom later he was entrusted with various offices such as the government of the March of Ancona and of Bologna. On Martin's death, Cardinal Condulmaro was immediately elected pope (3 March 1431) and crowned eight days later.

Martin had bequeathed to his successor a double task, the conduct of the newly-summoned Council of Basel and the union of the Greeks. Martin himself, throughout all the years of his reign, had been in regular contact with Constantinople working for union, and shortly before his death had almost concluded an agreement with the Greek Emperor, John VIII, and the Greek Church for a common council to be held in Italy at papal expense. He had, too, left to his successor a problem, in that he had put too much Church property into the hands of members of his family, the Colonnas, and they were disinclined to give it up, which involved Eugenius in war with them in and about Rome in the early months of his reign.

The Council of Basel was another problem. It opened with so few members and in such adverse circumstances that Eugenius thought he could dispose of it by transferring it to Bologna to meet again after an interval of eighteen months. But it would not be disposed of. The anarchy in the Church during the Great Schism[1] and the consequent complete lack of discipline and state of moral decadence had produced a reaction in the shape of the Conciliar

---

[1] From 1378 to 1417 there was not a time when, besides the true Pope, there was not one or even two antipopes.

Movement and the demand for ecclesiastical reform. The Conciliar Movement sprang from the widespread conviction that a General Council representing the whole Church had its authority directly from God and was superior to a pope at least in respect of faith, schism, and reform. As it seemed that the rival popes and antipopes could not or would not settle or sacrifice their claims, to give the Church a single, stable government, good men looked to a Council to impose peace and with peace the much needed reform. But, while all were agreed that reform was both necessary and urgent, all were equally of the view that it should begin with someone else, not with themselves. The Fathers met in Basel were ardent reformers, who also believed that the principle of the superiority of a Council over a pope had been defined in Constance, so with their few but rapidly growing numbers they refused to obey the papal dissolution and instead summoned the Pope to give an account of himself to them. Tension between Council and Pope grew. Eugenius, barely finished with the reduction of the Colonnas, was attacked by the troops of Milan (always hostile to him, as it was also at this time to Florence and Venice) and of Naples (where Alfonso of Aragon was trying to wrest the crown from René of Anjou, the papal nominee), with the result that, when later the harassed citizens of Rome revolted, he had to flee down the Tiber in disguise to Florence (4 June 1434). Meanwhile fifteen out of twenty-one cardinals and many other lesser clergy had thrown in their lot with the Council. So at the end of 1433 Eugenius withdrew his Bull of dissolution and gave a seemingly full approval to the Council of Basel.

As early as September 1431 the Council had urged Eugenius to make contact with Constantinople and to invite Greeks to Basel. Then, by-passing the Pope, the Fathers themselves sent two messengers to John VIII, and these in July 1434 returned with three Greek envoys, one of whom was Isidore, later Metropolitan of Kiev and All Russia. These, on the basis of the pact discussed with Martin V, agreed with the Council for the Greeks to come to the West to a place to be chosen from certain specific cities (not including Basel) at the expense of the Council. The agreement was put into the form of the decree, *Sicut pia mater*, which was solemnly ratified by the Council on 7 September 1434 and sworn to by the Greeks.

Eugenius, however, left in ignorance of these negotiations,

had in the interval despatched Cristoforo Garatoni to Constantinople and through him arranged with the Emperor for a council
to be held in that city. But, when he heard of the decree *Sicut pia
mater*, he sent Garatoni and two messengers of the Emperor newly
arrived in Italy to the Council, and as the Fathers were set on
retaining their own pact, he sacrificed his plan and acquiesced in
theirs, though with misgivings. Thereupon the Council sent three
new envoys to the Byzantine court to implement the decree and
also (though without success) to persuade the Greeks to accept
Basel as the seat of the future Council.

The more Eugenius conceded, the more the Council demanded.
In the name of reform, it forbade the payment of annates[2] to the
Pope, though it exacted them for itself. It set up all the machinery
of Church government, exactly parallel to the papal Curia. It
appointed 'legates *a latere*': it even decreed, in the name of the
Council, a plenary indulgence. Its grim determination to reduce
the papacy to a position of unimportant inferiority alienated many
of its own supporters, and cardinals, clerics, and theologians began
to rally to the papal cause. The climax came in an open split
within the Council over the choice of the city for the meeting
with the Greeks. In spite of its own convention *Sicut pia mater*,
the section of the Council more hostile to the papacy (and afraid
to hazard its pretensions to superiority by moving into Italy)
chose and decreed Avignon, though it was not one of the cities
mentioned in the agreement and was totally unacceptable to the
Greeks. The more moderate section simultaneously (7 May
1437) decreed Udine, Florence, or some other suitable Italian
town. The latter decree was taken to the Pope who, with the
approval of all the Greek envoys, accepted it as conciliar and
wasted no time in putting it into execution. A papal fleet sailed for
Constantinople arriving on 3 September. The Council's fleet put
in a month later. The Greeks chose to come to Italy in the papal
ships and set off on 27 November 1437.

By Bulls dated 18 September and 30 December, Eugenius
transferred the Council of Basel to Ferrara, where in fact the new
Council opened on 8 January, the Pope arriving two weeks later.
The Greeks reached Venice on 8 February and Ferrara on 4 and 7
March, the Emperor John VIII with his brother and royal suite,

---

[2] Annates were a proportion of a year's revenue payable to the Roman Curia
by all new bishops and beneficiaries.

the Patriarch Joseph II with twenty Greek metropolitans, representatives of Moldavia and Georgia, and a numerous gathering of
clerics and monks—in all about 700 persons. Isidore of Kiev
with the Bishop of Susdal and a few other clerical and lay envoys
reached the Council in the mid-August following.

One of the motives that had moved the Greeks to accept a
council in the west was the dire need of their country. If Constantinople was not to fall to Turkish arms, there had to be some
form of crusade to rally the western princes to its aid. A crusade
could be set on foot only by the Pope, and he would be more
enthusiastic in the cause if the Churches were united. There
was, too, a real desire for Church union for its own sake, because
all Christians, whether eastern or western, regarded the division
of the Churches as a tragedy. But the difficulties in the way of
union were not small. The Oriental Church believed that the
schism stemmed from Latin arbitrary action in adding to the Creed
and indeed from Latin heterodoxy. The Latins looked on the
Eastern Church as a 'daughter-Church', to be 'brought back' to
the bosom of the mother-Church which it had left and whose faith
it should in all points embrace. This difference of principle soon
showed itself. The Patriarch refused to follow the western custom
of saluting the Pope, as head of the Church, by kissing his foot, and
a little later the Emperor objected to the proposal that in the public
sessions the papal throne, and it alone, should be central and as it
were uniting the Churches, which would have symbolised
superiority to both. Eugenius, so as not to wreck the Council at
the start on points of etiquette, yielded so far as to accept a compromise.

The Council of union opened with a solemn session on 9 April
1438. Then, to satisfy the Emperor who wanted time for the
western princes to send their envoys, nothing was done for
months, during which, of course, the Greeks (and not a few
Latins) were living at papal expense, and the papal exchequer was
growing emptier and emptier. Inevitably the Pope's subventions
to his visitors fell into arrears, and they began to feel the pinch of
poverty. In June and July, to pacify the impatient Latins, there
were some discussions about Purgatory, but only between committees of ten. Soon plague fell on the city of Ferrara, but the
Pope and the Greek ecclesiastics did not leave it. Finally, on 8
October dogmatic discussions were started on the subject chosen

by the Greeks—the legitimacy of the addition of the *Filioque* to the Creed.

Again there was some little friction. Mark, Metropolitan of Ephesus, wanted to expose his whole case before the Latins answered and, as part of it, to read all the decrees of all the Councils that touched on the immutability of the Creed, which the Latins thought quite unnecessary. Eugenius refused to insist that it was for the Latin Church to say what and how things should be done (as many of his advisers urged him to do), and let the Metropolitan of Ephesus have his way. The sessions in Ferrara went on till mid-December. Eugenius missed none of them, though he would have had abundant excuse if he had. He was still, of course, directing the ordinary business of the Church; he was all the time being harassed by his enemies who possessed themselves in these very months of cities dangerously close to Ferrara; the Council of Basel had again refused to be translated and a remnant, now more viciously hostile than ever, lingered on to subvert the loyalty particularly of France and Germany to the Holy See[3] and in November 1439 to elect the last antipope in history; and the Council was lasting far longer than had been anticipated and was living largely on borrowed money.

Florence was Eugenius's chief creditor. It was also firmly opposed to Milan and at a safe distance from the activities of Milan's condottiere Piccinino. Eugenius therefore persuaded the Emperor to continue the discussion in that city and thither the whole Council moved in January 1439. Though the debates in Ferrara on the legitimacy of the addition to the Creed had been inconclusive, now to satisfy the Latins the subject of discussion would be the doctrine of the *Filioque*, whether, that is, the Latin dogma that the Holy Spirit proceeds from the Father and the Son was or was not sound.

There were eight public sessions in Florence ending on 24 March, which left the question still unsettled. Then began a period of private meetings, of discussions between committees, of comings and goings of messengers, of mutual dissatisfaction. The Pope was bitterly disappointed that so much time, talk and expense had produced no result and he expressed his feelings to the Greeks on 27 May. That speech proved to be a stimulus. Those among

[3] Both these countries adopted a policy of neutrality to both Pope and Basel. England throughout was steadily and consistently loyal to Eugenius

the Orientals who had been convinced by the Latin arguments of
Latin orthodoxy (and they were all the intellectuals among the
Greek clerics save one) redoubled their efforts to persuade their
fellows and, appealing to the teaching of the Fathers of the Church,
they succeeded. In this way the chief difference between the
Churches was solved. Other questions were still unsettled, but
there were more difficulties and misunderstandings. Finally,
agreement was reached also on them, the Pope yielding to Greek
and imperial insistence on a number of smaller points.

The decree was written, signed and, on 6 July, 1439, publicly
proclaimed in solemn session.

But the Council was not yet finished for Eugenius IV. There
was the 'Council' of Basel to be dealt with, for it had dared to
declare 'Gabriele Condulmaro' deposed (25 June 1439), and there
were other Orientals besides the Greeks. On 4 September in
solemn session the Pope renewed all the penalties formerly decreed
against the Baseler unless they repented, and not long afterwards
he had the subject of papal versus conciliar authority (the basis of
disagreement between him and Basel) thoroughly discussed in the
Council. At this same time delegates of Armenians from the
Black Sea area were in Rome for union and the 'Decree for the
Armenians' was promulgated by common consent on 22 November
1439. Isidore, Metropolitan of Kiev and All Russia, left Venice on
22 December as papal legate to make the union effective in Poland-
Lithuania and the Russian princedoms. Papal agents were already
on their way to invite the Copts of Egypt and of Abyssinia to
union: the former sent delegates who agreed to the 'Decree for
the Copts', promulgated on 4 February 1442. In Rome, whither
the Council had moved in September 1443, union with the Syrians
of Mesopotamia was celebrated on 30 September 1444 and with
certain Chaldeans of Cyprus on 7 August 1445.

Eugenius had promised material aid to the Greeks to help them
defend their imperial city. However, though he could cover part
of the expenses, he could not supply troops. For that he depended
on the temporal princes, and, to rally them to the cause, he
launched a crusade and sent his ambassadors to the princely
courts to win support. Unfortunately most of the princes were
too intent on their own affairs. England and France were just
emerging from the Hundred Years' War. The German Electors
were testing their strength against the German Emperor and, most

unfortunate of all, Austria and Hungary were divided on a question of succession to the Hungarian crown, which involved, too, Ladislas King of Poland. Exhortation and embassies proved unavailing till Elizabeth of Hungary died (1442). Then, with Ladislas ruling over Poland-Lithuania and Hungary, the crusade was set afoot, the Pope furnishing money and a fleet, the King supplying the land troops. But Eugenius's hopes were sadly disappointed, for after some preliminary successes the Christian army was defeated at Varna (10 November 1444), King Ladislas and Cardinal Cesarini, the papal legate, both being killed. There was no chance of another crusade on the same scale being put in the field in Eugenius' lifetime; all the same he still continued to encourage and support opposition to the Turk wheresoever it was manifested.

The issue of the battle of Varna meant, of course, that Eugenius's great effort to save Constantinople from the Turk had failed. It had other consequences too, in that it weakened the appeal of union among the Greeks and strengthened the opposition to it. Mark Eugenicus, Metropolitan of Ephesus, who enjoyed a reputation both for holiness of life and for learning, had never, even in Italy, concurred in the union. On his return to Constantinople he conducted a campaign of unremitting and clever propaganda against it, which, as it was so completely in harmony with traditional Greek hostility to the Latins, effectively won popular support against it. The majority of the prelates, who in Florence had let their heads lead their hearts, now in face of the general attitude obeyed their own inner feeling and prejudices, and once more let their hearts lead their heads. John VIII, though personally loyal to the union, did not impose it. Unionist patriarchs, successors of Joseph II who had died in Florence (10 June 1439), could not do much against imperial inactivity and popular opposition. During Eugenius's lifetime the union was never proclaimed in Constantinople.

The Council of union with the Orientals did more to unite the Latin Church within itself than it did to unite it with the Greek Church. The remnant at Basel with its antipope Felix V still existed (it survived Eugenius by two years), but it was receiving less and less support. France, though it did not abrogate its Pragmatic Sanction, drew nearer to Eugenius. Scotland formally acknowledged his 'obedience' on 4 November 1443. At about the same time Frederick III of Austria definitively rejected Basel in favour of the Pope. The German Electors, too, were moving in the same direction when Eugenius nearly alienated all of them by excommunicating two of them for their continued support of Basel. The crisis was passed, but only just in time. Eugenius was literally on his death-bed when their representatives read to him the instruments of their adherence, and so he died (23 February 1447) with the Latin Church at least united around him.

Eugenius was a simple-minded man, of the type who sees one line of duty clearly and is prepared to do that duty at all costs. His duty cost him dear—flight from Rome, constant military assaults, the bitter persecution from Basel, the desertion of 'friends' when his fortunes were low, the opposition of not a few good men like Cardinal Cesarini, the disloyalty of France and Germany, the lack of financial resources, and dependence on others—all of which he bore with endurance and courage.

His very simplicity had its defects. If he had given or withdrawn his trust, he was difficult to change, and was at times too loyal to unworthy friends and too hard on those he considered enemies. But he did forgive many such, like Cesarini who from having been the spokesman of the opposition of Basel became a leading figure of the Council of Florence. If he gave his word, he kept it as far as that was possible. At any time from 1431 to 1442, by abandoning his support of René of Anjou, he could have bought off the opposition of Alfonso of Aragon whose representatives at Basel were among the bitterest and the most redoubtable of his opponents and whose constant warfare was a source of great expense and anxiety, but not till Alfonso had actually captured Naples and René had fled from Italy obviously never to return did he make terms.

He was, too, conciliatory. Having withdrawn his Bull of dissolution of the Council of Basel, he tried to get along with the Fathers: he was ready to accept their *Sicut pia mater* instead of his own plan; he would have endured the loss of the annates if some compensation had been made (for even a Pope and a Curia need money if they are to direct a Church); when the Council was set on granting an indulgence, Eugenius offered either to provide the money himself or to proclaim the indulgence in his own name 'with the approval of the Council'—further he could not go in concessions—but the Council did not accept his offer. Similarly with the Greeks, without letting his action compromise the principles he believed in, he yielded on many points of detail where insistence might have prejudiced the attainment of the larger issues.

Eugenius has been blamed because, when the Church so badly needed reform, his Council of Florence did nothing to effect it. It is, however, an open question whether any Council could at that time have produced a general reform of the Church, because no one section of the Church, Curia, episcopacy, Christian princes, or laity, was willing to be reformed. Eugenius did a great deal to further reform where it was certainly possible. He seconded every effort of the many then being made, to build up the reforming elements, the 'Observants', in the great religious Orders, Franciscans, Dominicans, Benedictines, Camaldolese, and others. As a result, monasteries and convents all over Italy, in France, Germany, Poland, Spain and as far away as Caffa in the Crimea and Jerusalem, were brought to a higher level of religious life and became the nucleus of a growing religious revival, for the great missionary preachers of that age came from them. If Eugenius did not (and could not) reform the whole Church directly, he did much to reform it indirectly, beginning with what was most feasible and what would have most influence on the rest.

His heart was in that reform, because he himself had been a monk of a reformed monastery, and he retained throughout his life the spirit and, to a large extent, the habits of his early dedication of himself. He always had with him four chaplains, two of them monks of his old monastery of S. Giorgio, two monks of S. Giustina, a monastery that was the centre and inspiration of much monastic reform. With them he recited the breviary daily, using the copy that he had himself written out in his early years of religious life. He was very abstemious in food, taking only one meal a day and that mainly of fruit and vegetables, and never drinking wine. In his charities to the poor (and access to him of all in need was easy) he was most open-handed, so much so that he was an embarrassment to his secretaries who often found themselves in difficulties to find money to meet current needs. He rarely appeared in public, so reports a contemporary Florentine, but when he did, on such occasions, for example, as Easter to give the Easter blessing, such was the impression he made that 'it not only seemed that those people beheld the vicar of Christ on earth, but His divinity. Of a truth, at that time he seemed to be what he represented'.

The one duty that Eugenius had set himself was not to sacrifice any right of the Church whether to the soaring ambitions of Basel or to the exigencies of political life. His chief claim to fame in the Church is perhaps not so much his ardour for Church union as his courage, his indomitable courage, in withstanding the Conciliarists and safeguarding the traditional constitution of the Church.

CHAPTER FOUR

CARDINAL BESSARION

Though Cardinal Bessarion has many claims to fame—as a humanist, a diplomat, a reformer of monasteries—he is best known as the apostle of union between the Latin and the Greek Churches, and it is rather under this last aspect that we shall consider him here.

He was a native of Trebizond, born on 2 January 1402, at a period, that is, when the last Greek possessions were being threatened on all sides by the victorious arms of the Turks. What had once been a great empire, embracing all the eastern Mediterranean, was by this time sadly reduced. Africa, Syria and Palestine had been lost early, and then Turkish forces absorbed Asia Minor, crossed the Dardanelles, and encircled Constantinople also from the west and north. That city had been besieged for more than three years at the turn of the century and was relieved in 1402 not by the prowess of its own arms, but because the Mongolian invasion had temporarily challenged the Turkish power and defeated it. Trebizond, it is true, was then an independent Greek kingdom, but it would not long survive the eclipse of Constantinople and lived equally under an ever present threat of destruction.

Of Bessarion's early life little is known in detail. While still quite young he was taken by the Archbishop of Trebizond to Constantinople where he was educated under the care of the Metropolitan of Selymbria in one of the schools of rhetoric that flourished there. He took the monastic habit on 30 January 1423 with the name Bessarion, by which he has always since been known. Thereafter he began to make a reputation for himself as an orator, and in 1426 was in his native Trebizond on a diplomatic mission, perhaps concerned with the imperial marriage of John VIII to Maria Comnene, daughter of the Emperor of Trebizond. He was ordained priest in 1431 and shortly after went to the Peloponnesus whose Despot received him graciously. At Mistra he studied under George Gemistus, the great exponent of Platonic philosophy, as a result of which Bessarion too became an ardent Platonist and a great admirer and friend of Gemistus. In 1436 his mediation in composing one of the many quarrels between the Emperor John and his brother, the Despot Theodore, drew the attention of the authorities of Constantinople to his talents, with the consequence that he was soon called to that city and made head of the monastery of St Basil. Shortly afterwards he was elected to the See of Nicaea, at about the same time that Mark Eugenicus became Metropolitan of Ephesus, Isidore Metropolitan of Kiev and All Russia, and Dionysius Metropolitan of Sardes. The elevation of all these was not unconnected with the negotiations for a council of union between East and West, then reaching their climax, for they were outstanding among the Greek clergy for their philosophical and theological ability, whereas the general level of learning of the oriental hierarchy was not very high.

After the Greek arrival in Ferrara in the beginning of February 1438 and the solemn opening of the Council of union on 9 April, there was a lull in the proceedings till Latin insistence on action of some kind produced a reluctant acquiescence from the Greeks to consider such a possibility. In the preliminary meetings that followed between committees of ten members from either side, Bessarion was one of the Greek delegates. When Mark of Ephesus' reply to the opening speech of Cardinal Cesarini was censured by his colleagues as too rough and discourteous for such an occasion, Bessarion was put up to speak the next time so that his urbanity and polish might make up for the bad first impression. The result of those meetings was the decision to discuss the question of Purgatory, still between the two committees. On the Greek side the Emperor appointed Mark Eugenicus (of Ephesus) and Bessarion as sole spokesmen. The Latins opened the discussion on 4 June asserting that there is such a state as Purgatory and that in it there is purification by fire. Subsequent debate was largely centred on the second assertion, Bessarion speaking on 14 June to prove that Greek theological tradition did not accept it. The discussions on Purgatory continued for some weeks and then petered out, without any agreement having been reached, probably because by then everyone's attention was focused on the plague that had infested Ferrara.

The Greek ecclesiastics remained in the plague-stricken city all that summer, though without casualties. Fear of the pestilence, financial difficulties (for the Pope was already in arrears with his payments for their maintenance), prolonged absence from home

—these and other like factors reduced the Orientals to great distress and made them anxious now to get on with the dogmatic conversations and to get away. The date for the discussions was fixed. Six orators on each side were to act as speakers for the rest. The Greeks elected among their six Bessarion, Mark Eugenicus and Isidore. The choice of the exact subject of debate was left to the Greeks who, at the instigation of Eugenicus and George Gemistus, decided to impugn the legitimacy of the addition by the Latins of the *Filioque* ('and from the Son') to the Creed, whereas Bessarion and a few others would have preferred to start on the orthodoxy of the *Filioque* doctrine.

The honour of making the opening speech of the doctrinal sessions fell to Bessarion, a proof that he was considered by his own as their most accomplished orator. To the Fathers assembled in solemn session he extolled the greatness of the occasion, congratulating both sides on their goodwill for union and exhorting Pope, Emperor and Patriarch with all the other members of the Council to bring to a glorious conclusion what they had so happily begun. Mark Eugenicus then enunciated the Greek charge that the Latin Church was responsible for the schism by the addition of the *Filioque* to the Creed in defiance of the prohibition of the Council of Ephesus that forbade any change at any time to any part of the Creed, and added his proofs from the definitions of the Councils. Andrew, Bishop of Rhodes, answered from the Latins. Bessarion in a speech extending over the greater part of two sessions (1 and 4 November) replied to Andrew's syllogisms and reaffirmed the Greek position, that to add to or subtract from the Nicene Creed even a word or syllable was forbidden, not only to the Roman Church, but to the universal Church, and therefore much more so to the Church of Rome, because the Council of Ephesus had so enacted.

Writing later, Bessarion said that until Cardinal Cesarini began his defence of the Latin action (some two sessions later) the Greeks were having the better of the debate, but Cesarini's many and forceful arguments began to make him doubtful of the strength of the Greek position and then convinced him that the Council of Ephesus could not have tied nor have meant to tie the hands of the Church for ever. Not all the Greeks, and especially Mark of Ephesus who was the speaker of the Greeks for the rest of the time at Ferrara, were of the same opinion, and the sessions went on till mid-December, always on the same topic and showing no prospect of leading to agreement.

In January the Council was transferred to Florence. By mutual consent the subject of discussion was changed to the orthodoxy of the *Filioque* doctrine. Bessarion did not speak on this in the Council. Mark Eugenicus was the sole Greek orator. Eight sessions were held, but ended without agreement, and by that time it was already 24 March 1439 and the Greeks, by now away from home for full sixteen months, were beginning to be desperate. They refused to entertain the idea of further public discussions, a method that had so far proved fruitless. Some other way should be found to lead to union, they said, or else they should go home.

The public sessions, however, had not been entirely without result. The able arguments and wide patristic learning of John of Montenero, O. P. had convinced Bessarion, Isidore, Dorotheus of Mitylene, Gregory the Emperor's confessor and others, of the orthodoxy of the Latin teaching and of its compatibility with Greek doctrine. These now began to try to persuade their fellows, chiefly Mark of Ephesus, the only man of learning among the Greek clerics who still obdurately refused to acquiesce. The greater part of the Greek prelates, by tradition and sentiment inclined to hold the Latins as heretics, were yet impressed by Montenero's scholarship, especially in the Greek Fathers, though they were not on a high enough level of theological learning to assess all the arguments. They would follow a lead, and they got not one lead but two—Bessarion and his friends argued to Latin orthodoxy and union; Mark Eugenicus asserted that by Greek tradition the Holy Spirit proceeded from the Father only, and so the *Filioque* clause was heretical.

The Greeks, divided among themselves, argued this way and that. Half way through April, Bessarion addressed his *Dogmatic Oration* to the Greek synod—as all saints are inspired by the same Holy Spirit, their teaching, even if expressed differently, must be fundamentally the same. Latin saints declare that the Holy Spirit proceeds from the Father and the Son; Greek saints that He proceeds from the Father through the Son. These two assertions must therefore be of identical meaning, so both Churches are orthodox, 'from' and 'through' in respect of the Holy Spirit having the same signification. This thesis he demonstrated with copious quotations from the Greek Fathers, specially from those on whom Mark Eugenicus relied to rebut the Latin doctrine.

George Scholarius, a lay theologian in the Emperor's suite, followed with an exhortation in the same sense. The fruits were not immediately seen, but they were not long delayed. Meetings between ten delegates from each side, among whom was Bessarion, towards the end of April brought no result. Then the Latins sent a kind of profession of faith, which the Greeks amended in such a way that the Latins rejected it. A few days later, during a meeting of the Greek clerics with the Patriarch and the Emperor, excerpts from the Fathers were read by Bessarion on the lines of his speech; the prelates approved: all gave their opinions in writing and the upshot was that the Greek synod (always excepting Mark Eugenicus) accepted the equivalence of 'from' and 'through' in the formula of the Procession of the Holy Spirit and, therefore, the orthodoxy of the Latin doctrine. The first great step to union had been achieved. Unfortunately the general jubilation of the Council was overshadowed by the sudden death on 10 June of the aged Patriarch.

The Greeks would have been willing to consider that the Council had now accomplished its main object and that they therefore could sign a formula of union and depart. The Latins, however, insisted on agreement over the other outstanding points of difference, Purgatory, the primacy of the pope, the effective words of consecration in the Liturgy (the Sacrifice of the Mass) and the legitimacy of the addition of the *Filioque* to the Creed. These were treated of mainly by small committees, though there were, at the request of the Greeks, two more public sessions, on the primacy and on the Liturgy. There were times when agreement seemed to be an impossibility. In the general despair Bessarion, Isidore and Dorotheus of Mitylene, refusing to abandon hope, stimulated both Pope and Emperor to new endeavours, and discussion was begun again. The Latin method was to present the Greeks with a statement, to let them debate it privately, and then to discuss with them any difficulties that arose from it. The method proved effective. With slight modifications in the Latin statements on Purgatory and the primacy, and the omission of any formal pronouncement on the words of consecration, on which the Greeks were to make a declaration (read by Bessarion before the Latins on 5 July), agreement was reached on all four

E

points. The decree was written in Latin and Greek, Bessarion doubtless having a hand in the process; it was amended to suit the emperor, and solemnly promulgated on 6 July in a plenary session in the cathedral of Florence, Cardinal Cesarini reading it in Latin and Bessarion in Greek. It was an honour that Bessarion deserved, for he had played a large part in the discussions and negotiations. The Pope gave him a pension of 300 florins annually, to be raised to 600 florins if he resided in the Roman Curia. He returned, however, to Greece with his compatriots, and in his absence he was made a cardinal in the consistory of December 1439. He came back to Italy towards the end of 1440, never to return again to his native land.

Thirty years of life still remained to him, which he spent in various activities entrusted to him by the popes and in furthering the humanism of the time, which gave him also the opportunity of helping many an unfortunate compatriot in exile from the power of the Turks. One of the first things he did was to learn Latin, in which he acquired great facility. At about this time too he composed his 'Letter to Alexius Lascaris Philanthropinus about the Holy Spirit', at once a short history of certain phases of the Council of Florence, and a treatise on the Procession of the Holy Spirit. Eugenius IV gave him the revenue of certain monasteries for his upkeep and, after the return of the Curia to Rome, of a site for a suitable residence. Among the abbeys of which he had charge were some under the Basilian rule. In 1446 he summoned their superiors to a General Chapter in Rome to introduce needed reforms, and drew up for their use an epitome of the Rule of St Basil. A few years later he was empowered to act as visitor of all Greek monasteries in Italy, a task he was eminently fitted for from the fact that he was both a Greek and a monk.

Bessarion had been created Cardinal with the title of the church of the Twelve Apostles. In 1449 he was made Bishop of Sabina, but he retained his interest in his original church where in 1463 he substituted for the secular Canons a community of Friars Minor whose Protector he had become in 1458. In 1449, too, he was appointed legate to reconcile Venice with Milan, and the following year was sent as governor to the turbulent city of Bologna. One of the lasting effects of his rule there was the restoration of the once-famous university which had latterly fallen on evil days. While Bessarion was at Bologna, Constantinople was taken by the Turks (29 May 1453). Thereafter one of his chief preoccupations was to aid his fellow countrymen by fostering every, even faint, prospect of rousing the western princes to a crusade against the Turk, and by assisting unfortunate Greeks, some by providing ransoms to buy them or their families from captivity, others by receiving them in Italy and either giving them work to do or finding them a means of subsistence. It was at this time, too, that he conceived the project of gathering together as many Greek manuscripts as he could so that Greek learning should not perish with the fall of the empire.

Pope Nicholas V died in 1455. In the conclave that followed Bessarion seemed at one time likely to succeed him, but that was not to be. Under Callistus III, relieved of absorbing appointments, he gave himself for a few years to literary work, from which there issued among other things his *In calumniatorem Platonis*. At the death of Callistus (1458), Pius II was elected, an ardent promoter of a crusade against the Turks. In this he found a supporter, equally enthusiastic, in Bessarion. The Pope summoned the Italian States and the Christian princes to a congress at Mantua to arrange the crusade. The response was poor, but, as the German envoys asked for a papal legate to compose the ecclesiastical and political differences of their country and organize the levies for the crusade, Bessarion was the papal choice. He crossed the Alps in mid-winter, traversed large areas of Germany and effected reconciliation in Austria and Hungary, but he could not bring the various princes, intent only on their own immediate problems, to combine for a larger cause. He returned to Venice towards the end of 1461, to learn that Thomas Palaeologus had had to abandon his despotate in the Peloponnesus and that his native town of Trebizond had fallen to Turkish arms. But Pius II had not given up his determination to oppose the Turks. He sent Bessarion in 1463 as legate to Venice, where the Cardinal persuaded the Signoria to declare open war on the infidel, and then went with the Venetian fleet to the rendezvous of the crusade at Ancona. He was just in time to greet the Pope, who had come in person to assume its direction, before Pius II died (14 August 1464). With his death the crusade died too. It was little consolation to Bessarion that in the previous year he had been made Patriarch of Constantinople, in which capacity he addressed an encyclical letter (27 May 1463) to the Greeks living under Venetian rule, commending to them the union of Florence.

In the conclave that followed, Bessarion was doyen of the Sacred College. The new Pope, Paul II, rejected the conditions that the cardinals had drawn up and, as a consequence, his relations with the doyen were for a time somewhat strained. Bessarion retired to the abbey of Grottaferrata (he had become its archimandrite in 1462) which greatly benefited by his sojourn there, for he did much to re-establish it both spiritually and temporally and not least to reconstitute its once-famous library. He had not, however, forgotten the cause of Greece in the midst of his private studies and local activities. When the Emperor Frederick III came to Rome, Bessarion urged him to action against the Turks, who, he said, would not and could not cease from war. His warning was justified, for next year (1470) they captured the Venetian island of Negroponte (Euboea) and later attacked Carinthia. Bessarion's residence in Rome became the meeting place of the commission of cardinals appointed to combine a plan to meet the Turkish threat, but the measures started by the Pope were interrupted by his death (26 July 1471).

The new Pope, Sixtus IV, immediately made Bessarion (22 December 1471) his legate *a latere* to bring France, Burgundy and England together in a crusade, but soon his commission was changed to one of more limited scope, the preliminary settlement of outstanding questions between the Holy See and France. The Cardinal, for reasons of health, hesitated for some time before undertaking the arduous journey. His hope, however, of inducing France to take part in the Holy War, a consequence that might have resulted from a successful issue of his mission, finally led him to accept. But his hopes were not fulfilled. While on his return, he died at Ravenna on 18 November 1472. His body was taken to Rome and solemnly interred in the church of the Twelve Apostles where his tomb can still be seen.

Bessarion was a great man whose name has unjustifiably been blackened. It has been said that his support of the union was the fruit less of conviction than of ambition and of desire for papal rewards. The only proof ever offered of this assertion is the fact that actually he was given a pension and made a cardinal by Eugenius IV. That apart (and by itself it proves nothing), there is no incident in any contemporary document, not even in the bitter *Memoirs* of Syropoulus, that would suggest that Bessarion acted from any less worthy motive.

That he changed his views goes without saying. He began persuaded of the traditional opinions of his Church; he ended convinced by the arguments of the Latins, predisposed perhaps somewhat for this by a correspondence he had had before the Council with Andrew Chrysoberges, O.P., (Latin Archbishop of Rhodes) about the theology of hesychasm, which had made him wonder if the official approval given to this by the Eastern Church was altogether sound—if it could be wrong on one point, it might be wrong on another. He did not disguise his change of opinion. His 'Dogmatic Speech' of April 1439 was at once a proclamation openly made to the whole of the Greek synod that he had come to hold that the Latin doctrine was as sound as their traditional faith and an exposition of the theological reasons for his belief: it ended with a declaration that he would ever be true to his convictions, even if that brought persecution. His subsequent action in the Council, and indeed for the rest of his life, was the logical fruit of his faith.

Yet, even though he was soon held by many of his leading countrymen as a traitor both to his religion and to his fatherland, he was in fact one of his country's best friends. After the fall of Constantinople in 1453 Bessarion was ever active, through diplomatic missions, in letters, by personal contact, trying to persuade the western powers to realise that the destruction of the Byzantine empire would be but the prelude to Turkish designs on their territories, and that the danger of attack was imminent and immense. For their own sakes they must compose their differences and unite, in order to thrust the Mohammedan peril out of Europe. In so doing, they would restore Constantinople to the Greeks. The fact that the western princes were so involved in their own quarrels as to be blind to the larger issues defeated all of Bessarion's endeavours. But he was not to blame for that, nor was a succession of popes who likewise urged unity and the crusade, but in vain.

The Greek exiles also, and there were many of them, received the benefit of his patriotism. Not only did he supervise the education of the three orphan children of Thomas Palaeologus, but he aided with money, with counsel and, very often, with patient restraint many others seeking a living in the new country. Some of these, with Latin humanists, met regularly in his residence and formed his 'Academy', by whose means the translation, conservation and study of treasures of Greek literature and philosophy were greatly advanced. The Cardinal, in the course of years, spent large sums of money on buying and copying manuscripts and the (for those days) rich library that he thus acquired he gave before he died to St. Marks, Venice (1468), as a token of gratitude to that city for its constant goodwill towards him and so as to keep his collection of books together and make it more accessible to his compatriots, for Venice was the nearest great port to Greece and had a large colony of Greeks resident there. Not only his contemporaries, but posterity too, has reason to be grateful for his wise forethought.

CHAPTER FIVE

MARK EUGENICUS, METROPOLITAN OF EPHESUS

'This great beacon of life in the world, who proved himself to be also light and good salt to the Church of Christ, stalwart champion of the truth and sun that illuminates the whole earth, put forth his first beams from the great and imperial city, from this famous Constantinople that is, for in it he was born,[1] nurtured and educated, and finally here, too, in his transit to God he put off his holy body. His parents were George, deacon and Sakellios of the great church, whom the great city at that time enriched by giving a double charge—over the church of Christ and over a throng of youths, who from all parts gathered round him—and Maria Loucas, the daughter of a pious and God-beloved doctor. Enquiry revealed that their forebears on both sides were endowed with nobility, moderate wealth and worldly excellence, as well as piety and virtue.

'The boy, then, in the rite of regeneration by the divine Spirit, received the name of Manuel (no other, indeed, was suitable, for he was worthy of the first of all names), the name of the Lord, and later it was through him that there abode with us God and true religion and our ancestral faith. Till he was in his studies of rhetoric he had as his teacher his father, whom he shortly surpassed in wisdom and virtue; for indeed he excelled his father as much as his father (who gladly experienced what all fathers desire, to be out-distanced by their children) himself outdid all the rest. Orphaned, however, of such a father in his thirteenth year, he did not allow himself to turn towards ease, but preferred immediately to frequent the best and most famous teachers. These were, first, John Chortasmenus, who under the name of Ignatius later adorned the throne of the province of Selymbria; then, for the more advanced of the general and philosophical studies, George Gemistus. With them, by his extreme zeal, his industry and marvellous natural gifts, in a short time he gained great profit. Besides, his good, reverent and moderate disposition, his manner, too, as regards style of dress, gait, glance and gesture,

[1] Probably in the year 1394.

that had the gravity of riper years and added grace to his speech and appearance, made him an object of admiration not only to his fellow-students but also to his masters and, in a word, to everybody.

'So, after a good and saintly youth, he set his hand to many important tasks, wherein he achieved wondrous success. At one time he took over the school that had been his father's and the care of the young, from which there issued many a scholar and teacher; at another, throughout a whole year he never failed to be present daily at the holy celebrations in the great church, no matter the season whether winter or summer, practising thus in anticipation while he was yet a layman the life of the monk, altogether godly and enlightened and in reality being and seeming to be a philosopher while still in tender youth; at yet another, in night-long struggles meditating within himself and storing up for himself the wisdom of the ancients, he neglected nothing that would make for completeness either of the divine scriptures and the holy doctors or of secular knowledge.

'While yet in his twenty-sixth year, after having distributed generously and freely all his goods to the poor, he put on the goodly yoke and the light burden of the Lord that he had yearned for from boyhood. He embraced the solitude dear to Elias and John and their associates, the tranquillity that is the mother of interior calm and peace and quietude and the ascent to God and familiarity with Him, and having chosen the islands that lay before his native shores and were at that time adorned with many a godly man, he picked out for himself the best spiritual guide of them all, the late wondrous Symeon. As his disciple he straightway shaved his head in the style of monks and girt himself for spiritual combat and labours, having left behind unconsolable grief to his kin, his familiars, friends, the Emperor who desired and needed his wisdom and knowledge, to the dignitaries, to the clergy, to the throngs of youths whom he had educated—in a word, to all his fellow-citizens by whom his withdrawal from their life and the loss of the great man's high qualities that had been at everyone's disposal were obviously regarded as a kind of common bereavement.

'In his holy purpose he had had Dorotheus as co-operator and helpmate, a man reverent and earnest, of education and nobility of disposition, who was the son of Balsamon the Great Sacristan of the great church, in youth his intimate confidant, friend, companion of like age and associate in studies, who later had joined him in a pact that both, with God's help, should, no matter the cost, become monks. This came about shortly after, for at one time Jerusalem and the Holy Mountain of Sinai embraced Dorotheus, happily fulfilling there his aim, though shortly he returned and went and put himself under obedience to the above-mentioned Symeon; while the island of Antigone had lately received Mark under the same father and guide.

'But that holy routine of solitude and peace was not to continue for long. Before a second year had run its course, the foolish instability of the policy of that time was already throwing the common weal into confusion, and the new Arab beast, by now the only satrap left of the Ishmaelites, girt the great city round with an immense host. The danger for those in the islands was manifest. The marvellous one returned from the wilderness with his father and guide, and chose to make his abode in the holy and famous monastery of the Mangani, seeing that it, more than the others, offered greater facilities for the hermit's life so dear to him. There, then, he gave himself to harsh mortification, fasting, watchings and night vigils, especially when he was left in solitide, and he would say; "God is served by nothing so much as by the endurance of suffering". So he gained the victory in the struggle against the well-known adversaries and, raised to the heights of contemplation and holy illuminations and divine radiations (when he wrote many, most useful works) and become wholly venerable and Godlike, he received the priesthood, but only with reluctance and under pressure and after much urging, seeming to the onlooker, when he was offering the bloodless sacrifice to God, completely ravished, completely illuminated, completely out of himself in consecration to God, like some angel incarnate.

'There followed the far greater and more striking achievements and the brilliant and noble trophies of the thrice-conqueror. For, when our thrice-miserable nation besides others was about to sustain the disaster of the Church, and a union of that kind was on the point of being devised and accepted—when preparation for this was being made, yielding to earnest prayers and persuasions of all sorts he was raised to the lofty See of Ephesus, he who was in truth worthy of greater, and indeed of the very first, honours, great high priest, who proved himself the zealous imitator of the great and first High Priest and Shepherd, such as the great

Paul described him; truly another Basil the Great, both in appearance and in name. For when the Emperor with the Patriarch and all the clergy after the voyage had reached Italy, he alone from first to last proved himself a double-edged blade to destroy the bastard and evil cockle amidst the true harvest of the holy doctrine of the Church; herald too of godly theology and inexhaustible river of orthodox writings and definitions of the holy Fathers, with piercing and honey-sweet, nectar-burdened voice and fearless and noble disposition of soul.

'All people and nations of those there present know the sophistical twists and turns and modes and deceits and guiles of the others' arguments (to speak with as little bitterness as I can), and how by the pure theology of the Fathers, beginning from the first Theologian Himself and Head of theologians, the God-Word, and onwards, and by the oecumenical decisions and even indeed with the force of apodictic and undeniable syllogisms he dissipated them like smoke or froth, both in the discussions about Purgatory and in those on the Addition that they had dared to make to the holy Creed, and finally about the doctrine itself. Then he stood out more conspicuously than any monument and the holy theology of the great man and his learning and the grace of the most Holy Spirit that was in him and the whole force of truth, and the rottenness and the insecurity of the Latin beliefs were plainly disclosed, just as recently in his homeland in three conferences, even if those who think and say the contrary burst themselves.

'When the consent of the majority, procured by wiles and devices, had been brazenly given, and when as one condemned he stood before the so-called Supreme Pontiff two separate times (like in this to Basil before the eparch), on one of those occasions he answered joyfully and on the other he managed with prudent silence to soothe the irrational anger, after the fashion of the mild and innocent Jesus before the high priests and scribes of His time, so by the providence of God, against all probability, he escaped the danger and returned in safety with renown to his native land, openly admired and honoured by all. Having remained a short while he set off for his own flock, withdrawing from the bustle of the world—the good shepherd who laid down his life for the sheep, and the most genuine imitator of the true and first Shepherd —to visit his own children, the Christians in the midst of the infidel wolves.

'So, in long journeys, with sweat and toil, though in poor bodily health, visiting holy temples in distress especially that of the metropolitan church with its adjacent buildings, ordaining priests, helping the victims of injustice' even if it brought with it persecution and trials at times from the infidel, assisting widows and orphans, checking, chiding, exhorting, warning, converting, supporting, become all things to all men according to the apostle, he spent his time traversing in every direction the area that fell by lot to the great John, the evangelist and theologian. When the affairs of his flock were sufficiently set in order, stricken with a longing for the peace of that contemplation he had always ardently desired, he planned to cross from the East to the holy Mount of Athos to spend there the rest of his life on some desert spot. But while passing innocently through some strait, he put in at the island of Lemnos and there, having tarried a little for a moderate relaxation and having gone ashore, he was immediately recognised and, recognised, arrested on the spot.

'How could anyone sufficiently admire him in this place either for the magnanimity he showed and his endurance in evil plight, in resisting the fierce heat and the frequent lack of necessaries and in combatting diseases one after another, or for his patience in bitter confinement when the fleet of the infidel Ishmaelites girt the island round and was set on destroying it, and, in a word, in afflictions of all kinds for two full years.

'But seeing that he was not allowed to set foot in any way on Athos, the champion returned straightway from his exile to his fatherland, already the complete, new confessor of the faith, honoured and reverenced and justly acclaimed by all.

'There, then, after a life dear to God, a brilliant exemplar in all things—in his manner of life in youth before he assumed the monastic habit, in the holy monastic habit too, in the degrees of the high priesthood, in discussions for the orthodox faith and his bold profession of orthodoxy—in the course of the fifty-second year of his earthly life, on the twenty-third day of the month of June he departed with joy to Him with Whom, in the words of Paul, he desired to be dissolved and to be, Whom he had honoured with sound theology, had served throughout his life, had glorified by good works. With general concourse and honour and the reverence of the populace, to the glory of God Who is rendered glorious and admirable in His saints, the holy and precious casket and shrine of his sanctified soul was reverently set to rest in the same holy monastery of the Mangani of the divine martyr George, after he had laid many injunctions and paternal commands on those present, regarding the righting of the ecclesiastical situation and sound doctrine in us, and the public vindication of the right doctrines of the Church, and the subversion of the innovation. Then joyfully uttering as his last words: "My Lord, Jesus Christ, Son of the living God, into Thy hands I commend my spirit", so saying he passed to Him. By his intercession, Christ God, and that of all Thy holy Doctors and the Father theologians, preserve Thy Church forever in the orthodox faith'.[2]

Such is the brief 'life' of Mark Eugenicus that, a short time after his death, his brother John composed as part of a liturgical office in his honour. It is our chief source for knowledge of Mark's earlier years. About his activity in the Council of Florence and later, information is more plentiful. When the Turkish authorities refused to allow the three oriental patriarchs to attend the Council first he was chosen as his proxy by the Patriarch of Alexandria; then, to his chagrin, he became instead procurator of the lesser See of Jerusalem; in the end, owing to another change made after the arrival in Italy, he acted for Antioch.

He was looked upon as a leading theologian of his Church, and that was probably one of the main reasons why he was raised to the throne of Ephesus on the eve of the Council, at about the same time that Bessarion, Isidore and Dionysius were also consecrated archbishops. In the early months of inactivity at Ferrara, at the suggestion of Cardinal Cesarini but not on the lines or with the purpose proposed by the Cardinal, he addressed a composition to Eugenius IV, an exhortation in beautifully balanced, simple and impassioned Greek, urging that, as a pope had started the schism by putting the *Filioque* into the Creed, the Pope could easily, in the well-disciplined Latin Church, end it by removing the offending word. The address reached, not the Pope, but the Emperor, who would have had Mark punished by the Greek synod if Bessarion had not intervened to calm the storm. That effusion reflected

<hr />

[2] There are two versions of the 'life', the one published by S. Pétridès, *Le synaxaire de Marc d'Éphèse*, in *Revue d'Orient chrétien* 15 (1910), pp. 97–107, the other by L. Petit, *Acolouthie de Marc Eugénicos archevêque d'Éphèse*, in *Studi bizantini e neoellenici* 2 (1927), pp. 195–235. There is no contradiction between them. The second seems to be taken from the first and differs chiefly by the omission of a few sentences.

Mark's views perfectly, and he never changed them—the *Filioque* was heretical, and the only way to ecclesiastical peace was for the Latins to delete it.

Mark was a member of every doctrinal committee formed on the Greek side. He and Bessarion were the two appointed spokesmen for the Greeks, and Bessarion spoke but little—once in the preliminary meetings in May 1438, once about Purgatory, and during two sessions about the addition of the *Filioque* to the Creed (1, 4 November). In all the other sessions in Ferrara and in all without exception of those in Florence, Eugenicus was the Greek speaker. In the meetings about Purgatory, conciliatory at the beginning, Mark hardened in his opposition the more he went on. In the discussion about the Addition, his position was simple and final—the Council of Ephesus forbade any change for all time in the Nicene Creed, and he repeated that as an answer to every Latin argument. Quite arbitrarily, he treated the Constantinopolitan Creed as if it were the original Nicene, and blandly brushed aside all argument drawn from the fact that, whereas the Creed mentioned by the Council of Ephesus was specifically the Nicene, both his Church and the Latin Church had over centuries used not that but the Nicene-Constantinopolitan, i.e. the Nicene with many changes. In Florence, where the doctrine of the *Filioque* was in debate, five sessions were passed in fruitless assertion and counter-assertion about the wording of a few texts from the Fathers; in the sixth, Mark exposed his scriptural and patristic reasons for rejecting the Latin doctrine. He did not attend the seventh and eighth when Montenero ably developed the Latin case.

Not that it would have made much difference, even if he had been present at Montenero's exposition. Mark was impervious to argument. The Latin spokesman had quoted, besides scripture, a most imposing array of Latin Fathers who taught the 'and from the Son' and an equally impressive list of Greek Fathers who wrote of the Holy Spirit as proceeding 'through the Son' or either from the Father and 'flowing', 'bursting forth', 'issuing', etc., etc., 'through' or 'from' the Son, or 'from Both'. After the end of the public sessions Bessarion, George Scholarius, Isidore, Gregory, Dorotheus pressed the parallelism. They started from what was an axiom for the Greeks, for Mark as much as for any of the others —all saints are inspired by the same Holy Spirit and so teach the same truth even if in different words. Their conclusion was, the 'from' of the Latin saints means the same as the 'through' of the Greek. Mark should have been forced to the same conclusion. He accepted the axiom; he could not deny the testimonies from the Greek Fathers, because he was confronted with the codices that contained them; what he did, perforce, was to accuse the Latins of presenting garbled and deliberately falsified quotations from their own Latin Fathers, or at least quotations that could not be checked because he, Mark, with most of the Greeks knew no Latin. Not a few Latin treatises, however, especially those of that greatest advocate of the *Filioque*, St. Augustine, had long been translated into Greek, and there were, of course, some of the Greeks, like Scholarius, who knew Latin well and who tried to disabuse him. But he would not be disabused. The Latins were heretics, and that was that.

Mark's obstinacy would not have mattered so much if all the Greek prelates, or the most of them, had been of a high intellectual calibre. They were not. On a theological problem as intricate as that of the Blessed Trinity, they were fitted rather to follow another's judgement than to make their own. Mark's attitude was in line with Greek tradition. The greater part of the bishops were naturally inclined, sentimentally, to sympathise with it. They did, however, recognise by their votes the cogency of the arguments of Bessarion and the other Greek unionists, yet all the time Mark's rigid abstention was a permanent reproof that made them uneasy and left them with the feeling that they had betrayed the tradition of their Church. When to that was added the raucous condemnation of the monks and the mob of Constantinople after their return, they recanted one by one.

As Mark found himself more and more isolated in his hostility to union, he began to be afraid. In the past, those who did not submit themselves to the decision of an oecumenical council (and Mark recognised the gathering in Italy as oecumenical till he began to disagree with it) had often been severely punished. Eugenius IV and the Latins, and not a few of the Greeks, felt that Mark should either conform to the general decision of the combined Church or at least be impeded from open opposition. Mark was still determined not to yield and so, to avoid the alternative, he appealed to the Emperor John who promised him a return unscathed to Constantinople. He was as good as his word.

Eugenicus, who alone of the Greek prelates in Florence on 5 July 1439 did not sign the decree of union, travelled with the Emperor to Venice at the end of August and arrived safely in Constantinople on 1 February 1440 in the imperial ship.

This history of Mark Eugenicus' activity in Italy should explode once and for all the often repeated—far too often repeated, and that by people who should know better—myth that the Greeks enjoyed no liberty of speech in the Council of Florence, and signed the decree under compulsion. Mark did not sign. The rest need not have done so, if they had not wanted; and, if most of them had refused (the story is that most of them were forced to sign), there was nothing that the Emperor or anyone else could have done to make them. An isolated recalcitrant could more easily have been forced or eliminated. But the only recalcitrant in fact returned home with honour under imperial protection, completely unharmed. And he, the only obdurate and consistent adversary of union throughout the Council, was throughout the Council the speaker for the Greeks, approved of as such by the Emperor, who, it is said, was so set on union that he muzzled its opponents. At any time in Italy John VIII could have put Bessarion up to speak, or Isidore, instead of Eugenicus, for both of these were among the elected six orators, both were theologians enough to do honour to the Greek name and both would have been more sympathetic to the cause of union. He did not do that. He left the intransigent Mark to speak without any official restraint during all the sessions, and, the sessions over, with equal liberty to express his opinion in the private meetings of the ecclesiastics. John VIII's letting Eugenicus go on opposing what he himself certainly wanted is not easy to explain, but it assuredly cannot be interpreted as denying freedom of speech to his subjects.

Back in Constantinople after the Council, Mark was more than ever the symbol of anti-unionism. When Metrophanes, a unionist, was made patriarch, Eugenicus assisted at none of the ceremonies, and, fearing that pressure might be brought to bear on him to mitigate his opposition, he left Constantinople secretly for his diocese of Ephesus, which he had not yet visited. The 'life' written by his brother John portrays him as playing the part of the good shepherd there for some considerable time. Other sources suggest that the Turkish authorities made difficulties and that he departed again soon after his arrival. Then there was the two years' confinement on Lemnos and his final return to Constantinople.

In all these various circumstances, he was active with voice and pen persuading the hesitant, confirming the persuaded and exciting the convinced to open and undying opposition to union. It was not a very difficult task, because the Greeks at large had long believed that the Latins were heretics. But Mark performed his task well. He wrote an encyclical letter 'to all orthodox Christians everywhere and in the islands'; he composed an account of his action in the Council; he corresponded with various people. In the compositions he mingled deep reverence for tradition with scorn for the 'innovators', ardent love of his Church and vulgar invective against the Latins and their Greek supporters (he never, however, wrote a disrespectful word about the Emperor), serious theological reasoning with the most blatant *argumenta ad hominem*. He was writing primarily, not for theologians, but for the mass of the Greeks, and he was clever enough to adapt his style and method to the educational level of the ignorant monks and the amorphous populace—very successfully. But his greatest triumph was that he finally persuaded George Scholarius, who for a time had stood aloof from the controversy, to take up his prophetic mantle after his death, and he could not have chosen a better successor for his purpose.

If some one cause is to be assigned for the failure of the Council of Florence, that cause was Mark Eugenicus, metropolitan of Ephesus. He enjoyed a well-deserved reputation for austerity of life and learning. He had the strength of character to follow a single-minded, indeed a narrow-minded, purpose at any cost. To many of his fellow-countrymen he seemed the embodiment of all that was best in his Church. And he was proclaiming that the union was a betrayal of their faith, for by it the Latin doctrine of the Holy Spirit and the Latin rite in unleavened bread had been declared the equal of the Greek, whereas their Fathers and he knew that that was false.

He was formally declared a saint by his church in 1734.

CHAPTER SIX

ISIDORE, METROPOLITAN OF KIEV AND ALL RUSSIA

Isidore, whose family name is not known, was born probably in Monembasia, almost the most southerly town of southern Greece, between the years 1380 and 1390. Secure information about his earlier years is scarce. There are, however, hints and allusions in the few letters of his and other personal documents that have been preserved, sufficient to establish a landmark here and there. The writer of a eulogium to welcome Manuel II back to Constantinople after his long voyage in the West (1403) speaks of the previous lack of teachers as he himself had suffered from it —presumably in the years of siege—and is grateful for the return of the philosopher Emperor, the reopening of the schools, and indeed for a kind of scholarship which he enjoyed. That writer was probably Isidore, in Constantinople from some little time before 1403 for purposes of study. It must have been then that he met the Italian Guarino Veronese, one of the first of the many Italian humanists who journeyed to Constantinople to study Greek on the spot. In later years there was a correspondence between these two, mainly about the manuscripts that Isidore was procuring and sending to his friend in Italy. The well-known Xenophon, now in the library of Wolfenbüttel, was a gift of his to Guarino.

Isidore returned to the Peloponnesus in 1409, the bearer of an oration written by the Emperor Manuel for the anniversary of the death of his brother Theodore. He seems to have remained in the Peloponnesus for the next twenty years or so, in the course of which he became a monk in the monastery of St. Michael and the Angels of Monembasia, and came under the influence of George Gemistus Pletho. Gemistus lived in Mistra and was a phenomenon of the Greek humanistic world. He had given himself the surname, Pletho, to perpetuate the fame of his hero, the philosopher Plato, in whose thought he had so steeped himself as finally to have become more pagan than Christian. He enjoyed a great reputation for learning and possessed a wide influence in humanistic circles

F

in Greece. Mark Eugenicus and Bessarion certainly studied under him; Isidore probably did, for his writings at this time display a decided Platonic tendency and an antagonism to Aristotle, which was the characteristic of Gemistus's thought.

In 1429 Isidore, on behalf of the Metropolitan of Monembasia, wrote two letters to the authorities in Constantinople, exposing with great vigour the reasons why two dioceses of the Province of Monembasia should not be put under the jurisdiction of Corinth. In the event, the better to defend the integrity of his native place and to uphold the rights of his archbishop, he was sent to Constantinople to plead the cause in person. His return journey was adventurous. The ship he was in was forced as far out of course as Sicily, and so Isidore on 25 September 1429 gazed from the sea on 'the great castles of Sicily' as the ship fared from Palermo to Syracuse. In 1430 he was back in the Peloponnesus, for there is extant in his handwriting a complicated explanation, dating from that year, of a prophecy about the Hexamilion (the wall of fortification that spanned the Isthmus of Corinth), and the solution of another similar prophecy, founded on intricate mathematical calculations, in which he foretold the speedy end of Greece's enemies. These writings are interesting, not only because they add another fixed date to Isidore's very sparse biography, but also because they illustrate a lesser known side of his character, for Isidore was a polymath with an interest in all kinds of learned and semi-learned subjects.

In 1433 the Council of Basel sent two envoys to the court of John VIII, whereupon the Emperor appointed three Greeks to accompany them back to Basel to negotiate in his name. One of the Greek envoys was Isidore, not long recovered from an illness and by now Superior of the Constantinopolitan monastery of St Demetrius. Their journey was ill-starred from the first. They set out on 11 November 1433, but because of a violent storm had to return. More successfully they left again on 18 January 1434, survived very bad weather in the Black Sea, continued their journey overland by Wallachia (Rumania) and Hungary, fell among bandits and were robbed, but contrived to reach Buda where they managed to raise enough money to take them to Ulm to meet the Emperor Sigismund, for whom they carried letters from their sovereign. They entered Basel on 12 July.

By this time the relations between the Council of Basel and

Pope Eugenius were strained to the uttermost. The Pope's attempt to prorogue the Council had been resisted by the Fathers; most of the western princes and universities attracted by the Council's programme of Church reform had rallied to its support; the greater part of the cardinals, making as it were a 'friend of the mammon of iniquity', had openly or covertly pledged their adherence; the Duke of Milan, claiming to act for the Council, had produced revolt in Rome, and Eugenius by 24 July 1434 had taken refuge in Florence. The sending of conciliar envoys to Constantinople without reference to the Pope was part of the anti-papal policy of the Council, for hitherto it had been Popes Martin V and Eugenius IV who had negotiated with the Eastern Church. When therefore Alberto de Crispis returned with three Greek envoys, it was something of a triumph, and the Council showed its delight by the almost extravagant honour it paid the Greeks. They were met, on their arrival, outside the city walls by all except the Presidents, lodged sumptuously and, when they were formally presented to the Council, the President Cesarini made a long discourse. The Greek answer was given a few days later by Isidore, whose speech was translated into Latin by the humanist, Giovanni Aurispa. This speech displays Isidore as a master of Greek prose and an accomplished orator; courteous, polished, stressing perhaps a little excessively (intelligibly, however, in the circumstances) the extent and consequent importance of the Greek Church; like Cesarini, not insisting overmuch on the differences that divided the two Churches.

The Greek legation had brought with it the draft agreement made in the last days of Martin V. The arrangements arrived at with Basel were based on that. The Council of union should be held in some town of Italy, Buda, Vienna or, at the most, Savoy; and at the expense of Basel, provision to be made also for the defence of Constantinople. This pact between the Council and the Greek envoys was solemnly approved by the Fathers on 7 September 1434 as the decree *Sicut pia mater*, and the Greeks promised on oath to do their best to ensure its fulfilment.

Meanwhile the Pope had been in negotiation with the Emperor John VIII and had agreed to a council in Constantinople, which was very much more to the liking of the Greeks. John, therefore, wrote to tell his ambassadors in Basel to suspend operations pending the arrival of more envoys. The new instructions, however, came to the three Greeks too late. When the Fathers heard of them they suspected that they had been hoodwinked, and their former graciousness turned into suspicion and illwill. Isidore proclaimed his innocence, but it was not till there came to Basel the new Greek envoys, accredited to the Pope but sent on by him to the Council, that harmony was restored and the decree *Sicut pia mater* confirmed anew. Shortly after, Isidore went to Venice and thence to Constantinople in the company of three envoys sent to the Byzantine court by the Council.

The Greeks of the capital strongly resented certain words in the preamble of the decree that the envoys from Basel brought with them. They even proposed a new one, which a committee that included Isidore prepared. There were other frictions also in which Garatoni, the papal representative, was involved, and Isidore (so Ragusa, one of the Baseler envoys, reported) sided with him. In the nominations of procurators for the eastern patriarchates, Isidore was chosen for Jerusalem; later, however, he was appointed to represent Antioch instead. But the greatest sign of confidence in him that the authorities of Constantinople showed came shortly after, when they selected him to fill the vacant See of Kiev and All Russia. In 1436 he was consecrated and then he set off for Moscow, at that time the seat of the Metropolitan, arriving on 2 April 1437. His first task was to arrange for the Russian Church to be represented at the forthcoming council of union.

Vasili, the Great Prince of Moscow, was not particularly pleased to see him. For one thing, he had sent to Constantinople Jonas, his own candidate for the metropolitan See, but he was too late; for another, he was more interested in the union of all the Russian princedoms under his own hegemony than he was in union of Churches. Isidore had a hard time persuading the prince to let him return to a council of union, especially as he would be representing the Church of Russia and wanted other representatives and an escort on a scale befitting its importance. It is said that Vasili yielded only when the new Metropolitan swore not to bring back with him a faith different from that of the first seven Councils. It is more than doubtful whether Isidore took any such oath, but, even if he did, the faith of the union that he brought back four years later was in fact and in his belief the genuine faith of the early Church.

After a stay of only five months in Moscow the new Metropolitan started on his return journey. The company included Avrami, Bishop of Susdal, the Archimandrite Vassian, the priest Symeon, Gregory the Greek monk who had accompanied Isidore from Constantinople, and various other monks and servants. At Tver, Prince Boris appointed one of his nobles, Thomas, to join the mission. Arrived at Pskov, Isidore satisfied its inhabitants (and doubtless pleased Vasili of Moscow) by detaching that diocese from the jurisdiction of Novgorod and putting it directly under himself, for that purpose appointing a vicar. He reached Riga on 4 February, where, on being refused permission by Sigismund of Lithuania to cross his territory, he had to wait till the sea was unfrozen to go to Lubeck by ship (5 May). There the Bishop, who had temporally espoused the cause of Eugenius against Basel (Isidore was still under the impression that all were agreed in following *Sicut pia mater*), directed him to the Pope in Ferrara. The journey has been described by one of Isidore's Russian companions, who was full of wonder at the stone houses, bridges, vineyards and the rest that they saw in place after place along the way, till they arrived in Ferrara on 18 August 1438. There the plague was raging, and several of the Russians soon fell victims to it.

The Greeks had already been in Ferrara for more than six months and were beginning to be tired of their self-imposed inactivity. The prospect of the arrival of representatives from the western princes seemed remote; the Pope was running short of money and was behindhand with his payments; the Latins were anxious to get down to business and be gone, and so there was general agreement to proceed with the main purpose of the Council, the discussion of doctrine. Each side was to have six speakers. As one of theirs the Greeks elected Isidore. The only two of the six Greek speakers, however, who made set speeches were Mark Eugenicus and Bessarion. Isidore, it is recorded, made himself heard once in the altercation about procedure that occupied most of the second session, and there have been preserved drafts, incomplete, of three speeches that he set himself to prepare for use in the earlier sessions, as well as of a longer work, comprising fifty-two arguments, but still incomplete, begun on 14 November, in answer to Cardinal Cesarini's presentation of the Latin case. There is no record of his having delivered any of these in public; their unfinished state would also seem to preclude it.

The documents of the Council make no further mention of Isidore till the end of March 1439. The Russian, however, who told the story of the journey to Ferrara, describes also the journey from there to Florence, on which he found, apparently, some consolation amidst the hazards of mountain travel in winter in 'a very good, sweet red wine' produced in those parts. Isidore left Ferrara on 27 January 1439 and reached Florence on 4 February, the first of the Greeks to arrive.

The sessions in Florence were conducted by only one of the chosen orators from either side—John of Montenero, O.P. for the Latins, Mark Eugenicus for the Greeks. Each of these, towards the end, expounded at length the arguments for his view. When Montenero had finished his exposition (24 March), it was Isidore who replied in a few words, demanding time to consider it and requesting a written text, especially of the quotations made from the Latin Fathers.

That was the last meeting in the regular series of public sessions. The months that followed were taken up with private debates among the Greeks and occasional contact with the Latins. The morale of the Greek community was low. Most of them had not been persuaded by the Latin arguments, but they had been silenced because the Latins never seemed to lack for an answer. Now they were determined to undergo no more public discussions; if the Latins could not find some other way of producing agreement, they wanted to go home. Isidore was one of four delegates sent to convey this ultimatum to the Pope. There was, however, a compact group among the Greeks convinced that the faiths of the two Churches were in essentials identical. The best theologians were of its number—Bessarion, Isidore (both of the chosen six speakers), Gregory the imperial confessor, Dorotheus of Mitylene, and two out of the three lay 'philosophers' brought by the Emperor to advise him, George Amiroutzes and George Scholarius. The only Greek theologian of note on the other side was Mark Eugenicus, and he was adamant in his opposition.

The consequent tension among the Greek ecclesiastics made itself felt in all their meetings. The unionists, foremost among them Bessarion and Isidore, were harping on one theme—that the saints of both Churches, inspired as they were by the same Holy Spirit, could teach only one doctrine, even though it might be expressed in different ways. They were appealing to a principle which they themselves believed, which Mark Eugenicus believed, which all the Greek prelates believed. Towards the middle of April, Bessarion and George Scholarius delivered before the Greek synod long addresses to demonstrate the harmony of the saints. But for the time being their efforts produced no perceptible effect. Meantime an expedient suggested by the Emperor was resorted to, meetings between committees of ten to offer and discuss possible modes of agreement. Isidore was one of the Greek delegates, and it is likely that he put forward as a possible formula of union the 'Through the Son', that had been used by the former Patriarch of Constantinople, Tarasius; he certainly prepared a dissertation along those lines. The Latins, however, were suspicious of 'Through', and did not take up the suggestion.

The conferences petered out without producing any tangible result, except that they led the Latins to present to the Greeks for their acceptance or comment a formal statement of trinitarian faith. The Greeks were divided about it, and finally decided to produce a statement of their own, based on texts from St Cyril and the first Council of Nicaea that Isidore had quoted in one of their meetings. But the Latins found that, too, ambiguous, and so union was still unachieved. Another month went by of visits of the Emperor to the Pope and of cardinals to the Emperor, of meetings among the Greeks and arguments and squabbles, till on 27 May Eugenius addressed the Greek synod, recalling his high hopes of the previous year and his increasing sadness as time was frittered away and exhorting them to bring the blessed work of union of the Churches to a happy conclusion. The Pope's speech moved his hearers deeply, and Isidore spoke a few words in reply, pleading that the Greeks had not been inactive in a matter that needed much time and consideration.

The group of unionists was spurred on to renewed efforts, stressing always the necessary harmony of the saints and quoting the words about the Blessed Trinity of both Greek and Latin Fathers. Isidore with Bessarion and Dorotheus of Mitylene was always to the fore. The Emperor took votes from the prelates, and first (28 May) there was accepted the genuineness of the quotations made by Montenero from the Latin Fathers, which Eugenicus had senselessly challenged, and then (3 June), as an inevitable consequence, all the Greek prelates, led by the Patriarch, with the exception of only Eugenicus and three others, agreed that the Latin 'From the Son' meant the same as the traditional Greek 'Through the Son'.

Meantime the Emperor, seeing union now in the offing and mindful of one of his chief reasons for ever embarking on the enterprise of uniting the Churches, on 1 June sent Isidore to the Pope to discuss exactly what help His Holiness would furnish to Constantinople in its perpetual struggle against the Turk. Isidore brought back with him three cardinals, who gave satisfying assurances of generous aid. A few days later he was one of four delegates who twice spoke with the Pope about the other doctrinal questions that still had to be settled, and after the Patriarch's death (10 June), with Bessarion and Mitylene, he received the Pope's condolences and again discussed with him the outstanding problems. The doctrines of the primacy and the Eucharist were explained by Latin orators in public sessions, Isidore offering a compromise solution of the epiclesis difficulty, that John of Torquemada rejected. But the primacy of the pope was an obstacle that seemed to block the way to union, and there was general despair. Isidore, Bessarion and Mitylene with a few others rallied Emperor and Pope to further action. A meeting was arranged between committees of six, which included Isidore. Some concessions were made by the Pope. The Greeks, shortly after, acknowledged the papal primacy. Isidore with Mitylene visited the Pope to urge expedition; the Bull of union was drawn up and would have been promulgated on 29 June, if its wording had not caused difficulties. As it was the Greeks signed it on 5 July, Isidore doing so both as Metropolitan of Kiev and All Russia and as procurator of the Patriarch of Antioch. It is said that he imprisoned Bishop Avrami of Susdal for a week to make him sign.

The purpose for which the Russians and the Greeks were in Italy had now been fulfilled. They could go home and take the union with them. Isidore, on 17 August, was nominated by the Pope Apostolic Legate for Russia and the neighbouring territories, with the mission of establishing the union in all the area of his metropolitanate. In practice that meant persuading the kings and princes of Poland, Lithuania and the Russian principalities to accept it and to put it into effect, a difficult task because the tone of Poland and Lithuania was antipapal and pro-Basel. On 4 September Isidore was present at the solemn session of the council to promulgate the Bull, *Moyses vir Dei*, Eugenius's answer to

Basel's decree of deposition against him, and on the same day, accompanied by Avrami of Susdal, he had a farewell audience of the Pope. He set out two days later and reached Venice on 15 September where, owing to the death of Albert of Hungary, he still was when in the consistory of 18 December Eugenius made him a cardinal. He left Venice only on 22 December, after some of his suite had lost patience and departed without him. Arrived in Buda on 5 March, he issued an encylical letter explaining the union of Florence and its practical importance—identity of faith and equality of rites. In Poland he barely saw the King who was on the point of leaving for Hungary. Lithuania was very unsettled owing to the recent accession to power of a boy successor. Nevertheless he visited the more Ruthenian parts of those countries, being accepted everywhere as rightful Metropolitan. In Kiev, the historical cradle of his See, his rank was recognised and he was officially given its temporalities. He entered Moscow on 19 March 1441, taking with him the priest Symeon in chains for anti-unionist propaganda.

Metropolitan and papal Legate, he went in procession (behind, so it is said, a Latin cross) to the church of the Ascension, celebrated the Divine Liturgy in which at the appropriate place the Pope was prayed for, and, when the Liturgy was finished, he had the decree of union read aloud from the pulpit by the protodeacon clad in sacred vestments. Vasili accepted the letters that Eugenius had sent him by his Legate, but four days later he had Isidore arrested and confined in a monastery on a charge of heresy. Faced with the prospect of being tried by a committee formed from his own metropolitan synod (which included also Jonas, the unsuccessful rival for his See, and Avrami of Susdal), Isidore escaped to Tver, with, it is generally thought, the connivance of Vasili who desired nothing so much as to be rid of an influence that breathed peace and co-operation with the Latins, when he wanted rather to undermine the loyalties of Ruthenian Christians in other countries and make them look to Moscow as their spiritual, and consequently also political, home. In Tver, Isidore was imprisoned again and, with his companion Gregory, the Greek monk, gained his liberty only in March 1442.

He found the tone of Poland and Lithuania less friendly than before, since in the meantime many bishops had declared themselves openly in favour of Basel against Eugenius. Nevertheless he lingered in those parts for a full year. Details of his activity are scarce, but it is certain that he visited many parts of the area subject to him as Metropolitan, smoothing out difficulties, settling problems and promoting the union of Florence on all occasions, as, for example, by consecrating unionist bishops for those dioceses that were vacant. One major result of his labours probably was the decree put out by Ladislas, King of Poland and Hungary, granting the Ruthenians equality of civil rights with the Latins. Unfortunately Ladislas's death in November 1444 robbed the decree of its force.

Isidore reached Venice in June 1443 and on 11 July Siena, where the papal court then was, when he was invested with the insignia of a cardinal. At that time, the eve of the crusade against the Turks that ended so sadly at Varna, there was much coming and going on diplomatic missions. Isidore was soon involved in it. He left Italy towards the end of January 1444, sent by the Pope 'to Greece and Russia'. As far as is known, he spent the whole of the next four years, till 12 February 1448, in various parts of Greece, except for a short visit to Rome towards the end of 1445. He wrote several reports for the Pope of his observations, one of which, composed probably in the summer of 1451 apropos of a visit to Nicholas V of a Byzantine envoy, is still extant. In it he declared that the union was well established in all the Venetian colonies of the East and that in Constantinople, whereas there was a very small hard core of opponents—half a dozen and they were renegades of a kind in so far as they had either themselves signed the decree or agreed beforehand to the idea of a council of union —there were, too, very many well disposed to it, especially in high places. The plan he suggested for strengthening union was the dispatch of trained preachers to explain simply, and as far as possible only from Greek sources, what the decree of union taught, and to send a legate first to the Peloponnesus and then to Constantinople to recommend the union.

Nicholas V did send a legate, and it was Isidore. But by then the situation of Constantinople was almost desperate, for Mahomet II had already cut the city off from the north by his new fort on the Bosphorus. The papal Legate left Rome on 20 May 1452, visited Naples, and accompanied by the Latin Bishop of Mitylene reached Constantinople on 26 October, bringing with him 200 archers from Chios, for whose hire he had sold his personal estate. George Scholarius, now the monk Gennadius, kept up a series of letters and manifestoes to maintain opposition to the union, but the proximity of danger was too great. The ruling classes, throughout inclined towards union, needed little persuading. The populace, in general anti-unionist, was overawed by the circumstances. On 12 December 1452 at a solemn Liturgy in the church of St. Sophia the Pope was prayed for and commemorated in the diptychs, and the decree of union promulgated from the pulpit. On 29 May Constantinople fell to the victorious Turks, and the church of St. Sophia became a mosque.

Isidore had not brought to Constantinople archers from Chios for nothing. During the fifty-three days of the siege he fought with them in defence of the city and was wounded in the head, though fortunately not seriously, by a Turkish arrow. In the confusion of the capture of the city he was taken prisoner, was ransomed, managed to hide himself in disguise for a time, and finally escaped to Crete in one of the few ships that got away. From there he wrote anguished letters to Bessarion, the Pope and many others, lamenting the loss of 'that most hapless city', describing some of the atrocities committed by the Turkish soldiers, and warning Christendom that Mahomet had only just begun his career of conquest—Italy and Rome would be his next aim.

The days of Isidore's great activity were now over. For the future his life will be passed quietly in Rome. When he was first created cardinal, his titular church had been that of SS. Peter and Marcellinus. In February 1451 he became Bishop of Sabina, and on 24 January 1452, to give him the means of living reasonably according to his rank, on the death of Giovanni Cantareno, the Latin Patriarch of Constantinople, to whom no successor was appointed, he was granted the enjoyment of the temporalities of that See, on condition that he appointed a vicar to do the work that belonged to it. In 1458 he co-operated in a scheme, that probably first originated with him, aiming at salving for union what could be salved of his metropolitanate of Russia. Jonas, the disappointed Russian candidate for the archbishopric in 1436, in 1448 was without reference to Constantinople elected and consecrated by the Russian synod Archbishop of Kiev and All Russia, and was recognised as such in 1451 by Casimir, King of Poland and Lithuania, in respect of his Ruthenian subjects. It was a political move on Casimir's part, and it did not help him.

He was, then, willing to fall in with the scheme, prepared by Callistus III and executed after Callistus's death by Pius II, of dividing the metropolitanate of Kiev and All Russia into two, the one part with its seat at Kiev comprising the nine oriental dioceses in Poland and Lithuania, the other with its seat at Moscow. To facilitate this plan Isidore resigned into the Pope's hands his archbishopric and, when Gregory the Greek monk, his old companion, was consecrated for Kiev, where the union was still lively, he became Archbishop of only Moscow. A year later (20 April 1459), on the death of Gregory III, he was appointed Patriarch of Constantinople, which meant in effect that he had practical jurisdiction in the Venetian colonies.

But Isidore was never reconciled to leaving Constantinople peaceably in the hands of the Turks. When Pius II at Mantua tried to rally the Christian princes of Europe to a grand crusade, Isidore immediately set to work to put it into practice and the winter of 1459–60 found him busy at Ancona preparing ships, buying arms, and collecting men and material for an 'expeditionary force'. He still had hopes, even when the negotiations of Mantua came to nothing, of leading his little band to the defence of the Peloponnesus. But the Turks were there before him, and the only consolation he could then get was to welcome the Despot Thomas Palaeologus into exile.

On 1 April 1461 his health gave way and he became subject to a species of seizure. Yet he dragged himself (11 April 1462) from his sick bed to join the procession that was escorting the head of St Andrew, the reputed founder of the Church of Constantinople, to St Peter's, there to venerate it on his knees. He had always been poor and had kept up, for a cardinal, only a very modest household. Now his affairs became very involved, and the man whose career had been most like his own, the Greek Cardinal Bessarion, his very close friend, was appointed his administrator (13 December 1462). Isidore, the 'Ruthenian Cardinal', died on 27 April 1463.

Isidore has always had what nowadays is called a bad press. The Greeks consider him a traitor to Orthodoxy, some of them going so far as to suggest that the cardinal's hat was the bribe. The Russian chroniclers could not be expected to wax enthusiastic about him, and they did not do so. Even the Latin author of the 'Lives of Illustrious Men', Vespasiano da Bisticci, accused him of borrowing codices from the Vatican Library and failing to return them. More modern writers, like Pastor, have echoed the calumny. In consequence Isidore is now looked upon by most of the few that know anything at all about him as having been ambitious, imprudent, and not quite honest; astute rather than intelligent; unscrupulous himself and impatient of hesitations in others; a man of little education, more given to activity than to reflection. His worst fault was that he failed.

There is no proof whatsoever that he was ambitious. Nothing at all is known of the circumstances that led to his being chosen as Metropolitan of Kiev, although it is generally thought that, as the Emperor and the Patriarch of Constantinople were in favour of union of the Churches and a council to that end, they selected for Russia someone who, they knew, shared their views. In Italy he was one of those most active for union; he was made papal Legate for Russia—not unnaturally, as he was the Metropolitan of it and about to return there; he was created cardinal. These facts we know. To conclude to a nexus between them of ambition on the part of Isidore is completely unjustifiable. There is not the evidence.

The charge of imprudence is a deduction—since he failed to establish the union in Moscow, he must have been imprudent in the means he adopted and in particular in promulgating the decree immediately on his arrival. He had, however, written his encyclical letter of explanation and recommendation from Buda in 1440 and taken nearly another year to reach Moscow, having meanwhile found both his office and his message acceptable to the Christians of oriental rite wherever he went. Vasili must have been aware of all his movements and known of his success, and unquestionably he had determined on his own attitude before Isidore ever arrived. He was not going to have union, and the only conduct that would have secured Isidore peaceable possession of his See in Moscow would have been silence on what an oecumenical Council had established, what he had been commissioned to do and what he himself had most at heart. And that fact he learnt only after the event.

The imputation of dishonesty has been disproved at least twice. The registers of books borrowed in Isidore's time are still extant, and there is a catalogue of the Vatican Library of 1475. A comparison showed that, morally speaking, all the manuscripts that the Ruthenian Cardinal had borrowed had been returned. But other and more interesting facts also came to light in the course of the investigation, first that Isidore had enriched the Vatican Library, for it contains even now after sacks of Rome, fire, and the negligence of human beings, many manuscripts that once were his, and also that he had a wide range of interests in his reading. His own books (some of them containing works of his own composition) and the books he borrowed (sometimes with notes of his added in the margins) cover many subjects: theology, patrology, philosophy, astronomy, mathematics, etc. They show that Isidore was one of the group of Greek humanists that flourished in the first half of the XV century, and that he should be numbered as an equal with Bessarion, Scholarius, Mark Eugenicus and the rest.

His life-story is his best defence. He was sent by the Emperor and the Patriarch to Basel, made procurator for the Patriarchate of Jerusalem while still a simple monk, and chosen for the See of Kiev and All Russia. His fellows selected him as one of the six orators in Italy, a sign of their trust and an acknowledgement both of his learning and his powers of oratory. He was the trusted messenger of Emperor to Pope and of Pope to Emperor. He was twice papal Legate. He was one of Constantine's most reliable councillors during the siege of Constantinople, and he fought till the last defending its walls: a scholar, an orator, a writer, and yet a man of action indefatigable in the service of his religion and his country. The most bitter anti-unionists admired and liked him till he began to promote union. Syropoulos referred to him, on the occasion of his mission to Basel, as 'that most worthy of abbots'. Mark Eugenicus, later Metropolitan of Ephesus, in a letter of congratulation to Isidore on his elevation to the throne of Kiev, wrote among many other high praises these words: 'A man who really is a reflection of Christ, gracious in character and angelic in form; a happy and outstanding blend of simplicity and sagacity with a gift of speech that surpasses the flow of rivers; generous and liberal to such a degree as not to grudge even his own coverings, if occasion demand'.[1]

[1] G. Mercati, *Scritti d'Isidoro il cardinale Ruteno* (=Studi e Testi 46, Rome 1926), p. 155.

CHAPTER SEVEN

GEORGE SCHOLARIUS

How many men of the name of George Scholarius were involved in the controversies of the Council of Florence—one, two or three? The extremely learned Leo Allatius at the beginning of the seventeenth century was convinced that there were three; John Caryophilus, nearly as learned as Allatius and a contemporary of his, decided for two. Nowadays no one seriously upholds that there was ever more than one. The reason for this wide divergence of opinion is that during the Council a Scholarius spoke and wrote openly and forcefully in favour of union, and after the Council a Scholarius was the very leader of the anti-unionists, who by his action and writing did more that any other single person, with the exception of Mark Eugenicus perhaps, to defeat the union. It was, however, the same Scholarius, whose real name was George Courtesis, the title 'Scholarius', which he himself later used exclusively and by which he is now known, being rather the designation of a profession.

George Courtesis was born in Constantinople about the year 1405 from parents of medium station who had come from Thessaly to settle in the capital. He began his studies under Mark Eugenicus, but was self-taught as regards the humanities, philosophy and theology. He early learnt Latin, and, as his preferences were for philosophy and theology, he turned to the great Latin theologians, particularly to St. Thomas Aquinas. Of the Greek philosophers he was a disciple of Aristotle rather than of Plato, not so much because he was opposed to Platonism as because he found in Aristotelianism a better ally of religion. His admiration for Latin theology and particularly for St. Thomas was, then, the greater, because there he found Aristotle's philosophy not only made to subserve the faith, but purified and improved in the process. In a letter to the Despot Constantine of about the year 1433, after dismissing the philosophical learning of his Greek contemporaries as almost elementary, he continued: 'So I applied myself to the most ancient masters and their writings, reading not those most easy to grasp . . . but the most learned and the most profound who have penetrated to the core and marrow to provide nourishment both for themselves and others, namely Theophrastes, Alexander, Porphyry, Syricius, Simplicius. I did not stop even at these great names, but, thanks to my knowledge of Latin, suspecting that foreign learning (I mean that of the Latins) would be of great help for the attainment of my purpose, I perused many Latin works, many of the early period, a few of the middle period, very many of the most recent period where there is more rigour and accuracy. In fact the Latin masters knew not only Porphyry, Alexander, Ammonius, Simplicius and Themistius, but they had made for themselves translations of the writings of Averroes and Avicenna and of many other Arabs and Persians. I read those translations also. Everybody, I suppose, knows that Averroes is the best of the commentators on Aristotle and that, besides being a commentator, he was the author of many works worthy of serious study. The Latins, utilising these various sources of information, made many a discovery for themselves. They have in consequence added many improvements to Aristotle's philosophy. By questions and reflections of a high order, by distinctions of great subtlety, they have surpassed the explanations of our first commentators. Nay more, they have even managed to surpass themselves, and the later ones among them bear away the palm from their predecessors'.[1]

Scholarius more than once contrasted the vigorous philosophical thought of the West with the stagnation in Constantinople, where, he said, there were not more than three or four, not merely ready to study philosophy, but even capable of it. That defect he set out to remedy and to restore to the Greeks what had once been a chief Greek glory. He opened, therefore, a school to teach grammar and philosophy, where he commented on Aristotle, beginning with logic and the art of dialectics. For the sake of his pupils he translated in this period of his life several of St. Thomas's commentaries on Aristotle, and in his own commentaries and explanations he followed the Thomistic method—clear exposition of the question, difficulties, proof, answer to difficulties. It is, perhaps, small wonder, also since Latins frequented his school, that he began to be regarded as too friendly to Latinism and even to be suspected of being infected with Latin errors. To answer his calumniators he wrote a short discourse wherein he mingled

[1] SCHOL., VII, p. 3.

attack and defence: the philosopher in Greece is rare and unappre-
ciated, while Italians in numbers come to Constantinople to gain
what Greeks neglect; recognition of Latin learning is not the same
thing as accepting Latin dogmas (from which charge Scholarius
vigorously defends himself), though his accusers are probably
ignorant of what Latins teach; in any case no one can say what he
holds on disputed questions, because he has never disclosed his
mind on them. Suspicion, however, did not dim his appreciation
of western thought, for some ten years later, when he was already
launched on his anti-unionistic career, he translated for one of
his favourite pupils St. Thomas's *De ente et essentia*, in his introduction to which he wrote: 'I doubt if Thomas has any more
fervent disciple than me. The man who once has attached himself
to him will have no need of any other Muse, and if he manages
thoroughly to understand him, he can think himself happy
indeed. . . . Thomas is without any question the chief of all (Latin
teachers). That is why he has received the approbation of the
Roman Church, whereas the others are honoured only in the
schools'.[2]

While Scholarius was engaged in these activities of teaching,
writing and translating, he gained the friendship of the Emperor,
John VIII, and without relinquishing his teaching was made
imperial secretary and Judge General of the Greeks, and (though
still a layman) the regular preacher to the court, who every Friday
evening addressed 'the Senate and all the city' in the imperial
palace. It was the period when Constantinople was in close
diplomatic contact with the Pope and the Council of Basel over the
question of union of the Churches. Scholarius' opinion was
sought on the advisability of going to Italy. He was wholly in
favour, provided that the discussion there of the differences that
divided the Churches was frank and thorough; if the aim was only
a union of expediency, an arrangement between a few ambassadors
would be as good and less laborious and less costly. He was not
certain (as appears from a letter to a nephew) of a happy outcome of
the Council, but that he was optimistic about it is clear from a
letter of his dating from this period to Pope Eugenius. There,
after referring to some previous communication of his and a papal
answer, he tells the Pope 'as common father and shepherd of the
universe' of his desire to see and venerate 'the chair of Peter and

[2] Ibid., VI, p. 179.

G

you his successor' and conveys his good wishes for what the
Pope has so much at heart, namely the Council.[3] Whether
Eugenius replied also to this letter is not known, though it is very
likely that he did.

Scholarius journeyed to Italy for the Council as an adviser
of the Emperor, but he went after the main party. He was not
elected one of the six Greek orators to speak during the doctrinal
sessions, and, even more surprising, he was nominated to hardly
any of the many official Greek committees that were formed.
Indeed his name barely appears at all in any of the sources of
the history of the Council. That means, at least, that he took
no great part in the rifts and squabbles among the Greeks that
Syropoulus describes in such detail, and that he was on the whole
less active either for or against union than many others. Syropoulus, that anti-union apologist, is suspiciously silent about
Scholarius, which is almost enough in itself to show that he was
not anti-unionist. The little we know about his activity in Italy is
as follows.

In Ferrara he was consulted on the choice of subject for the
first doctrinal debates, whether it should be the 'illegality' of the
addition of the *Filioque* to the Creed, or the doctrine of the *Filioque*,
and he agreed with Bessarion (and his own principles enunciated
in Constantinople) that the doctrine should be discussed as being
fundamental. He himself claims to have written the discourse
that Bessarion delivered in two sessions of early November 1438
in answer to Andrew of Rhodes. When the Council was to move
from Florence, he wrote to Ambrogio Traversari, begging shelter
in a little corner of his monastery on the outskirts of Florence,
pleading in excuse his late illness.

In Florence the public sessions on the *Filioque* ended on 24
March 1439. For several weeks there was stalemate. In mid-April
first Bessarion, then Scholarius, addressed the Greek synod to
persuade the prelates that as the Fathers, both Greek and Latin,
were inspired by the same Holy Spirit, their doctrine must agree.
Scholarius exhorted, challenged, almost insulted his audience. He
was obviously in a state of high nervous tension, probably because
news had lately come from Constantinople of an impending
Turkish attack on the city. This discourse of his is usually entitled:
On the Need of helping Constantinople, but that is the theme of

[3] Ibid., IV, pp. 432-3.

only part of it. The gist of his words was as follows. The Greeks, knowing little of the learning and skill in dialectics of the Latins, had come to Italy thinking that they would easily vanquish them in argument. Instead they had found that the Latins had not only ably defended themselves but had brought forward the most famous of the Fathers, Greek as well as Latin, in support of their faith. The Greeks had no reply to make, because the Fathers cannot contradict each other; if any one of them seemed out of harmony with the rest, the one should be explained so as to agree with the many. Greek and Latin Fathers agree. The saints we may not deny, or say that they are mutually opposed—that would upset the whole of the faith; while to assert that the Latins had falsified them is the height of stupidity (a hit at Mark Eugenicus). The Latins had already reconciled certain apparent differences of the Doctors, but if doubt remained he (Scholarius) would do it in a couple of hours. So let there be an end to words. The Latins had proved their orthodoxy. The Greeks could now unite with honour, and should do so, and get help for Constantinople. The Barbarian feared nothing so much as their union with the Latins: their wives, families, were looking to them. The Latins erred in no point of the faith. So let them unite, get ships, return to Constantinople. Any other course would be shame to themselves and treachery to their people.

Both Bessarion's more measured exposition and Scholarius' impassioned exhortation must have helped to break down the prejudice against the Latins in their hearers' minds, but they did not by any means remove it entirely. At the end of April there was still a deadlock in affairs, when the Latins transmitted to the Greeks a formal exposition of trinitarian faith, which the Greeks could not bring themselves to accept. Scholarius composed a similar Greek statement on the basis of texts suggested by Isidore of Kiev, a statement designed to be ambiguous. Even Mark of Ephesus, later on, likened it to an actor's boot so shaped as to go on either foot. Needless to say, the Latins rejected it. The Latin statement was finally accepted after a series of Greek meetings when the Emperor enjoined on everyone to give his opinion in writing.

Scholarius, too, produced his written statement. Indeed, according to the anonymous *Description* of the Council, he was the first to read his aloud in public. It was a concise, unambiguous, and precisely-worded acknowledgement that the Council then sitting was oecumenical and that the Latin doctrine on the Procession of the Holy Spirit was orthodox. 'I declare that I submit myself to the decision of this our Council, rather of this present Oecumenical Council, and welcome and honour with the greatest veneration and gladness whatever decision it shall make both about union itself and about the kind of union, and I regard that decision as emanating not from men but from God. . . . Wherefore I consent to this opinion or proposition: The Spirit proceeds from the Father and from the Son, or from the Father through the Son, as from one principle and one cause, and I assert that this is most true and I say that in this way the inevitable agreement of the western saints with the eastern is attained and that anything else would make agreement impossible.'[4]

In the beginning of this same public statement Scholarius reminded his hearers that he had already made known his views about the *Filioque* in the exhortation he had addressed to them in April, and he then mentioned two other tractates 'composed earlier' and now produced for their perusal. How long earlier? He does not say. It might have been only by a few weeks, in the interval from mid-April; but the title of the first of them immediately takes the mind back to the advice he gave in Constantinople in about 1436, and one wonders whether these tractates 'composed earlier' may not be works written in Constantinople disclosing the long-held opinions of their author. For the titles under which these tractates go are: (1) *On the Character of Religious Peace, that it should be a Dogmatic Union and not a Peace of Expediency; the Solving of the Difficulties that impede such a Peace:* (2) *The Factors that will make for such a Peace.* Scholarius himself summed up their content in these words: 'I advised you not even to take into consideration the method of expediency that some have in view, but I declared that it was essential to effect a true union and community of doctrine, which I said was to accept a single opinion about the questions in dispute and to profess this also in the symbol of the faith, either by adding or by taking away according as the grace of God should indicate. Further, the reason for which some are disturbed and pessimistic about this union I showed to be utterly weak and logically to be far from hindering you from union. Then I added the factors that make for it without

[4] *A.G.*, pp. 430, 431.

dilating on them but for the most part just mentioning them, and these are, in a word, the union of the Holy Scriptures and the Teachers of the Church.'[5]

George Scholarius with George Gemistus accompanied the Despot Demetrius when he left Florence on 25 June, and so was not present at the promulgation of the union, whose decree in any case, as a layman, he could not have signed. Writing later, he said that, when he arrived in Venice, he found already there Greeks 'not a few, some on private business, others because they could not bear to witness the disaster' [i.e. of union achieved]: he does not say in which category he would have put himself.

Returned to Constantinople with the rest on 1 February 1440, Scholarius took up again his old way of life, still acting as secretary to the Emperor, still Judge General of the Greeks and preacher at the imperial court, and still carrying on his school of philosophy. The Council in Italy that had united the Churches had split the Eastern Church into rival factions of unionists and anti-unionists, the new Patriarch Metrophanes trying his best despite the passivity of the Emperor to promote the union, Mark Eugenicus with voice and pen directing a determined opposition. Scholarius remained neutral. At the request of Gregory, the imperial confessor, he showed the frailty of some of Eugenicus' arguments in the *Syllogisms against the Latins*, but that was more an exercise in logic than a manifestation of opinion. Mark Eugenicus wrote him a challenging letter, bidding him come off the fence of neutrality on the side of (Mark's) orthodoxy. Scholarius replied telling him, in effect, to mind his own business; but the friendship between them was not broken, for in 1443 Scholarius sent him an affectionate letter to accompany the gift of his essay *Against Pletho*. Mark saw in George his ideal successor for the leadership of the opposition to the union. On his deathbed (23 June 1445) he appealed to him, as the only one capable of the task, to undertake it, and Scholarius yielded, promising unfailing hostility to the union, a promise he ever afterwards faithfully kept.

He was soon to show his mettle. On the occasion of the presence of the papal legation in Constantinople in 1444–5 the Emperor allowed public discussion on the trinitarian question. In fifteen meetings Lapacci, bishop of Cortona, spoke for the Latins, Scholarius for the Greeks, and each side, of course,

[5] SCHOL., I, pp. 371–2.

afterwards claimed to have discomfited the other. Scholarius reproduced his arguments shortly after in a big treatise, of which he sent a rehash to the Emperor of Trebizond at the imperial request. But he was still a bit timid in his new rôle, for he tried to keep both of these volumes from a more general circulation, though a couple of years afterwards he followed them up with a *Dialogue on the Procession of the Holy Spirit*, which certainly was meant for public consumption.

As long as John VIII was alive, Scholarius' position was assured, even though there was for a time some little estrangement between them over his stepping into Eugenicus' shoes as arch-anti-unionist. But when the Emperor died (31 October 1448), Scholarius lamented, with him 'all my fortunes died too'. Scholarius' name was mixed up (and probably correctly) with the faction that refused to acknowledge Constantine's coronation till he had declared himself for their view of orthodoxy. So Scholarius retired from public life and in 1450 fulfilled what he said had long been his desire. He became a monk and took the name of Gennadius. Somewhere about this time Lapacci was again in Constantinople and again there were public discussions, in which both the Latin bishop and the Greek monk claimed the victory.

Scholarius may really have wished to withdraw altogether from affairs to devote himself to prayer as a hermit. What happened was that, whether forced by circumstances or from sheer inability to keep himself out of things, he became actually more than ever the very centre and core of the opposition to union, the willingly accepted dictator of the little group of ecclesiastics, calling itself the 'synaxis', which kept up an implacable resistance. He wrote letters, issued instructions, published manifestoes, each one ending with 'for the future I will be silent'. But the last thing he intended was to be silent. As he wrote to Demetrius of Mistra: 'And the excuse for the letter was a defence of the supposed silence; yet when was I ever silent in the preceding period?'. He tried to gain the support of the powerful Luke Notaras with letters of abject flattery, in the style of the time. When the Bohemian Platris accepted Orthodoxy, Scholarius, who had been his instructor, signed the document that the new convert carried back with him to his Church, last after the 'synaxis': 'The universal teacher of the Church of the orthodox, the humble monk Gennadius'. He sent ten chapters of argument to the Emperor Constantine. After the arrival of Isidore of Kiev as papal Legate (26 October 1452), on 1 November he retired to his cell—retired from all mundane strife—but he affixed to its door for all to read a notice that began: 'O miserable citizens, you have ruined everything, and now you abandon your religion', and continued in the same challenging and inflammatory strain. When Constantine summoned the anti-unionist 'synaxis' to discuss with Isidore the ecclesiastical situation, Gennadius wrote to them that he would not come if it were a question of merely approving what the people had already foolishly accepted; but if there were any new proposal put forward, they should not do anything without his presence and consent. He went all the same to that meeting and to several others, and his presence helped to strengthen the anti-unionist resistance. Despite his efforts, the union was proclaimed from the pulpit of St. Sophia's. Just before that Gennadius shot his last bolt, a circular distributed 'in the palaces, in the markets, and in all the monasteries of the city'. He challenged anyone to find any evil in his life; his only 'crime' was fidelity to the faith; faith was free and he would remain united with their holy Fathers; he had the well-being of his fellows at heart; 'if then, because I take no part in such a union and because I preserved my faith, which is the ancestral faith, uncontaminated by the heterodox and those who communicate with them, and because I do not alter ancestral ways under stress of emergency and because I keep silence—if for all these reasons you should wish to put no limit on what you say and do, my defence is already made before God, not only on the things about which I have before now spoken, written and advised, but also about the crime that you contemplate perpetrating against me, and I will with joy undergo the ordeal in witness to the ancestral faith and orthodox doctrine, even indeed death itself, to the glory of God'.[6] After this and the promulgation of the union (12 December) Gennadius shut himself up in his cell, where he remained till the Turks took the city. He was led off, a captive, to Adrianople.

His captivity did not last long. Some leading Greeks who remained free persuaded Mahomet that the best way of restoring order was to enlist the aid of the Church, and they suggested Gennadius as its head. Gennadius' owner learnt who he was, and took him back to Constantinople. In the autumn of 1453, having

[6] Ibid., III, p. 174.

been given back his old monastery, he tried to gather together the old community of monks, buying some out of captivity and seeking out others who had remained free. It brought him little joy of heart, for 'the monks, who even before [the capture of the city] used to fill everything with malice and disorder, now making the disaster to the Christian name an excuse for avarice and for the satisfaction of their passions, filled full the former holy order with disorder, the souls of the beholders with scandal, and the world with every evil'. He was elected patriarch against his will by a synod of bishops, and on 6 January 1454 enthroned, not however in the church of St. Sophia, for that was now a mosque, but in that of the Holy Apostles. The Sultan bestowed the insignia of office as once the Christian emperors had done. The new Patriarch wrote an encyclical letter to try to bring back the old regularity of life and to hearten the faithful to constancy. Mahomet, who through the restoration of the patriarchate had harnessed the Christian Church to the Mohammedan State, three times visited Gennadius to talk about religion, and as a result the Patriarch, always grateful for the tolerance shown to the Church, composed a short outline of the faith for translation into Turkish. Any hopes he may have had of the Sultan's conversion were vain, but he would not brook paganism from any other source. He violently attacked Gemistus's book *About the Laws*, burning all but a few fragments of the only copy that existed, because it advocated a kind of neo-Platonic naturalism to replace Christianity.

Gennadius was isolated in his endeavours. Cliques were formed against him; accusations and menaces followed. Laymen and even clerics embraced, or threatened to embrace, Islam if their greed were checked. He was not made of the stuff to bear contradiction and failure. He set his mind on retiring, but had to remain in office for some time longer. He served for a full year, perhaps two, before he was allowed to seek the quiet of Mt. Athos. Sadness followed him there in the death of his nephew whom he loved as a son. He moved on to the monastery of St. John the Baptist near Seres (Macedonia). There he spent the rest of his life, except for two more short reigns as Patriarch (not of his choice, but by order of the Sultan), the one probably in 1463 which he ended by flight, the other not long after, which lasted about a year and a half. His leisure in the monastery he passed copying his old works and writing new ones, works on the Scriptures, on philosophy, on theology, which included a return to his old love, for he made a résumé of St. Thomas's *Summa contra gentiles* and of the *Prima* and *Prima secundae* of the *Summa theologica* (in all 663 pages of large octavo in the modern edition). He died some time after 1472.

*　　　*　　　*

The above account has been written on the supposition that there was only one George Scholarius, the subject of all the experiences recorded. There is no doubt that the George who before 1437 was imperial secretary and Judge General went to Italy, in Florence composed the Greek statement on the Procession of the Holy Spirit (April–May 1439) and after his return to Constantinople continued as imperial secretary and Judge General and besides took over from the dying Ephesus the direction of the anti-unionist movement—for all these facts there is abundant documentary evidence. What has been called in question is whether that George was the author in Florence of the exhortation to the Greek synod, of the treatises in favour of union, and of the precisely-worded statement accepting the Latin doctrine. No one now seriously doubts that these two Georges were one and the same, but it is perhaps still worth while giving a few positive reasons for that acceptance, besides the negative one that there is no indication whatever to the contrary (apart from the change of religious front implied), for these treatises had always been attributed to the imperial secretary George till Leo Allatius, nearly two centuries after the Council, could not credit that one man could have defended two such opposite opinions.

Surely it was *a priori* likely that a man as steeped in Latin thought and as well disposed to the Latin Pope as was Scholarius would have accepted the orthodoxy of Latin doctrine. More than that. He had in his explanation of the preposition 'Through' in his *First Introduction to Grammar* (written about the year 1430) insisted that 'Through' implied a real, though intermediary, causality subordinated to a principal cause. This reasoning, if applied to the causality in the Trinity, leads precisely to the conclusion of the Council of Florence, namely that the Holy Spirit proceeds from the Father as principal cause, through the Son as the mediating cause that has its power of causality from the principal cause. The pronouncements of Scholarius, therefore, at

Florence involved no break with the past, though after the Council he changed his explanation of 'Through' in his *Grammar*, limiting it to material causality.

The pronouncements, however, of the Scholarius of Florence do not harmonise with the writings of the Judge General and the Gennadius of the years that followed Florence—except for his *Refutation of the Syllogisms of Mark Eugenicus*. There are, however, in those writings admissions of a change of view and of a less 'orthodox' past. Replying in 1440 to Mark Eugenicus who had reproached him for his disloyalty (apparently for a second time) to Mark's type of orthodoxy: 'We were filled with grief and desolation, when we heard that you had again turned round and were thinking and saying the opposite', Scholarius wrote: 'I have often hitherto repented of much of what I have said on various occasions, from which I know that I have been the cause of good to no one and of scandal to not a few, who taking up my words and understanding them, each after his own fashion, thought that I too had a variable opinion about things divine. . . . They could not distinguish between 'economy' [i.e. adapting one's conduct to circumstances] and rigour and the fit times for each of these, and so they blamed those who could. . . .'[7]—that is, a recognition that there was at least some foundation for what Mark had said, but that it had its excuse in Scholarius' suiting his behaviour to the times, and this from the man who in Constantinople before the Council had deprecated anything but the greatest sincerity in discussion and decision.

Several other times, too, the polemical Scholarius in veiled language admitted his 'fault'. For example, in his panegyric on the dead Eugenicus he said: 'But now, having at last come to our senses, we grieve for our past sins either of silence when that was not proper or of speech when silence was due'[8]; and, writing after 1448, he declared: 'But not even those of us that survive, are bound to be slaves for ever to the things in which we ourselves are conscious of having sinned.'[9]

Once at least in unveiled language—and once is enough, even if there were no other indication to support its assertion— Scholarius says plainly that he had upheld Latin orthodoxy in

[7] Ibid., IV, p. 448.
[8] Ibid., I, p. 251.
[9] Ibid., III, p. 91. Note the use of the first personal pronouns.

both speech and writing. The statement comes in a criticism of Bessarion's *Dogmatic Oration* of April 1439, written probably shortly before he finally decided to throw in his lot with the anti-unionists. Of that criticism only a long fragment survives, but that fragment contains these words: 'I found then that the western Doctors were right in their assertion [of the *Filioque*] and that some of ours supported them; and since it was impossible that the Doctors of the Church should be proved false, I concluded from that that there was no case for rejecting the communion of the Latins, seeing that they believed and professed a true doctrine. . . . That, then, is why in all simplicity and from the bottom of my heart I was reconciled with the Latins and constantly made the weight of my arm felt by those who unsparingly abused them. I undertook the defence of their faith in more than one treatise, and I cleared them of a quantity of absurdities that those who had written lengthy books against them fastened on them—or rather on the Doctors of the Church. In consequence, I was called a 'Latiniser' by some. . . . And doubtless, while I condemned the ignorance of such folk, perhaps on the spur of the moment I said things like a Latin and, as happens in such circumstances, gave the impression in the heat of the squabble of being too indulgent towards the Latins and too hard on my adversaries. So I was then considered to be completely devoted to Latinism and to be contemptuous of and openly hostile to our traditions'.[10] Scholarius is here letting us in behind the scenes and offering information that even Syropoulus refrained from giving. But by the time that Syropoulus was writing his *Memoirs*, Scholarius, if he was not already the head of the anti-unionists, was their hope for the future and, in either case, his reputation was to be preserved.

It can hardly be doubted, then, that Scholarius-Gennadius first of all and over a long time upheld the orthodoxy of the Latin doctrine on the Procession of the Holy Spirit, even though he regretted the introduction of the *Filioque* clause into the Creed, and then in many a polemical writing defended the Photian position, that the Holy Spirit proceeds from the Father only. One naturally asks why; but it is easier to ask than to answer. One reason may have been a sense of national pride, not to seem to betray the honour of the Greek Church which since the time of Photius had held, against the Latins, that the Spirit was from the

[10] Ibid. III, p. 116.

Father only. Another reason may have been a kind of thwarted ambition or wounded pride. Scholarius was an outstanding scholar. His writings include works on philosophy, theology, grammar, philology, history, poetry, sermons, panegyrics, as well as translations. He was a deep thinker, versed in both Greek and Latin theology, pre-eminent among his contemporaries. He himself could not help but be aware of this excellence; he seems to have been too conscious of it, so that he resented it if anyone else laid a claim to scholarship.

In his letter to Mark Eugenicus already quoted he mentioned: 'I suppose that no one is unaware that for rhetoric, philosophy and the highest science of all, theology, I learnt from none of our teachers. . . . And now how much am I not better than all others in learning?'[11]; and elsewhere: 'In respect of sacred theology, which all my life through has had the greatest interest and profit for me, no one at all of the men now living anywhere knows as much as I do.' Of the three or four contemporaries in Constantinople whom he will acknowledge to have some claim to scholarship (i.e. including himself), the majority (consequently all except himself) 'are content with seeming, instead of being' scholarly.[12] He attacked Gemistus with religious zeal for his neo-paganism, but it was a personal motive that made him belittle the older man's learning. In the sad days after the fall of his city his mind went back to the applause that had fed his soul before: 'How can I recall without tears my audience of that day, the Emperor, his brothers, the courtiers, the bishops, the ecclesiastics, the monks, men from the markets, the citizens, foreigners, to whom I used to proclaim the word of God as they sat before me in the imperial hall. . . . Separately one lauded this excellence of those homilies, another that . . . but all extolled the dexterity in words that God had given me. . . . Oh! the daily discussions, sometimes in the presence of the Emperor himself, sometimes without him, one putting forward one difficulty, another another, and all, as if in the theatre, anxious to hear the one man who would give a solution to all. Oh! the good will, the honour, that was paid me by every one, and the joy with which they awaited us, thinking the day that we were not to be found in the palace a day of mourning and, when we came on the next day, embracing us as if we had returned from a long journey. . . .'[13] But after the Council of

---

[11] Ibid. IV, p. 446.   [12] Ibid. IV, p. 406.   [13] Ibid. I, pp. 288–9.

Florence it was not Scholarius, but Bessarion who, it seemed, had the limelight, for he was made a cardinal; and the contrast rankled. In his comments on Bessarion's *Dogmatic Oration* Scholarius blamed his one-time friend for not having sought his advice and help in composing the oration, and, after lamenting the broken friendship, wrote: 'But now he adds brilliance to Italy, but we pass our days among citizens worthy indeed but, with very few exceptions, uneducated and with no love for letters, with no possibility of displaying any of our talents to such as them and attaining thereby some glory and favour.'[14]

If Pope Eugenius had offered Scholarius some honour, like the red hat, would the issue have been different? In the event it was Eugenicus, who doubtless long ago had noted both the strength and the weakness in Scholarius' character, who made the right psychological approach, by appealing to him as the only one capable of the task he wished to entrust to him: 'I have known him since his youth and have looked on him as my son . . . I believe that he alone of all men of this time can give the helping hand to right doctrine, buffeted by the storms of violence from those who have corrupted the perfection of doctrine, so as with God's help to set the Church right. . . . Seeing then that I must shortly depart this life and finding no one besides him capable of filling my place for the defence of the Church, the faith and the doctrines of orthodoxy, therefore I appeal to him. . . .'[15] Scholarius accepted the charge, promised to devote himself to the defence of what Eugenicus held so dear, and ever afterwards was faithful to his word.

Yet even his devotion to the orthodoxy of Eugenicus could not make him as abusive in his polemics as were some of his fellows. Though he claimed complete certainty for his views ('There is no fear whatsoever that I elect anything but the best or that I fall short of the truth in my quest of it'[16]); even inspiration from on high ('Established by divine providence in the ranks of those able to defend the faith'); and revelation in a dream ('The Lord knows, all this I heard recounted to me in a dream as I was then in that dismal city'[17]); still he never characterised the Latins as heretics, but was content to refer to them as schismatics, or heterodox, or separated. This, unusual, mildness in controversy

---

[14] Ibid. III, p. 115.
[16] SCHOL., II, p. 5.

[15] PETIT, *Docs.*, p. 487 (349).
[17] Ibid. III, p. 433.

came doubtless from his respect for Latin theology and the fact that he was never so certain of his viewpoint as to feel quite free from the danger of mistake. He held his opinion, he said, till another council (Florence, he rejected) should settle the matter, to whose decision he would submit himself whether it harmonised with his own teaching or not. Meantime—he played for safety: 'Hence it is extremely dangerous to make additions. Be satisfied with what from of old has been professed in the Church at large'.[18] Dangerous, not absolutely fatal: so the Churches should be kept sundered on a probability.

[18] Ibid. III, p. 433.

CHAPTER EIGHT

CARDINAL GIULIANO CESARINI († 1444)

Giuliano Cesarini figured in all the main historical events of his age, so that information about his public activities is not lacking. Details, however, of his private life, and especially of his earlier years, are scarce. For these there are two chief sources. One of them is the 'Life' written by Vespasiano da Bisticci in his precious book *Lives of 103 Illustrious Men of the Fifteenth Century*[1]; Vespasiano, however, was a boy in Florence when Cesarini was there as a Cardinal, so that his information on the youth of Cesarini is from hearsay. The other is the funeral oration of Poggio,[2] the humanist and papal secretary, roughly a contemporary of Cesarini, but a Florentine, not a Roman.

Cesarini was born in Rome of a good but impoverished family, in 1398 or 1389 probably the former, since Poggio says that he was not yet fifty years old when he died in 1444. He studied first in Rome, then in Perugia where he began law. His circumstances were very straitened. He earned board and lodging by acting as tutor in the Buontempi family, borrowed books to study from, which he often copied out in a beautiful handwriting, and, to be able to prolong his hours of work into the night, collected candle-ends from the table after big dinners. From Perugia he went to Bologna and Padua, where he gained his degree of Doctor in Both Laws (*in utroque jure*). He was admitted straightway to teach in the same university—an eloquent testimony to his attainments— which he did for about two years, having among his students the future cardinals, Domenico Capranica and Nicholas of Cusa.

In about 1419 he was taken into the family of Cardinal Adimari as vicar, and in 1422 he accompanied to Germany Cardinal Branda da Castiglione, one of the most active papal nuncios of the time. In 1421 a military expedition against the Hussites that he had arranged having failed, the cardinal went on a second mission in 1422 to renew the effort and to try to introduce disciplinary reforms into the Church of Germany. Cesarini thus

---

[1] A. MAI, *Spicilegium Romanum*, I (Rome, 1839), pp. 166–84.
[2] Ibid. X (Rome, 1844), pp. 373–84.

made acquaintance with both the scene and the style of his later activities, for he accompanied the cardinal, doubtless as a kind of secretary and adviser, to various parts of Germany—to the Diet of Nuremberg, to Mainz where Branda promulgated a constitution of reform. They returned to Rome in the spring of 1425.

Immediately Cesarini was despatched on another mission, this time as its head. He went to France to discuss with the Duke of Bedford the thorny question of the collation of benefices, and such were his powers of persuasion and the impression he made of complete sincerity that, to the general surprise, he succeeded in inducing the English Regent to modify his views and to accept the system imposed by the papal constitution of 13 April 1425, which by royal decree was made the official English procedure on 26 November. Poggio indicates one of the reasons for his success —his obvious integrity: 'Besides, he acted in a way that was most unusual and unheard of—he would not accept any gift, no matter by whom offered. He refused them all, though many were proffered, asserting that he had been sufficiently provided for by the Pope, so that he stood in no need of help from other sources. This attitude by itself brought him the highest reputation and honour.'

In the years that followed he held various posts in the Roman Curia and was given a number of benefices in different places for his maintenance. He was named cardinal after his return from the English embassy, but *in pectore* (24 May 1426). His public nomination to be Cardinal Deacon of S. Angelo was made only on 8 November 1430. He had spent the last few years in Rome at the side of Martin V, occupied in part in reviving an earlier project for the reform of the Roman Curia and adding various other, more general, suggestions, all with a view to the Council due to meet in 1431.

The Council of Basel had been announced before the close of the Council of Siena in 1424. Martin V duly convoked it, appointed Cesarini his legate for a crusade against the Hussites and president of the new Council, and then died on 20 February 1431. Cesarini was already in Germany when there reached him the Bulls nominating him president of the Council and giving him full powers to regulate it (which included those of deferring, proroguing or even dissolving it). Forced to choose for immediate action one or other of the tasks entrusted to him, he decided to finish first what he had already set in motion in Germany, the campaign against the Hussites. Martin's successor, Eugenius IV, had confirmed him in both missions, though Cesarini wrote asking to be freed from the presidency of the Council for which he had little taste. He toured about recruiting reinforcements, collected an army of 40,000 cavalry, marched out of Nuremberg on 7 July 1431 and on 14 August was caught in defiles in the mountains and disastrously defeated, himself barely escaping capture. With nothing else now to absorb his energies, he went to Basel to promote the Council which had already been formally opened on 23 July by his representatives, John of Ragusa O.P. and John of Palomar.

When Cesarini reached Basel on 9 September he found very few assembled to form the Council. His first act was to have urgent letters despatched to princes, bishops and universities demanding attendance at the assembly. A messenger, Beaupère, was sent also to Pope Eugenius to solicit his active support and if possible his physical presence, but he painted so dark a picture of Basel—fewness of numbers, especially of bishops; local fighting; doubtful orthodoxy of the citizens—that Eugenius, himself involved in a war with Martin V's nephews, partly paralysed after a stroke, and anxious to encourage the Greek readiness for a council in Italy, decided to prorogue the Council of Basel for a year and a half and to transfer it to Bologna. He embodied these proposals in a Bull, *Quoniam alto* (12 November) and sent it to Cesarini, leaving him discretion in its use. He then learnt that the Council, since the Hussite heresy could not be suppressed by arms, had in the mean-time actually invited the Hussites to come to Basel, though their doctrine had been condemned at Constance. Straightway he both issued and promulgated a new version of *Quoniam alto* (18 December) definitely dissolving the Council and convoking it afresh to meet at Bologna after eighteen months, and he bade Cesarini publish the Bull and then quit Basel.

Meanwhile, however, the Council had been solemnly inaugurated by Cesarini on 14 December. Shortly after, rumours began to circulate about the first *Quoniam alto*, and a papal messenger who tried to promulgate it in a public session was subjected to ill-treatment (13 January). The Fathers in Basel were determined that the Council should go on, for they held that it was the only way of checking the Hussite heresy and of achieving the much-needed reform of the Church. Cesarini saw their mood and largely shared it. Before even learning of the second *Quoniam alto*, he wrote two letters to Eugenius, and a third afterwards, all within less than a month, stating very forcibly and with the hint of a threat all the reasons in favour of the continuation of the Council, and pleading with the Pope at least to defer the impending dissolution. Eugenius saw things differently, and there began the struggle between Council and Pope for supremacy in the Church. Cesarini for a time declined to act as president of the Council, since he was at loggerheads with the Pope whom he was supposed to be representing and who had appointed him, but he continued to be the foremost personality present and the virtual head of the assembly.

The Council based its claims on the principle, first enunciated in the early months of the Council of Constance, of the superiority of a general council, representing the Church, over even a pope in matters of faith, heresy and reform. That principle it renewed and made its own in a session of 15 February 1432. Cesarini, at that time and for years to come, heartily agreed with the principle, acted according to it, championed the Council against Eugenius in regard to it (he reassumed the presidency openly in September 1432), and on account of it rejected the first concessions that Eugenius made, because they covertly denied it. Eugenius was finally forced to withdraw his dissolution of the Council. A formula was dictated by Cesarini. Eugenius at first modified its phraseology and with that its assertion of principle. The Fathers rejected his first Bull *Dudum sacrum* of 1 August 1433, insisting on an exact following of Cesarini's draft. They got it in the second *Dudum sacrum* of 15 December.

The Pope named four men to act as presidents with Cesarini, but they were not admitted till they had taken the oath of loyalty imposed on all new members. The Council was by now claiming to do all that any pope could do. It had formed its own Curia to replace the Roman Curia. It authorised its president, Cesarini, to grant marriage dispensations in certain cases. It sent its ambassadors and even its 'legates *a latere*'. It had reduced the Pope to some degree of dependence: it meant to keep him there. A pope without money would be innocuous, so it abolished all taxes on new appointments (annates) without compensation to the Pope for loss of revenue, and Cesarini alone of the five presidents did not walk out of the session that decreed this measure, but stayed to ratify it. The Council wanted the Pope to withdraw all existing indulgences in favour of one to be granted by itself, so as to encourage donations to meet the expenses of the forthcoming discussions with the Greeks. Eugenius, however, could not allow any but a pope to grant indulgences and offered instead a choice of two other methods for collecting the money. Again Cesarini was the only one of the presidents who approved when the Council promulgated a plenary indulgence.

By such persistent hostility the Council defeated its own object. The princes became more and more alarmed at the prospect of a new schism in the Church. There began the return of the cardinals and higher clerics who had deserted Eugenius for Basel, partly because the earlier Basel had been more Christian in its behaviour than it turned out to be later and had given bright promise of happier days in the Church, partly for fear of the penalties imposed by a victorious Council. Cesarini himself started to doubt whether a gathering like that of Basel could be the highest authority in the Church. The crisis came when the Fathers, afraid of losing power if the synod that had been arranged with the Eastern Church should meet in Italy and so fall more under the influence of the Pope, voted to locate it at Basel itself or at Avignon, though the contract made with the Greeks and solemnly ratified in public session ruled otherwise. The Council split—the majority voted for Basel or Avignon, the minority for a city of Italy. When the minority took their decree to Eugenius in Bologna, Cesarini who had voted with them, remained in Basel, but discredited. He tried to persuade the Fathers to put union with the Greeks before their own ambitions. He failed. So when he heard that the Greeks had arrived in Venice and were going to Ferrara, he left Basel to join the Pope, and the Baseler gladly wished him God-speed, for he had become a nuisance with his attempts at restraint.

He was welcomed by Eugenius in spite of the many hard words he had said in Basel in the past, for no one ever attributed personal hostility or personal ambition to Cesarini. What he had done, he had done from an honest, if erroneous, conviction. He was a man of great sanctity and of outstanding abilities, an asset to any cause. At Ferrara he was soon representing the Pope in negotiations with the Greeks. He headed the papal committee that settled the delicate question of the exact locations of the papal and imperial thrones at the sessions. He was spokesman for the Latins in the discussions of April–May 1438 that led to the conferences on Purgatory and he opened the debate on that subject in the first of the meetings. He was one of the six Latin orators appointed to expound western theological teaching in the public sessions. If the Greeks were allowed to follow their own methods in these sessions, it was (so says Andrew da Santa Croce) because Eugenius and Cesarini, despite much Latin opposition, were inclined to concession. It was, finally, Cesarini who most forcefully put the Latin case about the addition of the *Filioque* to the Creed. Andrew of Rhodes and Aloysius of Forli had already spoken in four sessions. Bessarion later declared that at that stage of the discussions the Greeks were in the ascendant, but that when Cesarini took the floor their case subsided; to his arguments they could only reply: 'It is forbidden. It is forbidden.' It was Cesarini that convinced Bessarion of the worthlessness of the Greek case over the addition, and with Bessarion many more. Cesarini urged discussion of the dogma of the *Filioque* and his very confidence shook the Greeks who, by now already away from their own country for more than a year, wanted to abandon the whole project of union and to return home.

The Council moved to Florence in January 1439, and Cesarini accompanied the Emperor on the journey. The first meeting in the new site, of forty representatives from each side, was held to decide on method. It was a dialogue between Cesarini and the Emperor. In the seven public sessions in which the dogma of the *Filioque* was discussed, Montenero alone spoke for the Latins. But the problem of union still remained unsolved and there followed in the months of April, May and June a series of meetings and negotiations in which Cesarini inevitably went to carry the Pope's answer to the Emperor and the Greeks, taking them to task, exhorting, persuading. On the eve of the promulgation of the union, it was he who made a long explanation to the Latin synod, in the presence of the Pope, recounting the history of the negotiations with them on the various points of doctrine. In other words, after Eugenius, he was the outstanding figure on the Latin side, the trusted adviser and representative of the Pope. That it was he who read out the Latin text of the Bull of union from the pulpit of the church of S. Maria del Fiore on 6 July 1439 to receive the *Placets* of the Council was but just.

Meantime the remnant at Basel had declared the Pope to be contumacious and deposed, and were on the point of electing an antipope. Eugenius replied by the Bull *Moyses vir Dei* of 4 September 1439, in which, besides recounting the history of his relations with the Baseler and condemning them, he outlined his explanation of the famous principle of the Council of Constance about the superiority of a general council, which was the corner-stone of the Baseler pretensions. He was not, however, content only with that. A little later he arranged a debate on the theological foundations of the conciliar theory. Cesarini expounded the position of the supporters of that theory, as well he could, having once been a wholehearted believer in it; and John of Torquemada replied. Torquemada later published his answer as a treatise, and so it is preserved. Cesarini's dissertation is lost, but as the answer to it in the treatise is made point by point and argument by argument, it is not difficult to reconstruct the scheme of his exposition. He had, as could have been expected of a man of his honesty, developed the Baseler thesis in full, defending not only the Council of Constance and its decrees, but Basel's legiti-macy and the validity of its enactments. It was a bold step on the part of the Pope, but a wise one, to show that a satisfactory answer was forthcoming to the most able statement of his adversaries' case.

Armenians followed the Greeks in Florence and Copts the Armenians, and Cesarini played a large part in the conversations with them and signed the decrees of union that resulted. As a token reward for his labours the Pope presented him with the original Bulls of union with the Greeks, the Armenians and the Copts, and he, having had a handsome casket made to hold them, donated them in his turn to the Commune of Florence. They are preserved still in the *Cassetta Cesarini* in the Mediceo-Laurenziana Library of that city.

On 1 March 1442 the Cardinal was appointed legate *a latere* to try to resolve a dynastic quarrel between Hungary, Austria and Poland, so as to prepare the way for the crusade against the Turks that the Pope was determined to set in motion to fulfil his promise of aid for the ever-threatened Constantinople. The death of one of the protagonists simplified his mission, whereupon Ladislas, King of Poland, became King of Hungary also and head of the crusade. John Hunyadi, leading Christian troops, fought a successful campaign against the infidel in the autumn and winter of 1443–4, in consequence of which the Sultan, Murad II, made overtures for a truce before he went to Asia Minor to quell a rebellion there. Ladislas, who on 15 April swore in the Hungarian Diet to continue the campaign against the Turk and on 24 July wrote to Bosnia of his plans for it, is said to have agreed on oath to the truce with Murad and within a week or less (4 August), under Cesarini's influence, to have announced the resumption of the crusade for 1 September 1444. If Ladislas did forswear himself, it is not proved that Cesarini was responsible; but even if he were, he would have been justified in advising the King that his later oath was contrary to his former one and not binding because it proposed a lesser good. The crusade set out on 22 September and on 10 November it met the vastly superior force of Murad at Varna. For a time it seemed that the Christians would win, but a rash charge of Ladislas resulted in his death and the defeat of his army. Cesarini disappeared for ever in the disorder of the fight. Rumours of his survival were so persistent for a time that the College of Cardinals did not acknowledge his death till 26 July 1445.

Vespasiano da Bisticci, who as a youth in Florence during the Council knew the Cardinal personally, waxes lyrical in his life of him about his hero's many virtues and recounts numerous striking examples of them. Cesarini was most open-handed in almsgiving, never refusing anyone and even selling his goods to have more to give away. Many a poor Florentine youth benefited from the fact that the Cardinal had suffered so as to be able to study, for when Cesarini heard of a clever boy being barred from a better education by poverty, he brought the lad into his own household for some months to give himself the opportunity of judging his character and then, if he approved, he supplied him with books, clothes, pocket money and maintenance for the seven years' course in one of the famous *Studi*. If anyone of his household fell ill, he had him attended by a doctor twice each day, and himself visited him to make sure that the doctor's prescriptions were being carried out, even when the sick person was no more than the servant of one of his ostlers. Vespasiano himself one day was asked by the Cardinal whether he had ever thought of becoming a priest and was advised to think about it for a fortnight and then to give his answer. At the end of that time he told the Cardinal, No; whereupon Cesarini did not press him but bade him apply to him in his needs and meantime to join a certain pious confraternity, similar to the one that Cesarini himself frequented every week. The Cardinal was naturally quick-tempered, as appeared occasionally in his debates with Mark Eugenicus at Ferrara, but for the most part he restrained himself admirably. When one of his ostlers through carelessness lost his favourite mule, the Cardinal sent for him and asked him if he had found it; the man admitted that he had not; whereupon his master stood silent for a minute, fighting for control, and then mildly replied: 'Ah well, it can't be helped.'

Vespasiano has many more stories, obviously true. He tells too of the simplicity of the Cardinal's mode of life, his few servants, his several chaplains with whom he recited the divine Office daily, his restraint in eating and drinking so that 'the wine he drank he put in just so much as barely covered the bottom of the glass and then filled it up with water, so that it was coloured water'. He went to confession daily to an old and reverend German priest, his chaplain, and said Mass daily. He was so sparing of time that, if he went to the Pope and, having dismissed his carriage and attendants, found that the Pope was engaged, instead of waiting till his carriage returned at the appointed time, he would go home immediately with his chaplains on horseback.

He wished everyone well, particularly spiritually. To the youths he helped so generously in their studies he said: 'I have done to you what was not done to me, for the sole purpose that you should become good men: above all, love and fear God and, if you do that, everything will be well with you'. He gave much time and trouble explaining Christianity to a certain Jewish doctor for whom he had a high regard and, when the man became a Christian, the Cardinal himself baptised him, took him into his house and provided for him. The monastery where he lived during his stay in Florence was not up to the standard of observance that he thought right. He arranged, therefore, with the Pope, who was more anxious than anyone else for monastic reform, had all but two of the monks sent away, and started there a régime of strict observance.

Vespasiano was not the only one to admire Cesarini so much. Eugenius, the Pope, did so also, and Traversari, the General of the Camaldolese, writing to the sovereign Pontiff from Basel on 21 August 1435, when Cesarini was less of a *persona grata* with the Pope than he was afterwards, described him as 'this outstanding man, and indeed unique, and most useful to the Church of God'.[3]

[3] TRAV., no. 11.

CHAPTER NINE

JOHN VIII PALAEOLOGUS

A CHARACTER STUDY

John Palaeologus was born on 16/17 December 1392,[1] the eldest of the six children[2] of Manuel Palaeologus and Helen, his wife,[3] into a world of great difficulty, for Constantinople was in the beginnings of its death throes. When John was but seven years old, his father on his way to Europe to seek the aid of the western princes, took him with his mother and his brother Theodore to Monembasia where he remained with his uncle Theodore for some years till the threat to Constantinople was lifted.

The city he returned to was 'enclosed within a stout and lofty wall, defended by many strong, high towers. . . . Though the circuit of its walls is thus very great and the area spacious, the city is not throughout very densely populated. There are within its compass many hills and valleys where cornfields and orchards are found and among the orchard lands there are hamlets and suburbs which are all included within the city limits. Everywhere through-

---

[1] On the date of John's birth there is some difference of opinion. SPHRANTZES (=PHRANTZES, p. 201) asserts that when he died on 31 Oct. 1448, he had lived 56 years 10 months and 15 days, which, with the correction indicated by R.-J. LOENERTZ, in *Autour du Chronicon Maius attribué à Georges Phrantzès*, in *Miscellanea Giovanni Mercati* III (=*Studi e Testi* 123), p. 287, and in *Une erreur singulière de Laonic Chalcocandyle*, in *Revue des Études Byzantines* XV (1957), pp. 176–84, would place his birth on 16/17 Dec. 1392. A. Th. PAPADO-POULOS (*Versuch einer Genealogie der Palaiologen 1259–1453* (Speyer a Rh. 1938) no. 90, p. 59) gives the year of birth as 1394, and perforce has to correct Sphrantzes. His reason for this seems to be because he states that John's parents were married in 1393. But this is not correct. Manuel was married in 11 Feb. 1392 (R.-J. LOENERTZ, *Autour du* etc., ibid.)

S. LAMPROS (III, p. XVI) assesses the year of John's birth as 1397, on the strength of a phrase in an anonymous panegyric according to which he won his campaign of 1417–18 in the Peloponnesus 'While still coming to youth and not yet having the down blooming [on his cheeks] (Ibid., p. 176). DUCAS (*Historia byzantina*, ed. I. BEKKER, Bonn 1834, p. 56) writes that in Dec. 1399 Manuel, en route for Europe, left his wife with John, a 'brephos', and Theodore, 'nepion', at Monembasia.

[2] LAONICUS CHALCOCANDYLES, *Historiarum demonstrationes* ed. E. DARKÓ (Budapest, 1922) I, p. 192.

[3] Helen died on 23 March 1450 under the name, taken in religion, of Hypo-mone (PHRANTZES, ed. Bonn, p. 210, where he calls her Irene Hypomone).

out the city there are many great palaces, churches and monasteries, but most of them are now in ruins'.[4]

What the effect of these shattered glories of the past had on
John's character may perhaps be gauged from a remark of his
father recorded by Sphrantzes: 'My son, the Emperor, seems to
himself to be a suitable emperor—but not for the present day.
For he has large views and ideas and such as the times demanded
in the heyday of the prosperity of his ancestors. But nowadays, as
things are going with us, our empire needs, not an emperor, but
an administrator. I am afraid that the decline of this house may
come from his poems and arguments, for I have noted his pro-
pensities and what he thought to achieve with Mustafa, and
I have seen also the results of his doctrines, to what danger they
have brought us'.[5] The reference to John's 'poems and arguments'
suggests that he had received a careful literary education. He
certainly quoted a line of Homer correctly in Ferrara[6] and took
with him to Italy a copy of the works of St. Basil[7]; Traversari
declared in a letter of 11 March 1438: *Vidimus apud imperatorem
pleraque graeca volumina digna memoriae.*[8] Other indications on
this point are few, though a suggestion is to be found in Ducas,
who recounts that the son of Bajezid, a hostage in Constantinople,
'was enamoured of Greek learning while with John, the Emperor's
son, and frequenting the school set his mind to letters and was
taught'[9]; and an anonymous panegyrist makes John out to have
been a prodigy of learning, educated in the military arts of riding
and shooting with various weapons, in military strategy and naval
tactics, in literature, rhetoric, theology and philosophy, 'consorting
daily with Aristotle and Plato'.[10]

As the territory of the empire round Constantinople became
more and more restricted by Turkish conquests, Manuel envisaged
the plan of strengthening his hold on and enlarging his possessions
in the Peloponnesus. He himself spent some three years in Greece
(1413–16) and in autumn 1416 he sent John there, who with his
brother Theodore took by conquest a large portion of Messenia
and Elis from Centurione, prince of Achaia. While he was away

---

[4] CLAVIJO, *Embassy to Tamerlane 1403–1406*, ed. GUY LE STRANGE (London, 1928), p. 87.
[5] PHRANTZES, p. 178.   [6] *A.G.*, p. 106.
[7] BESSARION, *Ad Al. Lascarin de Processione Spiritus Sancti*, P.G., 161, 326B.
[8] TRAV., no. 510.   [9] DUCAS, Op. cit., p. 98.
[10] LAMBROS, III, pp. 169–72.

his young wife Anne, a Russian princess whom he had married in 1414, died of the plague. John returned to Constantinople in 1418 and with the necessary dispensation from the Pope, on 19 January 1421, married Sophia daughter of the Marquis of Monferrato, a Latin princess. A mistaken policy in regard to the Turkish succession on the death of Mahomet I (1421) led to a short attack on Constantinople and John, who had on 19 January 1421[11] been associated as co-basileus by his father, set off for Hungary on 15 November 1423 to seek the aid of Sigismund, returning in the October of the following year.[12]

Manuel died on 21 July 1425, dividing the Byzantine possessions between his sons and leaving Constantinople to John. A little more than a year later (August 1426) John's wife, Sophia, fled from his capital and, after the necessary divorce, John married his third wife, Maria Comnene, daughter of Alexius king of Trebizond, in September 1427. A month later he was on his way to the Peloponnesus where war had broken out between the Greeks of Mistra and Carolo Tocco prince of the port of Clarentza and of most of Elis, whom he defeated disastrously. The result was a new Greek principality under Constantine, John's brother. An attack on Patras, a papal possession, failed, and in October 1428 John returned to his capital. The next major event in his life was the Council of Florence. Negotiations had been initiated by John's father and he continued them, first with Martin V, then with Eugenius IV and the Council of Basel. The result was his departure with the Patriarch Joseph II and some 700 clerics and courtiers in November 1437 for Italy where he assisted at the Council in Ferrara and Florence, at which agreement on union was reached. He arrived at Constantinople on his return on 1 February 1440 some six weeks after his wife's death. The union agreed to in Florence was not well received in Constantinople and the last years of John's life, marked also by an insurrection organized by his brother Demetrius and other family frictions, were spent trying to implement the agreement and to reconcile unionists and non-unionists. He died on 31 October 1448 and was refused the usual church rites by the ecclesiastical authorities.[13]

[11] F. DÖLGER, *Die Krönung Johanns VIII. zum Mitkaiser*, in *B.Z.* 36 (1936), pp. 318–19.
[12] PHRANTZES, pp. 121–2.
[13] SCHOL. III, p. 100. This may possibly mean no more than that John was somehow prevented from assuming the monastic habit before he died, as the emperors usually did.

This very brief biographical sketch gives some idea of the variety of external activity in which John Palaeologus engaged. The documents on which it is founded naturally deal with his public actions. To get behind them to his private life and to estimate his character, one has to take a hint found accidentally here and there and, piecing these together and fitting them into the general background of his official life, form a general picture of the man.

By the time that John Palaeologus entered upon the Byzantine scene the imperial family was living in reduced circumstances. His father several times had to appeal to the West for financial as well as military aid. In the negotiations with Martin V about union Manuel had to lay all the expense of a possible council on the papal shoulders. John himself on his journey to Sigismund of Hungary (1423) raised money in Venice by pledging certain articles.[14] The imperial palace, as it was in the year 1435, is thus described by Pero Tafur: 'The Emperor's palace must have been very magnificent but now it is in such a state that both it and the city show well the evils which the people have suffered and still endure. . . . Inside, the house is badly kept, except certain parts where the Emperor, the Empress and attendants live, although cramped for space.'[15] Perhaps because of this relative poverty the family life of the Palaeologi was the closer and the more intimate. John had a great respect for his parents. Manuel, when dying, had recommended to his special care Sphrantzes the chronicler, and for this reason the new emperor long refused both his brother Constantine's and Sphrantzes' appeal that the latter be allowed to accompany the despot to the Peloponnesus, declaring that to let Sphrantzes leave himself would be against his father's behest. He yielded finally, but only when the Queen-Mother had been persuaded to second the request. His mother's influence with him was always high. He consulted her about negotiations for ecclesiastical union[16]: he wanted her advice before the election of a new patriarch to succeed Joseph II who had died in Florence[17]; no one else dare break the news of his wife's death to him on his return to Constantinople in 1440.[18]

[14] LAMBROS, III, p. 353.
[15] PERO TAFUR, *Travels and Adventures 1435–1439*, ed. MALCOLM LEWIS (London, 1926), p. 145.
[16] SYR., p. 12.   [17] Ibid., p. 305.
[18] Ibid., p. 329.

His own married life produced no children though he was married three times. Anna, his first wife, was only 11 at the time of her marriage and she died three years later (1417). His second wife, Sophia Malatesta, though beautiful of body, was so ugly of face that John took an aversion to her and left her isolated and lonely in some distant apartments of the palace. Indeed he would have shipped her back to Italy had not his respect for his father stopped him. Sophia herself ended the impossible situation by fleeing to Italy in August 1426—and John did not try to stop her.[19] Bessarion was commissioned to find his third wife and he arranged a marriage with Maria Comnene, daughter of Alexius of Trebizond, a girl of ravishing beauty who won John's heart.[20] When she died in his absence, not even his brother had the courage to tell him but left it to his mother, and his grief was such that Syropoulus accounts it as one of the reasons that favoured the anti-unionists after Florence, because the Emperor was too stricken to take any action.[21]

His relations with his brothers, of whom he had five, were rendered difficult by the dispositions of his father's will and the question of succession to the imperial throne after his own death. He himself was set on having Constantine follow him in the capital city, though there were two other brothers older. He seems to have handled the delicate situation adroitly enough, however. When Theodore, the next eldest after himself, declared his intention of becoming a monk, John brought Constantine from the scattered Greek possessions round the Black Sea to the Peloponnesus and, when Theodore changed his mind, retained his favourite brother in that centre of Greek influence by giving him the territory newly acquired by the war of 1426–28. Constantine went to Constantinople in September 1435, to be followed a few months later by Theodore come to protect his rights.[22] John then arranged for Theodore to remain in Constantinople, which he was nominated to rule in John's projected absence,[23] while Constantine and Thomas were to share the Peloponnesus between them. The result was war in the Peloponnesus stirred up by Theodore against his brothers, a war that was settled by John's envoys so that

---

[19] DUCAS, Op. cit., p. 98 seq.; PHRANTZES, p. 125.
[20] C. DIEHL, *Figures byzantines* II (Paris, 1913), pp. 276–7.
[21] SYR., pp. 326–9, 347.
[22] PHRANTZES, pp. 162–3.
[23] Letter of John of Ragusa dated 16 Sept. 1436; HALLER, Op. cit. I, p. 376.

Constantine should reside in Constantinople and Theodore share with Thomas the Greek possession of the Peloponnesus. So Constantine returned to the capital and took over the government while John was absent in Italy. But the process was reversed in 1443, and only the death of Theodore a few months before that of John himself secured the throne finally for Constantine.[24]

The *enfant terrible* of the family was Demetrius. In 1422 he had fled from Constantinople with the intention of going over to the Turk, but went instead to Hungary.[25] When John left for Italy in 1437 he took him with him, probably to keep him out of mischief, but he found him there somewhat of a problem, for Demetrius did not share John's enthusiasm for union and retired to Venice. At the Emperor's insistent request he returned to the Council, only to renew his demands for leave to depart. John acceded, but was persuaded by some Cardinals to revoke his permission[26]: Demetrius left finally for Venice on 25 June 1439 with Gemistus and Scholarius, 'though to the displeasure of his brother and Eugenius'.[27] Back in Constantinople (his wife had died just before his return) he fled to his possessions round the Black Sea to effect a marriage that the Emperor and the Queen-Mother disapproved of (April 1441): in April 1442 with the aid of the Turks he besieged Constantinople in an effort to make himself emperor.[28] He failed in his attempt and suffered confinement in the royal palace for a time while Theodore took over his Pontic possessions. Later released and given the islands, he resisted Theodore's blandishments to join him against John. Theodore's death changed the situation and John's death shortly afterwards prevented his restoring to Demetrius his old Pontic cities. A faction in Constantinople wanted Demetrius to challenge Constantine for the succession, but he resisted the temptation[29] and was pacified by sharing with Thomas the Greek cities of the Peloponnesus. Scholarius, who recounts the above details in a letter to Demetrius written some two years after John's death, blames the late emperor for harshness to his brother in that he did not restore

[24] PHRANTZES, pp. 164, 194, 201.
[25] Ibid., p. 121.   [26] SYR., pp. 208, 266–8.
[27] SCHOL., III, p. 118.   [28] PHRANTZES, pp. 191, 193.
[29] SCHOL., III, pp. 119–21. Scholarius with the acme of tact (he is writing to Demetrius himself) says that Demetrius resisted the temptation 'even if there was some need of advisers': LAON. CHALC. (II, pp. 140–1) more openly asserts that he was prevented by his mother, the people and some of the royal counsellors, afraid of the war with Constantine that would inevitably have ensued.

to him immediately after the unsuccessful rebellion the area he had ruled before and instead kept him for a time under arrest, but it is hard to share such disapproval in view of Demetrius' treachery in invoking the aid of the Turk against his fatherland and of the unstable conditions due to the ever-present Turkish threat and to Theodore's uncertain loyalty. For Scholarius, however, Demetrius had one, at least, redeeming quality, that he was a steady anti-unionist, whereas John and Constantine were not.

As a soldier John seems to have been very competent. The two campaigns he engaged in in the Peloponnesus were eminently successful and even if he failed to take Patras at the first attempt (all three brothers John, Theodore and Constantine were engaged in it, but not very seriously)[30] the city was forced to pay a yearly tribute to Constantine. These two wars indicate that John was following up his father's policy of building up Byzantine strength in Greece. The plan was wise, but also it needed delicate execution so as neither to irritate the Turk too much and force him to reprisals nor to embitter relations with Venice. It proved sufficiently successful to let the Greek kingdom of the Morea survive the fall of Constantinople for seven years.

On his return from the Peloponnesus in 1428 he set about strenthening the defences of Constantinople which had suffered from war and neglect, for this enlisting the help of all able-bodied men (clerics alone were excepted, though some of these also lent a hand), and paying them. He first had all the ditches and trenches that surrounded the walls cleaned out and restored to their original depth. Then he completed a tower that had been left half-finished near the Royal Gate and built two new towers overlooking the Propontis. Finally he cleared of silt a large dock capable of holding 300 triremes.[31]

If he followed his father's policy faithfully as regards the Peloponnesus, he departed from it disastrously on one occasion, with regard to the Turk, while Manuel was still living, acquiescing though not approving. It was when, on the death of Mahomet I, he thought that by supporting the claims of Mustafa, the dead man's uncle, against those of his son Murad, he could help the fortunes of his country. In the ensuing conflict Mustafa was defeated and killed, and Constantinople suffered the siege of the

---

[30] PHRANTZES, p. 132.

[31] Anonymous panegyrics in LAMBROS, III, p. 186 seq., 296 seq., Introd., pp. 6–10.

summer of 1422 in consequence. It was John's first and last
attempt of the kind. Thereafter he tried to preserve good relations
with his Turkish enemies, even in 1437 advising the Emir of his
proposed departure for Italy, though he did not take his advice
to forgo the enterprise and be content with Turkish friendship.[32]
That attempt to restore union between East and West, which
besides its ecclesiastical aspect was also a political move to bring the
western Powers to the aid of the dying empire, was also against the
mind of the cunning Manuel, whose policy had been ever to keep
the prospect dangling before the eyes of the Latins but never to
put it into execution.[33] That it failed in both its aims was neither
John's fault nor the Pope's, but was owing partly to the opposition
engendered in Constantinople by Mark Eugenicus and a few
others, partly to the disastrous defeat of the Christians at Varna
(1444) and to the growing nationalism and divisions obtaining in
Europe. Here again the event seems to prove that Manuel had
the wiser political head, but had Varna been a victory instead of a
defeat (the Christian crusade had won a resounding victory shortly
before) Constantinople would have survived for many long years
at least, and John's policy been vindicated.

In spite of the poverty of his circumstances the Emperor did
not abate anything of the pomp and ceremony surrounding the
imperial throne. Tafur, after describing the limitations of the
royal palace proceeds: 'The Emperor's state is as splendid as
ever, for nothing is omitted from the ancient ceremonies, but,
properly regarded, he is like a bishop without a See. When he
rides abroad, all the imperial rites are strictly observed'.[34] There
are plenty of examples to illustrate John's insistence on the honours
due to him. In his correspondence over union (and in his addresses
to his prelates in Ferrara and Florence) he frequently asserted that
it was he, as emperor, who had summoned the Council. On his
arrival at Venice the Doge invited him to land by the Venetian
state-barge: John insisted that his own galley be towed to the quay
that he might step ashore from that.[35] In the preparation of the
church for the first public session (9 April 1438) at Ferrara, there
was altercation about the position of his throne relative to that of
the Pope.[36] Then he wanted to proceed on horseback right to his

[32] PHRANTZES, p. 179.   [33] Ibid., pp. 177–8.
[34] PERO TAFUR, Op. cit., p. 145.   [35] SYR., p. 83.
[36] A.G., p. 11; SYR., pp. 101–3.

throne (the sessions were now being held in the palace of the Pope) and when that was not possible a way had to be broken through the wall so that he could be carried to it unseen and without setting foot on the ground—meanwhile till this work was done the sessions were suspended.[37] This Byzantine ceremonial was misunderstood by a good man of Peretola who was honoured by the Emperor's resting and dining in his house on 27 July 1438, when on an outing accompanied by about fifty gentlemen and attendants to visit Pistoia and the Girdle of Our Lady at Prato. In his account of the incident he wrote: 'And because he had lost the use of his legs he entered right into our room on horseback, without being seen by anyone to dismount, unless by his gentlemen and attendants'.[38] In December 1438 there was the episode of the Burgundian envoys to the Council who brought letters to the Pope and addressed to him their speeches, ignoring the Emperor. John was not content till the 'insult' had been repaired in a special session by the presentation to him of a fictitious letter.[39] This same determination to be given the respect he considered due to him raised a difficulty in the framing of the Decree of Union. The earlier draft had mentioned only the Pope's name in the opening phrase. The Emperor protested that reference both to him and to the Greek church should be made, and he had his way.[40]

John's insistence on punctilio may seem exaggerated, but it was not pointless. Besides its being the traditional etiquette that surrounded the Byzantine throne, it served to create in the Latin mind an impression of the dignity, majesty and importance of his empire—an empire it would be worth while to preserve against the depredations of the Turk. As he said to the Patriarch about the appearance of the clerics: 'If it (i.e. the Church) makes a dignified showing there, it will be honoured by them and be a credit to us. But if it is seen to be shabby, it will be despised and counted for nothing by them'.[41] John himself had a special bed and carriage prepared for his sojourn in Italy.[42] Besides, John and

[37] SYR., pp. 167–8.
[38] LAMBROS, III, p. 328. The year, however, must have been 1439 because the account says that the Emperor was returning from Pistoia and Prato en route for Florence, whither in fact he went after his meal in Peretola. Besides, Pistoia, Prato and Peretola are near to Florence, but a long way from Ferrara where the Emperor was residing in July 1438.
[39] A.G., pp. 212–13; SYR., pp. 175–6; A.L., pp. 87, 95.
[40] A.G., pp. 454–5; SYR., p. 280.
[41] SYR., p. 61.   [42] Ibid., p. 63.

the Greeks came to Italy, not as suppliants or inferiors, but as equals, and that was why there was so much argument about the positions, heights and ornaments of the thrones for the public sessions—a question, that is, not only of dignity but of principle, and the Emperor's insistence (like that of the Latins) was for the defence of the principles involved.

But John was not always on his dignity. He was passionately fond of riding and hunting and was generous in inviting others, and among them young men, to share his pleasure. He hunted any sort almost of beast or bird and usually with horse and hounds.[43] Tafur was invited by the Emperor to hunt and was provided with a horse in the days immediately before the departure of the Greeks for Italy.[44] S. Lambros[45] has published two letters from Nicholas Notaras written to a friend in the entourage of the Emperor in Italy—there is nothing in either except talk of horses and hounds and beasts of the chase. In the second of them the writer hopes for the Emperor's speedy return safe and well: 'because besides the other high qualities that God has given him is his frequent exercising of young men in the chase by often going out for that purpose, which gives not only that pleasure and satisfaction, but is by its nature an introduction to almost all military training and soldierly experience'. On the way to Italy, while the Greek convoy rounded the Morea, John travelled on horseback from Cenchrea, joining his ship again at Navarino.[46]

Once established in Ferrara and having little to occupy his time owing to the decision to allow an interval for the arrival of the envoys of the western princes, John took up again his favourite pastime. Not satisfied with the horses offered by the Pope, he bought one from Gydeles, the envoy he had despatched with Isidore of Kiev to persuade the Slav princes to send representatives to the Council, lately arrived from Russia (and so about the middle of August 1438: Demetrius bought the rest of Gydeles' horses), and from his residence outside the city of Ferrara where the plague was raging occupied his time in hunting. To such a degree did he indulge in the sport that Syropoulus complains

---

[43] He sent to the legates of the Council of Basel during their stay in Constantinople in Oct. 1437 at various times hares, partridges and half a deer complete with horns; Report of the envoys to the Council; HALLER, V., p. 356. Cf. also LAMBROS, III, pp. 169 seq.; 188 seq.

[44] TAFUR, Op. cit., p. 124.   [45] LAMBROS, II, pp. 182, 184.

[46] SYR., p. 76; LAMBROS, III, p. 362.

I

bitterly of his neglect of his duties and of his lack of care for his ecclesiastical subjects languishing in the city, and reports that on two occasions the Marquis of Ferrara made strong representations to the Emperor, begging him to restrain his enthusiasm for the chase owing to the damage he was causing to the property of the countryfolk and to the decimation of the game that the Marquis had imported for his own pleasure—but without avail.[47] He continued with his hunting even when the public sessions had begun.[48] He was usually followed about by a favourite dog[49] and took back with him a number of hounds from Italy to Constantinople,[50] using them for a hunt on the way at Kotzinon.[51] Arrived back in Constantinople and learning of the death of his wife, John went into mourning. But as soon as he roused himself from his grief to tackle the problem of union, he went back again to his hunting.[52]

Syropoulus, from whom most of the references in the preceding section have been taken, reports the hunting episodes always so as to portray the Emperor as selfishly indulging his own pleasure and neglecting the due care of his subjects. Rightly to estimate the value of Syropoulus' *Memoirs*, which contain a wealth of detail and fact not found elsewhere, one must realise that they constitute his defence of himself for signing the Decree of Union. Even if every incident that he recounts were true (and that is not in fact the case), the motives he assigns or implies, and the suppression of what might have altered the perspective of the general picture that he draws, distort historical balance, and always to the detriment of those who favoured union at Florence and to the exculpation of himself. But even from Syropoulus' biased portrait of the Emperor it emerges that John was not all etiquette and hunting.

One of Syropoulus' reasons for lamenting that the Emperor resided outside Ferrara during the summer months of 1438 when the plague was raging in the city was that there he was inaccessible. His very complaint emphasises a fact, shown abundantly elsewhere, that the Emperor was approachable, not only by his higher courtiers, but also by lower ecclesiastics. And they availed themselves of that condescension freely, going of themselves or

[47] SYR., pp. 143, 191.
[48] Ibid., p. 173.
[49] Ibid., p. 265.
[50] Ibid., pp. 325, 328.
[51] Ibid., p. 326.
[52] Ibid., p. 338.

as the mouthpieces of the Patriarch or of the ecclesiastical section of the Greek contingent at the Council. On many occasions the Emperor summoned meetings to discuss the situation, sometimes in his own residence, more often in the apartments of the Patriarch, and there he invited opinions, advised, persuaded, encouraged, and occasionally lost his imperial temper and rounded upon individuals, even such a venerable figure as Antony of Heraclea, the oldest of the Greek prelates, but slow of mind, poorly educated and not a little obstinate. On the journey from Ferrara to Florence he took with him the oldest of the prelates, including Heraclea and Mark of Ephesus, so as to spare them as much as possible the fatigue of the journey.[53] Yet Ephesus was the most obstinate opponent and obstacle to his hopes and the only Greek prelate in Florence who did not sign the Decree of Union. Even so the Emperor always treated him with the greatest consideration and courtesy, refused to fall in with the Pope's twice expressed wish that Ephesus should be called to account for refusing to submit to an oecumenical Council and, at Ephesus' request (for he feared, he said, for his own safety), took him back to Venice and thence to Constantinople in his own immediate entourage.[54] Mark Eugenicus himself in his polemical writings after his return from Italy, though he comments scathingly on the action of the Patriarch, has no word to say against John; and Scholarius in his funeral eulogy on Ephesus wrote that his dead friend had had much to suffer 'and he would have endured worse evils still, had not the Emperor's kindness saved him, for the Emperor as much as any other had admired the virtue and the wisdom of the man'.[55] Scholarius, too, who took up the mantle left by Ephesus and became the leader of the opposition to union, though he fell into the royal displeasure for a time—more apparent than real, he suggests[56], after John's death looked back with regret on the esteem and happiness he had enjoyed under that Emperor 'with whom all my fortunes died too'.[57]

Throughout all this period of the Council, the Emperor, for all his hunting, did not enjoy good health. He was ill at Venice when the decision Ferrara-Basel was to be made[58]; ill at Ferrara

---

[53] Ibid., pp. 211–2.
[54] *A.G.*, p. 471; Syr., pp. 299, 303, 314.
[55] Schol., I, p. 252.   [56] Ibid., IV, p. 464.
[57] Ibid., I, p. 289; cf. also III, p. 153; IV, p. 471.
[58] Syr., p. 86.

when the question of discussion of the *Filioque* was to be settled[59] and at times away from the public sessions for reasons of health. One of the few kindly things that Syropoulus says of him is apropos of a Greek conference of 29 April 1439: 'He was so ill that he could not lift his head from his pillow, and he who was always ill and always insisting that he was well, then could say only: "I am ill and I don't know if I can manage to express what I want to say".'[60] One thing at least that he suffered from was rheumatism.[61]

The Emperor's attitude to religion is, as far as the documents that have come down to us are concerned, largely involved with the question of the union of the Churches. An anonymous panegyrist recounts that he was miraculously cured of paralysis by a forty days' stay in the church of the Saviour near the monastery of St. George.[62] He retired to the monastery of Stoudiou when Constantinople was afflicted by the plague.[63] At the instigation of Scholarius he summoned Mark Eugenicus, still a simple monk, to the church 'Pephaneromenon' to demand an explanation of some erroneous theological statements that Mark had written on the subject of predestination.[64] On another occasion too he showed his zeal for purity of doctrine in respect of a certain Juvenal. Scholarios had denounced the heretic to Gregory Mammas then Protosyncellus, 'And he immediately acting wisely convinces the Emperor, already convinced before me, to banish the godless man. May the Lord be gracious to the soul of the late Emperor (Scholarius was writing in the year 1451 or 1452), for he always hated the impious and persecuted impiety and was full of zeal to confirm and augment the faith of Christ by teaching and in other ways'.

But Scholarius immediately goes on to say: 'But for one thing alone could he be censured, namely this ecclesiastical confusion, and this he shared in involuntarily; voluntarily he stood apart from it. Under some pressure to dissimulate, all the same he showed what he really was by deeds and evident signs both to God and to the right-minded, and he, practically alone, was the cause for us of retrieving that defeat.'[65] If that statement of Scholarius is completely accurate, then John was guilty of a certain

[59] *A.G.*, p. 218.   [60] SYR., p. 235.
[61] *A.G.*, p. 218; DUCAS, Op. cit., p. 223.
[62] LAMBROS, III, p. 300.   [63] SYR., p. 11.
[64] SCHOL., I, p. 428.   [65] Ibid., IV, p. 479.

amount of double-dealing, in that his insistence on implementing
the union arrived at in Florence was, after his return home, due
more to policy than conviction, or at least to a mistaken point of
honour—having given his royal pledge, he would abide by it.
There are other phrases that hint the same thing. 'These (sc.
our reasons) we often took to the late most excellent Emperor, and
we well know how he thought about what he had done and how he
was satisfied with our answers and praised those who acted thus
and abominated those otherwise disposed. Of this we are all
witnesses, each and all having heard it from his own words and
lips. But he, filled with a groundless dread about his kingdom and
lest to the Latins he might seem dishonourable if the evil promises
were not kept, hazarding, alas! the salvation of his soul, would not
bring himself to effect the cure of his soul openly and to save
those who meanwhile were being destroyed by the dissimulation
of the Emperor. . . . He gave us leave to meet frequently in the
Xylalas palace and to make our defence for our pertinacity, in
the presence of the legate, even though he was bringing great
pressure to bear on behalf of union . . . but, not willing to help the
Church in any other way, he gave up both his kingdom and his
life in this simulation of Latinism and was rightly deprived of the
honours that the Church gives, to the advantage of which he had
devised nothing'.[66] Mark of Ephesus gives a possible indication
of the same, though not so clearly. Referring to certain monks'
insubordination to a unionist superior appointed by the Emperor
he writes: 'And when the Emperor learnt of it he said nothing but
confessed openly that he regretted the action and laid the blame on
those who had submitted and signed.'[67]

In view of the above statements it is necessary to examine
John's whole attitude towards union. That help for Constantinople was one of the motives, or at least one of the inducements,
for holding a council whose fruit, it was hoped, would be the
reuniting of the Church was not disguised from the beginning.
The popes proclaimed it: the Council of Basel referred to it[68]:
the Emperor spoke of it both at Constantinople before his departure for Italy and occasionally in his addresses at Ferrara and
Florence. It was taken for granted by all parties. But that does

[66] Ibid., III, pp. 99–100.
[67] MARK EUGENICUS, *Letter to Theophanes*, in PETIT, *Docs.*, p. 481 (343).
[68] E.g. CECCONI, doc. XXVIII.

not necessarily mean that it was either the sole or even the chief motive for bringing about union. It was also a common conviction, shared in by all parties, that disunion was regrettable and wrong, and all sincerely desired to put an end to it. The difficulty was how to do that in such a way as to render the results effective and permanent. Attempts had been made before and failed. The Council of Lyons was rejected by the Greeks as not oecumenical—the few Greek delegates there did not represent the Church. John V's submission was personal. The only way that could recommend itself to the Greeks was an oecumenical council and, if at all possible, with the presence of the pope. Both John and the Patriarch insisted on these conditions time and again,[69] and also that discussion should be free and untrammelled and both sides loyally accept whatsoever the Holy Spirit should inspire the Council to decide.[70]

As regards the oecumenicity of the Council the Greek demand was satisfied—the Greeks were present with Emperor and Patriarch, with most of their metropolitans, with representatives of the other eastern Patriarchates and of many of the eastern Churches: the Latins were fully represented with the Pope. Mark of Ephesus admitted as much when addressing the Pope in the Emperor's name on the question of voting in the Council[71]: Scholarius in his written *votum* of 30 May 1439 declared the same[72]: the Emperor several times asserted it, most solemnly in his *votum* of the same day when also he proclaimed it his duty to uphold each and every decision of such an oecumenical Council.[73]

But on the other hand it has been, and is, frequently said that in the Council there was no real freedom of speech and that the final Decree of Union was the result of Latin and royal pressure. Whether this charge, as levelled against the Latins is or is not true, does not concern us here,[74] but we must examine shortly the accusation against the Emperor.

At various times John VIII enunciated, according to Syropoulus, certain principles that should govern the whole discussion.

[69] E.g. SYR., p. 37; CECCONI, docs. LX, LXI, LXVIII, LXIX.
[70] E.g. SYR., p. 6; CECCONI, docs. IV, XIV.
[71] SYR., p. 148.   [72] A.G., p. 430.
[73] A.G., pp. 432–4; SYR., p. 264; cf. also pp. 196, 254.
[74] I discuss this point at some length in *The 'Acta' and the Memoirs of Syropoulus as History*, where also can be found a detailed examination of the voting in the Greek private conferences and something on the Emperor's action in general.

Firstly, sincerity; replying to Mark Eugenicus who had asked whether in the conferences on Purgatory the Greeks should speak with real contention and insistence or rather 'with economy', the Emperor replied: 'Declare with real contention all our rights'.[75] Secondly, till the Synod had settled the issue, they should preserve an open mind on both the Greek and the Latin doctrines'.[76] Thirdly, the opinion of the majority should prevail, both in the Council as a whole[77] and in the private conferences of the Greeks,[78] after which there should be no cavilling.

He defined his own office as follows: 'I am the defender of the Church. This function of defender ... in the present matter seems to me to have a double aspect—the one to preserve and defend the dogmas of the Church and to furnish liberty to those who wish to speak on their behalf so that they may bring forward without hindrance whatever sound doctrine they like to pronounce, and to restrain and rebuke those who assail it in a contentious and hostile spirit: the other to hold together and preserve ours in concord, that all may agree in one decision and opinion'.[79] These principles explain all of John's conduct at Ferrara and Florence.

There is no question but that John took his position of 'convener of the Council' seriously. He, not the Patriarch, was the head of the Greeks in Italy. He normally consulted with the Patriarch and often with all the Greek prelates on what was best to be done in the practical field, but no step was taken without his consent, a fact which the Latins too recognised for they addressed their requests, their demands and their grievances to him. This is so obviously true that there is no need to support the statement by quotations: both the *Acta* and Syropoulus' *Memoirs* furnish innumerable instances of it. All the same, he never ventured into theology—that was the province of the Church. He might, and did, appoint the exponents of the Greek doctrine and even approve or reject or combine various of their explanations (as e.g. in the discussion on Purgatory),[80] but, as he twice told the Pope, he would not act tyrannically to his synod.[81] If the Greeks elected among themselves speakers or a committee, the choice needed the Emperor's approval. For that reason it is all the more noteworthy that for most of the public sessions in Ferrara and for all those in

[75] SYR., p. 130.
[76] Ibid., pp. 198, 209, 285.
[77] A.G., p. 433.
[78] SYR., p. 271.
[79] Ibid., pp. 221–2.
[80] Ibid., pp. 133–4.
[81] A.G., pp. 418, 421.

Florence the spokesman of the Greeks was Mark of Ephesus, the only Greek prelate who was consistently opposed to the Latins, though there were others who could competently have exposed Greek theology—Bessarion, Georgius Scholarius, Isidore of Kiev or Gregory Mammas, all of whom in the event advocated union and so would have better suited the Emperor's supposed purpose of uniting the Churches by hook or by crook. The fact should not be overlooked, for it shows clearly that at least till 21 March 1439 the Emperor allowed freedom of speech.

At the session of 21 March 1439 Ephesus and Heraclea were not present. The reason was because the Greeks could see no prospect of any conclusion ever coming from the interminable dialogue between John of Montenero and Mark of Ephesus—the abstract theology of the Blessed Trinity was not, in any case, congenial to the Greek patristic mind. They wanted to end public sessions and were present at that of 21 March only because the Latins claimed the right to reply to Mark's long exposition of the previous session, and they did not intend to answer.[82] So they looked about for another line of approach and found it (after John of Montenero had to their joy roundly asserted that the Latins acknowledge not two but only one *principium* and one *causa* in the Blessed Trinity)[83] in a field where they were more at home, the writings of the Saints, with a passage of St. Maximus as a connecting link. Thereafter there was only one question before the Greeks —what did the Latin Saints hold. For it was an axiom with them that the Saints, whether they were Greek or Latin, could not disagree about the faith, for they were all guided by the same Holy Spirit. Such was the conviction of Bessarion,[84] such that of Isidore,[85] of Scholarius (it is the theme of his three discourses at Florence),[86] of Amiroutzes,[87] and indeed of all the Greeks— it was a self-evident fact for them that none of them would have thought of questioning. Mark of Ephesus (and Syropoulus) accepted it as fully as any of the others.

Perusing the Greek Fathers they found none who said that the

[82] Ibid., p. 394.
[83] Ibid., p. 390.
[84] BESSARION, *Oratio dogmatica pro unione*, addressed to the Greeks at Florence 13–14 April 1439; *P.G.* 161, 551–4.
[85] *A.G.*, p. 426.
[86] SCHOL., e.g. I, pp. 299, 356, 357–8.
[87] *Votum* delivered between 30 May and 3 June 1439, *E.O.* 36 (1937), pp. 177, 179.

Holy Spirit proceeded from the Father alone (St. John Damascene wrote: *Ex Filio autem non dicimus*, but curiously he was not quoted by them, not even by Mark,[88] though he did use this quotation in his later polemics)[89]; most wrote that He proceeded from the Father; some from the Father through the Son. The Latin Fathers in general spoke of the Holy Spirit as proceeding from the Father and the Son. But both the Latin and the Greek Fathers were Saints, so 'From the Father', 'From the Father through the Son', 'From the Father and the Son' must mean the same thing. On their own principles the Greeks at Florence ought as a conclusion of this argument straightway to have admitted the correctness of Latin doctrine. Most did, including all the theologians except Ephesus. Some hesitated, daunted by this seeming contradiction of the Greek theology, which, as a result of controversy with the Latins, had crystallised into the phrase 'From the Father alone'. Only Ephesus was adamant in refusing to accept the conclusion. (Syropoulus asserts that he too remained staunch, but no one else mentions his stand.) But it is interesting to note the reason why Ephesus refused to acquiesce. He did not deny the principle: he could not deny the words quoted from the Greek authors: he had to fall back on the excuse that 'We Greeks are unfamiliar with the Latin Fathers; their original writings have been falsified by the later Latins; so we must follow our Greek Fathers alone'.[90]

It was at this point that the Emperor introduced the system of having the opinion of each one recorded by the secretary—first of all on the question of the genuineness of the Latin Fathers, then on whether the *Filioque* was to be accepted or not as true doctrine. His purpose was clear. It was to make the vacillating come to a decision, which as it would be preserved in writing they could not easily go back on, and to discover the majority opinion of the Greek community. Probably there were a few among them who would have preferred to give no positive decision at all, because they had no definite opinion on the question but only a vague sentiment that the Latins were wrong and the Greeks right. But there is no sign anywhere that any voter was constrained one way or the other. Syropoulus complains that the archontes (laymen)

---

[88] Bessarion, *Ad Alex. Lascaris*; *P.G.* 161, 357a.

[89] Cf. his *Encyclical Letter*; Petit, *Docs.*, p. 451 (313).

[90] *A.G.*, p. 401; Mark Eugenicus, *Confessio fidei*, in Petit, *Docs.*, p. 438 (300); Syr., p. 218.

registered their votes (one such has been preserved, of Boullotes),[91] whereas the Staurophoroi, officials of the Great Church and deacons, were not asked. If that is true, it is strange. But it is almost equally strange that it seems to have made no impression of injustice on any one else: at least there is no reference to it in any of the later polemics against union where it would have been a useful proof of the iniquity of Florence, even in those written after Syropoulus' *Memoirs* were penned. In any case, both the *Acta* and Syropoulus are agreed that of the prelates by far the majority—15 against 5 and later increased to 18 'Ayes'[92]—voted for the *Filioque* and union, as did at least two out of the three lay-theologians, Scholarius and Amiroutzes. The Emperor was justified in holding that the Greeks, on the chief question that divided East from West, the question that had occupied all the public sessions of the Council, had agreed to unite with the Latins. When it came to the signing of the Decree, only Stauropolis (who had secretly left Florence) and Ephesus did not append their names, and the Emperor did not constrain Ephesus to sign nor did he enforce any sanction against him for his contumacy in resisting what was generally regarded as an oecumenical definition, or allow others to do so.

John's attitude to this union, after his return to Constantinople, is harder to define. Almost all the literature that we have that recounts the sequel in Constantinople comes from the pens of the anti-unionists, and we have seen what one of them insinuates. When the Emperor saw the tragic fruits of his attempt to bring harmony into the Church—that the old division remained and was now more than ever embittered—he may well have regretted that he had ever embarked on the project of union at all and in the practical field have decided that forcible repression of the opponents of Florence would not succeed. But there is no fact that can be pointed to that would support the idea that he too had in his inmost heart repented of his adherence to the Decree. His delay in taking practical steps to implement the union is explained, and satisfactorily explained, by Syropoulus as due first to his mourning for his wife's death, and then to the attack on his city by his brother.[93] The incident that the *Apologia* of the

---

[91] Revue des Études Byzantines, X (1952), p. 68.
[92] *A.G.*, pp. 436, 438; Syr., p. 263.
[93] Syr., pp. 346 seq.; *E.P.* doc. 243.

anti-unionists adduces as an example of his favourable attitude towards them—the discussion in the Xylalas palace[94]—is hardly convincing, because such discussions would depend also on the good will, and possibly even on the initiative, of the Latin legate.

On the other hand, it must be remembered that both the patriarchs elected during his lifetime were unionists, and that Scholarius, a great favourite and friend of his, suffered his displeasure for a time for his anti-unionist proclivities. Then, too, the majority of the Emperor's counsellors and of the court was unionist—even the Grand Duke Lucas Notaras whom Scholarius tried to woo to orthodoxy with frequent letters, even he was 'unsound' as late as 1451–52[95]—which was the reason why Scholarius so often lamented that they put their trust, even for the safety of Constantinople, in the wrong place, in western aid instead of in fidelity to the true faith. And the fact remains that, notwithstanding his knowledge of the fate meted out by the Orthodox Church after his death to the unionist Michael VIII, the Emperor John VIII died loyal to the union he had subscribed to in Florence and in his turn was refused the rites of his Church after death. In Florence, referring to his own Greek bishops, he had said: 'I am not master of the Synod and I will not unite ours by tyrannical action.' After his return to Constantinople he remained, it would seem, of the same opinion. He would persuade, but not force; and his anti-unionist subjects, who had expected more obvious and tangible signs of the royal displeasure, interpreted such tolerance as weakness and as evidence of the bad conscience of their sovereign.

If John on the one hand failed to satisfy the hopes of his anti-unionist subjects, on the other he disappointed also the popes—in this again like his predecessor on the path of union, Michael VIII. Nicolas V in 1451 wrote of him to Constantine, then Emperor of Constantinople: 'For we have not the least doubt that John Palaeologus, your brother and predecessor on the throne, in virtue of the prudence with which God had endowed him, could, had he so wished, have brought this business to a happy conclusion, but, because he was too intent on adjusting it to his temporal situation, he was taken from your midst.'[96]

[94] SCHOL., III, p. 99.   [95] Ibid., IV, p. 496.
[96] E.P., doc., 304.

'In the year 1448, the 12th indiction, on 12 March, the Emperor Kyr Constantine left the Peloponnesus and took possession of Constantinople after the death of our ever-venerable and thrice-blessed, mighty and holy, master and emperor Kyr John of the noble house of the Palaeologi. When he paid the debt it was during the year 1448, the 12th indiction, on 31 November (*lege*: October), Thursday, at the 10th hour of the day, and he was buried in the venerable monastery of our Lord and God and Saviour Jesus Christ the Pantocrator, in the tomb of his wife. May God lay his soul with the holy emperors. Amen. Amen. Amen.

He who wrote this is Demetrius Lascaris Leontaris.'[97]

[97] LAMBROS, IV, pp. 90–1.

CHAPTER TEN

THE PRINTED EDITIONS OF
THE PRACTICA OF THE COUNCIL OF FLORENCE

All the large collections of the Councils from the beginning of the 17th century onwards contain the Greek Practica of the Council of Florence and, as these are all the same, they give an impression of a clear and undeviating manuscript tradition before them. But, as a matter of fact, the manuscript tradition is not undeviating. It is divided into three large families, one giving only the discussions at the Council with no introductory description of the arrival of the Greeks at Venice or of the negotiations for the transfer of the seat of the Council from Ferrara to Florence and no account of the preliminary sessions on the subject of Purgatory; another, and this the most numerous, containing all that is contained in the Practica of the Collections but with the descriptive parts written in a slightly less polished Greek; and the third, the Practica as we have them in the Collections.

The collections of the Councils before the Vatican Edition of 1612—Merlin (1524), Crabbe (1538), Surius (1567), Nicolini (1585), Bini (1st edition, 1606)—have no Greek text but only the Latin translation by Abrahamus Cretensis, which first appeared in 1521. Abrahamus omitted most of the descriptive parts as well as certain of the disputes and controversies that the Greeks had among themselves, on the grounds that they were *ineptissime* included in 'the Acts of the divine Council'. The rest he claimed to have translated *fideliter ac fere de verbo ad verbum . . . e graeco in latinum*. He was, therefore, using a Greek text that included the description and, as he complained that the Practica *graecis litteris non minus barbare quam confuse relicta fuerint, ita ut vix intellegi possent*, it is not unlikely that his manuscript was written in the less polished language, though, perhaps with a view to enhancing the value of his own translation, he was probably greatly exaggerating the deficiencies in the Greek style of his original.[1] Abrahamus was a Cretan and Bishop of Ara or Arum in

---

[1] From his dedicatory epistle to Benedictus de Accoltis, Archbishop of Ravenna, who had set him the task. LEGRAND, *Bibliog. Hell. XV–XVI sièc.* III, pp. 306–8.

Crete. There is a manuscript in the Nationalbibliothek of Vienna (Hist. Gr. 14) written by a Cretan, Manuel Gregoropoulus, in 1506. It is of the less polished family. Manuel, it is true, was at the time in a kind of exile on the island of Carpathos,[2] but he made frequent journeys to Crete, where his father still was, and so probably was using a Cretan manuscript to copy from. One cannot, of course, assert that that manuscript was in Crete in Abrahamus's time, nor even that he used a Cretan manuscript at all; since the impulse to his task was given him in Italy, it may have been that there too he acquired his manuscript. Also the differences in the Greek of the two descriptive families are not great and consist for the most part in synonyms, which would not appear in a translation, and in any case Abrahamus's version is so free that it would obscure differences even much greater. It cannot therefore be asserted with certainty that his manuscript prototype was of the less polished family, but it is extremely probable that it was so.

The interconnection between the different Collections of the Councils has been traced by Dom Henri Quentin in his *Jean-Dominique Mansi et les grandes Collections conciliaires*. Mansi took his Practica of the Council of Florence from Hardouin (1714); Hardouin derives from the Vatican Edition (1612) and Labbe (1671-2); Labbe from Bini (1618, 1636) and the Vatican Edition; Bini from the Vatican Edition. The Practica of the Vatican Edition were edited by Johannes Matthaeus Caryophilus, who produced also a new Latin translation, for the Index of Volume III of that edition reads: '*Concilium Florentinum Graecum, juxta exemplar impressum, et diligentur recognitum cum versione nova, interprete Joan. Matthaeo Caryophilo Cretensi*'. Another edition of the Practica with the same translation was published in Rome in two volumes by the same editor in 1629.[3] It was this that was used by Dom Nickes for his edition published in two volumes at Rome in 1864. This last edition gives a few variant readings (the only one to do so) taken from undefined manuscripts of the Vatican Library, and the Latin translation is founded on that of Caryophilus.[4]

[2] Ibid., II, p. 262.
[3] LEGRAND, *Bibliog. Hell. XVII sièc.* I, p. 265; L. ALLATIUS, *Apes urbanae* (Rome, 1633), p. 163.
[4] By courtesy of Dom Ildefonso Passi, librarian of the Basilica of St. Paul's *fuori le mura*, I was allowed to see the notes of Dom Nickes, which are still preserved there.

All the published Greek texts, therefore, of the Practica go back to the *exemplar impressum* that was utilised by Caryophilus. That *exemplar* was an edition of the Greek text without translation, that appeared in Rome in one volume in 1577 from the press of Franciscus Zanetti. It was produced by two editors working together. One of them was Gasparo Viviano, an Italian born in Urbino in 1525, who had been bishop of Sitia with Hierapetra in Crete and knew the Greek language well. Recalled to Italy by Pope Gregory XIII, he set up a press for printing in oriental characters, was the effective founder of the Greek College, and became bishop of Anagni. The other was Nicola Stridoni, a native of Venice, where he acquired a thorough knowledge of Greek in the Greek milieu of that city. The correspondence of these two reveals that they had more than one copy of the text before them and that they were anxious to obtain yet another from the library of the Sforza family. The Sforza manuscript, even if they managed to get the loan of it and to use it, which is by no means certain, cannot now be traced, though an early catalogue of that library mentions two copies of the *synodus florentina*, both now apparently lost. Of the other copies in their possession they give no detail that would help towards identification, but as the text they produced was of the more polished Greek variety, it is safe to presume that one at least of their manuscripts, was also of that family.[5]

It could perhaps be thought that they, with the help of Matthew Devaris, of whom it was said by his nephew: *Florentinum Concilium, tum primum Graece editum, emendavit*,[6] were the originators of the third family of manuscripts. But that is most unlikely because there is a manuscript of this third family in Vienna (Nationalbibliothek, Hist. Gr. 108) that was bought in Constantinople by Augerius de Busbecke and presented with many other manuscripts to the Viennese library. Busbecke acquired these manuscripts when he was ambassador of Ferdinand, King of the Romans, at the court of Soliman II, an office he held from 1555–1562, which was at least ten years before Gregory XIII (1572–85) called Viviano from Crete. So it must be accepted

---

[5] These facts are taken from V. LAURENT, *L'édition princeps des Actes du Concile de Florence (1577)*, in *O.C.P.* XXI (1955), pp. 165–89. Cf. also J. GILL, *The 'editio princeps' of the Greek Acts of the Council of Florence*, in *O.C.P.* XXII (1956), pp. 223–5.

[6] LEGRAND, Op. cit. *XV–XVI sièc.* II, p. 57.

that an already existent manuscript gave the text that was published. As the edition was produced in Rome, the manuscript might have come from one of the Roman libraries. Of these there were not a few but, unfortunately, though the subsequent history of some is fairly well known, many were later dispersed and their contents scattered over various other libraries of Europe.

The most likely library to have furnished the manuscript was, one would say, the Vatican. But an inventory of 1545, *Index bibliothecae publicae Vaticanae confectus a Metello kal. sept. a. 1545* (Vat. Lat. 7132) gives only one manuscript of the Council of Florence. *Pluteus 4 ordine inferiore . . . Concilium Florentinum sub Eugenio habitum . . . 12 cap. quae Jo. Philosophus Italus asserebat damnata sunt p. synodum indictione. 9 De substantia et natura pauca pap. for. 8 L. sat. corr. rec. ineptis. Mancus est hic liber et sine initio. Post actiones additur epistola Jo. Palaiologi Imp. ad Patriarcham Alex. et item Georgii monachi et protosyncelli ad eundem. . . .* The alphabetical index compiled by Leo Allatius in the first half of the 17th century also gives only one manuscript (Vat. Gr. 837) and this corresponds exactly with the description of the inventory of 1545—it lacks the beginning and contains all the other items in addition to the Practica, and therefore it may safely be concluded that it is the same manuscript in both cases. So that, over the period when the edition was being produced, the Vatican Library had no complete manuscript of the Council.

There were, however, several manuscripts of the Practica in other libraries of Rome. When John Lascaris died in 1535 he left 128 Greek manuscripts of which Devaris made a list (Vat. Gr. 1414), and the first entry is 'Practica of the Eighth Council, No. 8 della 20'. Lascaris' library was not kept together but part came into the possession of Cardinal Ridolfi, part found its way ultimately into the library of Fulvio Orsini. The Ridolfi Library, after the Cardinal's death, was bought by Marshal Strozzi and finally reached Paris with Catherine de Medici, but an inventory of it[7] published by Omont makes no mention of a manuscript of the Eighth Council. Orsini received his part of Lascaris' library through Devaris and probably through the sale of Devaris' own library after his death. But neither the inventory of Orsini's original library presented to the Vatican (Vat. Lat. 7205) nor

---

[7] *Bibl. de l'École des Chartes* LXIX (1888), p. 309.

that of the books he acquired later[8] records any Practica of the Council.

Orsini, however, was not interested in manuscripts dealing with ecclesiastical history and freely gave such as came into his possession to any friend who asked for them, so that, even if Lascaris' manuscript of the Council did, in fact, come into his hands, he may easily have given it away. Lascaris' manuscript, with his siglum still plain to see, did reach Paris and is now in the Bibliothèque Nationale under the number Fond Grec 422, but, as it is of the second family with the less polished diction, it would not have served for the first printed edition.

Another great library of the time was that owned by Cardinal Cervini, later bequeathed to Cardinal Sirleto, Vatican librarian from 1570 to 1585.[9] On Sirleto's death most of it was bought by Cardinal Colonna (1588), then by the Duke of Altaemps (1611), then by Pope Alexander VIII (1689), and finally for the Vatican in 1740, where it became the Fondo Ottoboniano Greco. An inventory (Vat. Gr. 1207) made during Sirleto's lifetime, i.e. about the time of the publication of the first printed edition, records four manuscripts of the Practica—the first without beginning or end, the second with nine other items, the third with one other item viz. the 12 Anathemas of St. Cyril, the fourth has only the Practica. The present Fondo Ottoboniano Greco of the Vatican library also possesses four manuscripts of the Council of Florence, two of which (Ottob. Gr. 30 and Ottob. Gr. 171) bear the stamp of the Altaempsian library, a third (Ottob. Gr. 389) is so badly damaged by water that most of each of the earlier pages has been lost but it still retains the shelf and chest numbers and the initial letters of the Altaempsian mark. The fourth (Ottob. Gr. 78) has now no indication of ever having been in the Altaempsian library, but as it lacks the beginning of the Practica and the end of the second and last additional item, it almost certainly corresponds to the first entry of the Sirleto inventory. That the other three Ottobonian manuscripts of the Eighth Council are those mentioned in the same inventory is seen from their contents, for Ottob. Gr. 30 contains the Practica and the same nine other items, Ottob. Gr. 171 follows the Practica with the 12 Anathemas

[8] NOLHAC, *Bibl. de Fulvio Orsini* (Paris, 1887), app. 1.
[9] The history of this library is recounted by Mons. BATIFFOL, *La Vat. Bibl. de Paul III à Paul V* (Paris, 1890).

K

of St. Cyril, and Ottob. Gr. 389 has only the Practica.[10] Of these four manuscripts, two (Ottob. Gr. 30 and Ottob. Gr. 78) belong to the second great family and the other two (Ottob. Gr. 171 and Ottob. Gr. 389) to the first. The Sirleto library, therefore, at the time when Viviano and Stridoni were publishing their work, possessed no example of the third family and so cannot have provided them with their original.

The next most likely library that might have furnished a manuscript to serve as the basis of the printed edition was that of Cardinal Alexander Farnese. The Farnese palace, constructed in 1517, had become a centre of Greek studies and a refuge for Greek savants, and the Cardinal himself was a most accomplished Greek scholar. But his library, though rich in Greek manuscripts, had no copy of the Council of Florence, for neither the earliest-known inventory (1584) of its Greek manuscripts[11] nor the catalogues of the Library of Naples,[12] which finally became the home of the Farnese library, record any entry of the Acts of the Eighth Council.

There were several other libraries in Rome in the XVI century, but in none of those of which I have managed to find inventories —the libraries of Card. Bembo,[13] of Card. Grimaldi,[14] of Rudolfo Pio di Capua,[15] of Angelo Colocci[16]—is there any mention of a manuscript of the Council of Florence.

Yet it can, I think, be taken as a certainty that the printed edition of 1577 was the reproduction of an already existing manuscript, not only because editors and compositors must have a copy to work from, but also because to my knowledge six manuscripts with the same text as that of the book exist, though for various reasons I do not think that any of them was used by the two editors. The question, therefore, of the source of the first printed edition of the Council of Florence is still unanswered, and perhaps some time fortune may offer the solution that research has so far failed to find.

[10] If the identifications here suggested are correct, then Ottob. Gr. 30 and Ottob. Gr. 78 were in the Sirleto library before 1585 and cannot have been written in the 17th century as is indicated in the Vatican Catalogue of the Ottobonian manuscripts.

[11] *Mélanges d'Archaeologie et d'Histoire*, École française à Rome, XL (1923), pp. 175–83.

[12] E.g. Pascal BALBI, *Cat. Mss. gr. Bib. reg. Neap.* (1792) to be found in FABRICIUS, *Bibl. Gr.* V (3rd ed. Hamburg, 1796), pp. 774–93.

[13] NOLHAC, Op. cit., p. 109.

[14] Vat. lat. 3960.   [15] Vat. lat. 7205.

[16] *Mélanges d'Archaeologie et d'Histoire*, École française à Rome, XLVIII (1931), pp. 308 seq.

CHAPTER ELEVEN

THE SOURCES OF THE 'ACTA' OF
THE COUNCIL OF FLORENCE

'This conscientious reproduction of the speeches from the Greek records of the sessions in the centre of the above-mentioned history [i.e. the printed 'Acta'], the partisan attitude adopted in favour of the Romanising party and the whole arrangement, but especially the personal remarks introduced—particularly those in the diary-account of the further progress and the conclusion of the negotiations for union that followed the last of the general sessions —of the author who obviously was present and participated in them all up to the end, explain the general esteem that this Greek history of the Council of Florence enjoys in, at least, ecclesiastical circles of the West up to the present day'.[1] In this place and in others, too, Frommann recognises that there are two elements, the speeches and the diary-account, in the Greek 'Acta'[2] of the Council as we find them in the printed editions. He did not, however, follow up the line of investigation that this recognition opened up to him, partly because he did not trace the history of the text he was using back to the manuscripts; partly, I imagine, because he had concluded that the *Memoirs* of Syropoulus were far more trustworthy as a source. The purpose of this article is, first to show that there were two sources of the 'Acta' and secondly to try to determine their nature.

PART I.—THE SOURCES

(a) In the preceding essay I pointed out that there are three large families of Mss. of the Council of Florence: I. Those which contain only the discourses and omit the descriptive accounts of the arrivals at Venice, Ferrara and Florence, the discussions on Purgatory and the events that followed the public sessions in

---

[1] T. FROMMANN, *Kritische Beiträge zur Geschichte der Florentiner Kirchen-einigung* (Halle a. S., 1872), p. 50.
[2] Throughout this essay I use the word 'Acta' to denote the account of the Council of Florence as it is found in the printed editions, and the word 'Acts' in the sense of authoritative proceedings of a council.

Florence: II. Those which, with the discourses, give also the accounts omitted in I, in an ungrammatical and somewhat colloquial Greek—by far the largest of the three families: and III. Those with the same content as II but in a less ungrammatical Greek.

A comparison of the Mss. shows that the differences in the diction in II and III applies only to the descriptive accounts, i.e. to the parts omitted in I. The parts common to all three families, i.e. the discourses, are not only written in grammatically good Greek, but they all derive from the same source. This conclusion emerges clearly from a collation of the Mss. and it is confirmed by the fact that Joannes Plousiadenus, the copyist of a Ms. of the second Family (Cod. Laurenz. Conv. Sopp. 3), was considerate enough to add notes in his text stating that he had taken some of his material from 'another book'.

(b) These notes are not found with every variation between I and II, but there are sufficient of them to show conclusively that one of his books was a Ms. of the first Family (I). For the descriptions of the arrivals of the Greeks at Venice and Ferrara and for the discussions on Purgatory he gives no indication of his source. His first reference to another book occurs in the text at the exact point where Family I finishes its account of the proceedings at Ferrara. It is as follows: 'From this point on we are writing from another copy what was done privately and publicly at this juncture, on account of the transfer of the Council from Ferrara to Florence' (*A.G.*, p. 213).

He does not, however, indicate when he goes back to his first source, but he clearly must have done so, for later he interpolates two passages of unequal length into the text of Family I, noting at the beginning that they are from the 'other book' and at the end that he is returning to the 'first book'. Then, at the very point where all the Mss. of Family I came to an end, Plousiadenus comments in his codex: 'At this point we finish the first copy, the whole book; the following we found in the other copy'. These marginal notes, therefore, leave no doubt that the 'Acta' as we now know them in the printed editions are compiled from two separate sources.

(c) There is a notable difference in the character of the contents of the first Family and that of the additions made to it to form the second and the third Families. The first Family recounts almost exclusively the speeches and discussions of the public sessions. Sometimes these were lively, but the account given of them is a transcript of the words employed, not a general description or a résumé. On the other hand, the added parts are descriptive of scenes and events, somewhat verbose in the introduction, briefer and indeed diary-like in the later sections. Speeches are very rarely given in 'direct' form, usually they are synopsised; and the events dealt with are the relations between the Greeks themselves and their less official contacts with the Latins.

(d) At the same time the diction has changed and even more, judged on classical standards, the accuracy of grammatical construction. The grammar of the sessional accounts is above reproach and the diction is literary Byzantine Greek. The non-sessional sections of the 'Acta' even in the Mss. of the third Family, and much more so in those of the second, abound in unclassical and even ungrammatical constructions and use contemporary words as synonyms for classical words. Like the difference of character of the contents, so the difference of language and correctness between the two parts is obvious even in the printed editions, although editors have removed many of the solecisms and other non-classical usages that are of frequent occurrence even in the most correct of the Mss. of the second and third Families.

(e) The 'Acta' have been frequently condemned as being a 'partisan' account, by writers who thought them the product of one author. T. Frommann, for example, in the quotation already given refers to them as 'Romanising'. A. Warschauer was convinced that they were 'emperorising'.[3] Whether either of these scholars is justified in his contention will be considered in the following essay. What is of interest here is that all the examples and incidents they adduce to prove their views are taken not from the sessional sections of the 'Acta', i.e. the contents of Family I, but from the parts added by Plousiadenus from his 'other book'. There is, in fact, a difference of tone between them. The additional parts are more personal, more Greek; the sessional parts are impersonal, mere transcripts of dogmatic speeches. There is one exception to this. At the end of session VII in Ferrara, a short session in the 'Acta', there is a note to explain

---

[3] *Ueber die Quellen zur Geschichte des Florentiner Concils.* (Paderborn, 1891), pp. 9–11.

why it is so short. The three Greek notaries declare that because the Latin speaker was talking only to fill up time, 'We had begun to write, but when we realised that all this was off the subject, we stopped and indeed chiefly because our side did not bother to make any defence in the matter. Therefore, it is not written down in this record, like some other unnecessary items' (*A.G.*, p. 160).

(*f*) The quotation just given indicates that the writers were more than one in number and implies a group. Another remark, found in four Mss. of the first Family, 'These things were written by the principle secretary', with a variation of it in two other Mss., 'These things were written by the three ecclesiastical secretaries', explains who the 'We' were who stopped writing at the end of the seventh session. They were the three Greek notaries whose work it was to write down all the discourses of the sessions and to compare their accounts among themselves and with the Latin record, so as to produce an accurate transcript of the speeches delivered. Being Greeks they would, in any debate with the Latins, tend to be anti-Latin, as the quotation shows. They were not, however, 'authors' of any work, tendentious or otherwise, but as nearly as possible automata recording sounds. The non-session parts of the 'Acta', on the other hand, are plainly and openly the work of one writer describing what he saw and heard.

Conclusion of Part I

There is, I think, no doubt whatsoever that the 'Acta' as we have them are drawn from two distinct sources, the one furnishing the discourses delivered at the public sessions, the other providing the rest. It can still be asked whether there were not even more than two sources, i.e. whether all the rest comes from the same original, seeing that Joannes Plousiadenus makes no mention of his second book till nearly the end of the proceedings at Ferrara and after that point notes his new authority each time he changes over. The answer to this question is, I think, 'No', and for these reasons. The parts unaccounted for are the descriptions of the arrivals at Venice and Ferrara up to and including the discussions on Purgatory. The copyist gives no indications of his source for these, but he certainly did not take them from the Mss. of Family I which have their own very brief introduction. When he does mention a second book, he three times refers to *the* first book and three times to *the* second book, implying that he was using only two, not more. Nor is it likely that he himself is responsible for the introductory pages, for they are the description of a participant and an eye-witness and, more than that, of an archbishop, which Joannes Plousiadenus certainly was not in 1437. Further, the description of the arrival at Florence is so similar, though very much shorter, to that of the arrival at Ferrara—even to a few identical phrases, that one must conclude that they come from the same pen. And the arrival at Florence falls within a part taken from the 'other book'. Whether, however, the 'other book' contained copies of the official Bulls of the opening of the Council and of its transference to Ferrara is an open question. There is no reason why it should not, but on the other hand Plousiadenus might have had easy access to these and so have included them without more ado.

So it seems safe to conclude that there were only two, at any rate, main sources of the 'Acta' and from the arguments put forward it seems likely (personally, I should say, seems highly probable) that the two sources had two distinct authors, or rather that whoever wrote the non-sessional sections did not write the accounts of the sessions. From this it follows that, in judging the historical value of the 'Acta', a distinction should be made between the two parts and that the whole thing should not be lumped together and labelled e.g. a *Tendenzwerk*. The accounts of the sessions give every sign of being what they purport to be, an accurate and impersonal verbatim record of what was said, and as such they should be accepted as the primary historical source for the history of the Council. The other parts are more personal and on these each historian will doubtless have his own opinion. Mine will be found in the next essay in this collection.

PART II. THE NATURE OF THE SOURCES

(A) *The Discourses*

The discourses reproduced in the Mss. of the first Family and embodied in the 'Acta' may be the official Acts of the Council (or part of them) or they may be nothing more than a collection of the speeches with no official character. Reasons can be adduced in favour of both of these views.

I. The Discourses are the Acts

(*a*) All the Mss. of all the families (and all the printed editions) are entitled, *Practica of the Holy and Oecumenical Council held in Florence*. Now the word, Practica, had, at least by the time of the Council of Florence, come to mean official Acts. It is used in this sense several times in the 'Acta' themselves and it is never used in any other sense, e.g. *A.G.* pp. 11, 77, 457. It is used in the same sense by Syropoulus (e.g. pp. 170, 254), who speaks even of the 'Practica' of this council: 'I refer those who want detailed information about what was said in the sessions to the Practica' (p. 118), but as will be noticed later, he calls them also 'Minutes'.

This use, then, of the word 'Practica' in the title of the 'Acta' strongly suggests an official character. Whoever was responsible for the title in the original, knowing full well the connotation of the word, would hardly have had the temerity to label as 'Practica', within a few years or even months of the close of the Council, what was nothing more than an unofficial collection of speeches —even of speeches certainly made at the Council—put together privately by himself.

(*b*) It is universally admitted that official Acts were written. For that purpose *notarii* were appointed on both sides and their number was three.[4] References to them in the 'Acta' and in Syropoulus are frequent and, it is to be observed, these references are strictly to the secretaries or to their minutes of the proceedings and not merely to the occasions when notes were exchanged between the Latins and the Greeks, or when meetings were arranged to compare manuscript-books of the Fathers and the Councils to check the accuracy of the quotations made from them. From the 'Acta': e.g., at the end of session 3 in Ferrara, Cardinal Cesarini says: 'But so that you too may give a clear answer to all the points of the speeches, what today has been said and written down by your notaries must be read and compared with the version of ours. In this way, when remembrance of it has been refreshed and agreement reached, we shall in the next session make our reply on all that has been said' (*A.G.*, pp. 87–8); or in the last session at Florence, when the Emperor asked for the Latin books, he was answered by Cardinal Cesarini: 'What we

---

[4] *Tres vero fideles notarii erant constituti pro qualibet parte, qui omnia gesta in latino et graeco fideliter conscribebant* (Fantinus VALLARESSO, *Libellus de ordine generalium Conciliorum et unione Florentina*, ed. B. SCHULTZE (Rome, 1944), p. 21.

have said, the secretaries have noted down: that you have got, so examine that' (*A.G.*, p. 398). From Syropoulus: e.g., describing the scene at the first business session at Ferrara, he writes: (in front of the assembled Fathers were) 'the interpreter and the secretaries of the Patriarch and the Latin ones, writing the words of the speakers' (p. 165); or 'There was said . . . whatever is contained in the minutes which were being written there in detail by the appointed secretaries and, if anyone should desire further information, he will find it there' (p. 217).[5] An official account, then, of the proceedings was written and that by three secretaries on either side. The statement, therefore, already quoted: 'This was written by the three ecclesiastical secretaries,' should, it would seem, be taken as applying to these three official secretaries and as indicating that they wrote the discourses contained in the Mss. of Family I. But, the statements quoted above show that they wrote the official account of the Council or the Acts. Therefore, the discourses of the Mss. of I are the Acts.

(*c*) If the Acts did still exist, what would one expect them to contain? Not descriptions of arrivals and eulogies of towns— for the secretaries would not function officially until the Council was in session. Not private conferences of one side or the other or even semi-official meetings of small bodies of delegates—for the secretaries are officials of the whole Council and should be present in full numbers to note and compare what was said. No, the most natural content for Acts of a Council are the arguments and counter-arguments delivered at the public sessions, recounted in *oratio recta*, and transcribed in full and as nearly verbatim as is possible. And that is the content of the Mss. of Family I, i.e. the discourses.

(*d*) The Florentine Ms. Bibl. Laurenz. Conv. Sopp. 3 is one of the few dated Mss. of the Council. It was 'The property and product of John Plousiadenus, priest, head of the churches'. Plousiadenus was 'head of the churches' from 1463–70,[6] which means that some Ms. of Family I was certainly in existence at least before 1470.

It is most likely that a Ms. of that same family was in exist-

---

[5] Similar references are to be found in the account of Andrea da S. Croce, e.g. *Quia placet, ut breviter respondeatur et distinctim, ut vobis morem geramus, videtur, ut per vos relata per notarios adscripta auscultentur* (*A.L.*, p. 45); *Placeat plane dicere ut scriptores possint scribere* (Ibid., p. 197).

[6] A. PETIT, *Joseph de Méthone*, in D.T.C. VIII 2, c. 1526.

ence before c. 1444, the date which most critics assign for the composition of Syropoulus' *Memoirs*. Syropoulus himself indicates that he wrote not from notes taken during the council but from memory (cf. pp. 231, 345). He would then have been the more ready to avail himself of any documents he could find in Constantinople. It is, in fact, highly probable that he constructed his account of the public sessions from the Practica that he refers to so often, because his synopsis contains phrases and combinations of words found in the Mss. of Family I and repeated in the 'Acts'—e.g. SYR. p. 169, *A.G.* pp. 65–6; SYR. p. 174, *A.G.*, p. 160; SYR. pp. 175–6, *A.G.*, pp. 212–3; SYR., p. 216, *A.G.*, p. 242.[7] The obvious answer to this is that one would naturally expect a similarity of phrase and word when the one source gives an account *in extenso* and the other a précis of the same speeches—both could be drawn directly from the words of the speaker. But three of these examples are not of speeches, but of explanatory narrative. One of them is the account of the incident referred to earlier, when the secretaries stopped writing the Latin speech (*A.G.*, p. 160, SYR. p. 174). The Greek of Syropoulus has words and phrases that correspond so closely to the narrative of the Mss. that the conclusion of dependence is inescapable. Yet the account of the Mss. was obviously composed first, and so must antedate the *Memoirs*. Was, possibly, the copy that Syropoulus consulted the original, authentic Acts that the three secretaries produced for the Greek Church? That is quite possible, for that copy would have been consigned to the Emperor.

2.   *The Discourses are only a Collection*

(*a*) While it is true that Syropoulus on one occasion refers to the proceedings of the council as 'practica' (p. 118), on two others he calls them 'minutes' (pp. 167, 217), i.e. by the same word that he twice uses for the reports of the discussions on Purgatory (pp. 118, 132), which were in fact the written statements read at the meetings of the committees of ten a side by each side in turn and delivered later to the other.   Not only that, but the very secretaries, too, who were employed in recording the discourses in the council call their production, not 'practica', but 'minutes' (*A.G.* p. 160).

[7] For other similar passages cf. L. MOHLER, *Kardinal Bessarion* Bd. I, (Paderborn, 1923), pp. 73–4, n. 2.

But the force of the argument in the previous section lay in the use of the title at all, seeing (it was suggested) that that word had come to have a distinctive meaning. That the secretaries, writing while the Council was still going on, should call their work 'minutes' is easily understood, for it would hardly merit the title of 'practica' till it was complete and had received the approbation of the authorities. In any case, that both the Secretaries and Syropoulus do on occasion employ another word does not weaken the argument. In English, I could call e.g. the Acts of the Council of Chalcedon by some wider term—the 'minutes', the 'records', the 'proceedings'—without being understood to deny that I recognise them as the Acts in the narrower, official sense.

(b) There is a widespread opinion that the 'Acta' are untrustworthy as history. The main reason for this is that all the writers about them up to date have taken them as the work of one author and have judged them as a whole. One of the purposes of this article is to show that that is wrong, that they should be judged in parts—discourses and descriptions—and each part assessed on its own merits.

The Manuscripts

(c) It can be urged that the Mss. of Family I omit certain official items that Practica should contain and so they cannot be Acts. Such items would be the Bull for the opening of the Council and the Pronouncement of the Patriarch, which were read publicly on April 9th, 1438, and the Bull for the transfer of the Council from Ferrara to Florence.[8] To these might be added the *cedulae* exchanged between the Greeks and the Latins in the months April to June 1439 preceding the close of the Council, and the speech made by Bessarion before the Pope on the eve of the solemn declaration of the Union. The Mss. of I are silent, too, on the preliminary conferences between the two parties of delegates and on the discussions about Purgatory.

There is no real difficulty in the omission of the records of the committee meetings of May–July 1438, because these were not public sessions and the three secretaries did not function at them at all. As regards the other items mentioned, authentic copies of

---

[8] The Mss. of Family I contain the Decree of Union but without the signatures.

the Bulls must have been given to the Greek Emperor at least, possibly also to the Patriarch; the *cedulae* were certainly delivered to the Greeks; and presumably Bessarion left in the Emperor's hands a copy of the official statement that he made in the name of his Church. All these must have been taken back to Constantinople and would undoubtedly have been deposited in the imperial archives and possibly also in the chancery of St. Sophia.

Complete Greek Acts, with all the relevant documents, must have existed in Constantinople; it is inconceivable that the Emperor would have returned without them. How, then, do the Mss. of the first Family compare with those Acts? They contain almost none of the items of which the original could well have been preserved. They give only those parts in which the official secretaries were engaged, with the exception of the last sessions both of Ferrara and Florence—this will be discussed in the next section. The Mss. we have do not include the autograph document that resulted from the secretaries' combined work, but there is every likelihood that some of them are copies made from it and made either while the Council was still sitting or very soon afterwards. If, therefore, one takes the Acts to include all the official documents issued during the period of the Council, the Mss. furnish only an incomplete version of the Acts. If, however, the term is restricted to the events of the public sessions where the arguments were propounded and the Fathers discoursed, then there is every likelihood that the first Family furnishes a complete version of the Greek Acts.

(*d*) All the Mss. of Family I end abruptly with the arrival of the Burgundian envoys at Ferrara and in the sessions at Florence in the course of the last session but two, in each case without comment. The proceedings at Ferrara are continued in the 'Acta' with a session on December 4th, where it is mentioned that Ephesus spoke and that Cesarini 'began to speak a thousand words for every one of Ephesus's and he never stopped talking'— the whole session is dismissed in half a page. Two pages follow with a single heading: 'On December 8th, Thursday, there took place session 15', which one session corresponds to two sessions in the account of Andrea da S. Croce, those of December 8th and 13th. All these three sessions, omitted in the Mss., are given at great length by Andrea. Their tone is very acrimonius and, particularly in the first of them, there is a great lack of courtesy, mostly on the part of Cesarini who is not only abrupt but positively rude to the Emperor and to Ephesus. That the *notarii* were present and fulfilling their duties is attested by Andrea (*A.L.*, p. 124) who reports Ephesus as saying: '*Dicatis plane propter notarios*' and Cesarini's curt reply: '*Faciam.*' Why, therefore, no Greek record of these sessions is included in the Mss. is not easy to explain, unless they were omitted because they went over the same old ground again (all the sessions at Ferrara were on the one point of the addition to the Creed of the *Filioque*) and were of a tone offensive to the Greeks.

Where the Mss. cease their record of the proceedings at Florence, the 'Acta' continue the same session (No. 7) with short speeches for two more pages and record another two sessions in direct speech but at no great length—2 pages and $1\frac{1}{4}$ pages respectively. In the Latin *Acta*, after the end of the last session but two (the latter part of which corresponds only vaguely to the account of the 'Acta'), there are also two more sessions, given at great length. In these the Greek contribution to the debate is six lines by the Emperor at the beginning of the first and twenty lines by Isidore of Kiev at the end of the second, the whole of the rest being the eloquence of John of Montenero. In the first of these sessions Andrea da S. Croce notes the presence of the *notarii*: '*Interpr.: Placeat plane dicere ut scriptores possint scribere*' (p. 197). In the second it is possible that neither the Greek interpreter, Nicholas Secundinus, nor the secretaries were present, for Andrea remarks: '*Lecta est in Graeco per Generalem Camaldulensem qui has omnes auctoritates hoc die in Graeco legit*' (p. 216). Ephesus was not present at these last two sessions, having been forbidden by the Emperor to attend in the hope of avoiding argument and of reaching a conclusion: the Greek prelates were generally tired to death of debates. The silence, then, of the Greek secretaries may have been due to the fact that these two sessions were a Latin monologue and it seems to reflect the general feeling of futility.

There is now-a-days a general consensus of opinion that the Greek Acts of the Council, like the Latin, have been lost. The capture and sacking of Constantinople make it understandable that any copy that was taken there by the returning Greek delegates should have perished. It is, however, inconceivable that at least one copy was not left in the papal archives in Italy but, if the Latins could lose their own Latin official reports, they could undoubtedly lose also the Greek ones. Nevertheless Abrahamus Cretensis and later Caryophilus, who produced the second Latin translation of the 'Acta', believed that they possessed the Greek Acts. In this they were mistaken to this extent at least, that they took as the Acts the version that contained, besides the discourses, the descriptions and the diary-notes that certainly were not part of the official Greek Acts. That there existed within their reach Mss. containing only the discourses which, more than the longer version, give the impression of being Acts may have escaped their notice, or they may have concluded that the longer version, containing as it does the discourses, was the original whole and the Mss. of Family I were merely deficient.

To me, the arguments in favour of the discourses being the Greek Acts, or at least the sessional parts of the Acts, are very strong. They are entitled Practica. It is stated in them that they are the work of the three ecclesiastical secretaries and one copy was made by the 'principle secretary' (hypomnematographos). They contain matter characteristic of Acts and, if they show any prejudice, it is for the Greeks and not the Latins. (The Mss. we have go back to a very early archetype and themselves show signs of being of an official character.) They correspond in content, even in what they omit, to the records at Constantinople that Syropoulus terms 'Practica' and 'minutes' and show verbal similarity with the text he consulted there. That text must have been written before 1444, the date of Syropoulus's work, and may even have been the original, the archetype, from which our Mss. were taken, for where else would the original have been, if not in Constantinople?

(B) *The Descriptions*

All I propose to do here is to try to determine the content of the second source.

From the notes added to his text by Joannes Plousiadenus, it is clear that the 'other book' contained (1) a description of the conferences among the Greeks with regard to the transfer of the Council from Ferrara to Florence, (2) some speeches in session 6 in Florence that were omitted from Family I, (3) some speeches at the end of session 7 where Family I finishes, (4) a little of what was said in the last two sessions and (5) the account of the negotiations from then on up to the departure of the Greek delegates.

In this last section a certain number of short speeches are recorded in *oratio recta* but most are in résumé. To the above we may safely add, I think, (6) the description of the arrivals at Venice and Ferrara and (7) the résumé of the discussions on Purgatory, that occupy the early pages of the 'Acta'. Besides this, the second source, seeing that it is so detailed on the less official events, must have contained also (8) a more or less complete account of the speeches of all the public sessions, but whether they were in full and in direct speech or only in résumé is not clear.

That, I think, is as far as the material at our disposal allows us to go. Of the second source there is, as far as I know, no extant Ms., and so one can argue only from the parts included in the Mss. of the second and third families (II and III), both as regards authorship and as regards the nature of the original. Frommann's description of it as *tagebuchartiges* is, I think, amply justified, though to demonstrate that beyond fear of contradiction would take too long to do here and can fitly be left to another occasion. Frommann, however, meant his description to apply generally to the 'Acta' or, at any rate, far more generally than the text warrants, with the consequence that he sadly underestimates their historical worth. He recognised that the 'Acta' contain at least elements taken from the Acts,[9] but failed to realise that these elements are more than two-thirds of the whole, and that they are not cut up piecemeal and scattered throughout the work but are grouped in two solid, unadulterated parts, the one containing the discourses delivered at Ferrara, the other those at Florence. The diary-element is confined strictly to the sections drawn from the second source. The rest, the discourses, have no diary-character at all. Their characteristic is rather that of Acts, though whether of the official Acts of the Eighth Oecumenical Council or only of something like official Acts the reader may judge for himself from the considerations here proposed.

[9] Indess lässt sich dieser Verlust einigermassen verschmerzen, da die Acten zum Theil im Werke Syropuls, und in noch grösserer Vollständigkeit in dem erwähnten Geschichtswerk Aufnahme gefunden haben (FROMMANN, Op. cit., p. 48).

CHAPTER TWELVE

THE 'ACTA' AND THE MEMOIRS OF
SYROPOULUS AS HISTORY

There are two main sources for the history of the Council of Florence, the 'Acta' and the *Memoirs* of Syropoulus. Of these the former is not to be judged as a single work, but as divided into 'Discourses' and 'Descriptions', and since the Discourses have been discussed at some length in the previous essay, here we are concerned only with the Descriptions, i.e. the account of the arrival of the Greeks at Venice and Ferrara and the debates on Purgatory, the negotiations for the transfer of the Council from Ferrara, and the events after the close of the public sessions in Florence that culminated in the official union of the two Churches —in all, some 120 of the 472 pages of the 'Acta'. What value have these 120 pages historically? Unlike the Discourses they have no official character, still they are the work of an eye-witness and an active participant in the events they describe, particularly in those of the last few months before July 1439. Yet the picture they convey of the situation is so different from that offered by Syropoulus that the student is constrained to chose either the one or the other—he cannot wholeheartedly accept both. The 'Acta' are in favour of union and are conciliatory in tone to the Latins: the *Memoirs* are opposed to union and hostile to the Latins and the Greek 'Latinisers'. This gives rise to another difficulty for the student, for he himself comes to the question predisposed to the one attitude or the other and it is hard not to be influenced by one's sympathies.

Though the purpose of this article is to assess, as far as may be, the historical value of the Descriptions of the 'Acta', that cannot be done without at the same time passing judgment on the *Memoirs,* for the two accounts must be compared and in many cases an acceptance of the one necessarily involves a rejection of the other.

A.   GENERAL ACCOUNT OF BOTH SOURCES

The Descriptions of the 'Acta'. So accustomed have historians become to thinking and judging of the 'Acta' as a single whole, a

lengthy work of 472 columns, as long as, if not longer than, the
Memoirs, that it will be hard for them to appreciate how short is
the personal part of it, the Descriptions. These, let it be repeated,
occupy only about 120 columns and for the most part they are
only brief diary-notes. They give the impression that the author
set out to do something on a larger scale, for his account of the
arrivals at Venice and Ferrara are fairly elaborate, but he soon
desisted from that and in the 94 remaining pages he contented
himself with short résumés of the more notable events. His
narrative, with one or two exceptions, of the various conferences
and meetings that took place just before and just after the public
sessions at Florence is in parts almost schematic. That in itself
determines the kind of record he can give. It leaves no room for
personal impressions, for behind-the-scenes incidents, for gossip,
and in fact his account deals only with public or semi-public
conferences and meetings between the Greeks and the Latins or
among the Greeks. Doubtless his picture of the situation would
have been more complete if its background had been fuller, but
part at least of that background does appear in so far as it colours
the attitude and words of the participants in the conferences. He
shows that certain Greeks were actively disposed for union and
among them he himself is to be numbered. He mentions that
certain others voted against union and that Ephesus was to the
end hostile to it but, except in one phrase, he expresses no animus
at all against any of these. He speaks of the Patriarch's illness, but
only to account for delays in conferences or for the fact that
meetings were held in his and not in the Emperor's apartments,
and he portrays the Patriarch as generally conciliatory to the
Latins and increasingly in favour of union. The Emperor is
particular about the honours to be shown to himself but is not
above appealing to the hardships undergone to persuade the
Greeks to consider favourably the transference of the Council to
Florence. When the Patriarch, towards the end, was too ill to
direct, and especially after his death, the Emperor took the lead
in all the Greek negotiations, patiently striving to bring the Greeks
to agreement among themselves and then to union with the
Latins. When he lost heart, the leading Greek unionists threatened
to unite without him. The Pope is spoken of always with respect
and reverence. His financial difficulties at Ferrara are given as the
reason for the need to move the seat of the Council and for the

L

straitened circumstances of the Greeks who had been 5 months without their grants for maintenance. All this is background, but not background put in for its own sake. It appears incidentally, one might almost say accidentally, with the notices of the events. The author was favourable to union and does not attempt to disguise it, and the tone of his work is friendly to the Latins, but, apart from the five words mentioned above, it is no less friendly to all the Greeks. He indulges in no adulation of the Latins nor in any back-biting of the Greeks. For one thing, a bare diary-account of events does not lend itself to that kind of treatment; for another, the impression is given that the author was not interested in it.

The Memoirs of Syropoulus. Compared with the Descriptions, Syropoulus' work is very much longer. Some 230 columns of the *Memoirs* deal with the history of the events from the arrival of the Greeks at Venice to their departure from the same place—the period covered by the 'Acta'—of which only about 20 columns are devoted to official discussions, while most of the rest is background. To assess this justly, the situation in Constantinople must be taken into account. The Emperor on his return had been met with the news that his wife was dead and in his grief he neglected to take any measures to establish and promote the union. This neglect gave the anti-unionists among the returning Greek delegates the opportunity to get hold of the popular ear, an easy enough proceeding as the populace was already anti-Latin and, even in the most favourable circumstances for making the union a reality, would have been hard to persuade. As it was, a lively propaganda was begun and the majority of the Greek delegates, faced with popular hostility, changed position and recanted. But at Florence they had all signed the Decree. Some reasons had to be adduced to account for their acceptance of Union in Florence and their rejection of it in Constantinople and, the more they were suspected of treachery to Orthodoxy, the stronger those reasons had to be or, at least, to seem to be. It was being said that their concurrence had been bought. So the misery and poverty in which they had been left by the Latins—in part, at least, true—was pictured as a deliberate policy of duress. The Emperor's management of affairs was not merely undue, but overwhelming, pressure. No validity at all could be allowed to any of the Latin arguments at the Council, but the

Greek delegates had been ill-supported by the dead Patriarch and deceived by the wiles of Bessarion and the cunning of Gregory, the imperial confessor.

Syropoulus, too, had signed the Decree, probably very much against his will as he himself declares a thousand times, but nevertheless he had signed and he was having, it would seem, some difficulty in accounting for it and in living it down. His two solemn asseverations that the subscriptions to the Decree were not bought clearly implies that he, too, had had this accusation thrown at him: 'This He knows, who examines reins and hearts and who will give just judgment on the slanderers of those who signed—that they signed on asking for and receiving money' (p. 292) and on p. 307 he calls on God to witness the truth of a similar protestation. The atmosphere of suspicion is illustrated by a letter to Syropoulus from John Eugenikus, Mark of Ephesus's brother, who had left Ferrara secretly on September 14th, 1438, and reached Constantinople in the middle of the following year —he, of course, had not signed the Decree. The date of the letter is not determined but it was written after George Scholarius had become the monk Gennadius, 'the honest and noble, to me the completely venerable in fact and in name', i.e. after 1450. In the letter John hopes that God 'has firmly corrected Your Honour so that having got back your former, reverent and holy way of life after the terrible fall in Italy. . . .' He reminds him of Peter's repentance and David's sorrow, and exhorts him: 'just as you have already before made good and atoned for the fall in Italy, so by many a token you have shown most clearly in works and words both there and after that and constantly the soundness of your opinion. . . .'[1]

Syropoulus then, had to prove his orthodoxy: he had to defend himself for his signing, perhaps also to himself, certainly to others. He may have signed only under strong pressure from the Emperor, but he had signed. He was not of the stuff that martyrs are made of, not the equal of a Mark of Ephesus. He was writing largely from memory (apart from the dates of the sessions, taken probably from the Practica deposited at Constantinople, and the occasions when the Greeks received grants of money from the Latins, he gives very few other dates) and his memory was embittered by what he honestly conceived to be his treachery to his faith and by

[1] LAMBROS, I, pp. 191–5.

remorse for the guilt that that involved. This does not, of course, mean that everything he says is false or even that in the passages where he most shows his feelings there is no solid fact, but it does mean that one has to be constantly on one's guard against accepting what he says at its face value and in all its details, especially when he is speaking of the Latins, the 'Latinisers', the Emperor or even the Patriarch—and these make up a fair proportion of the leading personalities of the history. One has to be on one's guard even when he is speaking of himself, for it is then that his defence of himself mostly comes in—'He lets his own person play a large rôle in the forefront of events, so that at times one is in doubt whether he really acted the part that he ascribes to himself'.[2]

B.   More Detailed Examination

The above general account of the two sources may appear too lenient to the 'Acta' and too severe on Syropoulus, and the reader may conclude that, in fact, here is another case of prejudice upsetting historical impartiality. What has been stated, then, must be substantiated from the works themselves. This can, perhaps, best be done by contrasting the treatments accorded by the two authors to the personages or parties involved in the negotiations at the Council.

(1) *Diary-character of the 'Acta'*. But first of all the diary-character of the Descriptions must be demonstrated, for in my view it gives an *a priori* probability of veracity to the 'Acta'. The primary purpose of exposing in detail this characteristic is not to argue whether the Descriptions or Syropoulus is right on this or that date where they happen to disagree, but to show the detail of the Descriptions and the almost continuous chain of events they narrate, which in itself suggests a day-to-day diary-entry contemporaneously with those events and so less likelihood of slips of memory, not only as to the dates but as to what took place on those dates.

The date of composition of the Descriptions is not known but that they were written partly during the sittings of the Council can be inferred. Where the writer recounts the death of the Bishop of Sardis (*A.G.*, p. 26), who according to Syropoulus (p. 112)

---

[2] Mohler, *Kardinal Bessarion*, I, p. 70.

was buried on April 24th, 1438, he adds: 'This frightened us not a little, but by the grace of God only he instead of all of us, up to the present, departed to the eternal abodes'. The phrase 'up to the present' suggests that this first part of the Descriptions was written while the Greeks were still at Ferrara and the plague still rampant. The diary-character of the events between the sessions of Ferrara and Florence and, even more so, of those that followed the public sessions of Florence also leads to the same conclusion. The work was possibly finished and perhaps re-written in Constantinople for the Mss. end: 'All this being finished, we left Florence and went to Venice and leaving there went to Constantinople and there each one to his own abode'.

The date of the *Memoirs*, on the other hand, has usually been regarded as known. Mohler[3] considers that the last chapter was a kind of appendix added later to the main work, which itself was written before 1443.

Memory, however, can mislead. An example of how it can create a false impression, is Syropoulus' account of what purported to take place in the interval between the last session at Ferrara and the Greek resolution to go to Florence. The point here is not so much the definite events reported as having occurred, but the impression of a long period of frustration, misery and oppression, which the reader cannot help but get and which Syropoulus himself probably retained. Yet the period in question lasted for not more than 18 days and included the feasts of Christmas and the New Year, which, being spent away from home, may have increased the Greeks' longing to return, but which must have helped at least to fill in the time by the celebration of their Liturgies. Syropoulus does not even refer to them.

Here is a synopsis of the account. Every day without exception Cristoforo [Garatoni] came to the Patriarch in the morning and Andrea in the afternoon to persuade him to debate dogma (p. 185). We go to the Patriarch to complain about our empty idleness, our being on a foreign soil and the lack of victuals: the Patriarch made no answer at all (p. 185). We went to him the next day and the day after that and urged the same: in the end the Patriarch rounded on us (p. 186). 'On that we went away, but on many occasions and over many days having gathered together before the Patriarch and having sung the same song of misery and

[3] Ibid., p. 74.

heard the same [reply] from him, finally' he sent them to the
Emperor who only roughly told them that they could not expect
to achieve any success without some difficulties (p. 187). But
'after the passage of days, distressed at so much idleness and
neglect' they approach the Patriarch again (p. 187). 'And after
many days' supplication, he sent us with seemingly kind words to
the Emperor. But he again scoffed at us and was angry and with
the aforesaid words dismissed us. And that we endured for the
two months during which there were no sessions' (p. 188). Then
the Staurophoroi summon all the Greeks to 'force the Patriarch
to busy himself with the Emperor and free us from misery in a
foreign land'. The Patriarch 'pretended to receive their words
with joy' (p. 188) and sent a committee of them to the Emperor,
but the Emperor went to visit the Patriarch before the committee
arrived. On the next day the Greek dignitaries visited the
Patriarch to learn what had been arranged, but the Patriarch urged
that they ask the Emperor, who would more readily yield to the
opinion of the majority (p. 189), so the committee approached the
Emperor who was very angry (p. 190): 'the dignitaries therefore
were very annoyed with the Patriarch, thinking that so monstrous
a thing had been done by him on purpose' (p. 190). 'Again we
were in distress at our idleness and attacked the Patriarch', who
defended himself (p. 191). Later the Patriarch summoned most
of the Greeks to a meeting: 'It does not seem to me to be of any
benefit to you to sit idle and to put up with all that I hear of at the
hands of the Latins, for they are at home and act as they please,
but mine are miserable in a foreign country and oppressed by
want . . . . (p. 192). 'I know that ours proposed many strong
arguments about the addition to the Creed and almost unanswerable . . . but what the Latins said was rotten and weak . . .'(p. 193).
The Patriarch proposed an ultimatum of 15 days to be presented
to the Pope, within which time the Latins should agree to give up
the Addition, otherwise the Greeks would return home. Mitylene
and Syropoulus carried this decision to the Emperor (p. 194).
In a long discussion with the Emperor, Mitylene softened and 'in
everything agreed with the Emperor', but Syropoulus was firm
(p. 195-6). The next day the Emperor visited the Patriarch (p.
197). 'Some days went by' and the Emperor wished to convene a
meeting of the dignitaries and 'draw them willy-nilly to debate
on dogma'. But he was ill and so was the Patriarch. The latter,

therefore, was carried in a litter and next day there was a general meeting of the Greeks.

That day was December 31st at the latest, as can be gathered from the 'Acta' (p. 218 ff.), according to which for 16 days after the last session both the Emperor and the Patriarch had been ill and then the Patriarch was carried in a litter to the Emperor. On the next or the second day after, there was the meeting. The Emperor recovered and on Friday, January 2nd, there was another meeting in the apartments of the Patriarch who was too ill to move. The Emperor spent Saturday and Sunday in discussion with the Pope (Jan. 3rd and 4th): on January 6th the Feast of the Epiphany was celebrated, after which the Emperor showed them the written agreement arrived at. On January 10th the Decree of transfer was promulgated. The account of the 'Acta', then, hangs together and fits in with the date of the Decree known from other sources. Syropoulus is, therefore, recording the events of the period between December 13th, the date of the last session, and, at the latest, December 31st—an interval of 18 days. Even though the Greeks after the last session must have waited for some days —a week or more—before they decided they were wasting their time in idleness, he gives no indication of that in his narrative, because he had a general recollection of long periods without public discussions, which he wanted to make the most of, and transferred inaccurately his general impression to each particular occasion. And the casual reader he carries with him.

To return to the more immediate purpose of this section, here is a table of the events after the last session in Florence according to the two sources. The days (first column) or dates without brackets are stated in the narrative: the days or dates in brackets are arrived at by calculation.

EVENTS BETWEEN MARCH 24TH AND JULY 6TH

DESCRIPTIONS		page	MEMOIRS	page
March				
T	24 Last session	397	2 other sessions ...	217
Th	(26) Meeting to compare texts	399		
M	30 Meeting with Pat. ...	399		
T	(31) Emp. to Pat. in rain. Schism among Greeks	401–2		

	DESCRIPTIONS		MEMOIRS	
April		*page*		*page*
W	(1) Meeting with Pat. ...	402		
Th	(2) Meeting with Pat. ...	403		
Sa	(4) Pat. ill; anointed Meeting deferred ...	403		
F	(10) Meeting with Emp.: Bess., Isid., Charto., and Syrop. to Pope: oath suggested ...	402-5	Meeting with Emp.: Isid. Eph., Charto. and Syrop. to Pope: oath suggested ...	229-30
Sa	(11) Meeting with Emp.: Delegates report suggestion of oath ...	405-6		
S	(12) Delegates again to Pope	407		
M	(13) Speeches of Bess. and			
T	(14) Schol.	407-8		
W	(15) Meeting with Pat. 3 Cards. visit Emp. Choose 10 delegates	408-11	Meeting with Pat. 3 Cards. visit Emp. Choose 10 delegates	230-4 / 234
F	(17) Emp. to Pope ...	411		
?	First conference ...	411	4 or 5 conferences	234
?	Next day 2nd conf. ...	412	Pat. suggests 'economy' to Greeks ...	234
?	3rd conf.	413	(23) Feast of St. George passed	225
	1st Latin written draft of Union	413	1st Latin written draft of Union ...	235
W	29 Meeting with Emp. ill in bed	414	Meeting with Emp. ill ... ... Text of Latin draft Long discussions	235 / 236-237 / 237-43
May				
(F)	(1) 2nd Latin written draft of Union	414		
	2 days to frame reply	415	Committee to frame reply ...	243
	Synopsis of reply ...	415	Reply in full ... Gk. discussion on reply	243 / 244-5
	Latins criticise reply	416	Latin reply in full	245-7
S	(10) Meeting with Pat. Talk of return to Constant. Emp. ill ...	416-7	15 days later, ask Pat. for return to Constant. ...	248
W	13 Emp. to Pope ...	417		
F	15 Emp. to Pope ...	418		

DESCRIPTIONS			MEMOIRS	
May cont.		*page*		*page*
S	17 Meeting with Pat. who is ill	419		
Th	21 Emp. to Pope: visited by 3 Cards. ...	420		
(F)	(22) Cards. to Emp. ...	420	22 Money for 2 months given ...	251
S	(24) Emp. to Pope ...	420-1	Pope chides	
W	(27) All to Pope: all to Pat.: 4 to Emp.	422-5	Greeks	279
Th	(28) Meeting with Emp. in Pat.'s lodgings on agreement of Fathers: *vota*	425-7	Meeting with Emp. in Pat.'s lodgings on agreement of Fathers	251
			After 3 days, meeting with Emp. ...	254
			'On another day', Eph. calls Latins heretics (=*A.G.*, p. 400)	255-6
			2 days later, discussion in Pat.'s lodgings ...	256
			Next day, meeting with Emp. in Pat.'s lodgings ...	257
F	(29) Meeting to read Fathers	428	After one day, reading of Fathers (=*A.G.* pp. 390-91)	258
Sa	(30) Meeting with Emp. in Pat.'s lodgings: *votum* of Schol., of Pat. and Emp. and others	428-36	2 days later, meeting and *vota* ...	259-60
			For two days Pat., Isid. and Emp. cajole Greeks to consent	260-61
June				
M	(1) Isid. sent to Pope: returns with 3 Cards. to Emp.	436		
T	2 'After these events Tuesday, which was June 2nd, passed and on	437	2 Meeting with Emp. in Pat.'s lodging. *Vota* of Pat. and Emp.	262-8
W	3 Meeting with Emp. in Pat.'s lodgings: *vota*	437-8	Next day Emp. to Pope. Pat. speaks with Staurophoroi	271-6

An examination of the above table confirms the statement that the Descriptions give a diary-account of events. The days and dates correspond exactly, which is all the more striking as the author gives a wealth of days and not many dates, but they are never at variance. Further, his days are usually even more exactly stated than appears from the table, because he defined many by their incidence in this or that week of Lent, of Holy Week, or by their falling within the week following the Sunday of Thomas, of the Blind Man, etc., names taken from the Orthodox liturgical year. So consecutive is the list that it would be difficult to transpose any event without upsetting the whole sequence, and one must conclude that the Descriptions furnish an accurate chain of events. On the other hand, the account of individual incidents is, with very few exceptions, extremely brief—another indication that they are diary-entries—but they convey an idea of what took place.

In the corresponding account of Syropoulus there are only four fixed dates, two of which would be well-known (the death of the Patriarch and the date of the promulgation), a third was for a money-grant (for which he always gives a definite date), and the last is June 2nd when the most important voting took place. Syropoulus' account here will not fit in with that of the 'Acta'. For the business recorded in the 'Acta' as having occurred on May 29th and 30th, Syropoulus, in vague phrases like 'two days later', postulates a period of twelve days ending on June 2nd, when he narrates what the 'Acta' assign to May 30th. He must, presumably, have had some reason for asserting this isolated definite date (the only private Greek meeting in this whole period that he does date), but what that was we are not in a position to know. Were there extant in Constantinople the dated *vota* of the Patriarch and the Emperor?—Gennadius in a list of signatories to the Decree (which, incidentally, omits the name of Monembasia) says that the '*votum* of the Patriarch is still preserved nor is it altogether without malice'.[4] Or was Syropoulus only arguing from a current opinion that the Patriarch died within eight days of giving his treacherous *votum?* Until his reason can be indicated and assessed, preference must be given to the 'Acta', where days and dates are expressly mentioned in sequence.[5]

(2) *The Voting in the private Greek Conferences.* The author of the Descriptions is accused, not only of colouring his account to give a wrong impression, but of downright falsification of facts, which is proved, it is said, by comparing him with Syropoulus. The main instance 'sufficient in itself to undermine conclusively the trustworthiness of the "Acta"'[6] concerns the voting in the private Greek conferences. That voting was important, for on it the fate of the Council would, in the event, depend—whether it should continue its sessions at Florence and, once there, whether agreement could be reached on doctrine. With regard to the first question, there is no opposition between the two authors. It is on the second question that irreconcilable differences are alleged, but, before examining the sources, it will be well to see what the voting was about and why.

What was the situation? The Greeks as a whole were not, as it were, professional theologians. They could grasp the substance of the Greek argument against the addition to the Creed, for it rested on a categorical prohibition of apparently any and every change, but they were out of their depth in the theology of the Trinity. So the Emperor felt constrained to apologise: 'Even if ours do not express it clearly because of the ignorance of individuals' (*A.G.*, p. 418) and Scholarius, addressing the Greeks themselves, blamed them: 'How do you think they will regard us . . . (we) who are always at loggerheads and thinking that ignorance or 'many say so' or 'so-and-so denies it' suffices for the examination of the dogmas, shutting out learning and intelligence and wisdom,

---

[4] SCHOL., III, p. 194.

[5] There is extant the *votum* of Manuel Boullotes, and it is dated 3 June. Cf. V. LAURENT, *La profession de foi de Manuel Tarchaniotès Boullotès au Concile de Florence,* in *Revue des Études Byzantines* X (1952), pp. 60–9.

[6] A. WARSCHAUER, *Ueber die Quellen zur Geschichte des Florentiner Concils* (Paderborn, 1891), p. 11.

while the Latins cleave to them'.[7] That accounted for their refusal to re-open the public sessions, though urged thereto time and time again by the Latins (e.g. SYR., pp. 220, 229, 230, etc.), because they were consistently defeated in argument. Mark of Ephesus was the only speaker on the Greek side throughout all the Florentine sessions—the sole defender of the faith[8]—yet of him Scholarius declared: 'Our common teacher and master says all the argument must rest on two or three texts and that the political law establishes it', though the Latins bring forward the six greatest writers common to us both and expound and harmonise them with the Scriptures, 'and nothing has been said by us to them, to which they have not clearly answered with wisdom, honesty and truth'.[9] Bessarion said the same thing to the Greeks also during the Council: 'And we have replied through our experts to what they have said, by complete silence on some points and by an answer of no value at all on others'.[10]

Greek theological training and mentality were patristic and so the question at issue finally resolved itself into: 'Are the writings of the Latin Fathers genuine i.e. unfalsified?' and 'Do they agree with those of the Greek Fathers?' The latter question was really unnecessary, because it was an axiom that Saints cannot contradict each other in matters of faith; nevertheless much time was spent in comparing texts, and Scholarius asserted to the Greeks that he could demonstrate agreement within the space of two hours, if need be.[11] If the answer to these two questions was in the affirmative, then the solution was found and the 'through the Son' of the Greeks meant the same thing as the 'from the Son' of the Latins. The most important voting, therefore, of the Greeks (and the voting where Warschauer found falsification in the 'Acta') was on these two questions. Here are the relevant passages from both the 'Acta' and the *Memoirs*.

(a) *Conference to discuss the genuineness of the Latin texts: A.G.*, pp. 425–7; Thursday (May 28th); SYR., pp. 251–4; no date.

'*Acta*': Isidore, Bessarion and Mitylene read various passages from the Latin Fathers. The Greeks exclaim: 'Never (before) have we known the western Saints, never read them. Now, then, we know them, have read them and accept them. . . . The Emperor

---

[7] SCHOL., I, p. 303.   [8] Ibid., II, p. 493.
[9] Ibid., I, p. 297.
[10] *P.G.* 161, 549A. Cf. also 416D, 422B, 424C.
[11] SCHOL., I, pp. 299, 304, 324, 356, 367.

enjoined: If you accept them, all of you give your votes. All gave their votes with the Patriarch, that they accepted the western Saints and that their writings were genuine and not falsified.'

Memoirs: 'The first 5 or 6 having declared their votes, it was enjoined on the rest to say briefly, if each deemed the sayings of the Westerns genuine or false.' Syropoulus, nevertheless, spoke at length and concluded that, not knowing the western writings, he took as a criterion that those of them that harmonised with the letter of St. Maximus and the words of St. Cyril were genuine, the rest false. 'Those who followed me took my opinion. All the same, the majority of the votes were positive, and these were accepted as genuine' (pp. 252–3). 'The Emperor, therefore, perceiving that, except four or five of the higher clerics, the rest followed Russia and Nicaea and took them as guides, but that those after us for the most part attached themselves to our reasons and took their lead from us . . ., determined to exclude us from the voting and for that end had the Acts of the Councils brought in and read to see who exercised a vote in them. Only bishops and archimandrites had signed the Acts, and so he ordered only such to speak now and at the proper time to sign, all the rest to keep silence. And so he made us be silent or rather freed us from speaking' (p. 254).

(*b*) *Conference on the truth of the Filioque:* The two authorities record different meetings. The 'Acta' give the reading of the Greek Fathers for morning and afternoon of Friday, May 29th, and a full meeting on Saturday, May 30th, at which George Scholarius, the Patriarch and the Emperor gave their solemn *vota* and other Greeks voted, ten of them in favour. The Emperor, pleased at the progress towards union sent Isidore to the Pope. On the Monday of All Saints (June 1st) Isidore brought three Cardinals to the Emperor. 'After these events, Tuesday, which was June 2nd, passed and on June 3rd Wednesday', there was another meeting when the Patriarch gave another public opinion and 'all concurred in it and voted that the Holy Spirit proceeds also from the Son', Ephesus excepted. Syropoulus gives one date, June 2nd, for the meeting where both the Patriarch and the Emperor gave their solemn *vota*. He precedes this by another meeting two days before, i.e. May 31st, where a vote was taken too—this meeting has no parallel in the 'Acta', just as the meeting of the 'Acta' of June 3rd is not mentioned in the *Memoirs*.

(i) *Memoirs:* Meeting of May 31st (pp. 259–262). The Patriarch 'gave his *votum* though shadowed over and submerged, and he seemed to most not to accept the *Filioque*. Then the higher clerics gave their votes and with them the hegoumenoi. And there were 10 for and 17 against' (pp. 259–260). There followed two days, records Syropoulus, of remonstrance by the Patriarch to some that had not voted as he did (so clearly he voted 'for'), of dinners given by Isidore to cajole others and of similar action by the Emperor. Then came the meeting of June 2nd which corresponds to the entry in the 'Acta' of May 30th.

(ii) *A.G.*, pp. 428–36; Saturday (May 30th): Syropoulus, pp. 262–8; June 2nd.

'*Acta*': Speech (*in oratio recta*) of George Scholarius, not mentioned in Syropoulus. 'When Scholarius had said this, he went out. We, taking the books of the eastern teachers into our hands, read many passages of the Saints. So an end was put to the business. Votes were asked for; differences of opinion were disclosed; the truth was openly declared. First spoke the Patriarch' (p. 431) and then the Emperor, the 'Acta' and the *Memoirs* being in full agreement on both of the texts except for a few words of no importance: Syropoulus states that the Patriarch gave his opinion in writing. Then Isidore and Nicaea spoke. 'The opinions being put forward in order were not given in one sense. But Antonius of Heraclea, Mark of Ephesus, Dositheus of Monembasia and Sophronius of Anchialus opposed the opinion for union in everything' (p. 434). Then Dorotheus spoke. 'The higher clerics being asked their views, so as not to protract the account, some openly spoke out our view, others otherwise. Yet ten higher clerics were in agreement. They are as follows: Russia, Nicaea, Lacedaemon, Mitylene, Rhodes, Nicomedia, Drista, Gannus, Melenikus and besides . . . Gregory the confessor, proxy of Alexandria, and from the hegoumenoi, Pachomius the monk. Later were added to us Cyzicus, Trebizond and Monembasia, who was the procurator of the patriarch of Jerusalem' (p. 436).

Memoirs: The Emperor spoke to Cyzicus and won him over. The Patriarch gave his opinion in writing. The votes of the rest were written down. Heraclea said 'No': Gregory the confessor said 'Yes'. 'Then the rest of the higher clerics gave their opinions', but Trebizond was absent ill and refused to give an opinion. 'Except, therefore, for Heraclea, Ephesus, Monembasia, Trebizond and Anchialus, the rest of the higher clerics gave their opinions in favour of the *Filioque* and union with the Latins. The favourers were, therefore, 13 and they disassociated themselves from the 6' (p. 263). The emperor was then asked if he wished the hegoumenoi to vote. He replied that he believed the Patriarch was opposed to it as they were not ordained, and the Patriarch confirmed this. They did not vote. The Emperor then gave his *votum* and his dog whined all the time, and 'immediately some noted this as an unpropitious portent'. The Emperor's brother, though importuned, refused as a layman to express any opinion and the representatives of the eastern Sees agreed with the Emperor.

(iii) 'Acta' (*A.G.*, pp. 437–8). On Wednesday, June 3rd, there was a full meeting of higher clerics, the philosophers, the Staurophoroi and the hegoumenoi with the Emperor in the apartments of the Patriarch, who was ill. The Emperor spoke first, that as a majority accepted the *Filioque* and all accepted the Latin writings, and as 'the majority had written and delivered their opinions before yesterday, I say that the others must be asked and the vote of the majority prevail' (p. 438). The Patriarch gave his opinion first and 'all concurred in it and gave their opinions that the Holy Spirit proceeds from Father and Son. . . . These opinions having been written down, Mark of Ephesus did not wish to give his opinion on this and so the meeting closed. On Thursday, therefore, having met together, we gave our opinions and a document was made and written in three copies. And we sent one to the Pope, the Emperor took one and the Patriarch the third. . . On Friday we sent the document to the most blessed Pope. . . .') (p. 438).

The accusation against the author of the Descriptions is that in the votes of May 28th (*A.G.*, pp. 425–7; SYR., pp. 251–4), (a) the 'Acta' record an acceptance of the Latin Fathers by general acclamation and make no mention of the opposition which Syropoulus says consisted of four or five higher clerics and the three Staurophoroi; and (b) the 'Acta' do not refer to the exclusion of the Staurophoroi and the hegoumenoi from subsequent voting.

(a) It is not unlikely that the Greeks would have voted on some occasions by acclamation (cf. SYR., p. 223 for another instance), and acclamation does not necessarily mean unanimity. But Syropoulus says that there was an individual vote and division of opinion. The 'Acta' also record the individual vote ("The Emperor

enjoined: All of you give your votes') but do not mention the
result or suggest divided opinion, though it can be taken for
granted that at least Eugenicus did not agree. There is, unfortunately, no court of appeal, no third source apart from these two.
But that there was general agreement on the subject of this
conference, viz. the genuineness of the Latin texts, is asserted by
Amiroutzes in his *votum* delivered during the meeting: 'Further
the whole of this holy Synod has agreed on the two points—I say
those too who deny the Holy Spirit to be from the Son—that the
citations that the Latins bring forward in proof of this truth are
genuinely of the Saints and there is no doubt about it, and that
one must obey in all things the Saints in what they say'.[12] And
Mark of Ephesus, referring apparently to this occasion, records:
'But they said they did not doubt about the citations whether
they were genuinely of the Teachers', though he goes on to deny
agreement on the truth of the *Filioque*.[13]

(b) Mark does not refer to the exclusion from voting of the
staurophoroi, though he apparently speaks of the occasion of it.
Neither does any other of the anti-unionist writers, Syropoulus
apart. They frequently urge that opinions were not free, but they
lay the blame for this on the Latins and do not adduce this
instance to prove it. Gennadius in his 'Answer to the Discourse of
Bessarion' declares that before any one could reply to him: 'the
Emperor imposed silence' (even though it was on the same
occasion that he delivered his 'Exhortation'), but he adds no
reference to the Staurophoroi to illustrate further the Emperor's
tyranny. It would seem, then, that the exclusion of the Staurophoroi did not strike others as forcibly as it did Syropoulus, who
had a very exalted idea of the importance of his position and was
aggrieved that, in the arrangement of the seating for the public
sessions, the Staurophoroi, 'the 5 senses of the Patriarch', were not
given places close to the Patriarch, who did nothing to meet their
frequent complaints about it—'doing it on purpose, I think, and
putting a distance between us and him' (SYR., p. 108). Whereas
he refers to the exclusion time and time again, particularly when
he is recounting how he was forced to sign the Decree (where, of
course, it makes a very good argument), others of his own party,
who would have welcomed so apt a demonstration of injustice,

---

[12] *E.O.*, 36 (1937), p. 177.
[13] *Relatio de rebus a se gestis*; PETIT, *Docs.* p. 448.

M

if it had struck them as such, pass it over. In any case, it was not unreasonable. The Staurophoroi were only deacons and three of them were consistently blocking agreement among the Greeks. The responsibility of deciding questions of doctrine rested with the bishops only, and there seemed a fair chance of their reaching agreement, and that chance would be the more likely to be realised the less the number of discordant voices. Voices that had a right to be heard were not impeded. There is no sign whatsoever in either the 'Acta' or in the *Memoirs* (apart from the last two sessions at Florence, which the Greeks endured rather than participated in) that Mark of Ephesus was ever hindered from saying whatever he liked in public sessions, private Greek conferences or casual meetings—on the contrary, a special meeting was convened to persuade him (*A.G.*, p. 450) and, when he still remained unconvinced, he was subjected to no reprisals. The most one can say is that, if the three were silenced as Syropoulus says, it was then unfair to force them to sign the Decree of Union.

That there was, not merely a majority, but an overwhelming majority in favour of the truth of the *Filioque* is not open to question. Gennadius, after his change of heart, refers to Mark as the only defender of the faith, the only true archbishop. Mark himself says: 'When I saw them now enthusiastically rushing towards union and those who before had stood by me now fallen to them' he did not hand in his prepared, written *votum*, and this on the occasion when the *Filioque* was the question at issue.[14] It is apparent in the 'Acta' and in the *Memoirs*. The 'Ayes' according to the 'Acta' have already been given. Syropoulus agrees in substance. He records that Ephesus, 'when he realised that almost all were traitors and ready for acceptance of Latinism, was silent' (p. 258). In the final voting on the *Filioque* of June 2nd (according to the *Memoirs*), with Bessarion, Isidore, Mitylene and Gregory the confessor, who throughout were prime movers for union (cf. SYR., pp. 221, 223, etc.) and Lacedaemon (cf. pp. 238, 256, etc.), went Tornobus, Amaseia, and Moldoblachia won over by the Patriarch; Melenikus, Drama, Dristra and others beguiled by a good dinner with Isidore; and the legates of Trebizond and Moldoblachia and, later, Cyzicus, gained in pretty much the same way by the Emperor (pp. 260–1); and, the most important person of them all, the Patriarch. On the same side went the weight of

[14] Ibid.

the theological advisers, Scholarius[15] and Amiroutzes.[16] 'Apart
from Heraclea, Ephesus, Monembasia, Trebizond and Anchialus,
the rest of the prelates voted to accept the *Filioque* and union with
the Latins', (SYR. p. 263), i.e. 5 against, presumably supported by
Gemistus; 16 for, together with the Patriarch, and supported by
Scholarius and Amiroutzes. Neither the list of the 'Acta' (p. 436)
nor that of Syropoulus (p. 262) of those in favour is complete, but
between them they account for 15 out of the 16 'Ayes'—neither
list mentions Stauropolis, whose name also is not included in the
signatures to the Decree (*A.G.*, pp. 465-7) nor in the list of
signatories given by Gennadius. Syropoulus' explicit declaration
that only 5 were unfavourable removes any hesitation in accepting
these statements. In addition, the 'Acta' relate that later were
added to the 'Ayes' Trebizond (who, being ill, did not vote in the
meeting: SYR., p. 263), Monembasia (who had voted 'No' in the
meeting: SYR., p. 263, but who was selected to go with Bessarion,
Isidore and Mitylene to the Pope on June 9th: *A.G.*, p. 440), and
Cyzicus. Bessarion, however, later asserted: 'For all these reasons
union rightly followed and all, without any violence, freely and
voluntarily, assented to it. Those who were unwilling to assent
(there were only two, not more) were left in their own view without
violence or any oppression and returned to their own abodes with
honour and charity and at the expense of the Roman Church'.[17]
That gives, out of the higher clerics, 2 against and 19 for. Of the
Greek theologians, Ephesus was against union, with Gemistus;
Bessarion, Gregory the confessor, Isidore, Mitylene were for
union, with Scholarius and Amiroutzes.

(3) *The Enforced Idleness and the Poverty of the Greeks.* That
the Greeks were not given the agreed maintenance but were left
in poverty and misery is a constantly recurring theme of the anti-
unionists. Mark of Ephesus (referring to the period after the
Greeks had voted for the *Filioque* and union, i.e. after June 2nd):
'A long time passed after this and ours were bearing the delay
hard and lamenting their poverty and were being forced towards
famine. And indeed this was plotted against them, to give no one
anything of the agreed maintenance-grants, so that, being forced
by this, they might by degrees yield to them'[18] Scholarius: 'And

---

[15] SCHOL., I, p. 374.
[16] *E.O.*, 36 (1937), pp. 177-8. Cf. also SYR., pp. 175, 239, 257, etc.
[17] *Epistola ad Al. Lascarin*; *P.G.* 161, 424CD.
[18] PETIT, *Docs.*, p. 447.

in all, partly by promises, partly by pretended necessities in which he (i.e. the Pope) had the Greeks shut in, he persuaded them, though unconvinced, to agreement with the decision'.[19] John Eugenicus (referring to the period September 1438): 'With famine on top of plague, as by degrees practically the very necessities were lacking, since for four months we had had to live on our own resources'.[20] Syropoulus, it need hardly be said, is not silent on it; it would be too long to give here the 34 references I have collected from the *Memoirs*. Quite obviously, the Greeks did suffer both from enforced idleness and poverty. But the period of the Council—February 1438 to July 1439—should be divided into two periods, the first at Ferrara when long intervals passed with no business done or even attempted and when the maintenance-grants were very badly in arrears, the second at Florence when the Greeks had little excuse for idleness and were less hard-pressed by poverty.

That the Greeks had little to do from February to October 1438 at Ferrara is apparent from both Syropoulus and the 'Acta', and the fault was their own. The Pope wanted to get down to business immediately (e.g. *A.G.*, pp. 19, 422–32: SYR., pp. 99, 113, 115, etc.), but the Emperor insisted on a four months' delay. In June and July the Latins managed to arrange the semi-informal conferences but the Greeks would not touch dogma in spite of Latin pressure (SYR., p. 118 sq.). The sessions began in October only after strong Latin insistence (SYR., pp. 148, 158). One reason for urgency from the Latin side was that the Pope was paying for the upkeep of the Greeks during all this period and he was finding himself more and more pressed for money (*A.G.*, p. 220; SYR., p. 205). The result was that he could not provide for them as had been arranged. He paid the clerics 691 fl. on April 2nd, 689 on May 12th, 685 on June 30th and 1215 fl. as the maintenance of two months on October 21st. By the end of 1438 he was five months in arrears in his payments to them (*A.G.*, p. 222, SYR., p. 205). For that reason and because he feared the depredations of Nicholas Piccinino, who had captured some papal towns and might even attempt an attack on Ferrara itself, and because Florence promised financial aid (much of the money spent on the Council at Ferrara was borrowed from Florence), he pressed for

---

[19] SCHOL., II, p. 260.   [20] LAMBROS, I, p. 275.

the transfer of the Council from Ferrara to Florence (cf. *A.G.*, p. 220; SYR., p. 205).

In his account of the situation at Florence, Syropoulus continues in the same strain—idleness, misery and want. He alleges enforced idleness shortly after the last session of March 24th, 1439 (p. 231); about the Feast of St. George, April 23rd, (p. 225); after the reception of the Latin reply to the Greek answer, about May 10th (p. 249). A glance at the table (pp. 151-5) will show that there was plenty of activity among the Greeks at these times. With regard to money, in accordance with the agreement made about the transfer, on January 12th the Greeks received 2412 florins for four months' back-money—five months' was owing—(p. 211), as well as 340 fl. (2 each) for the journey, for which, in addition, the Latins paid the expenses (p. 212). By the Feast of St. George they were more than three months in arrears (p. 225). A few days later the Patriarch agreed that an end should be made to their distress (p. 227). Shortly after the Latin answer (circa May 10th) they are all upset about 'their misery, want and separation from their families' (p. 249), for now they were four months in arrears in respect of the money-grants (p. 250) and Mitylene addressed himself to the Pope's Camerarius about it, who said he was ready to order it to be given. 'The delay comes from the negligence of those appointed to ask for and receive it. We answered that from the time when Cristoforo had arranged a day and bidden us come to him to get the florins, we had been to him seven times and always it was put off till tomorrow. We were by no means negligent in going and asking for it.' The Emperor, however, was angry that they had approached the Camerarius (p. 250). Finally, on May 22nd, 1205 fl. were given for two months; 'Cristoforo saying on this, that nothing should be given to Ephesus as eating the bread of the Pope like a Judas' (p. 251). On the day after the voting (June 2nd) the Patriarch said to the three recalcitrant Staurophoroi 'that the Pope already is providing what (money) is short, viz. he is disbursing for the five and a half months and for five ships and another for the Emperor' (p. 271). Referring to the period during which the Decree was being written (i.e. after June 28th), Syropoulus notes: 'There was no mention of maintenance. For after the May grant no maintenance whatsoever was given to anyone, except when we were leaving to return to Venice, namely after doing everything the Latins wanted'

(p. 282). Mitylene, however, Cristoforo and Ambrose gave money from the Pope to some of the lower-ranking (poorer?) prelates and the Skevophylax cunningly managed to tap all three sources (p. 283). By July 5th the maintenance was five months in arrears: 'I call God to witness, who is over all, that no mention of it was then made by anyone, nor any request however slight by any of ours, or promise by the Latins. But even if we all were gripped by want, still, though lamenting and weeping in the hidden places of our hearts, the majority signed'—this with a view to the accusation that their compliance was bought (p. 292). After the signing the Emperor encouraged them to endure till they received the five and a half months' maintenance (p. 302), but the Pope was adamant till five copies of the Decree had been signed, though five and a half months' maintenance was due to all (pp. 305–6). 'Two days after the signing [which according to the 'Acta' was on Monday, July 20th], the first of the prelates departed and set out on the road to Venice. On the very day of their departure, not earlier, maintenance for five months was given only to those who were leaving': the rest received theirs similarly on their departure (pp. 306–7).

Syropoulus, it will be noticed, gives precise dates only for the payment of the maintenance grants. He probably was employed by the Patriarch to distribute the money and had preserved the accounts he had then made. Both his dates and the sums received from the papal treasury are correct as far as can be checked by the registers of the *Camera Apostolica*, which recorded not the sums paid directly to the Greeks but the refunds it made months later to the individual Italians who had lent money for the occasion. The truth was that the papal treasury was living from hand to mouth and that from at least April 1438 onwards it was existing mainly on borrowed money. That explains the irregularity of the payments to the Greeks in Ferrara. In Florence, however, the Commune had undertaken to provide for their upkeep (against future repayment from the Holy See), and why there was delay in delivering the stipulated sums there on the agreed days is very difficult to understand. Certainly that was not the Pope's fault. Whoever was responsible, it was hard on the Greeks, and Syropoulus is not unjustified in complaining about poverty and hunger, though the humanist citizens of Ferrara, and much more so those of Florence, must have been generous in their gifts and invitations.

At any rate, when the Patriarch died, 500 florins, the equivalent of twenty months' maintenance-grants, were found in his effects (SYR., p. 318); Cyzicus in July 1438 had plenty of silver articles (SYR., p. 313); the metropolitans did not return to Greece poor and so were accused of having bartered away their faith.[21]

The 'Acta', on the other hand, do not descant on the poverty and idleness of the Greeks, but references to these are not lacking when they arise naturally out of the context. When Denis of Sardis died in April, panic fell on the rest, for the Metropolitan's death was an early case of the plague that later did, in fact, infest the city. Apropos of the transfer of the council to Florence, it is noted that 'there was never a mention of the maintenance-grants', which serves as an introduction and explanation of the Pope's request for the transfer on the grounds that, with the loss of Bologna and of much of his revenues, he was quite unable to support the council in Ferrara, whereas Florence promised ready means (A.G., p. 220). The Greeks accepted, but on conditions, and the conditions that they set reflect also their circumstances. That the arrears of five months' grants should be paid off was one condition; four months was fixed as the maximum stay in Florence; payment there should be made to them through a bank, i.e. not through the papal treasury; freedom of movement was also to be guaranteed (p. 222)—implying their poverty, their nostalgia and previous restrictions on their liberty (Syropoulus says that in Ferrara they were not allowed to go beyond the gates of the city).

The writer's account also of the sojourn in Florence gives here and there a glimpse of some of their hardships. It is not that he is deliberately suppressing knowledge of them; he is recounting in diary-like notes the stages of union, and other things are mentioned only by accident if they happen to be closely connected. For instance, the picture drawn of the weeks from Easter till the end of May 1439 is eloquent. The Greeks were tired to death of public discussions on the grounds that they were both endless and ineffective. They refused point blank to endure any more and, practically speaking, to bestir themselves at all; the Latins were to devise an expedient that would lead to union, or the council should finish and its participants go home. Later the Latins presented them with a statement on the Procession of the Holy Spirit; the Greeks changed it and returned it. The Latins were

[21] DUCAS, Op. cit., p. 216.

dissatisfied and wanted explanations. 'We began to complain and to set about putting an end to it all' (p. 416)—on 10 May. Seven days later (it was also five days before the first maintenance-grant in Florence was forthcoming), they were asking the Patriarch how they were going to support life while the talking went on and on (p. 419). When the Patriarch died (10 June), the prelates found in that a ready excuse to press the Pope to bring things to an end (pp. 445–6). Even after agreement on the question of the Procession of the Holy Spirit, which for the Greeks was the fundamental difference dividing the Churches, there were moments when the Emperor gave up hope and demanded ships to take them all back home (pp. 449, 452) and when the prelates also were thoroughly despondent (p. 452).

(4) *Motives*—Money, according to Syropoulus, was never given without an ulterior motive, and he manages to suggest some 'concession' made by the Greeks for each particular occasion (pp. 105, 125, 139, 172, 211). He is free also in ascribing deceit. The delay of four months after the inauguration of the council on 9 April 1438 was agreed to, so that they *might pretend* to send ambassadors to the western courts (p. 104); yet a little later (p. 112) he records that the Pope did send letters to all the Latin nations. The Pope urged the preliminary conferences only to impress the Council of Basel (p. 115). Some of ours would not eat a meal provided by the Pope, fearing hemlock (p. 143). The fourth session in Ferrara (the only session that Syropoulus does not date and that is recorded neither in the 'Acta' nor by Andrea da Santacroce (in the '*Latin Acts*')) was hastened on because the Latins were afraid that some of their simpler followers were too much impressed by what Ephesus had said in the previous one (p. 171). Several times the Patriarch is said *to have seemed* to receive complaints sympathetically and then to have informed the Emperor with a view to having the complainants punished (pp. 188, 190, 248–9). Later to persuade them to compliance he showed them what purported to be a promissary note of the Pope and Cardinals about aid to Constantinople (pp. 271–2). The transfer of the Council to Florence was a plot of the Emperor and the Patriarch. After Heraclea, Ephesus and the Nomophylax had tried to return to Constantinople, 'from then on the Emperor and the Patriarch considered together and took counsel in private how they might lead us further inland and to a greater and safer

confinement. Therefore they secretly arranged with the Pope the journey to Florence' (p. 153, repeated on p. 184); so the Pope sent Ambrose Traversari 'who was clever and cunning, clothed in an outward appearance of reverence, not without some education in Greek letters, and a confidant of the Pope', with one of ours, the Cretan monk Macarius, to arrange matters at Florence: the Patriarch, on being questioned, said that Ambrose had gone only to obtain more books. Such is Syropoulus' version of the events, but the truth is that Ambrose got leave of absence from the Pope in the beginning of September for a fortnight to visit his mother who was sick[22]; that Cardinal Cesarini in a letter of October 17th urged him in the Pope's name to return, as his presence was needed, and to bring what books he could[23]; and that finally he received a peremptory order to return in a personal letter from the Pope, dated November 3rd.[24]

The 'Acta' relate the events and assign no motives.

In a similar way Syropoulus would seem to have had an uncanny insight into what was said when he was not present, and what was not likely to have been divulged to him by the participants. For example, he records (pp. 152–3) Bessarion's arguments to the Patriarch for the recall of Heraclea, Ephesus and the Nomophylax; he relates a plan that Isidore of Kiev proposed to the Patriarch to silence the opposition, together with the Patriarch's answer (p. 260); he informs us of the content of the Patriarch's expostulations to win over some of the archbishops to unionism and their replies (pp. 250–1); it was Mitylene, he says, who suggested the device put forward by the Pope of demanding opinions on oath (p. 230). His own speeches which, of course, he was in a position to know of in detail he records at great length, but, as most of them were made on the spur of the moment, he is not likely to have had them prepared in writing and so what we read in the *Memoirs* is the speeches as reconstructed after a lapse of years—may be as many as twelve. In them he appears always as being as uncompromising as Ephesus, on occasions even more so, e.g. p. 203–4. Yet in the end he yielded and signed. It is somewhat hard to reconcile the picture he gives of himself and of his relations with the Patriarch and the Emperor with other information narrated in the *Memoirs*. The impression got from reading the

---

[22] Trav., no. 53.   [23] Ibid., no. 848.
[24] Ibid., no. 846.

Memoirs is that the Patriarch was unsympathetic, as definitely unionist as Syropoulus was anti-unionist and, at least at the end, completely hostile to him, and that Syropoulus was one of those who most complained about conditions and who was a rallying point for the opposition; yet the Patriarch made him a member of all the delegations he sent to the Emperor (pp. 187, 189, 194, 227). The Emperor, he says, was forced to silence him in the Greek meetings because of his hostility to union, and that only after long argument, expostulation and entreaty (pp. 287–291) did he sign the decree: yet the Emperor appointed him to accompany Bessarion to the Pope on July 5th and, a few days later, with Bessarion, Isidore and the Great Chartophylax, to try to arrange with the Pope for the celebration of a Greek Liturgy. It is doubtful if the Patriarch and the Emperor considered him quite as uncompromising, as he would make himself out to have been, and the 'Acta' too suggest a doubt on the same score: 'What we have done has been a great deal and, besides, against the opinion of the three of our proxies. For Heraclea, Ephesus, Monembasia and Anchialus gave no votes for the letter of agreement that was sent, and also from the clerics the Great Chartophylax and the Protekdikos' (416–7). Is the omission of an express mention of the Great Ecclesiarches just an accident, or does it imply that, contrary to the impression repeatedly given by himself (SYR. pp. 204, 242, 253, etc.), Syropoulus was not the most ardent anti-unionist of the Staurophoroi, but the least?

(5) *The Emperor.* The picture given by Syropoulus of the Emperor is not very attractive. He upheld the honour of the Greek Church when he strengthened the Patriarch's opposition to following the Latin custom of kissing the Pope's foot (p. 94) and when he prevailed on the Pope and the authorities of Ferrara to provide maintenance in money and not in kind (p. 104). But generally speaking, he was unsympathetic and indifferent to Greek wants. After three months' sojourn at Ferrara (i.e. in the beginning of June) he went off to live in a monastery about six miles outside the town, so as to be able to hunt (p. 142). He remained there till at least the middle of December, in spite of requests from the Marquis of Ferrara to spare the game (pp. 144) and of complaints from the country people about damage to property (p. 191), and returned only because some Greeks were embroiled with the Ferrarese in a riot (pp. 191–2) 'and the trouble

of the son of Novacus was more powerful than the entreaties of the
Marquis, the Patriarch and the Pope' (p. 192). His absence from
Ferrara rendered it difficult to make arrangements and checked
easy Greek access to him (pp. 146, 147, 150–1). It seems, however,
that the Emperor must have been frequently in Ferrara, for he
directed the Greek conferences to discuss what subject should be
dealt with in the public sessions, to settle how the voting should
count and to supervise the seating arrangements (pp. 153–163).
He rode in to the first session and he was present at all the others,
so that his living in the monastery would not seem to have been
much of an inconvenience and, after all, six miles is only about
half-an-hour's distance on horse back. He often received complaints harshly (pp. 187 seq.) and was very severe even with the
most venerable and aged (pp. 223–4), and it is implied that he
was little concerned with underlings (p. 225). On the other hand,
he was considerate in offering to take with him to Florence some
of the older prelates (pp. 211) and was always kind to Ephesus
(p. 303) who, though with the Emperor's approval he did not sign
the Decree (p. 284), was defended by the Emperor from being
censured (though Syropoulus says that the Pope urged that he
should be) (p. 299) and was guaranteed safe passage back to
Constantinople (p. 284). He was vain and had a special door made
for his entry to the sessions at Ferrara (p. 167 seq.) and accepted
what all knew to be fictitious letters from the Burgundian envoys,
to save appearances (pp. 176–7). He was insincere: 'As long as the
city (i.e. Constantinople) remains in its present state, I accept the
union of the Churches; if anything else happens, I think it
immaterial whether there is union or not' (p. 128)—this in a
private conversation with the Pope: another example of Syropoulus' uncanny insight. He lied when he denied that negotiations were in progress about sessions (p. 148). He lied when he
said that a messenger had arrived announcing a large embassy
from France (p. 146), and again when he disclaimed any knowledge
of the proposal to move the Council to Florence (p. 203). He
cajoled some of the prelates and the embassies of Trebizond and
Moldoblachia to vote for union (pp. 261–2). He tricked the
Greeks into giving countenance to Bessarion's discourse of July
5th, 1439 (p. 293). He did all the managing of affairs with the
Latins. Though Greek representatives were chosen by free
election (p. 155), they had to report to him each day what had been

done (p. 116): 'Everything depended on his opinion and counsel, and without the will and mandate of the Emperor nothing ecclesiastical was done' (p. 123). Negotiations for the public sessions at Ferrara were made with him, perhaps because the Patriarch was passive: 'For they observed that the Patriarch contributed very little to this, but that everything was arranged through the Emperor' (p. 159). He persuaded the Greeks to discuss dogma (p. 201) and to go to Florence (p. 205). He presided at numerous meetings held by the Greeks after the close of the sessions at Florence, ordered them to give their opinions in writing and, in general, managed everything, partly because the Patriarch was very ill during most of the time. The Emperor, however, was himself frequently ill (cf. p. 199) and directed one meeting at least from his bed (p. 237). After the sessions at Florence he realised that there would be no result from more public discussions (pp. 229, 232, 233, etc.) and so tried to find other means such as the conferences of representatives (p. 234 seq.). He arranged the various meetings of the Greeks to try to achieve unity first among them: (after the Greek meeting of June 2nd) 'Behold with the help of God it has appeared that the belief of the Latins is good and the synod (i.e. meeting) has declared this and has come to the opinion that we should unite. No one, therefore, should dispute further about this. For before the decision of the synod everyone had freedom to say what he wanted, but after the decision no one has freedom to say anything other than the decision of the synod' (p. 271). He ordered that written votes should be given because 'I wish to have the written opinions of each, so that it may not be possible for any to change later' (p. 238). He silenced the Staurophoroi in the Greek meetings and his presence checked freedom of speech: 'no one had freedom to say what he wanted, not being able to stand up to the Emperor' (p. 163; cf. also p. 238). He urged that, till the Council had decided, all should keep their judgements on both the Latin faith and the Greek faith in suspense, but once it had spoken 'you must accept unhesitatingly what the Council has determined. For I have so disposed myself as I have said, though I am Emperor and I convened the Council' (pp. 285–6). In his formal *votum* of June 2nd he acknowledged the present Council to be oecumenical and therefore unerring, and 'it is necessary that we should follow it and its decision and especially that I, decked by the grace of God in imperial robes, should support and defend it' (p. 265). He forced the three Staurophoroi very much against their wills and convictions to sign the decree (pp. 287–291).

The picture of the Emperor given by the 'Acta' is not as full as that of the *Memoirs*. The 'Acta' begin with a glowing account of the arrivals at Venice and Ferrara, but omit the questions of kissing the Pope's foot and the arrangements about maintenance. The Emperor is meticulous that the Pope's throne should not be centrally placed, 'this befits the Emperor rather than the Pope' (p. 11), and is grieved over the lack of honour paid him by the Burgundian envoys (p. 213). He presided at Greek meetings (pp. 25, 390, 425, 428, 437), but all of these, when the Patriarch was too ill to move, were held in the Patriarch's apartments. After the sessions at Ferrara the Greeks were set on returning to Constantinople, and it was only the Emperor's patience and persuasion that prevailed on them to remain ('Acta', p. 217, confirmed by Bessarion *Ad Alex. Lasc.*; P.G. 161, 422 CD). He won them over to discuss dogma (pp. 218–9) and to go to Florence (pp. 221–3) by urging that, having already overcome the dangers and labours of the long journey, they should not now easily yield to circumstances and return empty-handed. He refused to entertain the suggestion of further public sessions (pp. 409, 410) and proposed that other means be found, so representatives were elected (p. 411). He encouraged the Greeks when they were downcast (p. 417) and, in his turn, was subject to pressure from Greek prelates when he was inclined to lose hope (pp. 425, 450, 452, 456). He declared to the Pope: 'I am not lord of the synod nor do I wish that union should be imposed by force, but our synod agreed of its own free will and sent this profession of faith' (p. 418 and again 421). He stood fast on Greek terms: 'We do not write or say anything else, except that we will unite if you accept that we have given you' (p. 420 cf. also pp. 447, 449, 452, 455) and several times yielded only after pressure from some of his prelates (pp. 450, 452, 456). He had several private colloquies with the Pope (pp. 417, 420, etc.) and reported to the prelates later what had been said (e.g. p. 419). He urged that the majority vote in the Greek meetings should prevail (p. 438). In his final *votum* he acknowledged the Council as oecumenical and that it was his duty to obey it (pp. 432–3). The only actions that might be considered as limiting freedom of speech were his approving the absence of

Ephesus and Heraclea from the last two sessions at Florence
(p. 393), his demanding written *vota* from the prelates, and his
suggesting that they bear in mind also the needs of Constantinople,
though they must give 'votes that do not harm the soul nor harm
the body' (p. 426).

Can these two pictures be harmonised? The Emperor's
insistence on the honours to be paid to him was, doubtless, due
to his considering that, even though the Pope was paying the
expenses, he, as Emperor and successor of Constantine the Great,
had convened the Council and was its head. The same reason,
together with the Patriarch's chronic illness, would account for
his managing Greek affairs, though it is to be noted that he
always held the meetings in the sick Patriarch's rooms, asked his
opinion first on the questions under review, and reported any
private conversations of his own with the Pope to his clergy. His
going out to the monastery, which according to Syropoulus was
after the close of the Conferences on Purgatory and so some time
after July 16th (A.G. p. 25) and not in the beginning of June as is
roughly calculated in the *Memoirs*, was probably due to a desire
to escape from plague-ridden Ferrara in summer when no business
was on hand, as much as to his love of hunting. In both accounts
he is shown as trying to put an end to internal squabbles and
frictions and as endeavouring to achieve unity—a well-nigh
impossible task if even only the half of Gennadius' criticism was
true[24a]—and to that end he ordered *vota* in writing. In both he
expresses no opinion on doctrine in any meeting and only urges
that the majority vote should prevail and be loyally accepted
by all. In both he gives no *votum* himself till the last occasion
and after the Patriarch, and then only to declare that in his opinion
the Council was oecumenical and that it should be obeyed in
whatever it decided, even by those not convinced by the arguments.
But in the 'Acta' he is not portrayed as harsh, indifferent, vain,
deceitful. That on occasions he was sharp (he was often ill) and

---

[24a] 'The Latins won by numbers, money and words. . . . And that nothing
humane, nothing Christian, right from the beginning, was done by us, but
everything was open betrayal of the truth, contempt of God, luxury, trifles in
what was not trifling, and quarrels and wars and jealousies and ignoble slanders
of each other and shame and jeers and confusion, from which some shamefully
became traitors, others, as it were in a cup of friendship, for too easily gave
away the faith of our Church—all this I pass over . . . those of higher rank early
betrayed everything and all the rest, some from simplicity others from fear,
followed.' Schol. II, p. 259.

diplomatic with so many vain, obstinate and often petty individuals can be taken for granted, but that such was his general disposition, as Syropoulus would have us believe, is at the least open to serious doubt. In spite of Warschauer's confident assertion that the 'Acta' are 'emperorising', it does not seem to me that this close examination of their account bears out the accusation. The 'Acta' do not recount all Syropoulus' censures of the Emperor and they portray him as patient and as striving for unity rather than union, but he is less persuaded of the possibility of union than many of his subjects and needed to be forced to agree on several occasions, which is probably a truer picture of the reality than Syropoulus' account.

*   *   *

We are now in a position to be able to sum up the evidence proposed and to draw some conclusions on the relative historical values of the *Descriptions* and the *Memoirs*. The *Descriptions* are documents contemporaneous with the events and, apart from the earlier pages recounting the arrivals at Venice and Ferrara, show every sign of being a diary written up daily. By contrast, the *Memoirs* are the recollections of Syropoulus composed some years after the end of the Council. Both authors were present at the events they describe. The writer of the *Descriptions* is more informative on relations with the Latins; Syropoulus on what took place within the Greek community in Italy. Their accounts of the voting in the private Greek sessions have been made out to be utterly opposed, but, apart from Syropoulus' declaration that the Staurophoroi were silenced, examination shows that there is agreement and that the actual number of votes and the names of the voters tally in both records.

Whatever be the truth about freedom of speech, the *Memoirs*, even more than the 'Acta', make it plain that apart from at the last two sessions at Florence there was no check at all on the liberty of Mark of Ephesus, who was the outstanding—in fact the only real—antagonist of union, to say whatever he wished both in the public sessions and in the private Greek meetings. Force is freely alleged by all anti-unionist writers, force exercised, so it is said, by the Latins through the withholding of the grants for maintenance. The only suggestion, that occurs in the copious writings of Gennadius that the Emperor used his authority unfairly is found in his *Against the Discourse of Bessarion*: 'This discourse those present did not criticise but, before they could do that, the Emperor enjoined silence, and he convicted them of great audacity, if they ventured anything about union that had not previously been approved by him, and enjoined penalties, if ever they managed to contravene his orders. Neither was it at all easy for them to contradict you without his previous knowledge; nor, if he knew, would he allow it'.[25] Yet Gennadius on this same occasion (i.e. the three days' interval of April 12th–14th) addressed his Exhortation to the same Greeks and in the same sense as Bessarion, and challenged them to disprove his assertion: 'I will show this not in long discourses, but two hours will suffice for me to convince all of you no longer to hesitate over the agreement of the Fathers'.[26] The latter quotation is of Scholarius the unionist: the former of Scholarius hesitating between Unionism and anti-Unionism. Which more reflects the truth?

The *Descriptions* say very little about the hardships endured by the Greeks, though they do not deny them: Syropoulus refers to them at length and repeatedly, and, as far as can be checked, he is accurate in his statements about money. Syropoulus is free in assigning motives, some certainly incorrect, others dubious: the 'Acta' give a simple recital of facts. The Emperor is differently portrayed in the two versions, though there is much agreement on his managing of affairs, the view he took of the Council and his endeavours to achieve unity of opinion and subsequent acceptance of it among the Greeks. That he possessed all the faults of character that Syropoulus ascribes to him is improbable.

In general, the *Descriptions* are too brief to be tendentious. Their omissions are to be ascribed, not to a desire to alter unpleasant facts, but solely to the diary nature of the work: they do not hesitate to mention those facts when they crop up naturally in the course of the narrative, but incidents and circumstances outside of the main course of events are not treated of for their own sakes. Syropoulus' *Memoirs*, on the other hand, do not purport to be a continuous narrative of even all the official or semi-official occurrences. The table given above shows that he records practically nothing of the relations with the Latins in the last months at Florence. They are recollections, and recollections almost entirely of inter-Greek relations. They err as much as, if

<hr>

[25] SCHOL., III, p. 113.
[26] Ibid., I, p. 299. Cf. also pp. 304, 356, 367.

not more than, the *Descriptions*, for, though the latter give little
of the Greek background, the *Memoirs* give too much—they are
all background with all the elements that might have relieved it a
little and modified its sombre hues omitted, background that is in
effect a treatise to prove, not just to record, that (as Creyghton
entitled his edition) it is a *Vera historia unionis non verae*. The
historian, therefore, when the sources are opposed should prefer
the 'Acta', remembering, however, though never fully trusting,
Syropoulus' description of the situation behind the scenes.

N

CHAPTER THIRTEEN

SYROPOULUS IN VENICE

Fr. Laurent's publication of a letter written from Venice on 16–17 February 1438 by the Patriarch, Joseph II, adds still one more precious date to the early history of the Council of Florence and offers another rare opportunity of checking the details of the information that Syropoulus furnishes in his *Memoirs*.[1] The question at issue was whether the Greeks, arrived in Venice, should go to Basel or to Ferrara.

Syropoulus' account of the events is briefly as follows. After recording the official reception by the Doge and the presents given by the papal representative, he reports that 'after some days' there came from the Pope the Cardinal of S. Croce and with him the Marquis of Ferrara, who visited both Emperor and Patriarch, and 'the Cardinal remained in Venice a few days and again returned to the Pope'. The question was then being generally discussed among the Greeks whether to go to the Pope or to the Council of Basel. The Doge of Venice bade the Emperor regard the city as his own and stay as long as he liked. He advised him to temporise and to sound both Pope and Council (who would rival one another in their offers to win his support) and to choose the more profitable proposal. Indeed he could hold the council in Venice itself. The Emperor, who was ill, sent for the Patriarch for consultation. The Patriarch was also ill and could not go. The Emperor was annoyed and sent two or three further pressing messages, to which the Patriarch replied that the Emperor should consult his counsellors and communicate the result to him, he would then offer his comments. That did not please the Emperor who wanted a full discussion for 'there were some opposed to those who held that going to the Pope would be more profitable, and till now those advising against going to him seem to give the better counsel. Let the Patriarch, then, come without fail because his advice on these matters is necessary'. Thereupon the Patriarch said that he knew that kind of thing was being said, but that he

[1] V. Laurent, *Les ambassadeurs du roi de Castille au concile de Bâle et le patriarche Joseph II (février 1438)*, in *R.E.B.* 16 (1960), pp. 136–44.

would confound all those people with one word. He informed the Emperor that he was feeling rather better that day, and that, if his improvement continued the next day, he would come the day after. On the day arranged, accompanied by the Doge, he first visited St. Mark's and its treasures and then went to the Emperor. He had a long talk with him before dinner and again after dinner, after which the imperial counsellors, six metropolitans and 'three of us' (Staurophoroi) were summoned to a meeting. 'It was then debated whether to go to the Pope and, much having been said on the question and with the majority speaking in favour', the Metropolitan of Heraclea advised awaiting the arrival of Cardinal Cesarini and consulting him. 'The Emperor, then, forgetful of what he had said before, was completely for going to the Pope, just as was the Patriarch before him. Although three of us (with whom was Boullotes second) said it was better not to go now to the Pope, all the rest gave a decisive opinion for going and that was settled. On the second day after that Giuliano (Cesarini) reached Venice'.[2]

From this account it appears that Cardinal Albergati came accompanied by Nicholas d'Este and shortly departed again; that the Doge advised a neutral, waiting policy; that the Emperor and the Patriarch were ill for several days, so ill that neither could venture out to visit the other on what the Emperor considered to be very urgent business; and that on the second day after the beginning of his recovery the Patriarch went to his sovereign, the meeting of the advisers was held when all but three favoured the Pope and a final decision was made, two days before the arrival of Cardinal Cesarini.

Cardinal Albergati arrived in Venice on 13 February, preceded by Este on 12 February; made his official visits to 'make known the intentions of our sovereign [the Pope], his great devotion and goodwill towards them';[3] and departed again for Ferrara only on 27 February, the day before the Emperor. Syropoulus, then, is not very accurate in respect of Albergati. Cesarini arrived on 20 February and therefore, according to Syropoulus, the meeting of the Greeks was on 18 February. The Patriarch wrote his letter to the Castilian ambassadors on 16–17 February: 'That you may know about our arrival in these parts, we are now completing the ninth day in Venice after we put in here [8 February] and we are

[2] SYR., pp. 85–6, 88–9.   [3] TRAV., no. 140.

still here awaiting passage to Ferrara to meet the blessed Pope'.[4]
As both Emperor and Patriarch were able to receive the Cardinal
on 14 February, their illnesses presumably began after that and (if
Syropoulus' memory of the events is accurate) continued some days;
there followed the three days of the Patriarch's recuperation,
which nevertheless ended on 16–17 February (when the Patriarch's
letter takes the journey to Ferrara for granted) or 18 February
(when Syropoulus puts the meeting of the counsellors).

There are, then, good reasons for believing that Syropoulus'
chronology about these incidents is inexact. In point of fact,
generally throughout his *Memoirs* he is generous in phrases like
'the next day', 'a few days later' and the like, and here again, as
in many other places, writing as he does from memory several
years after the events, he exaggerates and gives a false impression
of an anxious length of time.

He probably has exaggerated also the degree of hesitation of
the Greeks to choose between the Pope and the Council, for, in
spite of his repeating that there was much talk about it, in the
meeting there was unanimity except for three, of whom he was
one—the first occasion of the very many when he figures in his
own *Memoirs* as one of the chief opponents, if not indeed the most
consistent and outstanding one, of concessions to the Latins. In
reality, the Emperor and the Patriarch never seriously wavered.
The Emperor wanted the Patriarch's backing in the meeting and
waited till he got it, and the Patriarch was confident that he could
confound the doubters with a single word, and both, Emperor and
Patriarch, in the meeting were 'completely' for the Pope—just as
they had been in Constantinople in the previous October when
the Council's envoys, brandishing the Monitorium decreed at
Basel against Eugenius on 31 July,[5] wooed and threatened them.
They did not, then, have to go to Venice to learn that there was
serious tension between Pope and Council. Nevertheless it is true
that the Patriarch, some time before 17 February, in view of the
tension between Basel and Pope and, probably more so, between
Pope and princes, had asked the Senate's counsel, but he had been
reassured.[6]

---

[4] LAURENT, Op. cit., p. 144.
[5] *E.P.*, doc. 210, p. 103. The Monitorium was a long catalogue of the
council's accusations against Eugenius, ending with a summons to appear before
it within 60 days; cf. *M.C.*, II, pp. 1010–13.
[6] *A.C.A.*, doc. 30.

It is, however, quite certain that at no time was there any decision made by the Greeks to go to Basel, and no document, not even the *Memoirs* of Syropoulus, states the contrary. Letters, but not envoys, of the recalcitrant Council met the Emperor in Venice,[7] but it is very doubtful if those letters, which were not important enough to be mentioned by John of Segovia in his very detailed account of the Council, would have impressed the Emperor and the Patriarch more than the controversies in Constantinople of the previous October. What perhaps did make the Emperor pause for a moment was a letter from the King of France.[8] Charles, very annoyed that he was not going to have the council of union in Avignon under his own eye, wrote to protest that the choice of Avignon was legitimate and that the translation to Ferrara was illegal. 'Conforming ourselves to this, we have determined to allow no one at all to go from our kingdom to that city of Ferrara on the pleas of the so-called translation and election', and the princes related to him by blood, treaty or friendship, would act in the same way.[9] Even so, the hesitation on the part of the Emperor and the Patriarch was not serious. Traversari, writing to Eugenius on 20 February, told him in reference to the Patriarch: 'Neither has he any objection to going to Ferrara, as several of our company believed before they [the Emperor and the Patriarch] had replied to the proposal of S. Croce [Albergati]. Indeed, even before they made their public announcement, he exposed to me this as his intention, and time and again he assured me that he was ready to lay down his life, as he had already exposed it to the dangers of the protracted voyage, if only he might see the two Churches united'.[10]

The letter of Traversari of 21 February, as well as that quoted in the previous paragraph, refer to a kind of official announcement of the imperial decision, made on 20 February:[11] 'They [the Emperor and the Patriarch] declared that they had come for no other purpose than to meet with our Pope . . . that they were not

[7] The letter of Traversari already quoted mentions that: *A Basiliensibus redditae illis literae.* If there had been also envoys, he must have said so in the context.

[8] *M.C.*, III, pp. 52–3.

[9] Op. cit., p. 53, *Et principes sanguine, federe, amicitia nobis iunctos id ipsum facturos iustum est et nobis de vestra serenitate sentire.*

[10] TRAV., no 30.

[11] The Marquis of Ferrara departed that same night to make arrangements for the Emperor's voyage; JORGA, III, p. 28 n. 3.

concerned about the place of it, which would certainly be convenient to them if it was agreeable to His Holiness for expediting
the business of the holy union, which they did not doubt could be
brought to a conclusion only with him, and they announced their
proximate departure for Ferrara. . . .' That announcement was in
complete harmony with their previous attitude and exactly what
one would have expected them to say. The Emperor communi-
cated his decision also to Basel on 25 February in a letter in
which he reminded the 'Fathers' that he had repeatedly refused to
accept Basel as the seat of the oecumenical synod (even when its
claims were pressed by the Bishops of Digne and Oporto and by
Nicholas of Cusa, envoys of the Council and the Pope in Constantinople), and declared his intention of going to Ferrara for the
execution of the decree that had been promulgated in Basel (the
Sicut pia mater, of 7 September 1434); he exhorted the 'Fathers'
to join him there the better to promote the desired union.[12] Again,
this document is consistent with the previous conduct of the
Emperor and the Patriarch, as the letter itself states in unambiguous terms. The decision was also prudent, when considered in
the circumstances. On 5 December 1436 there voted in the
Council of Basel on the disputed question of the site of the future
council 51 'mitres', i.e. 3 cardinals, 2 patriarchs, 2 archbishops, 16
bishops and 28 abbots, and, after the dissension that culminated
in the split of 7 May 1437, two of the cardinals, one patriarch and
many of the bishops and abbots deserted the council. With the
Pope in Ferrara at the solemn opening on 9 April 1438, there were
118 mitres, including 10 cardinals, 2 patriarchs (Latin), 12 archbishops, 62 bishops and 31 abbots. In respect of the secular
princes, Basel, after a period of open support from them, had been
steadily losing their confidence because of its excessive hostility
to the papacy, whereas Eugenius was gaining ground, and no one
yet knew how many would rally to his council in Ferrara, which
had only just opened. Syropoulus reports that when the Emperor,
only a day's voyage away from Venice, learnt of the death of the
Emperor Sigismund, he declared that, had he known of that
while he was still in the Peloponnesus, he would not have continued
the voyage (p. 79). It is, however, very unlikely that John could
have been relying much on Sigismund's presence, for the same
Syropoulus also relates that the German Emperor, when his

[12] G. HOFMANN, *Orientalium documenta minora* (Rome, 1953) doc. 28.

advice was sought before the voyage, had counselled the Greeks not to go to any council in the West (p. 57).

That Syropoulus exaggerates also the illness of the Emperor and the Patriarch is highly probable. No other document refers to so serious a sickness of either of them as would have interfered with their ordinary business, and, if there had been such an illness, some of the documents could be expected to do so. The *Description*, included in the Greek *Practica*, does not mention it. The 'Latin Acts' do not speak of it and Ambrose Traversari, who had gone to Venice to meet the visitors, arriving on the day after them, and who had long conversations with the Patriarch, says nothing of it in the letters in which he records the events and his impressions of those days. Some Latins were irritated because the Emperor and the Patriarch pleaded fatigue from the journey as a reason for deferring the boon of union—so wrote Traversari; but, though he is writing to defend the Greeks against the irascible Latins, he offers no illness as an excuse, yet it would have been the perfect one: his letters are dated 20 and 21 February.

Syropoulus' account also of the attitude of Venice is not very convincing. According to it, the Emperor was to consider the city his own; he should play a waiting game and bargain with both sides; he could hold the council in Venice. The first statement might have been said in courtesy and have been nothing more than good manners. The fact is that, before the Emperor arrived with his seven hundred Greeks, the Signoria was alarmed at the expenses it might incur and told the Pope that it was he who had promised to pay the cost of the council and that they would entertain the visitors for not more than ten or twelve days and at an expense of not more than 3,000 ducats.[13] Indeed, if we can believe a diary of a contemporary Venetian, the city paid for only five days' hospitality of its guests and contented itself with gifts of sugar, wine, etc., to cover the rest.[14] Again, Venice was one of the very few powers that had been consistently loyal to Eugenius throughout the long and humiliating struggle with Basel. That makes it most unlikely that, when the Pope had regained the ascendancy and was rapidly recovering the prestige he had lost, and when the Greeks had already refused to take the way of Basel in the conciliar fleet but had come to Venice in the papal fleet precisely to join the Pope, the Signoria at that point would have

---

[13] *A.C.A.*, docs. 11, 17.   [14] JORGA, III, p. 28 n. 3.

begun to favour the Council that it had never favoured before.
The only document on this question (apart from Syropoulus'
account) is a letter from the Senate recording that it had firmly
advised the Patriarch to go to the Pope since the gathering at
Basel 'could not and ought not to be considered a council any
longer' and that of the princes only Alphonsus of Aragon and
Visconti of Milan were hostile to Eugenius[15]. It is what one
would have expected it to say in such circumstances, given the
historical background. As regards the third assertion of Syropoulus, Venice never showed any enthusiasm to be the seat of the
council of union. And later, when in August 1438 Eugenius
sounded the Signoria about moving from Ferrara to Venetian
territory to escape the plague, he was dissuaded by the Venetians:
'In regard to our territory for the council you must say that, as
his true and most devoted sons, we are always most ready for
everything that is pleasing and acceptable to His Holiness, but,
speaking with our filial sincerity and devotion and the great
affection which we have for his good and profit, we dare to advise
his Holiness that, taking everything into consideration, he should
not press this question at the moment', because he would find it
hard to get the Emperor and the Patriarch to move, and a change
of site before anything had been effected in Ferrara would
strengthen his adversaries. 'And with these and other words as
your prudence shall dictate, insist and obtain that His Holiness
rest content to persevere and stay in Ferrara'.[16] Syropoulus must
have been recording the gossip of the city, not the mature thought
of its government.

The letter of the Patriarch, besides illustrating once again the
need of checking details in all of Syropoulus' narrative, poses a
problem. Having said that the Patriarch was awaiting passage to
Ferrara, it continues: 'But when we shall be there and shall enter
into conversation with him [the Pope], we shall arrange both
about the place of the council and shall choose such a one as will
seem convenient to both parties and good and suitable for the
task proposed'. This seems to state that, in the Patriarch's view,
the place of the synod was still an open question, to be settled
between the Greeks and the Pope.

Joseph II, however, must have known that by two Bulls

---

[15] *A.C.A.*, doc. 30.
[16] Letter to the Venetian representative to the Holy See; *A.C.A.*, doc. 48.

Eugenius had transferred the Council of Basel to Ferrara, and that the fresh Council had opened in that city on the appointed day, 8 January. Even if all Venice had not told him that the Council in Ferrara was intended to accomplish the work of union, as the Bulls of translation declared, Cardinal Albergati, its first papal president, must have informed him of it when he made known the intentions of the Pope, and the Marquis of Este must have said as much when he welcomed his future guests. The Emperor seems to have been in no doubt, for in his letter of 25 February to the 'Fathers' of Basel, he asserts that he is going to Ferrara to fulfil their decree, i.e. to celebrate a council of union. Perhaps, then, the Patriarch's mind was really a little less clear than his words suggest. He was an old man and had preconceived ideas of how he and the Pope would settle things. Traversari wrote, apropos of this: 'He has a wonderful longing to meet with the Pope, in the hope that everything will easily be settled if they both come together in charity. . . . I gathered from his very cautious and prudent words that, in his views, the question should be settled by love and peace rather than by discussion, seeing that according to him the whole thing depends on the meeting of the two of them in body, mind and opinion; and he hopes for all this if the physical encounter takes place first'.[17] There might also have entered in a consideration of *amour-propre*. The Castilian ambassadors had put a clear question—where did he propose to go to celebrate the oecumenical synod? Had he replied: To Ferrara, because the Pope has fixed on that place, he might have seemed to be subordinating himself and his Church to the Pope. Saying: To Ferrara and then we'll see, he implied independence and equality in respect of his brother, the western Patriarch.

[17] TRAV., no. 140.

CHAPTER FOURTEEN

THE COST OF THE COUNCIL OF FLORENCE

An unknown member of the Council of Basel, some time before
the controversy about Avignon as the future seat of the Council,
drew up a memorandum to try to forecast what joint discussions
with the Greeks in Europe would cost. Two of the points he
considered at some length were the expense necessary for the
transportation and entertainment of some 700 Greeks and the
problem of how to raise the money for it. He took into account the
stipulations of the pact *Sicut pia mater* of 9 September 1434
entered into by the Council with the Greek ambassadors, which
laid down that 15,000 ducats for the expenses of the Greeks while
preparing to depart and 10,000 ducats to be deposited in Constantinople against emergencies in their absence were to be taken by
the Council's envoys to Constantinople. Then, for large galleys
for the passage of the Greeks and light galleys with 300 crossbowmen to defend Constantinople—their transport thither and six
months' stay—for the sending back of the two Constantinopolitan
ships (which he considered would be cheaper than paying the
wages of the crews for the months the discussions would last), and
for the journey of the Greeks from the port of arrival to the seat
of the Council by horse (he mentions 700 horses, which would
have been nothing like enough), he allowed 46,000 ducats—in all
71,000 ducats to bring the Greeks to the Council. The discussions,
he thought, would last at least a year; the cost of entertainment of
the Greeks he assessed at 5,000 ducats a month—60,000 ducats.
For a further 6 months' stay of the bowmen and their galleys in
Constantinople, for the transport of the Greeks back home and
the return voyage of the bowmen and of the empty ships he
calculated a cost of 55,000 ducats, which brought the total to
186,000 ducats, or roughly (so he says) 200,000 ducats to allow for
a variety of expenses he had not included and the approximations
he had made in guessing others. It is a very shrewd calculation
and not far from the mark. When, however, he came to the
problem of how to raise so large a sum, he was not so happy, but
still clear-sighted. The Indulgence, he noted, would not bring in

half of that sum, and certainly not in time. If a Tenth were to be imposed, it would probably clash with the Indulgence, so that neither would be fruitful, and in any case it was unlikely that it would be paid, people would appeal to Pope against Council. His only positive suggestion was that the collectors of the Indulgence-money should be more active and should go off to their appointed spheres of action and busy themselves collecting.[1]

In the event the problems faced by the author of the memorandum fell not on the shoulders of the Council of Basel (though this did in fact have great difficulty in trying to reimburse the citizens of Avignon for the expenses of the expedition to Constantinople of 1437) but on those of the Pope. And he found the case as difficult of solution as the unknown writer foresaw that it would be. How much in fact the Council of Florence cost to Eugenius cannot be exactly stated.[2] Fr. Georg Hofmann in his *Acta camerae apostolicae et civitatum Venetiarum, Ferrariae, Florentiae, Ianuae de Concilio Florentino* has published a long list of entries from the papal registers concerning payments made in connection with the Greeks. A few others can be found among the items listed by N. Jorga in *Notes et extraits pour servir à l'histoire des Croisades au XVe siècle*. If these two sources are combined and the account is limited to cover expenses till the Greek return was paid for, the following results emerge:

For the journeys of the Greeks and their entertainment	107,169fl.	23s.	6d.
For other Orientals	2,117	5	6
For embassies to Constantinople, France, Nuremberg, etc.	12,749	35	
For various small expenses	1,538	9	
	123,574	23	

This sum is barely approximate. The first item is probably fairly accurate. The second takes no account of e.g. Isidore's journey from Moscow to Ferrara (which took eleven and a half months) nor of his expenses on his return once he had left Venice;

[1] MANSI, 30, 1034 seq.

[2] Also because many known expenses were not booked in the registers of the *Camera Apostolica*; cf. A. GOTTLOB, *Aus den Rechnungsbüchern Eugens IV. zur Geschichte des Florentinums*, in *Historisches Jahrbuch*, München XIV (1893), p. 44.

it covers only maintenance in Italy. Whether the third item includes the sums of 15,000 ducats and of the 10,000 ducats' deposit stipulated in the decree *Sicut pia mater* which Eugenius accepted is not clear, but there can be no doubt that he fulfilled the obligations there expressed, for Garatoni in a letter from Constantinople dated 20 October 1437 records that Zeno and Lupari, the two papal banking agents, had sent letters of credit for 30,000 ducats and had before that transmitted another sum of 1,666 ducats.[3] Certainly the last item falls far short of the mark, for there must have been a myriad of incidental minor expenses not covered by it. Then, too, the Pope must have subsidized a large number of the Latins occupied with the Council. He certainly paid 24 florins a month to four separate Religious Orders for the maintenance of six theologians of each from December 1437 onwards and 12 florins a month from at least 10 March 1438 onwards to four Servite theologians[4] and he must have helped, too, many a bishop (Cardinal Cesarini received a gift of 1000 florins on 16 July 1438,[5] and on 1 October 1938 40 florins were paid for the rent of the house where Garatoni lived[6]), abbot, doctor, master, if not with regular maintenance, at least with timely subventions. What all that would amount to is completely uncertain.

In the agreements made with the cities of Ferrara and Florence it was stipulated that the Pope and his 'family', the Emperor, the cardinals and the Treasurer of the Pope should have free lodging, while Florence went further and provided free habitation also for all the Greeks. The rest—prelates, notaries, officials of the Camera and the Curia, courtiers—were lodged at a rent established by a committee of four members, two from the Pope's side and two from that of the city. Heads of Religious Orders and theologians were to be lodged in religious houses, which also were to take in cardinals and others. A further item in the agreements forbade any special taxes because of the occasion or the raising of existing taxes and dues. The price of commodities was fixed though it may be doubted if the price-list was adhered to when with such a crowd of strangers flooding the cities certain articles necessarily became scarce. Syropoulus at least laments that

---

[3] G. Mercati, *Scritti d'Isidoro il cardinale Ruteno* (=Studi e Testi 46) (Rome, 1926), p. 121.

[4] *A.C.A.*, docs. 13, 14, 16.   [5] Ibid., doc. 45.

[6] Ibid., doc. 52.

prices soon doubled[7]; but he need not be taken too literally for he is out to paint as black a picture of the situation as he can.

The price-list for Ferrara is given in full by Fr. Hofmann,[8] and it can serve to suggest an idea of the value of money at that time. The weight of gold in 123,500 florins of the Apostolic Camera would be 437,190 grammes.[9] (The Cameral florin, it is true, was worth less than a Venetian ducat, but not than a Florentine florin).[10] At present rates for gold[11] (which, it must be allowed, is purer than the purest gold of that day) this weight of gold would be worth about £175,163. But that does not convey a just idea of its worth then, so it may be useful to follow up the suggestion mentioned above. Here are a few of the items included in the price-list of Ferrara:

1 lb. of sucking veal	not more than 1 sol.
1 lb. of year-old veal	not more than 8 den.
1 lb. of pork	9 den.
1 lb. of freshwater fish, of size less than 1 lb. ...	7 den.
1 lb. of freshwater fish, of size 1–3 lbs.	10 den.
1 lb. of saltwater fish, of size less than 1 lb. ...	8 den.
1 lb. of saltwater fish, of size 1–2 lbs.	12 den.
1 lb. of saltwater fish, of size over 2 lbs.... ...	14 den.
Crabs per 100	8 den.
1 lb. oil	16 den.
1 cartload of 125 bundles of softwood	15 sol.

To these items can be added two entries about rents—in Ferrara 49 florins were paid as the rent of a furnished house for the Bishop of Corone for seven months, i.e. 7 florins a month[12]:

[7] SYR., pp. 104–5.   [8] *A.C.A.*, doc. 21.

[9] Taking a florin as weighing 3.54 grs.—the original weight in 24 carat gold of 1252—and I have found no evidence for thinking that it had changed. Cf. also H. HOBERG, *Taxae pro communibus servitiis* (= Studi e Testi 144) (Città del Vaticano, 1949), p. xi.

[10] There are many entries in the docs. published by Fr. Hofmann giving the equivalence between the Cameral and the Venetian florins, but none suggesting any difference in value between the Florentine and the Cameral florins. Cf. HOBERT, ibid.

A florin was divided into 50 solidi and a solidus into 12 denarii, so that a denarius was one 600th of a florin and a solidus one 50th. In 1453 the Venetian ducat was worth 39¾ English pence and in 1455 40¾ pence, roughly i.e. 6 to the pound, so that a solidus would be somewhat less than an English penny and a denarius $^{1}/_{15}$ of a penny.

[11] According to *The Times* of 25 Jan. 1956 gold stood at 249s. 2½d. a fine ounce: a fine ounce equals 480 grains or 31.1028 grs.

[12] *A.C.A.*, doc. 52.

in Florence 6 florins a months were paid for a house taken over by the Greeks.[13] To appreciate the meaning of these figures one should be a housewife. But even those who are not such can get some idea of the relative values of money then and now. Veal at 1 1/15 pence a pound; 1 lb. of pork for 4/5 of a penny; medium sized saltwater fish at 8/9 pence per lb.—on these figures the purchasing value of money then must have been some 40 to 50 times what it is now. So if the (roughly) 123,500 florins calculated earlier be taken as equal to 20,584 English pounds of that time and if that be multiplied by 46,[14] the result would be £946,864 of present-day value.

This sum, as suggested earlier, does not represent the complete cost of the Council to the Pope. Besides the other conciliar expenses, which cannot be assessed, there would have been, too, multifarious calls on his purse. For instance, he could not forgo the custom of presenting a ceremonial sword at Christmas and a golden rose in Lent to some outstanding personage (Henry VI of England received the rose in 1444), and these, between 1435 and 1441, cost him some 1470 florins. Then in the year 1437–8 alone he paid more than 3,384 ducats for the rebuilding of Rome.[15] And, of course, he had to meet the usual and regular costs of the upkeep of the Roman Curia, salaries of officials of all kinds both ecclesiastical and secular. A contemporary of Sixtus IV (1471–84) left a memorandum outlining the income of the papacy and its ordinary, administrative expenses, which Gottlob accepts as a fairly accurate assessment, if anything rather too generous in the calculation of income.[16] According to this the Holy See received yearly 260,000 ducats from all sources and paid out 161,000 ducats apart from the personal expenses of the Pope, this when there were no extraordinary charges to meet such as special embassies or wars, and when the Pope was in peaceful possession of all his territories and receiving the usual revenue from them. The reign of Sixtus IV was not that of Eugenius IV, but there would have

[13] Ibid., doc. 97.

[14] Having referred a housewife's question to an English housewife, I am informed (in 1956) that an average price per lb. for veal is 3s. 4d. and for pork 3s. 8d., i.e. respectively 37 and 55 times the prices noted above, 46 is the average between 37 and 55.

[15] E. Muntz, Les arts à la cour des Papes pendant le XVe et le XVIe siècle: Pt. I, Martin V-Pie II 1417–1464 (Paris, 1878), pp. 56–63, 37.

[16] A. Gottlob, Aus der Camera Apostolica des 15. Jahrhunderts (Innsbruck, 1889), p. 253 seq. This gross income compares unfavourably with that of many of the big Italian cities of that day (p. 257).

been a rough parallel if Eugenius' reign had been set in more happy times.

In point of fact Eugenius must have been far worse off than Sixtus. The Council of Basel had set itself to impoverish him so as to reduce him to surrender. Its reform decrees about taxation of all kinds and its suppression of the Annates, 9 June 1435, though they would not have been completely effective everywhere, were certainly adopted by France after the Pragmatic Sanction of Bourges of July 1438 and by Germany after the *Instrumentum acceptationis* of March 1439. But even before that, as well as after, Basel was running a Curia parallel to the Roman Curia and doing everything in the way of dispensations, etc., that usually depended on the Pope. Piero da Monte in a *Memorandum ad Henricum VI Angliae* of November 1437 wrote: *Item omnia officia curie Romane instituerunt [Basilienses] ibi, videlicet vicecancellarium, qui signabat supplicaciones de iusticia, camerarium seu thesaurarium, clericos camere, auditores rote et alios curie officiales, quod nil aliud est quam indicere quoddam tacitum scisma.*[17] The income from all those activities would go to Basel and not to Eugenius, and besides there must have been innumerable applicants who played off Pope against Council and Council against Pope and paid neither.

Then, too, in Italy itself the Pope was deprived of much of the revenues that would normally in times of peace have flowed into his exchequer. Hardly was he enthroned when the Colonna family about Rome revolted and only hard fighting reduced them to capitulate. But the papal Condottiere Nicolò della Stella, known universally as Fortebraccio, was so ruthless and brutal that Eugenius replaced him by another, Michele Attendolo, which drove Fortebraccio to ally himself to the Pope's enemies and the rebellion broke out afresh. Meanwhile, with the Patrimony of St. Peter thus invested and the Pope himself virtually a prisoner in Rome, Francesco Attendolo surnamed Sforza, another Condottiere in the service of Milan who claimed also to be the 'Captain of the Church' appointed by the Council of Basel, by a rapid campaign of a couple of weeks possessed himself of the March of Ancona and advanced into Umbria and the Patrimony. In this situation Eugenius chose the lesser of two evils. He bought off Sforza by granting him the title of Marquis of the March of

[17] A. ZELLFELDER, *England und das Basler Konzil* (=Historische Studien Hft. 113; Berlin 1913), p. 329.

Ancona and Gran Gonfaloniere (Standard-bearer) of the Church, letting him keep, as his 'Vicar', the places he had conquered in the Patrimony of St. Peter and in Umbria (25 March 1434).[18] The Duke Filippo Maria Visconti of Milan, who was behind all these attacks on the papacy as, so he said, the agent of the Council (and he had a letter to show for this, nor did the Council to which he reported his victorious campaigns ever repudiate his claim), soon found another brilliant Condottiere to replace the defecting Sforza, Nicolò Piccinino, who hastened to join forces with Fortebraccio round Rome. On 29 May the Romans, oppressed by the famine that resulted from the continuous warfare in the Campagna and incited by the propaganda of the Duke of Milan, Fortebraccio and Piccinino, broke into open revolt. On 4 or 5 June 1434 Eugenius fled in disguise down the river to betake himself to Florence. In July of the same year troops from Milan, reinforced by Piccinino and his band from Rome, occupied the Romagna and on 28 August defeated the papal forces united with Florentine and Venetian troops, when some of the best of Eugenius' generals, Pietro Gianpaolo Orsini and Nicolò da Tolentino, were taken prisoner and not more than 1,000 of the papal cavalry escaped. It looked as if Florence, the traditional friend of Eugenius and the avowed enemy of Milan, might have to come to terms with the Duke Filippo Maria. For the next few years however things went better with the Pope, but only at the cost of continuous fighting. The rebellion of Rome was at an end by 27 October 1434 but the campaign against the leading families behind it was savage and went on for years, complicated by attacks of the Prince of Aragon on Naples, which were foiled by the military astuteness of Vitelleschi, who was Eugenius' chief general around Rome. In the Romagna other papal condottieri gradually reduced the cities to obedience, till in 1438 Piccinino, profiting by the Pope's choice of Ferrara for his Council to the delusion of the citizens of Bologna, exploited the discontent of the Bolognese to take that city and others like Forlì and Imola. What all this meant in loss to the papal exchequer cannot be counted.

In the memorandum on papal income mentioned above, of the total of 260,000 ducats there assessed as incoming revenue,

---

[18] By the treaty of 19 Feb. 1439 Eugenius ceded to him also Assisi, Cerreto, Visso and all the territories he should take from the Duke of Foligno: N. VALOIS, *Le Pape et le Concile* II (Paris, 1909), p. 274 n. 2.

12,000 are calculated as coming from the March and Romagna, 6,000 from Perugia, 4,000 from the Patrimony, 4,000 from Bologna, 4,000 from Ferrara, 1,400 from Urbino, 1,000 from Faenza, 750 from Pesaro, 1,000 from Forlì, 300 from Imola, from Rieti and Norcia 1,500—a total of 35,950 ducats. Moreover the customs of the Patrimony and Rome on cattle were responsible for a further 56,000 ducats which brings the total to 91,950 ducats, that is, more than a third of the gross revenue. With the conditions prevailing during the first ten years of Eugenius' reign much, if not most, of those 91,950 ducats of annual revenue would never have reached the papal coffers. But that is not all. During all that time money was flowing out in vast quantities to pay the pontifical troops. Condottieri fought for a living and they and their mercenary troops had to be paid. The usual monthly salary of a fully-armed footsoldier was 3 ducats, of a 'lance' with three horses 9 or 10 ducats a month, and officers were paid at correspondingly higher rates.[19] Gottlob lists 13 contracts entered into by the Camera Apostolica with condottieri in Eugenius' first year as Pope for bodies of infantry and cavalry of different sizes.[20] To one of these, Rainuccio Farnese, between October 1431 and September 1433 he paid 13,491 fl., and yet by the close of 1433 he still owed him 11,900 fl. The only way left of extinguishing the debt was by ceding towns to his creditor that Rainuccio coveted to round off his properties, but which of course diminished Eugenius' revenue-paying possessions.[21] A contract made with Sforza on 29 November 1434 renewing a previous contract of 21 March of the same year, by which that general bound himself and all his troops, of 800 'lances' each with three horses and 800 infantry, to the papal cause for one year, obliged the Camera Apostolica to pay 10,500 ducats down and 50,000 more at the end of a month.[22] The same author mentions some items for 1441, which can serve to illustrate what must have been going on regularly in the previous years—14,566 gold ducats for troops

[19] GOTTLOB, *Aus der Camera*, etc., p. 123. A 'lance' 'consisted of a heavily mounted "corporal", of his attendant man-at-arms, and of a boy servant, the last being mounted only on a nag instead of a war horse' (P. PARTNER, *The Papal State under Martin V* (London, 1958), p. 154).

[20] GOTTLOB, Op. cit., p. 124.

[21] J. GUIRAUD, *L'État pontifical après le Grand Schisme* (Paris, 1896), pp. 130–6.

[22] GOTTLOB, Op. cit., p. 125: he had received 6,000 ducats from the Pope only a few months before for troops for the retaking of Rome; cf. B. NOGARA, *Scritti inediti e rari di Biondo Flavio* (=Studi e Testi 48) (Roma, 1927), p. lxix.

on 31 March; 22,592 fl. 12 sol. 6 den. on 27 May; 19,190 fl. on 30 June.[23] Other accidental expenses were involved too. In March 1457, 10,000 fls. were paid to Vitelleschi, who shortly before that had received 16,000 fls. from the papal treasury to extinguish a debt he had incurred with a Florentine merchant. In 1438 Piccinino asked the Pope for a loan of 5,000 ducats which Eugenius hastened to give, hoping to suborn him from his allegiance to Milan; the only result was the loss of the cities of the Romagna at the end of the same year, left unfortified because no longer considered threatened.[24] From May 1433 Sigismund, the Roman Emperor, was in receipt of a monthly pension of 5,000 fl. from the Pope. In 1434 Eugenius made a vulgar but successful condottiere, Baldassare da Offida, a knight and granted him a pension of 25 fl. a month.[25] There must have been many Offidas in the course of the reign of Eugenius, who tended to reward material success independently of considerations of personal character.

Where did the money for all these activities come from? This is a question more easily asked than answered. In the Bull of 1 September 1438 by which Eugenius imposed a Tenth in favour of the work of union, he justified his action by declaring that he had already expended 80,000 ducats on the Greeks and was paying at the rate of 5,000 ducats a month.[26] Assuming the monthly cost of the two ships permanently at the Byzantine capital as 1,200 ducats (which is probably an underestimate) and the pay of the force of crossbowmen as about 1,000 ducats, the upkeep of the papal troops at Constantinople would have come to about 2,200 ducats a month.[27] The maintenance of the Greeks while in Ferrara cost the Pope a minimum of 1,700 fl. per month and, as there he had besides to foot the bill for their lodgings, he was probably not far off the mark in assessing the monthly cost for the Greeks alone at 5,000 ducats.[28] The result of all these payments was, as the Bull referred to above hinted delicately,

[23] GOTTLOB, Op. cit., p. 126.
[24] MURATORI, Tom. XXXIII, Pt. I, pp. 50–1.
[25] VALOIS, Op. cit. II, p. 87.
[26] E.P., doc. 150. JORGA, II, pp. 351–2, gives the same figures as contained in a papal letter of 9 April 1438.
[27] Syropoulus reports the Emperor as telling the Pope in about May 1439 that he owed 11,000 florins for the upkeep of those forces at Constantinople (p. 220).
[28] Cf. above, The 'Acta' and the Memoirs of Syropoulus as History, p. 163 seq.

that the papal exchequer was bankrupt: *ne Ecclesiam in promissis deficere tantumque bonum neglegi defectu pecuniarum contingat.*[29] It was stated a little more openly in a letter of 24 September 1438 appointing John of Taranto and Antonio of Urbino as collectors of the Indulgence published the same day because *graves expensas subierimus et multo maiores quam suppetant facultates . . .;*[30] and even more bluntly in an earlier letter dated 6 July 1438 appointing the Abbot Bartholomew collector for Venetian territory: *magna subierimus onera expensarum, nunc adeo temporum causante malicia sumus pecuniis exhausti atque exinaniti, ut necessitas, nos, non voluntas, impellat ut fratres et filios excitemus,* and exhorting him to get by gift or loan on whatever conditions he thought fit financial help from the prelates of the district.[31]

In point of fact Eugenius had been carrying on with borrowed money already for some time. On 17 April 1438 he acknowledged and gave security for a loan of 10,000 florins of gold lately advanced by the brothers Cosimo and Lorenzo Medici.[32] A few months later (probably at the end of August) he applied to Venice for a loan of 20,000 ducats, though whether he received it is not disclosed by the published document.[33] On 5 June 1439 he acknowledged his obligation both to Florence and to Venice for loans lately made of 10,000 ducats from each.[34] On 11 July he wrote to Venice about an exchange he had transacted with the brothers Medici for 6,000 florins to pay for the ships of the returning Greeks,[35] and on 9 October 1439 he offered half the revenues of the Camera Apostolica as security for 12,000 ducats to be paid by the Medicis in Constantinople for the upkeep of the papal troops defending that city.[36]

Loans, however, are only a temporary expedient and have to be repaid. For this Eugenius saw no better way than that suggested by the unknown memorandum-writer of Basel—to make the most of the Indulgence that the Baseler had promulgated on 14 April 1436. In point of fact as soon as he learnt that the Greeks had elected to travel in his ships to his Council and not to Basel he claimed the money contributed by the faithful for the

---

[29] *E.P.*, doc. 150.
[31] Ibid., doc. 146.
[33] *A.C.A.*, doc. 48.
[34] *E.P.*, docs. 174, 175. T. FROMMANN, Op. cit., p. 37, also mentions these but assigns them to the wrong date, having misread *iulii* for *iunii*.
[35] *E.P.*, doc. 194.

[30] Ibid., doc. 151.
[32] Ibid., doc. 138.
[36] Ibid., doc. 221.

work of union of the Churches. A letter written in Bologna on 4 December 1437 declared that, lest the money so collected should be diverted to other uses and the intention of the donors be frustrated, 'we arrest and sequestrate the said sums of money and decree that they are arrested and sequestrated': those in whose power the sequestrated money lay were threatened with dire penalties if they did not observe the above declaration; archbishops, bishops and princes were required and exhorted to obey it.[37] A couple of months later, following up a suggestion put forward in the session of 11 February, Eugenius re-issued the above letter on the same day that in solemn session (15 February) he condemned again the remnant of Basel in the Bull *Exposcit debitum*.

To implement his sequestration of the Indulgence-money he appointed collectors. These were probably special and supernumerary collectors, for he had his ordinary collectors already in many, perhaps all, countries. In England, for example, Giovanni Obizzi had been collector since 1427[38] and the better known Piero da Monte was collector there and papal Nuncio from 1435–1440.[39] On 10 February four such collectors were appointed, with no particular territory being specified as their field of activity[40]. On 6 July the Abbot Bartholomew was allotted to the territory of Venice. On 31 July 1438 Louis Archbishop of Rouen was praised for having carried out the sequestration in his area and instructions were given as to how to transmit the money to the papal exchequer: on 17 October 1439 the same prelate was empowered to enforce the handing over of such money by ecclesiastical penalties. On 24 September Eugenius himself promulgated an Indulgence for those who assisted by their alms the work of union[41] and made such highly placed ecclesiastics and faithful supporters of his as the Archbishop of Taranto and the Bishop of Urbino collectors of its proceeds.[42] On 23 March 1439 the Pope allowed half of the money collected in the Duchy of Burgundy to be given to the Duke in gratitude for his support and to defray the expenses of his embassy at the Council.[43] Collectors to Castile and León were appointed six days later.[44] The Pope was at least not inactive,

[37] Ibid., doc. 103.   [38] ZELLFELDER, Op. cit., p. 206.
[39] G. HOFMANN, *Briefe eines päpstlichen Nuntius über das Konzil von Florenz*, in *O.C.P.* V (1939), p. 407 n. 1.
[40] *E.P.*, docs. 116–9.   [41] Ibid., doc. 152.
[42] Ibid., doc. 151.   [43] Ibid., doc. 172.
[44] Ibid., doc. 173.

therefore, in trying to put to their proper use the pious gifts of the faithful. But how much in point of fact came to hand to relieve his necessities is unknown. Gottlob was of the opinion that very little reached him.[45] With France and Germany neutral, and the German princes certainly 'freezing' the collections against both Basel and the Roman Curia, and Poland finding that too good an example to be missed,[46] with Castile following France, and Aragon and Milan hostile to Eugenius, it is more than likely that Gottlob's judgement, founded on the registers of the Apostolic Camera, is just. England, however, was an exception. Piero da Monte in a letter of April 1438 wrote that he had forwarded 600 ducats to the Camera Apostolica; loaned 200 to the papal Nuncio, Antonio of Urbino; transmitted 636 through his brother in Venice; sent 1,300 by messenger to Italy and had lent a further 200 to a Roberto Cavalcante (another papal official).[47] Later (May 1440) he speaks of having sent within three months after 9 January 15,000 ducats of Indulgence-money to Italy, a sum afterwards increased to 16,000 (though Piero himself was made later to restore 1,800 ducats that he was accused of having embezzled). All the same, this needed royal permission and he would not have dared do it without—*non audet absque speciali licentia in hac parte.*[48]

As the year 1438 wore on and Eugenius was finding his position with regard to money more than ever difficult, he employed other means too to ease the situation. Towards the end of May 1438 he decreed that bequests and legacies made in general terms for the poor, without any definite object or person being specified, should be devoted to the maintenance of the Greeks.[49] On 11 June 1438 he granted an Indulgence under the usual conditions to such as should visit the chapel Montroland (in the diocese of Besançon) on the feast of Pentecost and give an alms for its needed recon-struction, but half of the contributions should be sent to him for the Greeks.[50] Twelve days later he allotted to the Camera Apostolica one year's income of the episcopal *mensa* of the diocese

---

[45] GOTTLOB, *Aus den Rechnungsbüchern*, etc., pp. 52–3.

[46] *M.C.*, III, p. 116.

[47] J. HALLER, *Piero da Monte* (Rome, 1941), p. 58. Eugenius had to invoke the aid of the Doge of Venice to get hold of the sum that Piero sent via his brother (Ibid. Beiträge docs., 9, 10).

[48] Apropos of a royal licence of April 1440: GOTTLOB, *Aus der Camera*, etc., p. 201.

[49] *E.P.*, doc. 142 bis.   [50] Ibid., doc. 143.

of Posen, at that time vacant.[51] On 4 October of the same year he
alienated the revenues of the vacant churches of Seville and Leôn
for the same purpose and appointed an apostolic collector for
them.[52] On 17 August 1439 he did the same with regard to the
church of Massa, then vacant.[53] But he had already on 1
September 1438 taken a more important step, though, I imagine,
with great reluctance since he had waited so long before doing it,
and perhaps with no very sanguine hopes but rather as a counsel
of despair. He imposed *hoc sacro approbante concilio* on the
universal Church a Tenth, or rather he declared that the Tenth
earlier imposed by Basel but not to be enforced till the actual arrival
of the Greeks should now be exacted and from everybody no
matter what their privileges.[54] Collectors for it were appointed at
any rate for Hungary and Portugal.[55] The revenues from that
would have helped towards the maintenance of the Greeks while
they were in Italy.

But Eugenius' burdens did not cease with their departure,
though now he had a happier message to deliver, for he could
proclaim the joyous news that the long-hoped for union had
actually been achieved. That is the tenor of his two letters to the
Church, one of 5 August 1439, the other of 7 October of the same
year[56]: 'The all-merciful God has deigned to assist us labouring
untiringly in this most holy work. For He granted that those
who were divided from us by such vast distances of sea and land
should after toils, trials and many dangers reach this Apostolic
See and the Roman Church. In the first place our most dear son
in Christ John Palaeologus, illustrious Emperor of the Greeks,
and Joseph, Patriarch of Constantinople of happy memory, with a
large following of metropolitans, bishops, prelates, clerics, nobles
and others, these as well as the procurators of the three patriarchal
Sees of Alexandria, Antioch and Jerusalem and the envoys of the
Emperor of Trebizond, of the Georgians, of the Ruthenians and
Wallachians and of other nations he has led to us in like manner'.
The discussions had lasted fifteen months. The Fathers of the
Council had laboured day and night. 'Wherefore the Lord heard
and gave ear to our prayer; for His glory appeared on His people
and it was brought about by His disposition that they who for

[51] Ibid., doc. 145.   [52] Ibid., doc. 154.
[53] Ibid., doc. 205.   [54] Ibid., doc. 150.
[55] Ibid., doc. 153.   [56] Ibid. docs. 201, 220.

well-nigh five hundred years had been divided from the Western Church now should agree in one profession of faith with us as is manifestly contained in the decree lately composed on this and promulgated in solemn session'. Great and indeed unbearable expenses have been incurred for this and for the return of the Greeks and now for the defence of Constantinople in accordance with an agreement entered into. So the faithful are invited to partake in this great work and for those who do so, contributing the value of the salary of a crossbowman for one or more weeks according as their means allow, the Pope grants an Indulgence on the usual conditions.

The Fathers of Basel took in bad part another of Eugenius' expedients to raise ready money and made it the forty-fifth of the 150 charges that they formulated in the case that they were maturing against him during 1438—his alienation of papal property.[57] As regards their facts they were in the main right. Sforza had been left in the possession of the whole province of Ancona and other cities such as Todi, Gualdo and Corneto, to rid the Holy See of a dangerous enemy and deprive Milan of a redoubtable general. In June 1436 Nicolò d'Este received the three cities of Lugo, Massa and Zagonara, as a gift according to the Bolognese chronicler,[58] but a Ferrarese chronicler records the price paid for Lugo —14,000 ducats and 100 moggia of corn—and so probably all three were sold to provide funds for the forthcoming council.[59] Towards the end of 1437 there was such a strong rumour current that Eugenius had thoughts of selling Avignon that the Fathers of Basel took it under their own protection.[60] Massa (regained from hostile occupation) and Bagnacavallo were acquired by the Marquis of Este for 11,000 ducats,[61] and six months later Florence took over Borgo S. Sepolcro to cancel a debt of 25,000 florins loaned on various occasions to the Pope, until such time at least, as that sum was repaid in money.[62]

Syropoulus in many parts of his *Memoirs* laments the miserable condition to which the Greeks in Ferrara were reduced because the agreed monthly maintenance allowances were not forthcoming

[57] *M.C.*, III, p. 86.
[58] Muratori Tom. XXXIII, Pt. I, p. 47.
[59] Ibid. Tom. XXIV, Pt. VII, p. 22.
[60] *M.C.*, II, pp. 1024–5.
[61] Muratori, Op. cit., p. 25.
[62] 24 Feb. 1441; *E.P.*, doc. 246.

to them from the Pope, and there can be doubt that he had good reason for his complaints. But what he did not, and indeed would not, understand was that Eugenius was doing his best and that if he did not pay on the appointed days it was only because he had not the money to pay with. The Greeks themselves were in no small measure to blame. The papal ships had arrived at Constantinople in the first days of September; yet it was not till 27 November that the Greeks embarked. Then they pursued their leisurely way to Venice taking more than two months for the voyage and arriving only on 8 February. It was another month before they reached Ferrara and a further eight months before they would consent to begin the doctrinal discussions of the Council proper, despite the urgent prayers of the Pope and their own growing discomfort. By that time the Pope was living from hand to mouth and for the most part on borrowed money. He gave them their allotted portion when he could and before they went to Florence he had paid his debts to them. In Florence the situation was different. One of the attractions held out by the Pope to overcome the Greek reluctance to transfer to that city was that there they should have a 'bank', i.e. that the payment of their allowances should be direct and not dependent on his Camera,[63] and that was one of the conditions specified by them in their final acceptance of the proposed move of the Council. And they had it and yet their payments were still always in arrears, though now not because the Pope was to blame but because the Commune of Florence for some reason (which was not a lack of ready money) was at fault. Frommann, following Syropoulus, nevertheless lays this neglect still at the Pope's door, yet he himself publishes documents that suggest the contrary.[64]

What happened would seem to be this. On 28 April 1439 the city council of Florence deliberated: 'That the aforesaid Greeks after their arrival have received no money for their expenses in the city of Florence and that the aforesaid magnificent lords [i.e. the *Priores* etc. of the city] were requested on the part of the Supreme Pontiff that for the monthly payment and for the

---

[63] As the Emperor explained it to them: 'so that each might receive his allowance when he wanted from the bank, without any reference to the Pope, but he could send his own servant to the bank whether at the completion of the month or about half-way through it or weekly and receive his allowance as each wanted' (SYR., p. 207).

[64] FROMMANN, Op. cit., pp. 36–7. The docs. are given at greater length in *A.C.A.*, docs. 72, 88.

restitution of the 1,200 florins expended for their journey, payment should be made in accordance with the agreement entered into . . . wherefore the Camera-officials are held and must . . . give and pay 1,200 florins for the expenses of the journey of the Greeks from Ferrara to Florence, and also 1,700 florins per month for four months beginning the 15 February last for the expenses of the Greeks while they will be in Florence, and the payment should be made to him or those' agents on whom the *Priores* etc. had decided. However a month passed before this decision was implemented, for it is only on 18 May that the Register of *Uscite* (No. 268) of the Treasury of Florence records the payment to Cosimo and Lorenzo de' Medici of 1,200 florins for the journey, of 3,400 florins for Greek expenses for two months beginning 15 February at the rate of 1,700 florins a month, and of 1,700 florins for a third month—in all 6,300 florins.[65] On 22 May Syropoulus notes the payment to the Patriarch of 1,208 florins as the allowance for two months[66] and on 13 July the Camera Apostolica paid to the brothers Medici 1,208 and 2,212 florins remitted by them to the Patriarch and the Emperor respectively for their maintenance for two months up to 22 May.[67] On 22 August the Commune of Florence again discussed the case of the Greeks and authorized the expenditure of 3,400 florins for their expenses during their stay in Florence 'beyond the four months paid at other times', to the same agents as before, provided that the Pope accepted this in complete quittance of the obligation entered into by Florence in respect of the Greeks.[68] Again there was delay in putting this decision into execution, for the Register of *Uscite* reports the payment on only 30 September to Cosimo and Lorenzo Medici of 1,700 florins for the fourth contribution to the Greeks on the authority of the decision taken in April and of 3,400 florins in pursuance of the decision of August for the fifth and sixth months of Greek expenses in Florence.[69] According to Syropoulus the Greeks received no maintenance after 22 May till the day of their departure in July when they were paid for five months.[70] He does not state what the sum paid was, and as maintenance for at the most only four months was due, he is probably mistaken in giving the number as five, perhaps by counting a possible viaticum as a

[65] JORGA, II, p. 33. [66] SYR., p. 251.
[67] *A.C.A.*, doc. 76. [68] Ibid., doc. 88.
[69] JORGA, II, pp. 34–5. [70] SYR., pp. 306–7.

monthly payment. The Camera Apostolica reimbursed the Medicis on 24 October.

From these documents it appears that the authorities of Florence recognised that the responsibility for the upkeep of the Greeks while in Florence rested with them and that they used the merchant-bankers, the brothers Medici, as their agents, who because of the delay of the Commune first to authorise payments and then to implement their decisions had to advance money at the end from their own resources to cover the debts of the city before the Greeks departed. But there still remains some mystery about the money for the third month, authorized in April and delivered to the Medicis in May, but apparently not handed over to the Greeks till July.

However that may be, despite his financial straits, Eugenius did not let the Greeks depart with anything still owing to them. He had contracted to bring them to Italy, to maintain them while there and to restore them once again to their homeland at his own expense. He fulfilled his contract even if with unfortunate delays. They took their treasures back with them to Constantinople,[71] but he had yet in large measure to foot the bill.

Eugenius had no love for money; perhaps he had no real idea of its value. Before becoming a monk of the monastery of S. Giorgio d'Alga in Venice he gave away the rich patrimony of 20,000 ducats he had inherited from his father. As Pope he was so open-handed and so generous in his charities to all who appealed

---

[71] SYR. (ibid.) says that the first party of Greeks to leave Florence received payment for 5 months at the very moment of their departure, so that they cannot have had bad debts to pay off and must have set out home comparatively well off.

Major fuit, rex amplissime, opinione omnium impensa, maior diligentia magni Eugenii pontificis nostri; quam perducendis Florentiam septingentis cum Ioanne Palaeologo Graecis; quam ipsis importunis inverecundisque magis quam famelicis in itinere et in Italia pascendis; quam donandis ornandisque semper hiantibus tam malo quam magno auri profluvio consumpsit (BIONDO FLAVIO, *Ad Alphonsum Aragonensem . . . de expeditione in Turchos*, (Aug. 1453, in NOGARA, *Op. cit.*, p. 37).

'For they were in receipt not only of the money for maintenance but of much more, so that they returned to their homeland rich' (JOSEPH OF METHONE, *Reply to Mark Eugenicus' Judgement on the Council of Florence*; *P.G.* 159, 1080c).

Syropoulus reports that in the Patriarch's effects after his death there were found 500 florins, the equivalent, that is, of 20 months' maintenance grant (p. 318): and that the Metropolitan of Cyzicus on the day of his departure found his monastic habit and sacred pyx missing—of no value to thieves—though 'plenty of silver objects' that the thieves could have sold were not touched. But the whole story is a bit suspect, because Syropoulus also states that Cyzicus' baggage had already been consigned to the baggage-bearers (pp. 312–3).

to him as to be an embarrassment to his secretaries who had to keep him solvent.[72] He lived very abstemiously, drinking no wine but only sugared water and eating once a day, preferably fruit and vegetables, and that at no fixed hour but as he felt the need.[73] Yet he was enough of an Italian and Venetian to appreciate and love articles of beauty and the pomp of ceremony. In 1431 he paid only 49 florins 24 solidi and 8 denari for a tiara, but 7,053 florins and 22 solidi for baldachinos and hangings, for his coronation. In 1441, however, he commissioned the famous Florentine artist Ghiberti to make him a new tiara, which Ghiberti himself described in these words: 'Pope Eugenius came to live in the city of Florence. He had me make a mitre of gold, which weighed, the gold of that mitre, 15 pounds; the stones weighed 5½ pounds. They were estimated by the jewellers of our parts as worth 38,000 florins. There were balas rubies, sapphires, emeralds and pearls. There were in that mitre six pearls as big as nuts: it was adorned with many figures and very many ornaments. There is on the front a throne with many cherubs round about and a Nostro Signore in the middle; similarly behind, a Nostra Dama with the same cherubs round about the throne. There are in niches of gold the four evangelists and there are many cherubs in the border around the bottom. It was made with great magnificence'.[74]

By 1442 Eugenius had, perhaps, a certain right to symbolize the joy and satisfaction he felt for the success that had crowned his efforts in spite of all obstacles, a satisfaction that would assuredly have had a general echo in many parts of the Church. Henry of England had written to him on 3 October 1439 that he had ordered public thanksgivings *processiones, letanias ac orationes publicas per loca nostrae ditioni supposita* and four months later had expressed himself again in the same sense, this time for the added triumph of the reconciliation of the Armenians.[75]

---

[72] Eugenius, like other popes, had a private treasury besides the public *Camera Apostolica*. Cf. P. D. PARTNER, *Camera Papae: Problems of Papal Finance in the Later Middle Ages*, in *The Journal of Ecclesiastical History* IV (1953), pp. 55–68.

[73] VESPASIANO DA BISTICCI, *Vita Eugenii*, in A. MAI, *Spicilegium Romanum* I (Rome, 1839), pp. 5–23.

[74] E. MÜNTZ, Op. cit., pp. 56, 64, 53.

[75] THOMAS BEKYNTON, *Official Correspondence of Thomas Bekynton*, ed. G. WILLIAMS (London, 1872), vol. II, No. cciv, p. 49; No. ccxv (8 Feb. 1440), p. 51.

CHAPTER FIFTEEN

A TRACTATE ABOUT THE COUNCIL OF FLORENCE ATTRIBUTED TO GEORGE AMIROUTZES

George Amiroutzes, commonly called the Philosopher for his wide learning, was a native of Trebizond. In 1437 he accompanied John VIII Palaeologus, emperor of Constantinople, to Italy to the Council of Ferrara-Florence as one of the three erudite laymen (the others were George Scholarius and George Gemistus 'Pletho') that the emperor took with him to advise him on the difficult theological questions there to be discussed. As the events unfolded division arose in the ranks of the Greeks. First, in Ferrara, there was the question as to what should be the subject of the opening discussion—the addition of the *Filioque* to the Creed, or the doctrine of the *Filioque*. Bessarion, Metropolitan of Nicaea (later cardinal) and Scholarius (later the Patriarch Gennadius) wanted to start with the latter as the more fundamental; Mark Eugenicus, Metropolitan of Ephesus, and Gemistus preferred the former and their opinion prevailed. Amiroutzes agreed with Bessarion and Scholarius. In Florence, where the subject of debate was the doctrine of the *Filioque*, the rift between the two parties was more serious. It was a rift mainly between the leaders, for the majority of the Greek bishops, of a lower intellectual standard, was content to follow. For union the protagonists were Bessarion, Isidore, Metropolitan of Kiev and of all Russia, Gregory, the imperial confessor, and Dorotheus, Metropolitan of Mitylene. Against union, Mark of Ephesus stood almost alone but indomitable. George Amiroutzes was a staunch supporter of the unionists, who in several of the private conferences of the Greeks bitterly attacked Eugenicus and who gave a written vote in decisive and clear terms in favour of the orthodoxy of the Latin doctrine on the Procession of the Holy Spirit.[1] The decree of union of the Latin and the Greek Churches was promulgated in solemn session on 6 July 1439. It bears the signatures of the emperor, of all the prelates but two (Eugenicus and Isaias of Stauropolis), of five

---

[1] M. Jugie, *La profession de foi de Georges Amiroutzès au concile de Florence,* in *E.O.* 36 (1937), pp. 175–80.

deacons of the Great Church and of several monks. The three 'philosophers' did not sign because they were laymen. As is well known, after their return to Constantinople most of the Greek prelates, under the influence of Mark Eugenicus and of popular sentiment, repented of their adherence. George Scholarius, who had delivered in Florence as clear a decision in favour of Latin orthodoxy as Amiroutzes, even became the anti-unionist leader. It is said that Amiroutzes, too, made his recantation in the form of a letter or tractate entitled: 'About the Events in the Council of Florence to Demetrius, Duke of Nauplion, of Amiroutzes the Philosopher.'[2] It is the contention of this article that this tractate was not written by Amiroutzes and that it is most probably a composition of much later date, even though it purports to be written by a participant in the Council.[3]

The tractate was virtually unknown, if not completely unknown till the early years of the seventeenth century. The proof of this broad assertion is the fact that Leo Allatius, a man of vast erudition, particularly in the literature about the Council of Florence, who flourished in the first half of that century, had never heard of it till he came across a reference to it in a *contemporary* Greek polemic,[4] and then he obtained a copy of it from friends of his in his native Chios.[5] The manuscript he received bore the title attributing the work to Amiroutzes, and that is the only reference to Amiroutzes in the whole composition. Allatius, though critical of the work itself, accepted the attribution. Similarly, he did not question the name of the supposed recipient of the treatise, Demetrius, Duke of Nauplion. Yet who was that Demetrius who

---

[2] Edited by L. MOHLER, *Eine bisher verlorene Schrift von Georgios Amirutzes über das Konzil von Florenz*, in *Oriens Christianus*, neue Serie, IX (1920), pp. 20–35; and by M. JUGIE, *La lettre de Georges Amiroutzès au duc de Nauplie Démétrius sur le concile de Florence*, in *Byzantion* XIV (1939), pp. 77–93. Both editors have transcribed the sole extant MS., Vallicellianus 183, an 18th-century copy of an earlier MS. once in the possession of Leo Allatius. Allatius received it from Chios and gives several extracts from it, including the title, which amply prove the fidelity of the copy. References will be given to Fr. Jugie's article, as probably the more accessible to the reader.

[3] 'And, in the first place, I together with them put into Venice' (p. 82). The importance of this examination of the authenticity of this treatise ascribed to Amiroutzes will be apparent to the readers of my book, *The Council of Florence* (Cambridge Univ. Press, 1959).

[4] Of George Coresius who flourished in the first half of the 17th-century: L. ALLATIUS, *De ecclesiae occidentalis atque orientalis perpetua consensione* (Coloniae Agrippinae, 1648) cc. 877, 935.

[5] ALLATIUS, Op. cit., c. 1379. This copy, now lost, and the one in the Biblioteca Vallicelliana are the only known MSS.

had asked for a brief account of the Council of Florence? He could not have been Demetrius Palaeologus, both because having been an eye-witness of the events in Italy he would not have stood in need of enlightenment and because the letter speaks of him completely in the third person: 'The emperor went to Italy with the Byzantine patriarch and the patriarchal procurators and *his brother* and many nobles' (82). Modern writers say it was Demetrius Asan, governor of Mouchli.[6] The only reason I can imagine for such an assertion is that Demetrius Asan is the only other Demetrius of that time who might have been a possible recipient. He was active then in the Peloponnesus; yet he had no connexion with Nauplion, which had long been, and would long remain, a Venetian possession. In any case, even if he was ill-informed about the events of the Council, he would have been only too well acquainted with one of the main reasons why the Council was held at all—to get military aid for Constantinople— since he passed much of his life fighting against the Turk. Yet the letter begins by describing John VIII's despair 'since the Turk had subdued all the territories subject to the power of the kingdom of Byzantium' and spends the best part of two pages recounting, with a highly improbable speech of the emperor John, the actions and the sentiments of the Greeks that induced them to go to Italy—information completely superfluous for Demetrius Asan or any other contemporary Greek personage, but useful once the Council had become ancient history.

The letter, of course, purports to be more or less contemporary with the Council: the writer claims to have reached Venice with the emperor. If Amiroutzes were the author, he would not have written it before 1447, for in that year Mark Eugenicus's brother, John, addressed a letter to him trying to win him back to the ranks of orthodoxy.[7] He is not likely to have written it after 1453 when the fall of Constantinople spelt the end both of the Byzantine Empire and of the uneasy union with the Latins. In any case, during the years from the end of the Council till 1461, when Trebizond fell to the Turks (apart from an embassy to Italy in

---

[6] A. ZAKYTHINOS, *Le despotat grec de Morée*, I (Paris, 1932), p. 258 n. 5; II (Athens, 1953), pp. 114, 361, with assurance: N. TOMADAKIS, *Did George Amiroutzes become a Mohammedan?* in *Epeteris Hetaireias Byzantinon Spoudon* 18 (1948), p. 118, with more reserve.

[7] E. LEGRAND, *Cent-dix lettres grecques de François Filelfe* (Paris, 1892), pp. 304–5.

1448-9), Amiroutzes was back in his native city and immersed in political activity, a stranger to the bitter controversy that troubled Constantinople, dwelling at the other end of the Greek world from the Nauplion of which Demetrius was supposed to be the duke.

These preliminary considerations cast serious suspicion on the authenticity of the tractate. There is, however, one statement contained in it that changes suspicion into certainty. The writer states that Isidore of Kiev did not sign the decree of union (86). That assertion is an error that any active participant in the Council could hardly have been guilty of; one that Amiroutzes could not have been guilty of. For, as has been earlier stated, Isidore was one of the most energetic, if not the most energetic, promoter of union in Florence, who time and again encouraged, persuaded and exhorted his fellows to union; who was an active delegate on many committees; who was the chief go-between of emperor and pope; who did not return immediately after the Council to Greece but went as papal legate to announce the union to the oriental Christians of Poland, Lithuania and the principalities of Russia; who solemnly commemorated the pope and promulgated the act of union in the Great Church of St. Sophia on the eve of the capture of Constantinople. And Amiroutzes was an ardent supporter of his, and on occasion a bitter critic of his adversary, Mark Eugenicus. Amiroutzes could not have failed to know that Isidore not only approved of the decree of union that he had done so much to bring into being, but that he had signed it in his own name and in that of the Patriarch of Antioch, whose procurator he was: and, therefore, he could not have stated the opposite a few years later. Nor could anyone else who was at the Council.

This mistake can hardly be a deliberate falsehood, for it makes no appreciable difference to the writer's argument, and is included only incidentally. It is a mistake of ignorance, due possibly to a misreading of a list drawn up by George Scholarius. At some time after 1444-5, when he took over the leadership of the opposition to union from Mark Eugenicus, Scholarius made a list of the Greek signatories to the decree of union with comments on their later attitude to it. This list is preserved in two manuscripts, both in the handwriting of Scholarius himself. As the document is printed (reproducing Cod. Dionysiacus 150—Mount Athos), in a column on the left are the names, in one on the right are the comments of Scholarius. Isidore's name follows that of Mark of

Ephesus. Opposite the space between them is 'Procurators of Antioch'; opposite Mark's name there is 'He did not sign'; opposite Isidore's there is no comment, but underneath there is written 'He was later honoured by the Latins with the rank of cardinal'.[8] This, as it were, note easily escapes the eye (as it did mine for some time and) as apparently it did that of the author of the tractate, who took as applying to both Mark and Isidore both the marginal comments and so turned Isidore, the enthusiastic unionist, into an anti-unionist rivalled only by Mark Eugenicus for obduracy.

There are also other mistakes in the tractate, though not so glaring. Even so, one would not have expected a man of Amir-outzes's intelligence and position in the Council to have made them. It is said, for example (82), that 'the pope right from the start of the discussions makes the question of the addition the matter of dispute through John and Julian who were trying to show that the *Filioque* was added under the stress of necessity'. It was the Greeks, of course, who chose the subject of discussion (when Amiroutzes sided with Bessarion against Eugenicus), not the pope; and John Montenero, O.P., made no public appearance in Ferrara in favour of the addition, though he was the Latin spokesman throughout the sessions in Florence. Again, the writer asks: 'In what way was it (i.e. the Council) oecumenical, when the exarch of the Synod, that is the Metropolitan of Ephesus, who was also procurator of the Patriarchs both of Antioch and of Jerusalem, did not sign?' Mark in Constantinople had been appointed procurator first of Alexandria, then of Jerusalem, and finally in Ferrara he was made procurator of Antioch, but he never held two proxies simultaneously—neither did any other procurator of the patriarchs.

Apart from the above inaccurate assertion there is very little other reference to the events in this 'About the Events in the Council of Florence'. However, the author on two occasions quotes what purport to be words uttered by the pope and on another some words of a Greek prelate, which are so like the account found in the Greek *Practica* of the Council as to make one believe that they are not founded on the author's memory of events, but are in fact direct borrowings.

[8] SCHOL., III, pp. 194–5. The other MS., Cod. Barrocianus Oxon. 85 fol. 3r–3v, is drawn up in the same way.

It should be borne in mind that the Greek *Practica* as we now have them are compiled from two main sources, the official protocol of the speeches made in the public sessions and excerpts from a general account written by some Greek metropolitan who took part in the Council, probably Dorotheus of Mitylene.[9] This latter source, which I call the 'Description', was originally a separate work which is now lost, no copy of it being now known to exist. But at some date between 1463 and 1470 a scribe, John Plousiadenus, filled out the lacunae in the history of the Council as recounted in the protocol by introducing in various places long extracts from the 'Description'. This 'Description', to judge from what Plousiadenus has thus preserved to us, is concise, made up for the most part of diary-entries strung together. Events are narrated briefly; of speeches only a *précis* is given.

Two of the quotations found in the tractate addressed to Demetrius are from a speech of the pope that is recorded in *précis* in the 'Description'. According to the text of 'Amiroutzes' they are as follows: 'Everywhere before my eyes I see division, and I marvel as to how division is going to be of any help to you. Still, if that is to be the case, how will the western princes receive it, and We, how much grief must We not feel in Ourselves? Nay, you, how are you going to depart to your native land?' (86). The only difference between this version and that of the *Practica* (423) is that 'Amiroutzes' wrote 'princes' where the *Practica* has 'lords'. 'But once union is accomplished, both the western nobles and We shall help you, and our help will free you from captivity' (86). The corresponding text of the *Practica* is much longer (423-4): 'But once union is accomplished, both the western kings and all of us will furnish great help and we shall greatly help you; and our help will bring great relief to the Christians dwelling in the East and to those in the power of the pagan.' The words of the prelate are these: 'What then are you after with this departure of ours at the expense of the pope? Do you want us to betray our faith?' (86). The *Practica* for 'What then' has 'And what', and after 'this departure of ours' adds 'to our native land' (400).

The similarity between the two versions for the first and the last quotation is so great as to amount to identity. One explanation of this striking correspondence could be that each writer independently was faithfully recording the speaker's words and incidentally proving the other's historical reliability. But in the

[9] *A.G.*, pp. liii–lxix.

P

case of the first quotation it is not the speaker's words that are being quoted, but part of a *précis* made by a casual individual, the author of the 'Description', so that one is forced to conclude that the writer of the letter-treatise to Demetrius borrowed from the 'Description'. If he borrowed in the one case, we need not hesitate to affirm that he borrowed also in the other two. The 'Description', however was probably written during the Council and no more is known of its later history except that the original or a copy was in the hands of Plousiadenus some thirty-five years later. Thereafter the protocol-'Description' as he contrived it was frequently copied, but it is not likely that copies would have circulated in the Turkish-dominated territories, at least for a considerable time after the establishment of Turkish rule there, before, that is, a certain degree of peace and a *modus vivendi* had been established between conqueror and conquered. By that time the *Practica* had become even more accessible, for they were printed first in 1577 and then, with a Latin translation by John Caryophilus, again in 1612 in the third volume of the Vatican Collection of Councils, and this edition was published separately in two volumes a few years later in 1629. One cannot conclude from this argument alone that the treatise to Demetrius is a late production and not by Amiroutzes, because it is just possible that an anti-unionist writer in the decade after the Council could have had access to a copy of the 'Description'. But it is so unlikely that the presence of these quotations indicates that the letter to Demetrius was put together long after the Council, when the Greek *Practica* after frequent copying, or more probably after being printed, were easily come by.

There are other considerations, of a more general nature, that should make the reader who is well acquainted with the documents of the Council of Florence regard this tractate with reserve. From its title one would expect a treatment that has constant reference to the events of the Council. What one finds is what I have frequently called it, a treatise. There is, of course, incidental mention of the accusations that have been current among the Greeks from the end of the Council to this day, that the union was bought, that it was the fruit of duress, etc., but they do not indicate that the writer was a participant in the Council, only that he was an anti-unionist. These, with the 'quotations' discussed above, are used to prove that the Council of Florence was not oecumenical. Something, too, is said about the addition of the

Filioque to the Creed, but with the purpose as much as anything of showing that no pope could lawfully have introduced it on his own initiative. The bulk of the treatise is directed not to discussion of the *Filioque*, which was almost the exclusive theme of the debates in Italy, but to disproving the papal claims to primacy, and that by arguments which are certainly not drawn from the records of the Council of Florence. Appeal is made to canons of the Council of Nicaea and of the Third Council of Constantinople, called also the Council in Trullo, for the oecumenicity of which Peter Lombard is quoted. A parallel is drawn between Moses as 'teacher of the race of the Jews' and the Patriarchs of the Pentarchy, with references to the books of the Old Testament. Various Fathers, including Jerome and Cyprian, interpret 'Feed my sheep' and 'Lovest thou me more than these' as applicable to all the Apostles: exact references are given. The treatise ends with a list of deposed patriarchs (with references to sources) and of errant popes—Zephyrinus was a Montanist; Marcellinus sacrificed to idols; Liberius and Felix were Arians; Celestine was a Nestorian; Honorius a Monothelite—so 'it is not an article of faith to believe in the pope', 'remove then the *Filioque* from the Creed and say it as before', 'for the third hypostasis has his being from the Father only, though he comes forth through the Son as through a second hypostasis. This, most honoured leader, I am able to put before you in brief, and if you need anything of me, command me'. So it ends. The arguments are far, far removed from those of Florence in matter and spirit, and, I would say, also in time.

If this treatise had come down to us with no title and without the phrase in it that makes the author reach Venice with the emperor, no one, I think, would for a moment have imagined that it was from the pen either of Amiroutzes or of any other participant in the Council. On the contrary, its false statements and its general tone would suggest some controversialist not very familiar with the history of the Council, writing at a date long after its close, when controversy about the papacy had already been coloured by the Protestant Reformation.[10] And this view is, in my opinion, the correct one. The title and the phrase that connect the treatise with Amiroutzes and Italy are, I believe, deliberate falsifications designed to give the document a spurious authenticity.

[10] This idea, of its relation with Reformation theology, occurred to me before I had actually traced any possible physical connection.

If that is so, it is not the only imposture of the kind. Credit was long given to the so-called acts of a council that was supposed to have been held in St. Sophia in 1450 to depose the patriarch Gregory and reject the union of Florence. C. Papaioannou has shown conclusively that these are fabrications and, both for other reasons and because the first mention of them came from the pen of George Coresius, he concluded that Coresius was the one who fabricated them.[11] Coresius, born in Chios c. 1554–63, studied medicine and philosophy in Padua, taught Greek and practised as a doctor in Pisa and Leghorn, and returned to Chios where, c. 1624, he founded a monastery. In 1633 he was called to Constantinople to conduct discussions with Antony Leger, the Dutch Calvinist. He died about 1654.

Can it be no more than a series of coincidences that in the same phrase in which Coresius makes the first known mention of the spurious acts of the council of 1450 he mentions too, and again it is for the first time, the treatise of Amiroutzes and a treatise of Gemistus which also makes the strange assertion that Isidore of Kiev did not sign the decree of union[12]; that Coresius (like Allatius) was a native of Chios; that Allatius received his copies of the spurious acts and of the treatises of Amiroutzes and Gemistus from friends of his in that island[13]; and that these works, till then so rare as to have been quite unknown, became suddenly available at the same time? Coresius was the most active Greek opponent of the Latin Church of his day and the writer of an imposing list of polemical works.[14] Allatius and Caryophilus were just as active on the other side. It looks as if Coresius did not hesitate to provide himself with 'authoritative' answers to his opponents' arguments and to make sure that his adversaries read them.

[11] C. PAPAIOANNOU, *The Acts of the so-called last Synod in St. Sophia* (A.D. *1450) and their Historical Value*, in *Ekklesiastiki Aletheia* XV–XVI (1896–7) passim. Allatius (Op. cit. cc. 1380–95) had already indicated a number of blatant contradictions and absurdities, and had come to the same conclusion as to their worthlessness.

[12] PAPAIOANNOU, Op. cit., XV, pp. 397–8; ALLATIUS, Op. cit. cc. 877, 935. All we know of the treatise of Gemistus is a quotation in Allatius (cc. 908–9). He mentions Chios as the source of what must have been this treatise in c. 937, whose opening words are nearly, but not quite, the same as those of the treatise generally recognised as genuinely by Gemistus: cf. c. 936.

[13] ALLATIUS, cc. 1379, 1380, 937.

[14] Cf. K. N. SATHAS, *Biographies of Greeks Distinguished in Literature (1453– 1821)*, (Athens, 1868), pp. 249–50. One is entitled: 'About the Primacy of the Pope'; it would be interesting to compare its arguments with those of the treatise addressed to Demetrius.

CHAPTER SIXTEEN

THE CONDEMNATION OF THE COUNCIL OF FLORENCE BY THE THREE ORIENTAL PATRIARCHS IN 1443

It is generally believed that in 1443 the Patriarchs of Alexandria, Antioch and Jerusalem met at the instigation of a certain Arsenius, Metropolitan of Caesarea in Cappadocia, and condemned the Council of Florence. The late Fr. Hofmann published the text of the condemnation and Leo Allatius gives both that document and also a letter addressed to the Emperor, John VIII.[1] Of these documents the late Archbishop of Athens, Ch. Papadopoulos, wrote: 'As is well-known, this synod did actually meet, but the documents about it that are preserved are not genuine'.[2] These two documents are the only source of information about the synod that we have. It they are not trustworthy, there is no proof whatever that such a synod took place. They merit, therefore, serious examination.

The letter to the Emperor is dated December 1442. It does not state who was (or were) responsible for it, but, as it is written in part in the first person singular, it was not the product of three patriarchs. Indeed, it makes no mention of any patriarch at all, or of any synod of patriarchs, and, therefore, not of any condemnation of the Council of Florence by the three patriarchs. Admittedly, the conclusions of the council are castigated, but on the grounds of a supposed letter from the Patriarch of Constantinople, Joseph II, alleging against it all the complaints that characterise later Greek polemics—duress, fraud, perjury, etc. Whatever else this document of 1442 may or may not prove, it is no evidence of a synod of the three patriarchs in 1443.

The other document, which purports to be the synodal letter of the three patriarchs, is certainly less extravagant. It is addressed

---

[1] *Orientalium documenta minora*, ed. G. HOFMANN (Rome, 1953) doc. 45; L. ALLATIUS, *De Ecclesiae occidentalis et orientalis perpetua consensione* (Coloniae Agrippinae, 1648), pp. 942–7; MANSI, 35, 55–64.
[2] *The State of the Orthodox Church of Antioch in the 14th and 15th Centuries*, in *Epeteris Hetaireias Byzantinon Spoudon* XIII (1937), p. 149 n. 2.

to no one in particular, but reads as an authorisation of a certain
Arsenius, Metropolitan of Caesarea in Cappadocia, to uphold the
ancient faith. It is dated April 1443, and entitled (in Fr. Hofmann's
text): 'Decree of the Holy Patriarchs in Syria, Philotheus of Alexandria, Joachim of Jerusalem and Dorotheus of Antioch against
the synod that took place in Florence, that is, the eighth and the
execrable', or (in Allatius' text): 'Of the Patriarchs in Syria'. The
names of the Patriarchs occur again in the course of the text and
in the same order. Various other names are found that give an
impression of reliability, as names always do, scil. (besides the
name of the Metropolitan of Caesarea) Pope Eugenius; Metrophanes of Cyzicus, the new Patriarch of Constantinople; and the
dioceses of Amasia, Neocaesarea, Tyana and Mocessus, where
Metrophanes is said to have intruded unionist bishops. These
data seem to offer a chance of checking the genuineness of the
document. The names of the patriarchs are correct. Arsenius of
Caesarea is known only from this document. Metrophanes
certainly consecrated Pachomius as unionist bishop of Amasia,
but as far as I know, there is no evidence from any other source
that he filled also the other dioceses. At the least, then, one of the
positive facts stated is certainly true, and the others cannot be
disproved.

The general content of the document is not decisive either
way, but on the whole it suggests either that it is completely
spurious or at least that it has been seriously interpolated. Here
are a few of the reasons for this judgement (which is more or less
the judgement also of Ch. Papadopoulos):

1.   The Greek style is poor and in places ungrammatical.

2.   The tone is one of haughty superiority and condemnatory.

3.   The order of the patriarchs is given as Alexandria, Jerusalem, Antioch.

4.   In a genuine title, the Council of Florence would not be
called the 'Eighth synod', since it is claimed that it was not a
synod at all.

5.   The council is said to have 'allowed us to sacrifice in
unleavened bread and by that means to commemorate the Pope',
and

6.   'to have written the addition on to our divine and blame-
less symbol of the faith' (these are stated as the reports brought
by Arsenius).

7. The Emperor is referred to as 'Latinophron'.

8. The document suspends all those who have received any Orders 'not on account of virtue and right doctrine', i.e. from unionists, and

9. excommunicates the disobedient.

10. Arsenius is bidden preach the truth 'without respect for the face of the Emperor or the Patriarch'.

Negatively, the document makes no reference to the fact that each of the Patriarchs had had procurators in Florence who had signed the decree of union, still less does it contain any specific repudiation of their procurators' signatures; nor does it indicate that they had received copies of the decree from Pope or Emperor with, in the case of Alexandria at least, an explanatory letter, and so had personal knowledge of the council, for according to the document all their knowledge is founded on the reports said to have been brought by Arsenius.

The contents of the document, then, do not suggest that it is genuine. It is dated April 1443. The original is no longer extant, but copies are not rare. There is, however, no evidence that it was known in the fifteenth century, though one would have expected the knowledge of so important an event as a condemnation of the council by the three patriarchs of the East to be widespread. It was not known in Constantinople before that city was taken by the Turks in 1453—ten years after its written date—nor by the Patriarch Gennadius for as long as he was writing polemical works, which was till his death in about 1472, and, if he, the leading controversialist against the union, was ignorant of it, one may fairly conclude that no one else had any knowledge of it either. This is, admittedly, the conclusion of an argument from silence, but, I think, a valid argument. Scholarius-Gennadius and the other anti-unionists, like Theodore Agallianus, even Manuel the Orator, born about 1460, who wrote a kind of biography of Mark Eugenicus, could have found no better way of attacking the union of Florence than by proclaiming from the housetops that all three patriarchs of the East had, in solemn session, repudiated the signatures of their procurators and had roundly condemned the Council of Florence with all its works and pomps. Time and again in their writings such an announcement would have been the perfect culmination of long argumentation—and they had to be content with the condemnation of Beccus by the eastern patriarchs, which had taken place as much as a century and a half before, in 1285.

Here are a few examples drawn from the polemics of Gennadius. References are to *Oeuvres complètes de Gennade Scholarios*, 8 vols., ed. L. Petit, X.A. Sidéridès and M. Jugie (Paris, 1928–36) and the dates are those assigned by the editors.

The following passages occur in 'A Short Apology of the Anti-unionists', of date 1451/2. (Vol. III, p. 89, lines 13–26) 'Observe how great is the difference between the Council of Florence and the one that met in Constantinople against Beccus. The latter is in complete agreement with the faith of the oecumenical synods, both the eighth and the rest; the former is in disagreement with them all, both that one and the rest. At the latter the Pope of Alexandria was present and the other patriarchs agreed with and approved of the result as a sound and lawful decision; at the former, there were indeed procurators of the patriarchs, but they were limited by their letters [of appointment] and by oaths to accept union only if it was in conformity with the ancient faith but, if the Latins insisted on the addition, they were to return with no concession made. And now that they have negotiated what pleased themselves, not what was according to the minds of their principals, the patriarchs remain in their former opinion, but to their fine procurators they meted out a return worthy of the paternal doctrine and they do not till now cease meting it out'.

(P. 90, lines 24–6) 'These did everything against the will of the Patriarchs whose procurators they were. And no law bids us pay attention to them in this regard, even if in other respects they are not without merit or unworthy of honour.'

Further, in the same tractate, the formal rejection of the Council of Florence by the patriarchs would have suited the argument admirably on p. 86 line 28 and p. 100 line 11—but no mention is made of such an event. Similarly, in his 'Against the Union of Florence' of 1451 (Vol. III, p. 138), and again in his account, 'Against the Union, to Constantine', dated 12 March 1452 (Vol. III, p. 154), Scholarius, had he known of a condemnation by the patriarchs, must have quoted it. Also, at some unknown date, he drew up a list of the Greek signatories of the decree of union and after each name noted whether that individual had recanted or not. The names of the patriarchs' procurators are mentioned and that they were procurators, but no reference is made to a repudiation of their signatures by their patrons (Vol. III, pp. 194-5).

In November 1452, a group of anti-unionists sent a report to the Emperor Constantine. They advocated a new council, to be held in Constantinople to settle the ecclesiastical differences and pretended that there could be no difficulty, provided that the Latins did not act as in Florence. 'It is obvious what the most holy patriarchs think and wrote about the union that has been made, and every one of the Eastern Church' (Vol. III, p. 192, line 8).

In that same month, when Isidore, who had signed the decree of union as procurator of the See of Antioch, was in Constantinople persuading Emperor and people to a formal promulgation of the union and when Gennadius and his fellows of the 'synaxis' were doing all they could to influence the populace against that, the argument that the three patriarchs of the East had officially repudiated the union and, in particular, that Dorotheus of Antioch had condemned Isidore's unionism would have been devastating. It was never made in any of the many letters and manifestoes that were issued. For instance, Scholarius as the last shot of his broadside against Isidore, put out a manifesto on 27 November 1452. In it he challenged anyone to find evil in his (Scholarius') past life. His only crime, he said, was to be faithful to the doctrines of the Church, to the council that condemned Beccus, to the pledge he had made to the dying Mark of Ephesus and to the various manifestoes published by the anti-unionists, and so on (Vol. III, pp. 171 f.).

A short time before that, on 15 November, he had written to the opponents of union: 'In conformity with the doctrines of the holy Fathers and my own conscience, I regard that Synod of Florence as God and the truth and all genuine sons of the Eastern Church regard it. To speak clearer, I look on a council of that kind as like the pseudo-council of the time of Constantine, which, so it is said, abolished the 'homoousion'. Since such is my opinion, I shall judge whosoever commemorates the Pope or is in communion with one who commemorates him or who advises or counsels such an action, as the holy, big Synod of Constantinople did, the one, that is, that censured the Latin dogma and deposed those who held it, namely Beccus and his fellows' (Vol. III, p.

167). Gennadius cannot possibly have known that the three oriental patriarchs, some eight and a half years before, were supposed to have 'censured the Latin dogma' of the Council of Florence 'and deposed those who held it', and that thereby they had equivalently condemned Isidore and his mission in Constantinople.

One of the signatories of the report to Constantine of 1452, mentioned above, was Theodore Agallianus, author of at least two treatises against the Council of Florence and its doctrines, who was singled out by Leonardo of Chios as being at the very centre of the anti-unionist opposition. In neither of them does he make mention of any condemnation of Florence by the three patriarchs, though occasion offered (e.g. P.G. 158 1045 C). Another signatory was Syropoulus, the author of the *Memoirs*, which are really a thesis to demonstrate the iniquities of Florence. At the very end of his most interesting account, he lists seven factors which were 'the bigger and principal hindrances that occurred, as often as they planned and tried to establish and defend the union' (XII, 11, pp. 349–350). The last hindrance mentioned took place in 1444–5 —the debates between the Dominican Lapacci and Scholarius. Is it credible that, if Syropoulus had known that the three patriarchs had condemned the council in 1443, he would not have put that into his catalogue of hindrances, and indeed as the most important?

The conclusion that emerges from these considerations is that no one of the many controversial anti-unionists showed any knowledge of the supposed patriarchal condemnation of Florence. There may, however, have been an exception. John Eugenicus at some date (to judge from internal evidence) after 1453, wrote a hymn of thanksgiving for the survival of Orthodoxy, entitled in S. Lambros's edition of it: 'Of the same author, a Doxology to God for the Ecclesiastical Restoration'. It consists of a list of favours shown to the Church by God, and at the end contains the following: 'But before God and His chosen angels and all right-minded persons on earth, we are set firmly in safety in the renewal of our salvation and restoration, owing to the grace of the all-holy life-giving Spirit and the prayers, blessing and pardon of the Patriarchs of the East as from a common synod and canonical decision, in order that, as long as the Almighty favours the complete amendment of the Church, also in the metropolis, and utterly casts out from our midst the rotten and bitter compromises and hesitations, we may no longer have the slightest leaning towards the innovations and the innovators, but may abide in the good profession, which we issued to the holy Patriarchs and all the orthodox Church of Christ'.[3]

The words, 'the prayer, blessing and pardon of the holy Patriarchs of the East as from a common synod and canonical decision', could refer to the letter of the patriarchs of Syria of 1443; that is, the latter half of the phrase could do so, but the earlier half, 'prayer, blessing and pardon', is surely not an apt description of the letter that has come down to us as the decision of the patriarchs, for there is neither prayer nor blessing nor pardon in it. Further, if John were in fact referring to a formal condemnation of Florence by the patriarchs, would he have confined his lyrical pen in this Doxology to such a milk-and-water description of it? Moreover, if he knew of a condemnation, all those who shared his views and his anti-unionistic activities must have known of it too, and especially Gennadius with whom he was in frequent correspondence; yet none of these breathes a word about it. Finally, nowhere else, and he wrote much and bitterly about the Council of Florence, does he mention any such condemnation.

For instance, some time after the death on 23 June 1445 of his brother, Mark, and probably long after, since in his many published works (Lambros, Op. cit., I, pp. 49–218) which cover his life till after 1453 he never refers to it, he composed a *Logos antirrhetikos*, a refutation of the decree of union of the Council of Florence. His plan was to take each phrase of the decree and by his comments show its falsehood and absurdity. That gave him ample opportunity to produce the condemnation of the patriarchs; indeed several of the phrases cried out aloud for it—if it existed. E.g. '4. *Oecumenical*, in what way? The first and genuine letters of the patriarchs authorising their procurators still exist' (viz. those originally issued, later changed at the demand made by John of Ragusa to John VIII) . . . 'on condition that they never consent to submit to the Latin defilement and their lawless and ridiculous ways, and, as regards the Creed, neither to concede in any way the innovation nor to accept it. It is quite clear from this that the voice of not one of the patriarchs was heard there, without whom how is it oecumenical?' Therefore, there was 'the outward

[3] LAMBROS, I, p. 187.

rather than the oecumenical form, and a shadow and image was produced rather than the real'.[4] And that is all: he refers to no condemnation. When, shortly after (p. 214), he reached the phrase, 'and of the procurators of our venerable brethren the patriarchs', he was morally bound to report their rejection of the council, had he known of one. Instead he indulges in a diatribe about extravagance of living and of dress and brings in the episode about Eugenius wanting the Patriarch Joseph to kiss his foot. There is no hint that the patriarchs took any action afterwards. Similarly, he reports that the metropolitans on their return to Constantinople repented of their signature, but says nothing of the patriarchs having repudiated the signatures of their procurators.

The necessary conclusion seems to be that John Eugenicus had no knowledge of the so-called condemnation of 1443, and that the apparent reference to it in his Doxology must have another context, either the old condemnation of Beccus of 1285 or some other event in John's lifetime of which we are today ignorant.

If none of the writers against the union of Florence knew of its condemnation by the three patriarchs, it is not unfair to conclude that no such condemnation ever existed. They, the champions of the orthodoxy that Arsenius was supposedly being authorised to defend, would have been the first to be informed of such a condemnation, because they were the protagonists of the same form of orthodoxy, because it would have confirmed them in their opposition to the union and because it would have put a powerful weapon into their hands. That they were not informed means that there was nothing to inform them about, and that the document now purporting to be the condemnation of the Council of Florence by the patriarchs in 1443 is spurious.

It is difficult to say when the document was composed and by whom. It is to be found in many manuscripts of uncertain date, but, as far as I know, its first dated appearance was in the *De Ecclesiae occidentalis atque orientalis perpetua consensione* published by L. Allatius in 1648. It was Allatius who, by printing them in this same *De Ecclesiae, etc.*, gave a wide circulation to the 'Acts of the Council of Constantinople of 1450', which were certainly a forgery perpetrated by George Coresios of Chios. He mentioned also receiving, together with the 'Acts', a copy of the 'Letter of

[4] Dositheus of Jerusalem, *Tomos Katallages* (Jassy, 1692–4), pp. 209–210.

Amiroutzes', which was also a forgery and probably from the same pen. It is possible that the spurious 'Condemnation of 1443', even though Allatius does not connect it with Chios as he does the other two documents, had the same origin and was no more than another weapon forged by the Chiote, George Coresios, for his defence of Orthodoxy.

CHAPTER SEVENTEEN

THE YEAR OF THE DEATH OF MARK EUGENICUS

The day and the month of Mark's death, 23 June, are attested by John Eugenicus in the 'life'—synaxarion—that he wrote as part of the liturgical office—acolouthia—of his dead brother.[1] John, however, did not give the year, but contented himself with stating Mark's age: he was in his fifty-second year, i.e. he was fifty-one, when he died. The late Mgr. Petit, whose opinion is now generally accepted, fixed the year as 1444. He had only one real proof for this assertion, but that very solid. It is this. The Paris codex Coislin gr. 101 contains a treatise-letter composed by Scholarius for John Basilicus, in which the author refers to two books of his about the Holy Spirit written against the Latins.[2] Scholarius, however, did not begin to write against the Latins till after Mark's death. But the copy of the treatise in Coislin gr. 101, in the hand of Syropoulus, is signed and dated: 'in the year 6953, in the month of August, during the eighth indiction', i.e. August 1445. From this Mgr. Petit concluded that, as between Mark's death and, at the most, the end of August two long treatises on the Holy Spirit had issued from Scholarius' pen as well as the short one addressed to John Basilicus, which Syropoulus had then needed time to copy, Mark could not have died on 23 June 1445— two months would not have been nearly enough—but he must have died not later than 23 June 1444.[3] On the data the reasoning is sound and does not admit of rebuttal. All the same, there are

---

[1] There are two versions of the 'life', the one published by S. Pétridès, *Le synaxaire de Marc d'Éphèse*, in *Revue d'Orient Chrétien* 15 (1910), pp. 97–107, the other by L. Petit, *Acolouthie de Marc Eugénicos archevêque d'Éphèse*, in *Studi bizantini e neoellenici* 2 (1927), pp. 195–235. There is no contradiction between them. The second seems to be taken from the first and differs chiefly by the omission of a few sentences. A translation of the 'life' is given on pp. 21–2 above.

[2] 'It is not hard to solve and control, seeing that it has been sufficiently developed by us in the two books'; SCHOL., III, p. 210. The same treatise also speaks of 'the late blessed Ephesius'; p. 212.

[3] PETIT, *Docs.*, p. 322 seq.; L. PETIT, in *Dict. Théol. Cath.* IX c. 1970 seq. s.v. Marc Eugénicos.

The year 1445 was favoured by G. MERCATI, *Appunti scolariani*, in *Bessarione* 36 (1920), pp. 134–43; and in *Scritti d'Isidoro il cardinale Ruteno* (=Studie Testi 46) (Rome, 1926), pp. 122–6.

so many indications that point to a different year that the question
cannot yet be said to be closed.

i. The 'life' that furnishes the day and the month of Mark's
death contains also other chronological details. Mark was in his
fifty-second year when he died. 'Already in the course of the
twenty-sixth year of his age' (*Acolouthie*, p. 214), 'he had left
behind the twenty-fifth year of his age' (*Synaxaire*, p. 101), when
he went off to the island of Antigoni to be a monk. But 'before a
second year had run its course, the foolish instability of the policy
of that time was already throwing the commonweal into confusion,
and the new Arab beast, by now the only satrap left of the Ishmaelites, girt the great city round with an immense host. The
danger for those in the islands was manifest. The marvellous one
returned . . .' (*Acolouthie*, p. 214; *Synaxaire*, pp. 101–02). The
year of Mark's return to Constantinople would, therefore, seem
to have been 1422. Mahomet I died in the spring of 1421. The
Byzantines aided Mustafa to hegemony over the Turkish possessions in Europe by taking Gallipoli in September 1421. Mustafa
crossed to Asia in January 1422 where he was defeated. Murad
came to Adrianople and, to revenge himself on the Greeks,
besieged Constantinople from 8–10 June to 6 September 1422.
The events, therefore, that caused Mark to abandon Antigoni and
return to Constantinople date, at the earliest, after Mahomet's
death and, at the most reasonable (since the death of Mustafa
and the siege are specifically noted), in the months before June
1422. With 1422 as a basis of calculation, Mark survived this
incident 51 minus 26/27 (according as he had one or two birthdays
in Antigoni), i.e. 25 or 24 years, which would make the year of his
death 1447 or 1446, or, if his birthday fell between the day of his
departure from Antigoni and 23 June, even 1445.

ii. George Scholarius added a note at the beginning of a copy
of his first treatise about the Holy Spirit against the Latins: 'This
was composed after fifteen discussions held in the palace with the
papal envoy, the Bishop of Cortona, . . . in the presence of Domnus
Gregory the Patriarch, of the Cardinal, and of many Latins and
Orthodox, before the Emperor John and the Despot Theodore.
. . .'[4] Scholarius did not take the lead in anti-unionist activities till
after Eugenicus' death,[5] and Sphrantzes affirms that Gregory

---

[4] SCHOL., II, p. 1–2.
[5] PETIT, *Docs.*, no. XXIII, p. 486 seq.

became Patriarch in 1445. The year, however, 1445 for Gregory's accession does not fit in with the theory that Mark died in 1444, which rests on the supposition that the discussions, at which Gregory was present as Patriarch, took place in the autumn of 1444. Only so could Scholarius have been able to write his first treatise in late 1444 or early 1445. Mgr. Petit, therefore, held that Sphrantzes was mistaken in putting Gregory's accession in 1445, but that his mistake is easily explained. He had let his narrative of the events of 1444 run on to the battle of Varna (10 November 1444), i.e. into the new Byzantine year of 1445 which began on 1 September of (our) 1444. When, then, he proceeded: 'In July of the same year . . .', he ought to have noted that he was going back in his account to the preceding Byzantine year, but that he forgot to do.

Sphrantzes may have made a mistake: it would not be the only time. But his mistake here, if indeed it is a mistake, is not to be explained away. The description of the campaign that ended at Varna is not to be found in the *Chronicon minus*. It cannot, then, be attributed to Sphrantzes, or made into an explanation of a possible error of his. His sequence of events refers only to the Byzantine year 1445: 'So I reached Euripos, but not finding the ships I managed to arrive as far as Lemnos in another vessel and there, having found a royal ship, I reached Constantinople at the beginning of November 6953 [1444]. On the 17th, then, of June of the same year there was a universal burning heat, worthy of mention. In which summer, indeed, also the Confessor Domnus Gregorius Melissene became Patriarch. And on 15 August there was born to me a son, Andronicus by name, who lived only eight days. And in the year 6954 [1445], in the month of December . . .'[6] Sphrantzes connects Gregory's accession with his own presence in Constantinople and with the birth of his son who, as the father had been away from Constantinople for more than a year before his return in November 1444, could not have been born before summer 1445. If the order in the narrative of the events implies the real chronological order, then according to Sphrantzes Gregory became Patriarch between 17 June and 15 August 1445, and, if he was present at the fifteen discussions as Patriarch, as

---

[6] PHRANTZES, pp. 195, 198. It should be noted that Mgr. Petit offered this explanation of Sphrantzes's 'mistake' before the relation of the *Chronicon maius* to the *Chronicon minus* had been thoroughly investigated.

Scholarius declares, then Scholarius' first treatise could not have been written in late 1444 or early 1445.

iii. Neither could Mark Eugenicus have died before summer 1445, for on his deathbed he made his mind quite clear that he did not wish, on any account, that the Patriarch should be represented at his funeral, and the Patriarch was to be warned of this betimes.[7] So there was a patriarch, who was Gregory, the first successor of Metrophanes who died on 1 August 1443.

iv. Scholarius' first treatise was composed after fifteen discussions with Lapacci, in the presence of the Cardinal Francesco Condulmaro. How long fifteen discussions would have taken is uncertain, but at the least a week and most probably not less than a month. Condulmaro left Venice on 22 June 1444, and Methone on 20 July. Jehan de Waurin, the Burgundian admiral who left Venice at the end of July, found the papal fleet at Gallipoli, and he and Condulmaro, each with two galleys, went together to Constantinople. Exactly when they arrived is not known, but probably towards the middle of August. The Cardinal was papal legate, not only to regulate ecclesiastical affairs connected with the union, but primarily to be in charge of the combined fleet for the crusade organized against the Turk both on land and sea. Murad I had left Europe for Asia on 12 July. Ladislas on 4 August announced a new anti-Turkish campaign to begin on 1 September. The task of the fleet was to patrol the Dardanelles and the Bosphorus to prevent Murad's return to Europe. The land forces were late starting. They crossed the Danube only on 22 September. Murad, in alarm, was at the straits towards the second half of October. Checked at the Dardanelles, he managed to cross the Bosphorus and met and defeated the Christians at Varna on 10 November 1444.

It is most unlikely that, in the period immediately preceding the campaign and especially during it, the Cardinal would have had either the strength of mind or the leisure to detach himself from these absorbing cares on which the future, certainly of Constantinople, probably of Europe, rested to take an academic interest in fifteen theological discussions. And if he could have done so, it is incredible to think that John VIII and his brother Theodore could, for they, having lived under the Turkish threat at close quarters all their lives, hung upon this campaign for their

[7] PETIT, *Docs.*, p. 485 (347).

Q

salvation. Yet Scholarius, in the same note, asserts that they were present. After Varna, all was uncertainty. King Ladislas and Cardinal Cesarini were missing. Rumour said they were still alive. The fleet spent much of the winter looking for them. Condulmaro, doubtless, stayed in Constantinople, but neither he nor the Emperor John were likely to be theologically minded for some time.

Syropoulus, in the list of seven factors that favoured opposition to union and that in date range from 1439 to 1444/45, added a little information about Condulmaro's arrival in Constantinople that makes even more remote the likelihood of his having assisted at fifteen discussions in the late summer of 1444. He says that the unionists in Constantinople were so elated at the news of the arrival of the Pope's nephew that the anti-unionists were afraid: 'But the demand that the legate made that, when he went on horseback to the palace, he should dismount only where the Emperor was accustomed to do so, and the Emperor's resistance to this, which were the reason why so much time passed before the legate went to the Emperor, lessened the impact of the legate and the confidence of the proponents of union and made ours more resolute in their resistance. After this, having come to discussion, those who were zealous for union could not uphold it as they hoped'.[8]

If the fifteen discussions, owing to the friction over protocol and anxiety for the success of the expedition, were not held in late summer and before Varna, and not immediately after Varna, they probably took place in 1445, when a little peace of soul had returned to both Greeks and Latins after the shattering of their hopes in the crusade. Condulmaro departed for Italy with the fleet only towards the end of 1445, reaching Venice on 10 January 1446. Lapacci was still in Constantinople on 26 October 1446.

v. Whatever was the date of the discussions, it was not before 23 June 1444, for Cardinal Condulmaro was still in Venice on 22 June 1444. Yet St. Antoninus, states that Bartholomew of Florence, O. P. (i.e. Lapacci), Bishop of Cortona, went to Constantinople with the Venetian Cardinal (i.e. Condulmaro) and stayed there a considerable time during which at the order of the Emperor he had a public discussion with Mark of Ephesus, who being discomforted in the argument died a few days later.[9] If Mark died

---

[8] SYR., p. 350.
[9] Quoted by Mercati in *Bessarione*, p. 139 n. 8.

on 23 June 1444 after fourteen days of atrocious pain, he could not have assisted at any of the discussions with Lapacci and so the latter part of St. Antoninus's statement must be wrong.

There are, however, two hints, very obscure and of uncertain reference, that tend to support his statement. John Eugenicus in the 'life' has the following: 'Then [i.e. in Italy] he stood out more conspicuously than any monument and the holy theology of the great man and his learning and the grace of the most holy Spirit that was in him and the whole force of truth, and the rottenness and the insecurity of the Latin beliefs were plainly disclosed, just as recently in his homeland in three conferences. . . .'[10] Scholarius in his eulogium of Mark declared: 'And now, had he survived and were come to strip on our behalf for the contest, seeing that those that occurred over three days (or 'three days ago', or even perhaps 'some little time ago'—πρότριτα) were only a kind of skirmishing and an exhibition of knowledge rather than a trial on behalf of truth. . . .'[11] Chalcocandylas believed that Ephesus and Scholarius were both engaged in the discussions with the Latins: 'But the supreme Pontiff sent some of his doctors to Byzantium to the Greeks, to enter into discussion with Greek doctors who had not acceded to the synod held in Italy, viz. Mark of Ephesus the prelate who from the start had in no way at all attached himself to the dogma of the Latins and Scholarius who at that time was pre-eminent among the Greeks for learning'.[12]

vi. Mgr. Petit, writing of Scholarius' two treatises on the Holy Spirit against the Latins so as to show that their author must needs have begun on them from late 1444 if they, as well as the tractate to Basilicus, were completed and copied before August 1445, dilates on their length: 'imprimés, le premier ne comprendrait pas moins de 250 pages d'un fort in-8⁰, et le second, 180 pages du même format.' When the treatises came to be printed in 1929, several years after Mgr. Petit's lamented death, it was found that his forecast was very close—268 and 179 pages respectively. One would say, therefore, that there could not have been any great interval between the finishing of the two big treatises and the starting on the shorter letter to Basilicus, if all three were

---

[10] *Acolouthie*, p. 214, *Synaxaire*, p. 103, where John used the word 'diálexis', employed also by Scholarios (II, p. 1) and Chalcocandylas (cf. below) to describe this same occasion.

[11] SCHOL., I, p. 250.

[12] CHALCOCANDYLAS, Op. cit., II, p. 69.

the product of less than a year's labour. Yet the mention 'the two books' is casual and seems to take it for granted that the 'books' were well known: 'this point has been sufficiently developed by us in the two books'. What makes it even more unlikely that Basilicus or others would know anything of those two treatises is that Scholarius had done his best to keep them private. In the introduction to the second treatise, the one he composed for the Emperor of Trebizond, he wrote: 'But you, most mighty Emperor, having learnt of the former book, repeatedly asked that it should be sent to you. We, however, conscious that it had been somewhat ambitiously elaborated and that in many points it assailed those who were going contrary to us, gave it out to but few of the citizens of this city.' He had decided, therefore, to compose a simpler and shorter treatise for the Emperor. But even that the Emperor was to keep private and secret: 'Do not let even this book become common property for all and sundry, but let it be a treasure set apart for you, that is opened and shows itself and speaks before you only and then is hidden away again.' The reason for such secrecy was: 'There is much in this composition that must lie hid from those who differ from us [both Latins and Greeks], in case they ever again want to reopen discussion. We have, as you know, a commandment not to put our reputations in another's hands and our advantage in those of strangers, and success lies in doing everything at the appropriate time.'[13]

It would seem therefore that a fair interval must have elapsed after the writing of the first treatise and before Kaloianni of Trebizond heard of it and repeatedly asked for it. Afterwards, if he was in any way obedient to Scholarius' request for secrecy, more time was needed before Scholarius could write of 'the two books' as common property. And that process could hardly have been completed by August 1445.

vii. When Mark Eugenicus died, his brother John was in the Peloponnesus, where he wrote a funeral oration on the deceased. Some time later he returned to Constantinople, from which city he sent copies of his composition to various people. He sent one to the Emperor of Trebizond with two letters, one addressed to David Comnenos the Emperor's brother, the other to George Amiroutzes. The beginning of David's letter is as follows: 'Just as earlier there were not a few reasons that inclined me to silence

[13] SCHOL., II, pp. 270, 271.

—the unrest in our affairs and my living away from my native place and the grief and the double mortal wound, the one, that is, common to all and the other private to me that occurred a little before it; nay, rather, this too a common one, for the beacon, the leader, the father, the champion has departed from our midst to God; so now many are the reasons inviting me to write . . .' Later in the same letter, recommending his oration, he talks of 'having written it then, but we send it now since we have the opportunity'.[14]

His letter to Amiroutzes was written at the same time, because he bids his correspondent read the panegyric he was sending to the Emperor. He repeats much of what was in the letter to David: 'after a double loss and disaster, the one common to all, that is, and before that my own, nay rather, this too in reality common, receive us graciously, though only by word and letter, after my return from the island of Pelops. . . . Receive likewise the funeral oration on the late most blessed father and common leader, which we wrote there after the wound. . . .'[15]

It is not difficult to determine what was the 'mortal wound that was common to all'. It was the Turkish invasion of the Morea and the destruction of the Hexamilion that Constantine had rebuilt not long before. In several letters John explains the reason for his having abandoned the Peloponnesus and returned to Constantinople—explains and regrets his action. To Gemistus he wrote: 'Would that I had not, in my panic at the common grief and misfortune of Christians and my despair of the future security of life in those parts, would that I had not been torn away from the delights in the island, not least among them the sight and company of you, and run back to my native place, on the excuse of putting my private affairs in order.'[16] The Turkish expedition was to punish Constantine for his sallies into northern Greece in 1444/45 in support of the crusade that ended so tragically at Varna, and to prevent any future danger from the same quarter. The Turkish force attacked in spring 1446 and took Corinth on 4 December of the same year, a year's campaign that gave them, so it is said, 60,000 prisoners. No wonder John Eugenicus was afraid. His departure from the Morea can be set some time in 1446, perhaps half way through the year.

---

[14] LAMBROS, I, pp. 155–6.   [15] Ibid., pp. 156–7.
[16] Ibid., p. 154; cf. also his letters to Scholarius and to Serapion, ibid., pp. 159, 162, etc.

What interval between Mark's death and the 'common wound' are we to allot to justify the phrase, 'a little before'? John must have set about writing his panegyric soon after he got news of Mark's death. He did not write it solely for his own sake; he obviously meant from the start to send it to a circle of notables and friends. He found time for that only at Constantinople. Is it more likely, when all these considerations are weighed, that eleven months passed between Mark's death and John's departure, or a year and eleven months? That is, does the information gathered from these letters indicate 1444 or 1445 as the more likely year of Mark's death? To me, 1445 is far the more probable.

CONCLUSION. The seven considerations outlined above all lead to the same conclusion, that Mark Eugenicus did not die in 1444. That date is incompatible with the chronological information contained in John Eugenicus' 'life' and with the statement of St Antoninus, and, accepting Scholarius' assertion that the discussions were held in the presence of the Patriarch Gregory, it is contradicted by Sphrantzes. It is, too, hard to harmonize with what we know of Condulmaro's mission; it would make Scholarius' two very long treatises—kept secret, yet generally known—a very prodigy of industry; it fits in with what John Eugenicus says about his funeral oration less well. And so it has, I think, to be abandoned in favour of 1445.

There remains, however, the evidence on which Mgr. Petit based his opinion, the 'two books' and the 'late blessed Mark' in a treatise finished by Syropoulus in August 1445. The simplest answer is to say, *tout court*, that Syropoulus made a mistake in the year. It is not a desirable solution to the difficulty, but it is not an impossible one. Rather one would prefer to deny that the 'two books' of the letter to Basilicus are identical with the two long treatises that Scholarius wrote 'after fifteen discussions', if Scholarius himself in the introduction to the first of those treatises had not implied that that was his first writing against the union.[17] But that is an implication, not a statement, and the introduction can be read intelligibly, even if less easily, without accepting it. Or it could be supposed that, in the course of the conferences, Scholarius dashed off a couple of *aide-mémoires*, schemes from which to speak and on which perhaps he later wrote his treatise, which, when he came to write the introduction, he had forgotten

[17] SCHOL., II, p. 5.

about or considered too slight to be worth mentioning. Or it is not impossible that he began his first treatise during the conferences, and so could suggest that it was his first writing against union, and then, finding that composition on that scale was too slow for the pace of the conferences, he sketched out two schemes for both present and later use. If, then, the difficulty of the 'two books' is got out of the way after this or some other fashion, the reference to Mark's death becomes just a plain indication of fact. He died on 23 June 1445; the copy of the letter to Basilicus at any rate, even if not the original, was made in August 1445.

Whichever date one adopts, 1444 or 1445, there are difficulties. For 1444, an answer has to be found for each of the seven considerations outlined above. For 1445, one has to hold that Syropoulus mistook his year (and that is my own preference), or devise some explanation of the 'two books'.

The order of events, therefore, was probably this. Manuel Eugenicus was born about half-way through the year 1394. He studied under his father till 1406, when at the age of twelve he was left an orphan. In mid-1420, perhaps in May, he was 25 years old and, free now from any further legal tutelage, went to Antigoni to follow his vocation as a monk, taking the name of Mark. Some time before the start of the siege of Constantinople on 8–10 June 1422, troop movements were so threatening that not later than the end of April he returned to the capital. He became Metropolitan of Ephesus, went to Italy and returned, fled from Constantinople on 15 May 1440 to his see, but after some time, while going to Mt. Athos, was kept in confinement on Lemnos for two full years. Released at length he reached Constantinople. Soon the papal crusade was in motion. The fleet with Condulmaro and Lapacci arrived at Constantinople somewhere in mid-August 1444. The delay over etiquette and the business of war precluded theological discussion before Varna, and distress at the defeat and anxiety about Ladislas and Cesarini put it out of the question for some time after. The disaster to the papal force heartened the anti-unionists who prevailed on John VIII to sanction the conferences. These took place in early summer 1445 after Gregory's election as Patriarch (exact month unknown). Mark Eugenicus was there at the start; his mortal illness developed; he persuaded Scholarius to take the lead in his place; his sickness increased; he endured atrocious agony for a fortnight and died on 23 June 1445.

Meanwhile Scholarius, having perhaps sketched out 'two books', wrote the treatise-like letter to Basilicus, spoke in the discussions that lasted for weeks and, finally, at his leisure composed the two big treatises.

CHAPTER EIGHTEEN

GREEKS AND LATINS IN A COMMON COUNCIL

THE COUNCIL OF FLORENCE (1438–9)

The arrival of the Greeks in Italy in February 1438 was the culmination of a long series of negotiations. The possibility of a council of union, held in common, had been mooted often in the previous century. In the thirty years or so before Florence, it had several times been on the point of realisation. Manuel II of Constantinople, at the invitation of Sigismund, King of the Romans, had sent representatives to the Council of Constance, who in an optimistic mood discussed union with the new Pope Martin V, elected on 11 November 1417. Martin was so impressed that he appointed the Cardinal of S. Sisto as legate to Greece, who however died on 10 June 1419 while still in Bohemia. An embassy from the Byzantine court in 1420 confirmed the Pope in his belief that the Greeks were ready for union. He appointed therefore another legation to go to Constantinople in the person of Cardinal Fonseca and he raised money for the project by demanding 6,000 florins from each of Cologne, Mainz and Trier and 4,000 from Liége. But Fonseca did not reach Constantinople either, because meantime the Turkish Sultan had laid siege to it. The Pope, however, was so set on bringing the work of union of the Churches to a conclusion that, nothing daunted, he sent an Apostolic Nuncio, Antonio da Massa O. F. M., to learn accurately what was the mind of the Patriarch and the Emperor on the question and to set the wheels in motion towards the encounter in Constantinople of the Latins and the Greeks. The message he got back showed that the Greeks were not as ripe as he had thought for the type of union that he was contemplating, for they demanded open discussion of all the old problems and a decision, under the guidance of the Holy Spirit, based on those discussions. There was no knowing what would be the issue of a council composed of few Latins and many Greeks meeting on Greek territory. Martin's efforts, therefore, slackened, but not his enthusiasm. He met every overture readily and finally persuaded the Greeks to consent to a council of union in Italy. Greek envoys were on their way to Rome with the agreement embodying that consent already signed in Constantinople, when at Gallipoli they heard of the Pope's death.[1]

Martin's long-continued readiness to hold the council of union in Constantinople was due to his optimism about the results. The Latins thought and spoke of the ending of the schism as the *reductio Graecorum*, the 'bringing back' of the schismatical Greeks to the true Church. Sigismund, writing to Manuel II of Constantinople to invite his adherence to the Council of Constance, hoped to see the Oriental Churches 'reunited, joined to the sacrosanct Roman Church as a daughter to a mother and as members to the head'.[2] On 1 February 1418 a letter from Constance to the University of Vienna was sanguine about the 'hoped-for reduction of the Greeks'.[3]

It was natural for the Latins to think in that way for, of course, they had always blamed the Greeks for the schism and held that the Latin Church was orthodox, the Greek schismatical. At Constance their optimism about the 'reduction' of the Greeks came from the fact that now the Greeks also seemed to accept that version of history. A letter from Constance to the University of Cologne of 25 March 1416 mentioned: 'Lately there have come ambassadors from Constantinople . . . promising . . . that the Greeks themselves will conform to the Roman Church in their rite and articles of faith'.[4] Martin V, through Antonio da Massa, said outright to Manuel II and John VIII of Constantinople that the two Byzantine envoys who had visited him early in 1420 had 'proposed and said openly . . . that it was the will of the most venerable Patriarch of Constantinople and of the most serene Byzantine Emperors to procure and arrange without fraud or guile the most holy union of the Greek with the Latin Church under that faith which the holy Roman Church holds and under obedience to the same Roman Church'.[5] Consequently, the regular

---

[1] For further information and ampler references cf. J. GILL, *The Council of Florence* (Cambridge, 1959).

[2] H. FINKE, *Acta Concilii Constanciensis* I (Münster, 1896), p. 397.

[3] Quoted by R.-J. LOENERTZ, *Les dominicains byzantins Théodore et André Chrysobergès et les négociations pour l'union des Églises grecque et latine de 1415–1430*, in *Archivum Fratrum Praedicatorum* IX (1939), p. 20.

[4] E. MARTÈNE et U. DURAND, *Thesaurus novus anecdotorum*, etc. (Paris, 1717) II, 1661.

[5] RAYNALDUS, ad annum 1422, IX.

Greek demand for a general council as essential for the establishment of union was regarded as only a face-saving device to cover their submission. Such were the views certainly of Martin V till 1422 when John VIII's reply through Antonio da Massa disillusioned him. But John's answer was forthright. Thereafter the Pope knew that union meant open and free discussion of all points of difference. He did not, however, cease to work for union, but he was now not going to hazard a debate except in conditions when the Latin Church could be fully represented— no longer in Constantinople, but in Italy.

The Greeks, it need hardly be said, thought about the Latins in the same way as the Latins thought about them. The Palamite controversy of the fourteenth century, which issued in downright persecution of non-Palamites, whether they became Catholics or not, had embittered feeling against the Western Church. Joseph Bryennius and the brothers Eugenicus regarded the Latin Church not only as schismatical and also as heretical. Even such strong unionists as Isidore of Kiev, Bessarion and Dorotheus of Mitylene, as late as 12 June 1439 when the Greeks had already agreed on the doctrine of the *Filioque*, said about its inclusion in the Creed: 'As regards the addition, we will never accept it, but we allow you to have it in your churches, but not in those of the Eastern Church'.[6] The persistence, however, of Pope Martin, of Eugenius IV and of the Council of Basel in promoting a council of union certainly persuaded the Greeks of the sincerity of the Latin desire, and perhaps made them to some extent think that Latin intransigence had been softened. In any case, at that time the position of the papacy was very much in debate in the Latin Church itself, but the question of the primacy was not the one that the Greeks then regarded as the greatest and most fundamental difference between the Churches. That was the *Filioque*, as doctrine and as an addition to the Creed.

Not less than the Latins, the Greeks also, it would seem, harboured illusions about the tractability of their separated brethren. Syropoulus reports the Patriarch, Joseph II, as saying that if the Pope were older than he (Joseph was an octogenarian), he would regard him as a father; if a contemporary, as a brother; if younger, as a son[7]; and, according to Traversari, the Patriarch thought that once he and the Pope got together the whole business

[6] *A.G.*, p. 446.   [7] Syr., p. 92.

of union would be quickly settled by love and peace rather than by discussion.[8] Others besides the Patriarch were optimistic. George Scholarius in the exordium of the exhortation that he addressed to the Greek synod in mid-April 1439 told them: 'I am well aware that some of you thought that you would prevail against the learning of the Latins and persuade them to abide by the conditions that obtained of old, and I marvel much. . . . Grant it then that all had the same opinion and came in the hope of convicting the Latins of ignorance and error and of persuading them willy-nilly to deny their doctrine and so of achieving union with them'.[9] Under such conditions, with each party thinking itself to have preserved integral Catholic truth and the other to have departed from it, there would be no question of an easy 'reduction' of either the one or the other, but union, if it was to be achieved, would have to be the fruit of keen and even obstinate debate.

For that, Greeks and Latins came together in Italy in 1438. Indeed it was the presence of the Greeks that rendered the Council in Ferrara possible, for Eugenius had transferred the Council of Basel to Italy only when the Fathers had split over the location of the future unionistic council, and if, when both papal and conciliar fleets were at Constantinople in the autumn of 1437, the Greeks had gone aboard the ships of Basel, the Pope's project for a council in Italy would almost certainly have collapsed. The Greeks, then, were not summoned, they were invited, almost wooed, to attend the western council. Moreover, the Emperor claimed on several occasions that his was the right of convoking councils, and that the council of union should have been in Constantinople. He yielded about the site of it because his capital was in constant danger from the Turks, because he had not the money to support a council, and because he wanted to come into contact with the western princes so as to persuade them to help him against his enemies. But he, and his, still retained the conviction that the Emperor of Byzantium called councils.[10]

The Greeks, then, came to Italy convinced that they were doctrinally superior to the Latins and equal as a Church. The Latins welcomed them, conscious to themselves of doctrinal rectitude and ecclesiastical superiority; to their minds the

[8] TRAV., no. 140.   [9] SCHOL., I, p. 296.
[10] RAYNALDUS, ad annum 1422, XV; SYR., p. 6; A.L., p. 244.

'daughter' Church was returning to the 'mother' Church. There was a certain attitude, therefore, of reserve on both sides. So, while the Greeks were still in Venice, some of the Latins took it ill that they hesitated for a short time between Basel and Ferrara, and that neither Emperor nor Patriarch either doffed his hat or rose to meet Cardinal Albergati, the papal legate sent to welcome them, as he entered.[11] They had more reason for misgivings shortly afterwards. When the state-barge carrying the Patriarch was approaching Ferrara, he was informed by a messenger from the Emperor that the Pope expected him to conform to the Latin custom of salutation by kissing the papal foot. Joseph was astonished and grieved, and refused point-blank, asserting that he would return straight to Venice if the Pope insisted. For a full day messengers came and went, but the Patriarch was adamant, and in the end, so as not to render the whole expensive project abortive on a point of etiquette, the Pope yielded. But the solemnity of the reception accorded to the Patriarch was reduced. The Greeks were presented in groups of six, and the Patriarch was not allowed to wear his head-dress or to carry his staff, the signs of his dignity. This incident may seem trivial and even spiteful. That is to misunderstand it. At the first encounter of the Churches, the head of each was upholding the rights of his Church, on the one side the Latin superiority, on the other the Greek equality. Neither yielded on his principle, the one by not kissing the foot, the other by not giving a public reception.

A similar trial of strength arose over the Council hall. The Pope wanted his throne to be central at one end with Latins and Greeks ranged the length of the hall on his right and left. The Greeks would not hear of it. In the end the gospels were placed centrally and the Latins—the Pope, Roman Emperor, cardinals, patriarchs, bishops—had their thrones down the one side, and the Greeks—Emperor, Patriarch, metropolitans—down the other. But the Pope's throne was just a shade in advance of the others and isolated (everything was done by exact measurement), and the Greek Emperor's was exactly equal to and opposite the throne allotted to the Roman Emperor (but the throne was vacant, as Sigismund was dead), and the Patriarch was opposite not a Pope but a cardinal.

[11] TRAV., no. 140.

Most, however, of the combined activities of the Council were arranged without much friction, the Pope more often than not yielding for the sake of peace. In the inaugural session of 9 April 1438 a papal Bull was read in Latin and Greek declaring the Council oecumenical and convened in Ferrara. The announcement was in the Pope's name only, probably owing to an oversight on the part of the Greeks. Before it, there was read, also in both languages, an announcement from the Patriarch, who was absent ill: 'Since by the grace and benevolence of Him who arranges everything for the best, God, a divinely inspired desire fills the minds of the western and the eastern prelates of the Church here present with the common aim, that, after study of the Holy Scriptures and divine oracles by every possible and reasonable means, we may be able to examine the questions proposed in no spirit of strife and contention, but, in the fear of God and coming together in the single will of God, we may be united together with the truth triumphant. . . .' The document went on to say that it was fitting that the Greeks should have come for that purpose, and ends with the Patriarch permitting his subjects, the procurators of the other Eastern patriarchs and the other prelates and ecclesiastics, to take part in the Council.[12] For his part the Emperor had stipulated as a condition of the proclamation of the Council a delay of four months to allow time for the representatives of the western princes to arrive.

To fill in that interval usefully the Latins finally persuaded the Greeks to discuss something, at least by committees. Representatives met to decide what and, as the Greeks refused to allow the introduction of the major differences, the Latins chose to examine the question of Purgatory. When the public sessions were at last begun in October 1438, the Latins gave the honour of making the opening speech to the Greeks, and also left the exact subject to be discussed to their choice. They chose the addition of the *Filioque* to the Creed, and Mark Eugenicus began for the Greeks. The Latins wanted to answer, statement by statement, immediately. Mark claimed the right of exposing his case fully before any reply was made. He insisted, too, on reading the decrees of the early Councils. The Latins declared this to be unnecessary. Two sessions were frittered away in useless bickering. In the end the Pope, supported by Cesarini, but in spite of

12 *A.L.*, pp. 30–1.

much feeling on the Latin side, let the Greeks have their way. Mark deployed his arguments in full, and read and commented on the decrees of the Councils.

For the public sessions six orators were appointed from either side. In Ferrara, for the Latins there spoke Andrew of Rhodes O.P., Aloysius of Forlì O.F.M. and Cardinal Cesarini; for the Greeks, Mark Eugenicus in all the sessions but two, when Bessarion was the Greek spokesman. In Florence there was only one speaker on each side, John of Montenero O.P. and Mark Eugenicus. In Florence the Latins opened the debate to the chagrin of the Greeks, who thought that their Emperor had thereby made an unnecessary and undesirable concession, for to their minds they were present rather as judges deciding on the sufficiency of Latin doctrine and as such should have had the precedence.[13]

All the public sessions of Ferrara and of Florence (except for two in June 1439) were concerned with the *Filioque*. Even though the doctrinal truth of the Procession of the Holy Spirit also 'from the Son' had been defined at the second Council of Lyons, no appeal was made to that definition by either side.[14] The discussion in Florence was conducted as if the question were still open, Montenero and Eugenicus proposing and counter-proposing proofs from metaphysics, the Scriptures and the Fathers to support their respective views. That the discussion should have been of such a nature was inevitable once it had become apparent that the Greeks insisted on a genuine, and not a token, general council. First of all Martin V, and then Eugenius IV, were quite aware of the Greek determination. Both Popes nevertheless persisted in their pursuit of union and so accepted the condition on which union might be attained.

There was, then, a general equality in the external position of

---

[13] Syr., p. 215.

[14] Fantinus Vallaresso, Op. cit. calls only those councils oecumenical in which the Greeks took part, for *durante divisione et schismate supradicto non potuit ycumenica synodos congregari, quia orientalis ecclesia non obediebat Romano Pontifici, sine cuius auctoritate huiusmodi concilia secundum sacros canones congregari non possunt* (p. 18). Apropos of the Council of Lyons he wrote: *Et a tempore huius divisionis usque ad hec nostra tempora quibus domino inspirante unio facta est in concilio ycumenico Florentino . . . fluxerunt anni CCCCLXXIIII, licet tempore Gregorii pape decimi et Michaelis Paleologi Constantinopolitani imperatoris unio facta fuisset in concilio Lugdunensi, anno scilicet domini MCCLXXV. Sed quia huiusmodi unio quinque vel sex annis tantummodo perduravit, potest pro nichilo reputari* (p. 17).

the two Churches. There was nothing to suggest that the Greeks were held in less esteem, either as a Church or as individuals. They spoke turn and turn about with the Latins, expounded their arguments and developed their proofs at length. When they said that they would have no more public sessions (March 1439), public sessions ceased till they chose to attend two more, and, as the Ferrara-Florence Council had as its sole purpose the union of the Churches, all conciliar activity also came to a temporary standstill. That they finally accepted, first the doctrine of the *Filioque*, then the other disputed points, was because they were persuaded of their truth. Nobody forced them. Nobody could have forced them. Nobody tried to force them.

There was no hesitation on the Latin side to referring to the Greek ecclesiastical community as a 'Church'. The word is to be found time and again in all sorts of official documents. The convention agreed to between Martin V and the Greek envoys in 1430 lays down: 'Similarly, that they should come from the kingdom and territories subject to the Church of the Greeks'.[15] The decree *Sicut pia mater* of the Council of Basel (accepted also by Eugenius IV) speaks of 'the most fervent desire of the Emperor and the Patriarch and of the whole Oriental Church' and of a universal synod 'where both the Western Church and the Eastern may meet'.[16] Eugenius IV, in the Bull *Doctoris gentium* of 18 September 1437 by which he translated the Council of Basel to Ferrara, spoke of the division of, and the union of, the Eastern and the Western Church,[17] and in the letter he sent to all princes, bishops and universities of the West, summoning them to attend his Council, he gave the purpose of it as 'the union of the Eastern and Western Churches'.

All this time, of course, the Latin idea was still to bring about the 'reduction' of the Greeks. The question of the primacy cropped up from time to time, each of the Latin speakers at Ferrara referring to it in passing, and thereby provoking a sturdy challenge from both Bessarion and Eugenicus. It was discussed only in the last months in Florence and was the last of all the points of difference to be accepted by the Greeks.

One of the things that, before ever the Council began its dogmatic sessions, caused concern to the Greeks in Ferrara was the

[15] *E.P.*, doc. 26.   [16] *M.C.*, II, p. 753.
[17] *E.P.*, doc. 88.

method of voting to be employed. The Greeks were afraid that, if decisions were arrived at merely by a majority in numbers, they would be outvoted every time. Mark Eugenicus was sent to express their misgivings to the Pope. Having granted that the gathering was oecumenical, he went on to point out a difference between this Council and earlier Councils. In the latter 'all were united and of one mind, and the party that was not so was very small and was judged and condemned by the large number. Here, however, those congregated and judging in this Council are themselves the ones with the difference in comparison with those earlier oecumenical Councils. So neither the procedure of this Council nor its conclusions should be like their procedure, but there should be a suitable variation, for, as you are numerous and on your own territory, whereas we are few, you must know what we say and we know what you want'.[18] The Greeks on several occasions urged that this point should be settled betimes, proposing that conclusions should depend not on mere numbers of votes but that the two sides, as such, should be equal, so that 'the votes of our twenty should have as much weight as the two hundred of theirs'.[19] The Emperor and the Patriarch undertook to discuss the difficulty with the Pope and did, in fact, do so. But what arrangement, if any, was arrived at there is no knowing. When the Oriental prelates demanded to be told the result of the conversations, the Emperor and the Patriarch did no more than repeat, 'We have done very well', and vouchsafed no further details to satisfy their (and our) legitimate curiosity.

In point of fact, as far as we know, there never was a counting of heads throughout the history of the Council. Concord with the Greeks was arrived at in another way. The public sessions produced no unity. In the course of negotiations afterwards the Latins presented the Greeks with *cedulae*, i.e. accurate doctrinal statements, on the Procession, Purgatory, the Eucharist, the primacy. The Greeks considered these among themselves, met the Latins either in informal conversations or in committees to discuss differences and difficulties, and finally accepted, as a Church, the Latin statement with in some cases minor modifications. The decree of union promulgated on 6 July 1439 in the Duomo of Florence was nothing more than those statements put

---

[18] SYR., pp. 148–9.   [19] Ibid., p. 154.

R

together and rephrased as a decree, with the addition of an introduction and a conclusion. In the event, therefore, whether that
was the arrangement that the Pope had arrived at with the Emperor
and the Patriarch or not, the agreement was between the two
Churches as such, and 'the votes of our twenty did have as much
weight as those of their two hundred'. If the majority of the Greeks
had refused agreement, it is quite certain that there would have
been no union.

Thanks to the *Description* that the copyist, John Plousiadenus,
combined with the Greek Acts in his two manuscripts on the
Council of Florence and thanks, though in a lesser degree, to the
Memoirs of Syropoulus, we know a fair amount of detail on how
the Greeks came to agree that there was no essential difference
between their doctrine and that of the Latins. Unfortunately
we know practically nothing of events on the Latin side. The
Latin Acts are lost and, though many a Latin participant must
have written an account or a copious diary about the Council,
none is known to have been preserved. So what went on behind
the Latin scenes is wrapped in mystery. Whether there were
many meetings of the Latins alone, and whether in them there
was formal voting is not known. It is, however, certain that the
machinery for such voting was set up, and because the Council of
Florence was different somewhat in composition and purpose
from those of Constance and Basel, the arrangements for deliberation and decision were also different.

At Constance the questions as to who should vote and how
were fiercely debated. Objection was raised against only bishops
and mitred abbots having a deliberative vote, and it was claimed
that representatives of bishops and abbots and of chapters and
universities, and that masters of theology and doctors as well as
the princes and their representatives, should enjoy a like vote, and
this was accepted. The members of the Council were divided into
four (later, five) 'nations'. From each 'nation' a certain number,
clerics and laymen, was selected as the acting committee. Those
committees met separately and considered the questions submitted
to the Council, communicating to each other their views. When
there was a general atmosphere of agreement, the solution was
proposed at a general meeting of all the 'nations' and, if approved
there, was submitted to, and approved *conciliariter* at, the next
session of the Council. In such a procedure, bishops, abbots,

masters, doctors, princes and lay representatives would seem to have had the same standing in the deliberations of the Council.

The Fathers of Basel adopted another method. All the members of the Council, no matter their rank, whether prelates, abbots, doctors, monks (about 500 in 1433, amongst whom, by 5 February 1434, there were 105 'mitres', i.e. bishops or mitred abbots), were divided into four 'deputations', three of them to treat of faith, heresy and peace respectively, the fourth being the 'general deputation'. The four 'nations' (the English did not form a separate 'nation' at Basel) were divided equally between the deputations. All members had an equal vote. Measures were discussed first in the appropriate deputation, and conclusions were reviewed by a special committee of twelve, three from each deputation. If all four deputations, or at least three, agreed on any matter, that matter went before the full Council, when, of course, though objections could still be raised, its acceptance was practically a foregone conclusion. The number of 'non-mitres' at Basel always greatly outnumbered the 'mitres', which gave some justification for Traversari's jibe that the 'voice of a cook has as much value as that of a bishop or archbishop', and Eugenius' complaint to the princes that, whereas at Constance *extitit permissum ut procederetur per nationes*, in Basel the meanest cleric in the deputations could withstand and prevail by his impudence over cardinal or bishop, and so the prelates retired from the Council till barely twenty-five were left, leaving the field to the fanatics.[20] For example, on the question of the site of the unionist council with the Greeks, 353 voted on 5 December, 1436, viz. 3 cardinals, 2 patriarchs, 2 archbishops, 16 bishops, 1 protonotary and 28 abbots; the other 301 who voted were non-mitred.

When the Council met in Ferrara, the method of voting was fixed for the Latins before the Greeks came. This is how Andrea da Santa Croce described it: 'In the beginning when the Council was gathered in Ferrara and the Fathers were discussing whether the settlement of business should be by means of 'nations' or 'deputations', it was agreed, since the matters under debate would never be brought to a conclusion if all were present together, that the Council should meet in three Estates, i.e. Cardinals, archbishops and bishops; abbots and other Regulars; and clerics who were doctors or who held dignities in cathedral churches, graduates

---

[20] RAYNALDUS, ad annum 1436, VIII.

also in theology, and in canon and civil law. It was also determined that the will of any Estate should be said to be ascertained
if two-thirds of it were in agreement, and nothing was to be
considered conciliar unless it had the assent of each Estate'.[21] It
is to be presumed that in the course of the Council the Estates met
regularly (the Pope seems to imply that the Estates had approved
each *cedula* separately),[22] but we have knowledge only of three
or four occasions when Eugenius convened all the Latins together
and of an injunction to the different Estates to meet to select,
each of them, four of their number to collaborate with the Greeks
in formulating the final decree of union. Indeed it is apropos
of that injunction that Santa Croce happily recorded the division
into Estates as described in the above quotation. The Estates,
it is true, were composed of clerics according to rank. The authority and powers, nevertheless, of the Estates would seem to have
been equal, despite the difference of rank, so that theologians and
cathedral dignitaries would seem to have had the same vote—no
more, no less—as cardinals, archbishops or bishops.

The decree of union was drawn up in the Pope's name. It
was read to the full Latin assembly on 4 July, when Eugenius said:
'This decree, seeing that it is composed of the *cedulae*, has been
approved already by the unanimous vote of all, and so is *ipso iure*
approved'.   But the first draft of it roused opposition in the
Emperor, for it made no reference to him or the Eastern Church.
It was pointed out to him that the Bull inaugurating the combined
Council on 9 April of the previous year had opened in the same
way, but John would not yield till there was added 'with the
agreement of our most dear son, John Palaeologus, illustrious
Emperor of the Greeks, and of the procurators of our venerable
brethren the patriarchs and of the others who represent the
Oriental Church'. The substance of the decree is to declare the
identity of the Latin and Greek faiths in the Blessed Trinity,
Purgatory, the Eucharist, and the authority of the Pope in the
Church. The faiths, therefore, of the two Churches were the
same; the rites were of equal standing, dignity and validity.

The decree is signed for the Latins by the Pope: *Ego Eugenius
catholice ecclesie episcopus ita diffiniens subscripsi*, 8 cardinals, 2

---

[21] *A.L.*, pp. 256–7. The passage continues: *Sicque, ut concludi conciliariter
potuisset, necesse fuerat ut constituta forma auctoritatem preberet.*
[22] Ibid., p. 257.

patriarchs, 2 bishops representatives of Burgundy, 8 archbishops, 50 other bishops, the Archdeacon of Troyes as envoy of Burgundy, 4 heads of Religious Orders, and 41 abbots. For the Greeks the decree bears the signatures of the Emperor, 4 procurators of the eastern patriarchs (one of whom was a simple monk), 15 other metropolitans (3 also as procurators of other bishops), the Russian bishop, 5 Staurophoroi—deacons, officials of the church of St. Sophia and a kind of curia of the Patriarch—and 7 heads or representatives of monasteries.

As far, then, as one can judge from history, the Greeks that came to Italy in 1438 had no sense of inferiority as a Church, no feeling of guilt that they had departed from traditional doctrine, no confession of schism. Indeed, it was the other way round. They came rather to act as judges, convinced that the Latins were at least schismatics, if not heretics, in so far as the *Filioque* seemed to be an illegitimate addition to the Creed and a doctrinal error. What is more, they departed home again with much the same convictions, by which I mean to say that, when they admitted the orthodoxy of Latin doctrine on the Trinity, the Eucharist, Purgatory and the primacy, and signed the decree of union to testify to that admission, they were not thereby confessing that their Church had ever been doctrinally in error, they were only asserting that now they had come to accept that the faith of the Latin Church was the same as their traditional faith (which they had not realised before), and so they could unite.[23] They were still, in their own minds, the standard of orthodoxy. Some words of the Patriarch illustrate this. He did not live to see agreement over anything but the Procession of the Holy Ghost, but about that, a few days before his unexpected death, he made the following public statement in a Greek synod: 'Never will I change or vary the doctrine handed down from our fathers, but will abide in it till my last breath. But since the Latins [rely on Scripture] . . . I both unite with them and am in communion with them'.[24]

---

[23] 'And so all [the Greeks], with the lord Patriarch of happy memory while he was still living and the whole synod, with the approval also of the Emperor for the step, received the Latins into our communion and union, preserving intact and inviolate our customs in the celebration of Mass and in the sacred rites, the Creed and in other ecclesiastical customs; in the same way, they too preserve their customs, for we found that they were reasonable'—letter of the monk Gregory, procurator of the See of Alexandria, to the Patriarch of Alexandria (HOFMANN, *Doc. Minora* (Rome, 1953), p. 44), quoted also in *M.C.* III, p. 1174.

[24] *A.G.*, p. 438.

This conclusion may seem to be contradicted by the fact that the decree of union declares the pope to be *doctorem omnium Christianorum*, and to have the power *pascendi universalem ecclesiam*, which means, in fact, that it is he who is the standard of orthodoxy. There are, however, several points worth noting in this regard. (1) Concord was reached on the Procession of the Holy Spirit on 8 June 1439. By 27 June the other three points, as well as a compromise over the *Filioque* as an addition, had been discussed in public and in private and agreed upon. The process was rapid and could not have been very thorough. (2) In the *cedula* on the primacy, and in the decree itself, far more stress is put upon the primacy of jurisdiction. The Pope has the primacy, is successor of St. Peter, Vicar of Christ, head of the Church, father and doctor of all Christians, has the power of pasturing (convening, also, in the *cedula* but not in the decree), ruling and governing the universal Church. The element of teaching is rather overshadowed in the text by that of governing. (3) The arguments put forward by Montenero mention the usual scriptural texts that are the foundation of the Petrine claims, but the main burden of proof was drawn from the Councils principally and then the Fathers, examples, that is, of papal directives to councils and of popes acting outside of the 'Western Patriarchate'.[25] (4) In the discussions, as far as our meagre sources disclose them, there was the same tendency. The objections put forward by the Greeks were about the Emperor's power of convening councils, the undesirability of summoning patriarchs to Rome to answer charges, the area, whether patriarchal or complete, of papal authority and such like, and the Latin answers stressed the jurisdictional rather than the magisterial aspect of the papal prerogative.[26] In other words, it would seem that the Greeks were concerned rather with the relation of Rome to the other patriarchates than with the position of the pope as such. The controversy about the place of the pope in the Church was, at that time, an acute problem, but it was a Latin problem. For the Greeks 'Pope' meant 'Rome'. Was Rome one of five equals jurisdictionally, or was it, as the seat of St. Peter whose successors were the popes, a court of appeal for the whole Church? They had come to Italy believers in the theory of equality. That Rome, by itself and without even consultation with the rest of the Church, let alone discussion in a general Council, had

[25] *A.L.*, pp. 231–6.   [26] Ibid., pp. 241–7.

added to the Creed was one of their main grievances in respect of the *Filioque*. They went away, having acknowledged, on the basis of their own Church history (which in this respect was also Latin Church history), that Rome, as the See of Peter and his successors, held a primacy in the universal Church and was a court of universal appeal.

The Latins, at least in theory, regarded the Greeks as both schismatics and heretics. Gerson in his sermon before Pope Alexander (19 June 1409) said: 'How large a part [of the human race] are the Greeks, and them evil times have torn away from the See of Peter and sullied with the stain not only of schism but also of a certain degree of heresy'.[27] Opinion on this point had, of course, not changed by the time of the Council of Florence. It showed itself, however, but little; but it was there. It accounted for the readiness of some Latins to condemn the lack of deference of the Greek Emperor and Patriarch to the papal legate in Venice. It accounted for the various ways in which the Latins tried to assert the superiority of their Church. It accounted for the determination of the Latins in the first public sessions of Ferrara to impose their ideas of procedure on the Greeks and the dissatisfaction felt by some of them (including Andrea da Santa Croce, the writer of the 'Latin Acts'), when the Pope let the Greeks have their own way. It accounted perhaps for why the Metropolitan of Sardis was buried outside the church of S. Giuliano when he died in Ferrara in April 1438, whereas on 11 June 1439 the Patriarch was buried inside the church of S. Maria Novella. Andrea da Santa Croce wrote about this: 'So many and such were the signs of his complete return that the Supreme Pontiff . . . decreed that he had been admitted to the communion of the Church. With a great cortège of prelates and all the most reverend cardinals assisting . . . he was laid to rest in the church of S. Maria Novella'.[28] It explains doubtless, also, why the Latins persistently tried to have their *cedulae* accepted without change, though an added reason here would have been that the Latin *cedulae* were far superior to anything the Greeks produced as precise theological statements.

Yet, in spite of all this, the Latins undoubtedly regarded the Greek Church as a Church. They spoke and wrote of it as such

---

[27] JOANNIS GERSONII *opera omnia*, ed. Lud. Ellies du PIN (Antwerp, 1706), II 134D–135A.

[28] *A.L.*, p. 225.

in official and unofficial documents, and clearly that was how they thought about it. The Council was convened as a result of previous negotiations carried on as between equals. In Italy there was nothing in the external arrangements to discriminate between the two Churches. In other words, theory and practice were not altogether harmonious. Various factors had led to this anomaly, which are well illustrated in the writings of John Gerson, Chancellor (and often spokesman) of the University of Paris.

By the time that Gerson was writing the Western Church had become accustomed to schism, but not, assuredly not, reconciled to it. For thirty years or so there had been pope and anti-pope, rival courts, rival curias, rival cardinals, and the most thorough-going division. Pope excommunicated anti-pope and *vice versa*, with all supporters and abettors, and the penalty of excommunication thus multiplied (it had, in any case, even before this been used far too freely and often for unworthy purposes) had lost much of its terror. With the rivals for the papal throne both unable and unwilling to put a stop to schism, men looked for a higher authority which might impose peace and unity, and found that authority in the Church, which, at least in emergencies of this type, was thought to be independent of any pope. The solution would be for both 'obediences'—despite the mutual excommunication—to come together, whether the heads of the 'obediences' liked it or not. 'The Catholic and universal Church extended over the whole world does not consist in actual obedience to either of the two rivals, but in an humble, devout and pious attitude and promptitude of mind to obey it, as having the authority to rule in the place of Christ on earth, which can rightly and canonically be brought together, even if the two rivals either oppose that from malice or ignore it'.[29] Gerson wrote the above to prepare the ground for the Council of Pisa, which met on the initiative of cardinals of both obediences (1409). The Council of Pisa unfortunately did not end the schism (though Gerson for a time thought it had done so), but its failure did nothing to shake the general conviction that peace and unity would come only through a council, as indeed it finally did through the Council of Constance. But if a general council was the cure for the Latin schism, it could be the cure too for the Greek schism especially as the Greeks

---

[29] Z. Rueger, 'Le "De auctoritate concilii" de Gerson', in *Revue d'Histoire Ecclésiastique* LIII (1958), p. 792.

insisted on a council as the only means of achieving union. Gerson in the sermon he addressed to the King of France, entitled *De pace et unione Graecorum*, while he was still sanguine about the effects of the Council of Pisa and in view of the next council decreed to be held within three years, among many other pertinent things said: 'Men of good will ought to work valiantly that the Council which has been decreed should be held within the three years. And because the Greeks can and wish to join in, there is (so it would appear) no more apt arrangement for the peace of which we speak than the said council should be, nor could this business be accomplished in any better way, just as the last Council was necessary for the peace of the Latins'.[30]

In the Council of Pisa (as later in the Council of Constance) the contending Latin parties met as equals and without previous formalities, the various mutual excommunications notwithstanding. The same attitude was extended, or tended to be extended, to the Greeks, for, after all, the Latin Church divided by schism had been no happier a spectacle than the universal Church divided by schism. In his sermon before Alexander V, the antipope of Greek origin, Gerson had called the Greeks both schismatics and heretics, but he straightway went on to say that, though the Latin Church was 'purer and more stainless' because of the promise to St. Peter, still it 'had been sadly stricken by many, long and violent schisms both frequently in days gone by and in our day'.[31] And, even if the Greeks had the stain of 'a certain degree of heresy', there were nevertheless excuses, and judgement on them should be mild. 'If they [the Greeks] allege that they were not sufficiently invited or that they appeal from that decision [i.e. about the Holy Spirit] to a general council of both Latins and Greeks, for this they ought not to be held as pertinaciously obstinate or anathematised. Here careful consideration should be given to what they wish to say; or a suitable means should be found of reducing everything to harmony, not insisting on the thorough proof (*probatione omnimoda*) of the truth of this article against them; for men, who want to fight back, would hardly be convinced'.[32]

That attitude of mind, and the appeal to *epikeia* (i.e. not insisting on the letter of the law), were not confined to Gerson, who in his writings very frequently uses both the word and the

[30] JOANNIS GERSONII etc. II, 152C.
[31] Ibid., 135A.   [32] Ibid., 147C.

idea. He was doing no more than express the thought of the University of Paris and of a larger world outside, for it would have been impossible to restore peace to the divided Latin Church without some spirit of concession. So the Greeks benefited from an indulgence that the Latins had first to evoke for themselves. That was the more easy as relations between East and West had never for long been broken off. Time and again in the XIVth century ambassadors had gone between the court of Constantinople and the papal court. Their main mission had been military aid for the East, but that message was always softened by parleys about Church union, the popes usually insisting on it as a preliminary condition, the emperors holding out hopes of it, but through a general council. In 1397, when Constantinople was in imminent danger from the Turk, Manuel II's appeal to the West produced not only a small French force under Boucicaut, but letters from Pope Boniface IX to the Church (1398, 1399) urging that, though Manuel was not within the obedience of the Roman Church, yet help must be accorded to him as a Christian. Manuel himself toured the courts of Europe from 1400 to 1402 soliciting aid. At about the same time western humanism became enamoured of Greek letters. Manuel's agent, Manuel Chrysoloras, was invited to teach Greek in the *Studio* of Florence in 1396. From then on the passion for Greek learning grew apace. More and more centres in Italy taught it; Italians began to go to Constantinople to study, Greeks to come to Italy to teach.

All these contacts tended to put the Greeks in a class apart. Schismatics and heretics they might be, but with a difference. The Council of Basel had inadvertently included in the preamble to the decree *Sicut pia mater* a phrase that offended the Greeks, for it seemed to put them on the level of the Hussites: 'to extinguish completely as much the recent Bohemian discord as the ancient Greek one'[33]: first the Council's envoys in Constantinople, and then the Council itself, did not hesitate to disclaim any suggestion of equality between the two and to change the offending wording. The eastern heresy and schism were old and in any case had never been formally condemned; the Greeks of the day were not the instigators; they appealed to a general council, which was for

---

[33] Eugenius was enthusiastic to bring the Greeks to a general council; but, when he heard that the Council of Basel had invited the Hussites, he dissolved it forthwith.

contemporary Latins high orthodoxy; to them 'we Latins owe much'.[34] There was a number of converts from the Greek Church in the course of the fourteenth century. They doubtless made a profession of faith and presumably an abjuration of heresy. Pope Urban V, at least, was in no doubt. In a letter of 18 April 1365 he congratulated Maximus Lascaris on having understood 'that the ancient schism of the Greeks is damnable and cut off from participation in divine grace', and on having been converted to the Roman Church 'outside of which there is no salvation'.[35]

The same Pope Urban V in 1370—before the Great Schism of the West—in a reply refusing to the expectant Greeks the convocation of a general council, gave as his reason, 'lest there be brought into the examination of doubt and prying discussion points in which you differ from the Westerns and not a few eastern faithful, though, according to the faith and teaching of the holy Roman Church, these are known to be certain in that they have been approved by the evidence of Holy Scripture, by the sayings and opinions of the holy Latin and Greek doctors and by apostolic faith'.[36] Eugenius IV—after the Great Schism—was less unbending. In the summer of 1434, while he was arranging with the Byzantine Emperor for a council in Constantinople, the Council of Basel was in negotiation with Greek envoys for a council in Italy. Both succeeded. The Baseler, having learnt of Eugenius' step, rejected it, because, as they had no intention of being dissolved in favour of a new council, a synod in Constantinople could have been only a local council; but in any case 'it seemed most unsuitable that a universal synod should be held in Constantinople by which there would be defined what was to be held as of Catholic faith'.[37] Eugenius did not share their view, though in his zeal for union and peace 'it does not matter', he wrote, 'where and by what means union ensues' so long as it does ensue. He would have preferred a general council in Constantinople where, as was laid down in the agreement made by him with John VIII, Latins should have complete freedom to propose, argue, prove their views, and Greeks should have a like freedom; 'Also that the prelates and others who had come together from both sides should use the method of disputation, proposing and replying as above, and, as is the custom of those disputing,

---

[34] JOANNIS GERSONII etc. II, 136A.

[35] Quoted by O. HALECKI, *Un Empereur de Byzance à Rome* (Warsaw, 1930) doc, 5, pp. 363–4.

[36] RAYNALDUS, ad annum 1370, III.   [37] *M.C.*, II, p. 785.

supporting their arguments with texts from the Gospels and the other sacred writings and also from the holy Fathers and Doctors. Also that whatever shall be concluded by common agreement of both of the two sides about the differences that exist between the two Churches should be inviolably observed by each side and put into execution to be inviolably observed and preserved intact under the necessary penalties and censures by all the subjects of the two Churches, both Western and Eastern'.[38] That agreement he recommended to the Council of Basel and, while accepting their solution as a second best if they would not follow his way, he urged that 'a legate of the Apostolic See with prelates and other of our most learned men be sent to the city of Constantinople, where the prelates and other notables of the Greeks with the Emperor and the Patriarch should meet in a similar way, and there by the method of disputation, just as at an earlier time was done in the sixth Council, with the truth made plain, each of the two Churches should reach the desired result of union and peace'.[39]

Apart from siting the council in Constantinople, Eugenius was proposing to do no more than what Martin V had been prepared to do after John VIII had rejected all suggestion of a token-council, when he agreed to a council with the Greeks in Italy 'peaceful, apostolic, canonical, without force or contention, free'.[40] It was what the Council of Basel, the inheritors of Martin's pact with the Greeks, whose terms were defined in the Baseler decree *Sicut pia mater*, was arranging—a general council where 'without force' and 'free' should mean 'that each may freely declare his judgement without hindrance or violence from anyone', and where 'the Emperor of the Greeks and their Church should have its honours, that is, those that it had at the time when the present schism arose, provided always that the rights, privileges and honour of the Supreme Pontiff and the Roman Church and of the Roman Emperor be respected and, if any doubt should arise, that it be submitted to the decision of the aforesaid general council'.[41]

When the Council of Basel split over the question of the unionistic council, Pope Eugenius IV, by the Bull *Salvatoris et Dei nostri* of 30 May 1437, undertook to carry out the provisions of the decree *Sicut pia mater*,[42] which he had, in any case, approved

[38] Ibid., p. 794. Cf also pp. 761, 791.
[39] Letter to Basel of 15 Nov., 1434; *M.C.*, II, pp. 763–4. The sixth council was, of course, an oecumenical council.
[40] *E.P.*, doc. 26.　　　　　　　　[41] *M.C.*, II, pp. 755–6.
[42] *E.P.*, doc. 135.

two years before. The result was the coming of the Greeks to Italy and the Council of Ferrara-Florence. There can be little doubt that, in the atmosphere engendered by the schism in the Latin Church, Eugenius IV, the Fathers of Basel (the inheritors, both, of the thought of Martin V), and, of course, the Greeks themselves considered the Oriental metropolitans present at the meetings in Ferrara and Florence as true members of the Council, and that both Greeks and Latins in Ferrara and Florence thought their Council oecumenical. The Emperor,[43] the Patriarch,[44] Mark Eugenicus,[45] Scholarius[46] and others, even before the proclamation of the decree of union declared it so. Eugenius held it to be the continuation of the Council of Basel. At the inauguration of the solemn Council on 9 April 1438 he said: 'We decree and declare, with the assent of the said Emperor and Patriarch and of all those here in the present synod, that it is a holy, universal, that is, oecumenical synod in this city of Ferrara. . . .'[47] On the occasion of its transfer to Florence his Bull declared: 'We should have desired indeed that this universal Council which we initiated in this city, should have continued in the same . . . [But] with the approval of our most dear son, John Palaeologus, Emperor of the Greeks, and of our venerable brother Joseph, Patriarch of Constantinople, and with the approbation of the sacred Council, as from now we transfer . . . this oecumenical, that is, universal synod from this city of Ferrara to the city of Florence. . . .'[48] And, of course, the Bull of union of 6 July 1439 hails it as oecumenical with triumph: 'Let the heavens rejoice and the earth exult' that there had been broken down 'the middle wall of partition that was dividing the Western and Eastern Church. . . . For, behold, western and eastern Fathers . . . joyous and prompt came together . . . to this sacred oecumenical Council', wherein 'after long and painstaking investigation, finally by the mercy of the Holy Spirit they have reached this most desired and most holy union'.[49]

---

[43] A.G., p. 432. [44] A.L., p. 31.
[45] SYR., p. 148. [46] A.G., p. 430.
[47] Bull *Magnas omnipotenti deo*; E.P., doc. 135. Cf. also: 'But with the arrival of the Greeks and, as We are assured, their agreement to the aforementioned place of Ferrara for the celebration of an oecumenical council' (Bull *Doctoris gentium* of 18 Sept. 1437; E.P., doc. 88): 'We transferred the Council of Basel to the city of Ferrara, where also, by the providence of God, with the Western and the Eastern Church We established an oecumenical council (Bull *Moyses vir dei* of 4 Sept. 1439; E.P., doc. 210). Cf. also E. P. docs. 75, 76, 104, 124 etc.
[48] Bull *Decet ycumenici concilii*; E.P., doc. 160.
[49] Bull *Laetentur caeli*; E.P., doc. 176.

CHAPTER NINETEEN

AGREEMENT ON THE *FILIOQUE*

Everyone knows that the Council of Lyons, though it seemed to the Latins of that time to promise union of the Churches, was doomed to failure from the start. The acceptance by the three Greek delegates (there were not more) of the Latin *Filioque* indicated that Michael VIII, the Greek Emperor, was willing to pay a high price for protection against the eastern ambitions of Charles of Anjou; it did not mean that the Greek Church was willing to pay the same price. Before the council, the Emperor had tried to persuade it to accept the idea of union: it had refused. After the council, it met with an uncompromising rejection the union that the delegates brought back.

It is sometimes said that the Eastern Church was no more behind the Council of Florence than it was behind that of Lyons. Such a judgement cannot be supported by history. Before ever they set off for the West, the Greek ecclesiastics were on the whole in favour of the encounter with the Latins and of union. That does not preclude the other motive of finding help for their fatherland, but neither does it allow that the political motive was the only one, or even necessarily the chief one, that moved them.

The letters of the western envoys from Basel, who had gone in 1435 to Constantinople to implement the agreement made between that Latin council and the Greeks, bear ample and eloquent witness to the desire for union. John of Ragusa especially describes the processions, prostrations and protracted prayers offered for that end by Patriarch and people, and he assured the council that had sent him of the good will and, indeed, enthusiasm of the Byzantine capital for the speedy and successful fulfilment of the decree *Sicut pia mater*.[1] Scholarius' letter to Pope Eugenius is sanguine of happy results and his letter to a scholar of his, if not optimistic, is hopeful.[2]

In the event the Orientals went to Ferrara in Italy and not to Basel. There things did not go as smoothly and quickly as they had hoped. First, there were long delays, mostly due to the

[1] CECCONI, doc. LXXVII. [2] SCHOL., IV, pp. 414–5.

Emperor's desire to allow time for the envoys of the western princes to arrive, since he much wanted to meet them to obtain military aid for his Empire. The protracted delay produced difficulties for the Pope, for he was paying some 1700 florins a month for the maintenance of his guests and he soon was dependent on borrowing. His payments were, in consequence, irregular. The Greeks began to feel the insecurity of it, the lower-ranking clergy and court servants even the pinch of poverty. The discussions were long drawn out and the Latins had much more to say for themselves than the Greeks, surprisingly, had anticipated. Neither side would admit defeat. There was an atmosphere of stalemate, frustration and a growing nostalgia among the Greeks, especially when rumours reached Italy of dangers impending over Constantinople. When a year had passed after the solemn inauguration of the Council on 9 April 1438 with union apparently no nearer, the Greeks were almost in despair.

It was at this stage, when things seemed so bad that they could hardly have been worse, at the end of May 1439, that unity was achieved on the chief point of difference between the Churches. That was such a surprising and unexpected turn of events that one is tempted to conclude that the unity thus arrived at was not genuine, that on the side of the Greeks it was the result of the hardships they were enduring, in particular of their longing to be finished with it all and to return home to country and kin. Here, however, instinct is at fault. The documents, on which we must rely for the history of the Council, describe the various, though rapid, stages of this concord and show that it was sincere on the one side as on the other.

The point at issue was the Procession of the Holy Spirit, not as an addition to the Creed, but as a dogma. It was, then, a purely theological question, devoid of complications of prestige and authority in so far as it did not immediately implicate the further question of the primacy of Rome. It had been the subject of discussion during the eight sessions in Florence, five of which were largely wasted in squabbles about the genuine reading of a few texts. In the sixth session Mark of Ephesus had expounded at length the Greek arguments from Scripture, councils and Fathers in favour of his view—Procession from the Father only: in the seventh and eighth, John of Montenero had done a like service for the Latins.

These last three sessions had brought the argument to the domain where the greater part of the Greek ecclesiastics (and probably the greater part of the Latins too) could understand— the domain of patristics. The metaphysics of the Blessed Trinity, especially with the subtle differences of terminology and of outlook between Greeks and Latins confusing the issue further, were beyond the capabilities of most of the audience. The Greeks distrusted syllogistic reasoning, particulary in connection with 'Theologia', the knowledge of God. Montenero's arguments, therefore, in the first five sessions had probably done more harm than good to his cause, for they made his Greek hearers more suspicious of him. In the last two sessions, however, he showed a mastery of patristic learning. He quoted freely from Councils and from Latin Fathers venerated also in the Greek Church, and in particular from Greek Fathers, to show that these nowhere denied the Latin doctrine, but rather implied it by their less precise, more metaphorical phrases. He ended by asserting roundly that the Latins, like the Greeks, held that there is only one cause and principle in the Blessed Trinity and anathematised those who held two.

Montenero's words, of the latter part of the month of March 1439, did not bear immediate fruit, but were a seed. Bessarion, in his *Oratio dogmatica*, delivered before the Greeks probably in mid-April 1439, and Scholarius, with his Exhortation of about the same time, followed the same general lines as Montenero, the harmony of the Latin and the Greek Fathers. Again there was no immediate result. As a last resort to solve the deadlock, the Pope, Eugenius IV, addressed the Greeks and the Latins, exhorting, chiding, encouraging. His speech was the stimulus needed. The Greeks set themselves to new efforts, and the seed sown by Montenero, Bessarion, Scholarius and others began to bear fruit.

The soil in which the seed was set (if I may continue with the same metaphor) was an axiom, that saints cannot contradict each other about the faith, because they are all inspired by one and the same Holy Spirit. To say otherwise would be to assert that the Holy Spirit can contradict Himself. All the Greeks admitted this axiom. Bessarion, Isidore of Kiev, Dorotheus of Mitylene enunciated it. Scholarius stated it positively both in his Exhortation and his written judgement about the Procession of the Holy Spirit. George Amiroutzes included it no less in his written judgement. Mark of Ephesus, as much as the rest, granted its truth, but, when the axiom was applied to the question of the patristic evidence for the Procession of the Holy Spirit, he was in a quandary. Bessarion, Scholarius and others argued that, though Latin saints and Greek saints expressed themselves differently about the Procession, yet as saints they were inspired by the same Holy Spirit and must have said the same thing about the faith. Their expositions of doctrine, therefore, must have the same general content, though couched in different terms. In respect of the Holy Spirit the Latin saints assert that He proceeds from the Father and from the Son; the Greek saints, that He 'comes forth', 'issues forth', 'bursts forth', etc., 'from the Father' or 'from the Father through the Son' or 'from both' etc. Whatever the expression, the meaning is the same, more or less clearly expressed, and therefore the doctrine taught by the Latin Fathers and by the Greek Fathers is the same.

For the Greeks in the Council of Florence there was no refuting that reasoning. The axiom was universally admitted. Quotations from the Latin Fathers and the Greek Fathers had been provided in abundance by Montenero and Bessarion. Mark of Ephesus, to avoid the obvious conclusion, was reduced to having recourse to what Scholarius called 'the height of stupidity'. Unable to challenge the quotations made from the Greek Fathers, he was forced to assert that the Latin Saints could not have said what Montenero and his associates declared they had said—that is, he accused the Latins of falsifying their own Fathers, or, an even weaker defence, he refused to accept the quotations from the Latin Fathers because he personally, not knowing Latin, could not check their accuracy, though Scholarius and probably others, well versed in Latin, could have set his doubts at rest in a minute and probably did try to persuade him.

But Mark was in a minority. Because of his intransigence on that point, the first question to be settled among the Greeks was precisely the question of the genuinity of the quotations from the Latin Fathers. There was no argument against the genuinity except Mark's bare assertion, and it is an indication of his influence that the question was ever seriously raised. Mark himself, in his *Relatio de rebus a se gestis*, says that the majority was in favour of the genuinity. The *Description* (i.e. the addition to the protocol in the *Practica*) and the anti-unionist Syropoulus both

S

say the same. The vote was taken on 28 May and, that point settled, Greek acceptance of the orthodoxy of the Latin doctrine of the Procession of the Holy Spirit was a foregone conclusion. The Latin saints said 'from': the Greek saints said 'through' and a variety of other expressions. Latin saints and Greek saints must declare the same doctrine, so that 'from' and 'through' in respect of the Procession of the Holy Spirit mean the same. There was no way of escaping the conclusion and only two or three of the Greeks tried to do so.

There are, in the different sources, different accounts about the voting on this point of the orthodoxy of the Latin doctrine about the Procession of the Holy Spirit, but the facts related in all of them are substantially the same. The *Description* narrates that ten prelates voted in favour and four against, and that later three more joined the 'Ayes'. Syropoulus puts six as voting against the Latin doctrine (one of whom was sick and did not vote at all) and thirteen in favour. Mark Eugenicus in his *Relatio* does not give numbers, but records that when he saw all those who before had supported him gone to the other side, he discreetly suppressed his written, negative judgement. Certainly at the signing of the decree on 5 July 1439, only two Greek prelates did not append their names, the indomitable Mark and Isaias of Stauropolis. Of the Greek Church in Italy the Patriarch, four out of five procurators of the other eastern Patriarchs, all the bishops but two, the five Staurophoroi (three of them, so says Syropoulus, only under pressure), and half a dozen superiors or representatives of monasteries signed the decree of union that was at the same time a statement of faith. The Emperor signed it also, and George Scholarius and George Amiroutzes, the 'philosopher' counsellors of the Emperor, gave written judgements in public approving the Latin doctrine. Syropoulus in his *Memoirs* does not mention this fact. Neither does he make any note of Gemistus's decision, so that one is inclined to conclude that Gemistus, who certainly would have recorded a vote, also was in favour of Latin orthodoxy on that occasion.

In view of the basic harmony of the documents and of the logical march of events, the only conclusion to be drawn is that at the end of May and the beginning of June the Greek bishops, with hardly an exception, were genuinely and freely in favour of accepting the orthodoxy of the Latin doctrine about the Procession of the Holy Spirit and did in fact freely accept it. A little more than a month later they all, with only two exceptions, signed their names to the dogmatic statement.

What, then, is to be said about the duress that their prolonged separation from home, their distressing financial condition, and their sense of frustration and waste of time certainly exercised upon them? It can without difficulty be admitted that it made them most desirous of returning home and ready to accept the first honourable solution that offered. But, in face of the documents on which our knowledge of the Council rests, it cannot be admitted that it took away their liberty and that it forced them to give approval of the Latin doctrine against their wills. Such a theory of yielding under coercion is disproved by the events of the months March to June 1439.

The public sessions on the Procession ended on 24 March with no union achieved. The Greeks asked for time to consider their answer and, after Easter, on being pressed for a reply, twice sent an ultimatum to the Pope: 'We will undergo no more public sessions, which are a waste of time. We have the seven councils with us. Do you find some other way out of the impasse, otherwise we go home.' There is no sign of fear or of cowering under the force of threats or circumstances. That situation continued till the end of May. Various expedients were tried to find a means that would lead to union. The Emperor addressed his subjects. Bessarion delivered his *Oratio*. Scholarius exhorted. Meetings were arranged between committees of ten from each aside. The Latins presented a concise and carefully worded theological statement about the Trinity and the Greeks returned an amended and imprecise version of it. Subsequently, harrangued by cardinals, they refused either to endure fresh public sessions or to clarify their theological statement. Urged by some cardinals in the name of the Pope, John VIII replied: 'We neither write nor say anything more, except that, if you accept what we have given you, we will unite; if not, we shall go home'.[3] That was on 21 May 1439.

In all this there is not the slightest sign that the Greeks were wilting, hesitating, yielding under pressure. On the contrary, they were consistently firm, even stubborn, in refusing to give way to the insistence of the Latins. The Latins wanted more sessions, as

[3] *A.G.*, p. 420.

union had not been achieved: the Greeks said, 'No', and stuck to it. The Latins then urged a clarification of their theological statement, several of whose phrases were designedly ambiguous: the Greeks would not, and did not, accede. Then the meaning and application of the axiom about the saints came home to them, and they were relieved to find that the long-hoped for key to union had been discovered.

It is said that Greek freedom was impaired in another way, that they were not allowed to say what they wanted. The *Greek Acts* (which are the official Greek protocol compiled by Greeks) show conclusively that in the public sessions the visitors enjoyed equal rights with the Latins, so that in the public business of the Council their liberty was not curtailed by any action of the Latins. But Syropoulus asserts that the Emperor restrained free expression of views among themselves, because he was determined to bring about union of the Churches as a means to gaining western help for his Empire.

The best comment on this accusation is the history of Mark Eugenicus. Mark was the only consistent and noteworthy opponent of union among the Greeks. From his first contact with the Latins, his panegyric to the Pope, to his refusal to sign the decree, he was openly and eloquently the adversary of union. Yet he was the speaker for the Greeks in all but one of the private sessions on Purgatory, in all but two of the public sessions in Ferrara on the addition of the *Filioque*, and in all without exception of the public sessions in Florence. He declared his mind freely in the subsequent private meetings of the Greeks and he asked and received imperial protection when he feared that reprisals might be taken against him for refusing to sign the decree. If John VIII, who after all was Emperor and a Byzantine Emperor, was as determined as Syropoulus suggests to have union at any cost, he would have replaced Eugenicus by Bessarion or Isidore, who were both good theologians and, at any rate by the end, sincere upholders of union. That the Emperor allowed Mark, the only serious threat to the union, to continue as public orator and private speaker to the very end disposes of any accusation that he stifled freedom of speech.

By 8 June, then, real concord had been reached on what was the chief difference between the Churches, the doctrine of the Procession of the Holy Spirit. The Patriarch, by then a very sick man, would have been satisfied with that. He wanted the agreement to be proclaimed in solemn session and the council closed. But the Latins insisted on agreement also over the other controverted points. Between 11 June and the end of the month, these were considered, in public session and out of it, and formulas acceptable to both sides were found. We know little in detail about the process, but it followed the pattern adopted by the Latins for the question of the Procession. A very carefully and precisely worded Latin formula was presented; it was discussed and perhaps amended, and then became the mutually accepted formula, ultimately incorporated into the decree. To dispose of Purgatory, the Eucharist, the primacy and the question of the addition of the *Filioque* to the Creed in three weeks, after a year of haggling, seems incredible and a *prima facie* proof that the Greeks had given up struggling and would admit anything at all so as to get home. But it should be borne in mind that, once they had admitted the orthodoxy of that 'rock of offence', the Latin doctrine on the Procession of the Holy Spirit, the ice was, so to speak, broken. They must have been more receptive of the idea that the Latins could be right also on other points and they had no longer to bring themselves to a first recognition that they had misjudged the Latin faith. Besides, on Purgatory, Greek doctrine was altogether vague and fluid. The main point of controversy with the Latins in the discussions in Ferrara had been about the punishment of fire, and nothing on that was included in the decree. Similarly, about the Holy Eucharist, the definition was restricted to the uncontroversial points of matter, minister and rite: the necessity or not of the *epiclesis* was not mentioned. The question of the primacy caused more trouble but, though the decree and the exposition of it given by Montenero in public session were uncompromising about the Pope's position (as one might have expected in view of the opposition of the 'Council of Basel'), the difficulties against the formula raised by the Greeks in the second public session touched mainly one point, the question of appeal to Rome from a decision of a patriarch, and the jejune account of the *Description* records the gradual Greek softening on that point. Acknowledgement of the legitimacy of the Latin addition of the *Filioque* to the Creed 'for the sake of making the truth better known and under the spur of necessity' was added presumably because the Greeks, having agreed on so much, could hardly refuse that

last *amende honorable*. So all things considered the mutual acceptance of the common formula of faith on the points of controversy
within so short a time, though admittedly surprising, is not quite
so astounding as at first sight appears.

The decree was signed on 5 July and promulgated on 6 July.
The Greeks reached Constantinople on their return on 1 February
1440 and had already, according to Syropoulus, Ducas and others,
begun to repent of their acceptance of union. That was not true
of all of them.   At least eight of the prelates[4] with Gregory the
Confessor and the monk Pachomius, remained ever faithful to the
union; perhaps even others. The defection of the rest can easily
be explained without accusing them of either cowardice or
duplicity. In Florence they had come to a point of great boredom
and depression when an argument in favour of Latin orthodoxy
was put before them and pressed home, an argument which, on
their own accepted principles, was really unanswerable. A wave of
enthusiasm and rejoicing swept over them, for this meant release
and return, with the truth not betrayed. Mark of Ephesus,
however, stood out. However illogically, he refused to change
from the opinion he had always had and that they too hitherto had
had. His intractability was a challenge and a mute accusation of
treachery to their traditional faith. Though their heads were
convinced at least temporarily of Latin orthodoxy, they felt
unhappy about it. Sentimentally they could not rid themselves
of a feeling of instability and disloyalty, and that perhaps the
ascetic Eugenicus was right. When, then, the atmosphere of
Florence that favoured rapprochement changed to the hostile
atmosphere of Constantinople, intellect yielded to sentiment and
those who needed to be led in Italy followed the lead again in their
homeland, only this time it led the other way. They were not men
of strong intellect or strong character, but average men placed in
very difficult circumstances.

To say otherwise is to judge that a large proportion of the
metropolitans of the Greek Church was so lacking in moral
stamina, that in the face of moderate hardship they accepted what
was to them heresy, and that out of them all one alone, Mark
Eugenicus, was found with sufficient moral courage and spiritual
hope to be ready to face the consequences of fidelity to his Church.

---

[4] Bessarion, Isidore, Dorotheus of Mitylene, Cyzicus, Lacedaemon, Rhodes,
Moldo-Wallachia, Monembasia.

I do not think that that was the case. What documents we have show clearly enough that, on the question of the Procession of the Holy Spirit, the Greek prelates joyfully, freely and honestly admitted Latin orthodoxy, and that on the other questions, where documentation is scarce, there is nothing to indicate dishonesty on their part.

CHAPTER TWENTY

THE DEFINITION OF THE PRIMACY OF THE POPE
IN THE COUNCIL OF FLORENCE

The ecclesiastical question of first importance in the first half of the fifteenth century was undoubtedly the position of the Pope within the Church. But it was primarily a Latin question, because first the residence of the popes in Avignon and then, and to a much greater degree, the Great Schism of the West had brought Conciliarism into being, which was a theory (also put into practice) that declared nothing less than that, by the ordinance of God Himself, the highest authority in the Church was a general council and that a pope was merely the council's chief executive officer. The principle of the superiority of a council, and so of the inferiority of a pope, was first officially enunciated in the Council of Constance (6th April, 1415). It reached the climax both of its success and of its vociferous publicity in the Council of Basel. It received its *coup de grâce* in the Council of Florence in that part of the decree of union with the Greeks—an infallible document—which treats of the papacy:

Item diffinimus sanctam apostolicam sedem et Romanum pontificem in universum orbem tenere primatum, et ipsum pontificem Romanum successorem esse beati Petri principis apostolorum et verum Christi vicarium totiusque ecclesie caput et omnium christianorum patrem et doctorem existere, et ipsi in beato Petro pascendi, regendi ac gubernandi universalem ecclesiam a domino nostro Iesu Christo plenam potestatem traditam esse, quemadmodum etiam in gestis ycumenicorum conciliorum et in sacris canonibus continetur.

Also in the same way we define that the holy, apostolic See and the Roman Pontiff holds the primacy over the whole world and that the Roman Pontiff himself is the successor of blessed Peter prince of the Apostles, and that he is the true Vicar of Christ, head of the whole Church and father and teacher of all Christians, and that to the same in blessed Peter was given plenary power of feeding, ruling and governing the whole Church, as is contained also in the Acts of the oecumenical councils and the sacred canons.

In formulating that decree the Latins in Florence had their eye as much on the rump-council of Basel as on the Greeks, for Basel at that moment was still carrying on relentless war against Pope Eugenius and had just declared him contumacious and deposed. One may doubt if there would have been quite so much detail in this part of the Florentine decree, if only the Greeks had been envisaged. Not that that makes any present difference about its import also for the Greeks. The position of the Pope there defined is thus defined for Latins and Greeks, no matter who it was that was being chiefly considered.

Whatever the Greeks of today may think, the Greeks in the Council of Florence did not consider the primacy of the Pope as the difference between the churches of the greatest theological importance. That for them was the question of the Procession of the Holy Spirit. Given the choice of subject for the doctrinal debates, they chose to discuss in Ferrara the legitimacy of the addition of the *Filioque* to the Creed. In Florence, after the transfer of the Council, all the public sessions (March 1439) were about the doctrine of the Procession. In 1444–45 the anti-unionists in Constantinople had the opportunity of debating with a Latin theologian in fifteen public conferences: the subject throughout was the Procession. Again in 1449 similar public discussions in Constantinople revolved again about only the Procession. The argument must have continued there, because Pope Nicolas V replied on 12th, April 1450, to Bartolomeo Lapacci, O.P., Bishop of Cortona (the Latin speaker, incidentally, in both sets of conferences mentioned above), to resolve doubts put to him about the decree of Florence, but not about all of it, only about the definition of the Procession. Almost at the same time, or perhaps in 1448, Isidore of Kiev, newly returned from Greece, made a report for the Pope on the reception of the union in the East and on the best means to promote it—to send good preachers who would with arguments drawn from the Fathers, and especially from the Greek Fathers, explain the Procession; and he himself wrote a short treatise on those lines. Finally (lest it be thought that the absorbing interest in the Procession after the Council was due only to the fact that it had been the chief topic of debate in the Council) Syropoulus, who wrote *Memoirs* of the Council, that give much interesting detail not recorded elsewhere, recounts an illuminating event of May 1438, before any public session at all had been held.

The Emperor John VIII had stipulated for a wait of four months between the solemn inauguration of the Council on 9th April, 1438, and any discussion about 'doctrine'. After a time it was decided to hold some conversations between committees of ten a side. Cardinal Cesarini enumerated as 'the more important and the greater differences between the Churches, the Procession, the use of leavened and unleavened bread, Purgatory, the primacy of the Pope'. The Emperor insisted on the observance of the condition that had been mutually agreed on, and so the Procession was ruled out; since the question of leavened and unleavened bread 'seems to be a very big difference', that too had to be deferred; 'but about Purgatory and about the primacy of the pope let them propound whichever they prefer from these two, and we will hear them and reply'.[1] The Latins chose Purgatory, which was discussed on and off for about two months.

All the same the question of the primacy of the Pope, even if it was not the biggest of the obstacles to union between the churches, was one of the obstacles to union. The Greeks did not accept the supremacy of Rome in the Church. They believed in the theory of the Pentarchy, that the five patriarchates of Rome, Constantinople, Alexandria, Antioch and Jerusalem were all substantially equal, even if in practice Rome had a predominance in the West and Constantinople in the East. They resented that Rome did not abide by that equality but had arrogated to itself a supremacy over the rest, which it tried to impose on them. Mark Eugenicus, the Metropolitan of Ephesus, in his speech in the first dogmatic session in Ferrara (8th October 1438) formulated the Greek accusation:

> The Roman Church disregarded and lightly valued one of these, the love, I mean, that it ought to have shown towards its sister Church of the East; for it sanctioned and put forward on its own account a dogma that is neither expressly found in the Holy Scriptures, nor acknowledged by the oecumenical councils, nor approved by the more eminent among our Fathers.[2]

The Greek case against the legitimacy of the addition of the *Filioque* to the Creed, as put forward in Ferrara, rested on the prohibition of the Council of Ephesus, but it was always coloured by the attitude to Rome. Bessarion expressed this concisely:

[1] SYR., pp. 123–4.   [2] *A.G.*, p. 52.

About the authority of the Western Church much could be said, if we had not another subject at present under discussion. We are, indeed, not ignorant of the rights and privileges of the Roman Church; but we know too the limits set to these privileges. We wish your Reverence to know that we withhold this permission from every Church and synod, even oecumenical, and not from the Roman Church alone, since no matter how great is the Roman Church, it is notwithstanding less than an oecumenical synod and the universal Church: and we withhold it from the whole Church, much more so then from the Roman Church do we withhold it. But we withhold it not as by ourselves, but we consider that this had been forbidden by the decrees of the Fathers.[3]

Aloysius of Perano, O.F.M., who spoke after Bessarion, vindicated for 'the Church and its head who enjoys every power and right over the universal Church' the right of modifying the Creed if circumstances demanded; and Cardinal Cesarini, arguing with Mark Eugenicus, several times alluded to the same authority so that Mark in the end proposed that the question be discussed at length and disposed of in the next session ('for we have many, forceful arguments in support of our right'),[4] but Cesarini preferred to finish with the one topic of the addition first, before embarking on another.

As things turned out, it was some considerable time before the formal discussions about the primacy began, because the doctrine of the *Filioque* occupied the minds of the Council till 8th June, 1439. No sooner, however, was the subject settled than Pope Eugenius, somewhat to the discomfiture of the Greeks, who had thought that they could consider the Council over and that they could go home, began to press them to bring the other points of difference to a harmonious conclusion, and he instanced as still outstanding differences the primacy, Purgatory, the Eucharist and the question of the divine essence and operation, i.e. Palamism. The four Greek metropolitans to whom he was talking replied:'As regards the primacy of the pope, at any rate, it was arranged in this way, that he should have whatever privileges he had from the beginning and before the schism'. Two days later (10th June, 1439), again in conversation with the Pope, they answered:

[3] Ibid., p. 159.   [4] Ibid., p. 211.

We say that the first point is most wicked, for how may we affirm that the Roman Church has the power of adding or taking away without its brother patriarchs? So, though what was added is orthodox, all the same he who dared to do it without conciliar approval will not be accounted guiltless. But, if you wish, admit that you acted wrongly and agree not to do it again, and so you will gain pardon. . . .[5]

—they were not answering officially when they said this, but were offering their comments 'as friends'. This time, however, it must have been the Pope who was disconcerted, for their comments 'as friends', not put forward to plead any cause but expressing the inmost conviction of four of the most convinced unionists among the Greeks, showed the degree to which the theory of the Pentarchy was taken for granted. Again on 12th June the Pope urged the settlement of the remaining differences, and the next day the Greeks decided to discuss with the Latins in public session the questions of the primacy, the Eucharist and the addition.[6]

The Latin method of reaching union, at least in the months that followed after the dogmatic sessions of March 1439, had been to prepare a carefully worded theological statement, a *cedula*, about each of the theological differences and to present it to the Greeks for their consideration. The queries and objections that arose were then discussed either informally or formally or both, in public session or in committee. This method was followed duly in the case of the primacy, though quite when the *cedula* about it was delivered to the Greeks is not clear. At any rate, by the time that the Greek decision to discuss this problem synodically was put into practice on June 16th, the Greeks already had it, for the Latin orator, John of Montenero, O.P., contented himself with taking the *cedula* and explaining and proving each of its phrases.

The *Description* does not mention any *cedula* on this subject, and about Montenero's speech it gives nothing more than the bare information that he spoke. The *Latin Acts* fortunately give both what purports to be the very *cedula* and a full synopsis of Montenero's speech.[7] But if the formula given as the *cedula* is compared with the phrases explained by Montenero, differences appear. It would seem that the text that Andrea of Santacroce gives in the *Latin Acts* is the text as it emerged with certain emendations from

[5] Ibid., p. 443.   [6] A.G., p. 447; A.L., p. 231.
[7] A.L., pp. 231–6.

the discussion, and this conclusion is confirmed by comparing it with the decree of union, which is nothing else than the catena of the *cedulae* prefaced by an introduction. The text originally offered to the Greeks can easily be reconstructed from the Latin orator's explanation. It read as follows:

Also in the same way we define that the holy, apostolic and Roman Pontiff is the successor of Peter and Vicar of Jesus Christ, head of the whole Church and father of all Christians, our teacher too, and that he holds the primacy over the whole world, and that to the same See and Roman Pontiff in St. Peter, the Prince of the Apostles, there was given plenary power of feeding, convening, ruling and governing the whole Church.

Montenero drew his proofs from the Holy Scriptures and the councils with a few quotations from the Fathers. Very briefly they were as follows. *Successor of Peter:* Pope Adrian's letter to Constantine and Irene (VII Council, II actio; *Mansi* XII, 1057 CD). *Head of the whole Church:* Adrian's letter to Tarasius (*Mansi* XII, 1081E; PL96, 1240A); Council of Chalcedon (*Mansi* VI, 579D, 147A–D, 154C). *Father of all Christians:* the same Council (*Mansi* VII, 106C); St. John Chrysostom (PG 59, 480); the synodical letter of Pope Agatho to the VI Council (*Mansi* XI, 242D). *Teacher:* the letter of the pseudo-Athanasius to Pope Felix (PG 28, 1475A). *He holds the primacy over the whole world:* Adrian's second letter to Tarasius (*Mansi* XII, 1081E); the decretal letter of the pseudo-Anacletus quoting: 'Thou art Peter', etc. (PG 2, 813B); the letter of the pseudo-Julius to the oriental bishops (PG 28, 1452B). *Feeding:* Jn 21:17; Adrian to Tarasius (*Mansi* XII, 1081B); Agatho's letter to Constantinople quoting Lk 22:31–2 (*Mansi* XI, 239DE). *Convening:* the Council of Chalcedon to Pope Leo (*Mansi* VI, 150B). *Ruling:* words from the pseudo-Anacletus (PG 2, 815A); a sermon of Leo I (PL 54, 149C–150A). *Governing:* the same sermon of Leo I (PL 54, 145C–146A). *Plenary power:* Mt. 16:19; Jn 21:17; Leo's words commenting on these texts (PL 54, 146BC). Cardinal Cesarini added that oecumenical councils, which included Orientals, had approved the letters of Popes Adrian and Agatho.

This skeleton of Montenero's speech will give an idea of his line of argument, a line suited to the patristic preferences of the Greeks that, so it would seem, achieved its object in persuading many of them. At any rate, the *Description* reports that after it they went to the Emperor's residence 'and examined the demands of the Latins and found that they were five and all of them just and good'. Whereupon they pressed the Emperor to concur: 'We accept them all; let there be an end of the business. . . . But he would not'.[8] The *Memoirs* of Syropoulus, the third chief source for information on the Council, are very confused about this period, recounting episodes and remarks haphazard, and stressing the disagreement (everything is disagreement in Syropoulus) of Latins and Greeks about the *epiclesis*-question, in particular between the Emperor and Cesarini, and the convocation of general councils, almost to the exclusion of everything else.[9] The *Latin Acts* record that, on the day following this first explanation, Cardinals Capranica and Condulmaro with a number of theologians visited the Emperor apropos of the expositions of Latin doctrine about the primacy and the Eucharist that John of Montenero, O.P., and John of Torquemada, O.P., had made the previous day. In the discussion that ensued the Emperor, both personally and by the mouth of Bessarion, made several objections to the teaching and perhaps some positive suggestions. The upshot was that on Thursday, 18th June, there was another public session when Montenero and Torquemada replied to the objections made and clarified the Latin doctrine further. This second speech of Montenero about the primacy is of particular interest, as from it we can gather the nature of the difficulties that his first exposition had aroused in the minds of the Greeks.[10]

Before tackling the specific objections that had been urged against the Latin *cedula*, Montenero wished first to dispose of a general difficulty that clearly had been aired at length by Bessarion. The Greek had suggested that the three conciliar letters that Montenero had made so much of in his first discourse were no sure foundation for dogma, for the effusive approvals they contained were probably the expression more of oriental politeness than of interior conviction, and he had demanded a basis of proof taken from the canons of councils. Montenero replied that the letters of Chalcedon to Leo and of Popes Adrian and Agatho to the councils were synodical letters, i.e. letters approved by the councils. The definitions and canons of councils are the result of study of the writings of the Fathers and the letters quoted in the

councils, which therefore have at least equal authority with the
canons. Agatho, for instance, imposed his letter on the sixth
Council (*Mansi* XI, 235E), that is, imposed the decision of a
Roman synod, and the Council obeyed (*Mansi* XI, 666CD). The
Fathers recognized the authority of papal letters; St. Augustine,
for instance, put them among the catholic scriptures (PL 34, 40D).

After this justification of his method, the Dominican orator
approached the first objection, which had been proposed by the
Emperor apropos of the phrase: *Successor of Peter and vicar of
Christ and father and teacher of all Christians.* Bessarion in the
Emperor's name had asked if this meant 'a certain reverence' as
first among all the patriarchs, or something more. Montenero
replied: 'Not only reverence, but a certain power of a certain
obedience' and proceeded to prove, first that St. Peter was 'head'
with the implication that 'head' meant also power, and then to
inquire what that power was in the case of St. Peter and his
successors. 'Feed my sheep' (Jn 21:17) shows that Peter was head
with authority, and Chrysostom's commentary (PG 59, 478)
and the *allocutio* of the Council of Chalcedon to the Emperor
Marcian (*Mansi* VII, 455C) leave no doubt as to the fact. All
the Fathers, e.g. Leo I in sermon 73 (PL 54, 395B), agree. Agatho
quoted the testimony of the Byzantine Emperor Justinian I
(*Mansi* XI, 270CD), who among other things had called the
Roman Pontiff 'head of all the Churches'.[11] What then is the
'power' of this 'head'?

Hence this power, which is in Peter and his successors, is
called a power of spiritual jurisdiction, which is directed to
the salvation of the souls of all Christians, so that by means
of this power the sacraments may be administered duly to
the faithful, and in respect of this power all, whether clerical
or lay, are subject—laymen in what concerns the salvation
of their souls, e.g. if they have committed mortal sin, it
belongs chiefly to the spiritual shepherd to correct them and
bring them back, as a father, and so if they should act against
the faith, like some of the emperors who were heretics and
persecuted metropolitans, and there was need to have
recourse to the apostolic See, and in similar cases, since the
aim of the apostolic See is the peace of the ecclesiastical
order, so that by this peace it may arrive at heavenly glory.

[11] *Corpus Iuris Civilis*, vol. II, *Codex Iustiniani*, ed. P. KRUEGER, p. 11.

For this reason Christ said: ' To thee I will give the keys' and made him shepherd, to lead the sheep to the pastures of the heavenly life, and all councils are full of examples of this kind.

Athanasius, Chrysostom, Flavian had recourse to popes as heads of the Church, and this without prejudice to the authority of emperors which is over civil and temporal affairs, whereas papal authority is over things spiritual. The ecclesiastical and civil powers are likened to the sun and the moon, the sun meaning the spiritual which is the more sublime, the moon the temporal.

The next objection proposed by the Emperor was about the power of convoking synods. Montenero repeated the testimony of Chalcedon to Leo I 'who had hastened to unite together the body of Christ' (*Mansi* VI, 150B) and added another from the supposed letter of Pope Julius to the Orientals (PG 28, 1452A), arguing from these that the Pope's authority to feed the flock inevitably involved the power to bring the flock together to be fed.

> And these convocations are not made except in times of the greatest need for the whole Church, as when great heresies arise, since it is the business of the pope, who has authority over the [whole] earth and over the Church, and the other patriarchs not so, except over only a certain area.

Two difficulties (he said) have been raised, the first in respect of emperors, the second as regards other patriarchs on the supposition that the Church is founded on five patriarchs. To the first difficulty he replied 'that though emperors brought the councils together, since they had the sole power of dominion, this we say they did, putting that into execution which had the consent and authority of the pope', and he instanced the action and words of Pope Leo both before and after Chalcedon (PL 54, 899AB; 1029AB). About the second difficulty 'as regards the other patriarchs, I never read in any book or council that the government of the Church is in three or five patriarchs', but the Church must have the best government by Christ's ordinance, viz. the monarchical, as He put the power in one apostle, not in four or five. Then quoting and paraphrasing the decretals of the pseudo-Anacletus he referred to the history of patriarchates—Alexandria instituted by St. Peter and held by Peter's disciple, Mark; Antioch, Peter's first See: later Constantinople and Jerusalem were introduced but, in reverence to the canons of Nicaea, Rome did not acknowledge them till Pope Leo consented, and later Justinian embodied the new dignities in a law, so that by ancient right even Constantinople (like Alexandria and Antioch) is the daughter of Rome, which is 'the origin of the laws, the culmination of the high priesthood and the source of priesthood' as Justinian wrote.[12]

It was then asked by my lord of Nicaea whether this power, which is given to the head, is such as is given to a metropolitan in his province or a patriarch in his patriarchate. I reply that it is not such, because the powers of the metropolitan churches [and] of patriarchs are limited to certain areas, in such a way that one patriarch has no power in the territory of another and *vice versa*. But the successor of Peter has the immediate power of a superior over all, but he has it so that all may be done with order, as when cases of greater importance and difficulty arise . . . recourse can always be had to the apostolic See, and doctrine, decision and judgement obtained. . . .[13]

Leo (PL 54, 671B), the pseudo-Anacletus and the pseudo-Clement lend their corroboration.

When Montenero ended, a Greek commented: 'No one among us denies that without the authority of the Roman Pontiff a council cannot be summoned; but on the other hand the Pope cannot do it without the patriarchs.' Cesarini retorted: 'And if others deny that in their canons, will it then be convoked if the Pope so orders?' The Greek replied: 'On that ground they could not stop it from being a council.' The Cardinal: 'And without the Pope there will be no council. . . . Have you not got the Donation of Constantine which he made to Sylvester?' Whereupon the Donation was read out and with that Torquemada took Montenero's place to speak again about the Eucharist.

The history of the agreement must be continued from the *Description* for it gives the chronology of the progress made, even if it adds little detail to the story.[14] Friday, 19 June, was passed studying the 'books' (presumably the Acts of the councils) and Saturday, after a meeting with the Emperor, was passed in the same pursuit, but without result. On Sunday morning

we wrote and approved of the privileges of the Pope, save two: he should not convene an oecumenical council without

[12] Ibid., vol. III, *Novellae*, ed. R. SCHOELL and G. KROLL, Nov. CXXXI.
[13] *A.L.*, p. 247.   [14] *A.G.*, p. 451 seq.

T

the Emperor and the patriarchs, if they would come; but if they are informed and will not come, the synod should not be held over for that reason: and secondly, if someone should consider himself unjustly treated by one of the patriarchs and should come lodging an appeal, the patriarchs should not come answering and being judged, but the Pope should send examiners to the spot and there, where the business is, give justice locally to the injured.

The Emperor took this decision to the Pope on Sunday evening, who deferred his answer till Monday, 22 June, so as to have time to consult his synod.

The Pope's reply was taken to the Greeks by three cardinals. He insisted on all papal privileges without limitation. The Emperor was in despair and bade the cardinals have ships made ready for the Greeks' departure. Tuesday passed without any contact between the churches. Wednesday was a great day in Florence, for it was 24 June, the feast of St. John the Baptist. Isidore of Kiev, Bessarion, Dorotheus of Mytilene and others urged both Pope and Emperor not to give up, with the result that a meeting of six delegates from each side was arranged for Friday, 26 June. Details of that meeting are lacking, but on the evening of the same day the Greeks agreed upon another formula, which they wrote and sent to Eugenius:

> About the primacy of the Pope, we profess that he is supreme Pontiff and representative and guardian and vicar of Christ, shepherd and teacher of all Christians, that he directs and governs the Church of God, without prejudice to the privileges and rights of the patriarchs of the East, he of Constantinople being second after the Pope, then the Alexandrine, and after him the one of Antioch, then the one of Jerusalem.

That was really an acceptance of the Latin *cedula* with the addition of the order of the Patriarchates. However the account continues: 'When we had written this we determined neither to write nor to do anything else, but if this should not be accepted by the Pope, nothing further would be done. And having sent it on the evening of Friday we learnt that he had received it with pleasure and then we were relieved'.

Cesarini in a speech before the Latin synod, convoked on 27 June to approve the various *cedulae* before they were incorporated into the definitive decree, recounted briefly the history of the negotiations with the Greeks. Apropos of the primacy he said:

The last difference was about the primacy and this seemed to surpass human possibilities, because subjects stray from their head, and in point of fact till now they have not been well disposed about the power of the Roman Pontiff, saying that he was like the head of some one entity, like a dean. And after an exposition of the Holy Scriptures and the sacred councils, the truth appeared, that the apostolic See and the Roman Pontiff is the successor of St. Peter; then by the disposition of the divine goodness it was brought about that the Greeks agreed to the *cedula* presented by the Latins. Finally they said that we should make some deliberation about the patriarchal Sees, viz., that Constantinople should be second, etc., as had been determined in the constitutions of the councils and, in the Lateran Council when Alexander III presided, he renewed the privileges of the patriarchal Sees.[15]

The phrase in the Bull, therefore, about the order of the patriarchal Sees was inserted at the instance of the Greeks, and the omission from it of *convocandi* (which Cesarini forgot to mention) was presumably in deference to the Emperor's strong objection.

The Latins approved. Twelve representatives from each Church met to formulate the decree, and all seemed about to end peacefully. But there were more difficulties yet in store. The decree was drawn up in the Pope's name only, without mention of the Greek Emperor and the Greek Church. John VIII objected strongly. Also the section of the decree that treated of the primacy ended that to the Pope 'in Blessed Peter full power was given by our Lord, Jesus Christ, of feeding, ruling and guiding the universal Church, *as is contained also in the sacred Scriptures and the words of the saints*'. These last words probably had not been in the original *cedula*. At least they did not figure in Montenero's first speech when he explained the *cedula* phrase by phrase. In his second speech he had preluded his replies to the objections raised by the Emperor by disposing of a fundamental difficulty, which was precisely what is contained in this phrase, and so it seems most likely that the Latins, having once found the Greeks rather hesitant on this point, added it to the *cedula* without further

[15] *A.L.*, p. 255.

T.I

consultation, as being, after Montenero's exposition, mutually acceptable, and then automatically included it in the decree.

Montenero's explanation, however, had not dispelled the Emperor's prejudices, and he still objected that 'if any one of the saints shows respect to the Pope in a letter, is he to take this as a privilege?' Eugenius sent cardinals. They agreed without much difficulty to add in the preamble of the decree 'with the assent of . . . John Palaeologus, Emperor of the Greeks . . . and the others representing the Oriental Church', but they stood out for retaining the offending phrase about the primacy. The Emperor was equally determined. The cardinals with his permission addressed the Greek synod which, so reports the *Description*, took common counsel and wrote: 'that the Pope should have his privileges in accordance with the canons, and the words of the saints, and the Holy Scriptures and the Acts of the councils'. The *Description* is here clearly wrong, for according to it the Greek prelates conceded what the cardinals were demanding, with the addition of two more sources—the canons and the Acts of the councils. It must have been these last two, and not the 'Holy Scriptures and the words of the saints', that they were insisting on, because the Bull of union reads: 'as is contained in the Acts of the oecumenical councils and the sacred canons', and it is inconceivable that the Latins, if they had been given what they were demanding with so much persistence, would then have declined to avail themselves of the concession.

The solution of the difficulty may be hidden in the next paragraph of the *Description*: 'Next day, Wednesday, the cardinals went to the Emperor and said to him: "The Holy Father has received the two documents and has bidden us choose one out of the two. So let the statement be read and examined so that a final decision may be given to the question"'. What happened, perhaps, was that the Greeks offered two variations of the phrase in dispute and that the Latins, really wanting neither of the forms presented, chose the less objectionable, the one later inserted into the decree, 'as is contained in the Acts of the oecumenical councils and the sacred canons'. In this, then, the Pope gave way to Greek opinion.

The result, of course, was that the decree had to be engrossed afresh. That was done on Thursday, 2 July, and the parchment was taken to the Pope and the Emperor for inspection and approval. It was the Pope's turn this time to object. By mistake the word 'all', not in the *cedula*, had been inserted in the Greek text before 'privileges and rights' of the oriental patriarchs. Eugenius was for having it deleted. Presumably the Emperor refused, for it is still to be found in the final decree, which is the result of another rewriting, on Saturday, 4 July, to include *omnibus* in the Latin text, since both texts had to correspond exactly. That was the end of the alarums and excursions. The decree was signed by Latins and Greeks on 5 July and promulgated in both languages on 6 July.[16]

Two reflections come to the mind after studying the history of the primacy-debate in Florence. The first is that the Latins did not put before the Greeks a minimalist, but rather a maximalist, interpretation of the primacy. Montenero was almost brutally frank—'not reverence, but a certain authority of a certain obedience'; Peter was head and that meant authority; the Pope is successor of Peter and head with a like authority; it is a 'spiritual jurisdiction'; the pope convokes synods and the emperor (even a Byzantine emperor) executes; 'I have never read that the government is in three or five patriarchs' but in one; the Pope is not like a metropolitan with a limited power 'but the successor of Peter has the immediate power of a superior over all'. The Pope was no less uncompromising. When the question could have been settled by his accepting the relatively small limitations to his prerogatives in respect of the convocation of general councils and the exercise of his rights as court of appeal, though he must have been strongly tempted to yield so as to bring the discussion to an end, an action that would at once have gratified the Greeks and have assured

---

[16] The decree of union also declares: 'We also define that the explanation of the words *Filioque*, for the sake of clarifying the truth and under the impulse of necessity at the time, was licitly and reasonably added to the Creed.' How the metropolitans, who, speaking 'as friends', had earlier condemned the addition wholesale, came to accept this cannot be said for lack of documents. The *Description* says no word on this point. The *Latin Acts* give a *cedula*, in the words of the decree, and Cesarini's remarks in his recapitulation of negotiations, which do not really add very much light either: 'Then, when this subject was settled, the next came up, because ever since the subject of the addition was moved, it seemed right to define synodically that the addition was licit; and in this there was great difficulty, which four hours would scarcely suffice to narrate. Finally it was agreed to profess that that addition was justly and rightly made' (pp. 230, 254). The illegitimacy of the addition obviously died hard, and one may be justified in thinking that the Greeks consented because, once they had accepted papal primacy in the words of the *cedula*, they could less easily refuse the addition, but that it went sadly against the grain to break with their traditional attitude towards it—and, with the agreement of the Latins, they did not insert it into their Creed.

him of the union of the Church which was his chief boast against the Council of Basel that was still hanging on and about to elect an anti-pope, he refused that easy way out and instead threw everything back into the melting-pot by insisting on all or nothing. The Greeks, therefore, were left in no doubt as to what papal primacy meant. There was no deception, no ambiguity, no understatement. When in the first place by their various written answers, they agreed as a Greek synod to the Latin *cedula* on the primacy and its explanations, and then when they signed the decree, they were accepting something whose terms were plain.

But (and this is the second reflection) they brought a Greek and not a Latin mentality to their appreciation of the question. For the Latins (as has been said) the great question of Church polity was the position of the Pope within the Church, which for them was coterminous with what the Greeks called the Western patriarchate.[17] The Greek difficulty was with the position of the Western patriarchate itself, the Latin Church, whose patriarch was the Pope, within the whole Church, composed, in their view, of the five patriarchates. When they spoke of the *Filioque* and the right (or not) of introducing it into the Creed, they blamed 'the Roman Church' (also perhaps because no one was quite clear as to which pope was responsible). So Mark of Ephesus in his speech in the first dogmatic session and later when arguing with Cesarini; so Bessarion denying to the Roman Church what he denied to the universal Church. Even after agreeing with the Latins about the Procession, the four Greek prelates, speaking 'as friends', could tell the Pope: 'How can we say that the Church of Rome had the power of adding or subtracting without its brother patriarchs?'; and a few days later: 'We will never accept [the addition].' Later the difficulties raised by the Emperor and Bessarion against the Latin *cedula* all reflected the same preoccupation with the position

---

[17] That is, the relations between Pope and general council. An illuminating side-light on the primacy-definition in the decree of union is given by some words contained in a speech to demolish the pretensions of Basel, delivered months after the promulgation of the definition about the primacy by John of Torquemada in the presence of the Pope: 'If indeed the case should occur that ·the totality of the Fathers meeting in a universal synod should unanimously make some definition of faith and that the person of the Pope alone should contradict it, I should say, in my judgement, that one should stand by the synod and not the person of the pope. For the judgement of so many Fathers of a universal synod in a matter of faith seems rightly to be preferred to the judgement of a single man' (JOANNES DE TORQUEMADA, O.P., *Oratio synodalis de primatu*, ed. E. CANDAL, (Rome, 1954), p. 58).

of the other patriarchates in relation to the Roman Church—the Pope a *primus inter pares?* the power of convoking councils independently of emperor and the other patriarchs? papal power like that of a metropolitan or a patriarch? Greek hesitation after Montenero's speeches to accept the Latin claims stemmed from the same cause—reserve with regard to the convocation of councils without emperor or patriarchs; reserve in respect of appeals to Rome; later insistence on a clause to safeguard in some way the 'privileges and rights' of the other patriarchs, which was added to the *cedula*; the Emperor's demand for mention of the Greek Church in the Bull of union; and the limitation of the grounds of papal prerogatives to councils and canons of the councils; finally the intrusion of the word 'all' before 'privileges and rights' of the patriarchs.

This attitude of thinking almost exclusively in terms of the 'Roman Church' led the Greeks to concentrate their attention on one aspect of Montenero's explanation of the primacy to the exclusion of another—to stress the jurisdictional authority and to neglect the teaching authority of the Holy See. It is true that the *cedula* (and also the decree) was couched in terms that more readily suggested jurisdiction, and that Montenero had expatiated at length on that aspect of it though he had also introduced the teaching authority into his explanation of several of its clauses. The one phrase that clearly refers to teaching, 'teacher of all Christians', was indeed the subject of the Emperor's first difficulty, and that the Dominican solved in his second speech. But John VIII saw no query in it about a primacy of teaching:

> You say that he is 'father and teacher and master of all Christians'. We should like to know if by these words there is signified a certain reverence, because he is the first among all the patriarchs, as we pay honour to a great lord, or if there is implied some power beyond reverence, because in the *cedula* he is said to be 'head of the Church'.[18]

Montenero's reply was to prove that Peter was head with an authority to which all were subject, i.e. jurisdiction as 'head', not as 'teacher'. And all the other difficulties and hesitations of the Greeks (as far as the documents disclose them) were of a like nature.

Two possible conclusions could be drawn from this observation, that the Greeks raised no objection about the teaching

[18] *A.L.*, p. 243.

authority of the popes, either because they accepted it or because, owing to their absorption in the aspect of jurisdiction, they had not realized that it was being taught by the decree on the primacy. The second of these alternatives is the more probable, and for this reason. The Greeks at that time looked on the whole question of the western patriarchate's relations to the other patriarchates as a canonical one, and not as a dogmatic one. Being canonical, it ranked less highly than the doctrinal questions of the Procession and of the Eucharist, and in the Emperor's opinion, when in May 1438 Latins and Greeks were looking for a subject of discussion between their committees, it did not fall under the ban that forbade all dogmatic discussion in the four months' interval of waiting. The Greek case against the Latin addition to the Creed rested, not on a definition, a 'horos', but on the prohibition, a canon, of the Council of Ephesus. The bishops later expressed their horror and amazement that the western patriarch had acted without his brother patriarchs, whose existence and rights were established by the canons of Nicaea, Constantinople and Chalcedon. The objections the Greeks made to the *cedula*, which Montenero answered in his second speech on the primacy, were all jurisdictional, i.e. canonical, and they demanded from him proofs from the canons, and insisted on the insertion in the decree of 'as is contained in the Acts of the oecumenical councils and in the sacred canons'.

Surprise is nowadays often expressed that the Greek prelates in Florence accepted the primacy at all, but, even more, that they accepted it with relatively little debate and in so short a time— eight months for the Procession: one month for the primacy, the Eucharist and Purgatory. The explanation is that the Procession was the dogmatic question *par excellence*—it was debated at great length in Italy, and interminably and exclusively afterwards; on the question of the Eucharist, the *epiclesis* was not defined and the other points were of very minor importance; about Purgatory the Greeks had no very clear views[19]—Mark Eugenicus to some extent made up his theology about it as he went along; the primacy was canonical, not doctrinal—it had not yet entered into oriental dogmatics about the Church, that the Church must not have a visible head on earth.[20]

[19] *A.G.*, pp. 25, 447; SYR., p. 130.
[20] 'Therefore the principle of 'Autocephalous Churches' . . . is the very essence of Catholicity itself. Where is the Catholic Church? . . . *the Catholic Church is there where is the equality of local churches, their full communion with*

However, even if what is here suggested is true, that the Greeks thought 'Roman Church' where the decree read 'Roman Pope', it makes no substantial difference to the Greek understanding of what they were accepting when they discussed the primacy and signed the Bull of union. If they failed to grasp the full import of the Latin formula, it was not (let it be repeated) for lack of lucid explanation and intransigent insistence from the Latin side. What they could not fail to understand on any hypothesis was that the Roman Church was, not the equal, but the head of the other Churches, because founded on St. Peter, the Christ-appointed head of the Apostles; that it had the right of governing the rest, and that with authority; that it had a universal jurisdiction and was therefore a court of appeal from all the world. If the separated Churches of the East would now accept as much as did their fathers at Florence, the end of the schism would be in sight, for the transition from 'Roman Church' to 'Roman Pope' would not be insuperable.

APPENDIX

THE PRIVILEGES AND RIGHTS OF THE PATRIARCHS

The phrase in the decree of union, 'Renewing also the order given in the canons of the venerable patriarchs, that the Patriarch of Constantinople should be after the most holy Roman Pontiff, third he of Alexandria, fourth the Antiochene, and fifth he of Jerusalem, namely without prejudice to all their privileges and rights', was unquestionably added to the original Latin *cedula* to meet the Greek request for mention of the order of the patriarchates, and was modelled on a formula proposed by the Greeks to the Latins on Friday, 26 June 1439 (cf. above p. 274). The words 'without prejudice to the privileges' are found both in the Greek proposal and in the decree of union. The question arises, what was meant by them.

Probably Greeks and Latins did not mean the same thing, and probably neither party could have defined on the spot exactly

each other, and their unbroken communion and link with the Apostles, under one Head—Christ' (Vladimir RODZIANKO, One and Catholic, in Barriers to Unity, ed. M. BRUCE (London, 1959), p. 38).

what it did mean. If asked, both would perhaps have explained
the phrase as referring to such privileges as had existed in history,
the idea, that is, that they had of the situation before the schism;
but Greek ideas and Latin ideas on that were not the same. The
formula in which the Greeks proposed the order of the patriarchs
and their privileges begins: 'About the primacy of the Pope, we
profess that he is supreme Pontiff . . . shepherd and teacher of all
Christians, that he directs and governs the Church of God', but
ends 'without prejudice to the privileges and rights' of the other
patriarchs. The patriarchal 'privileges and rights', then, for them
were a sort of limitation of the Roman primacy that they were
accepting.

The kind of limitation they had in mind is suggested by the
two restrictions that they had tried to impose on the papal privileges, restrictions that the Pope refused to accept. Those were
that appeals to Rome against a patriarch should be tried on the
spot and not in Rome, and that a pope should at least consult the
other patriarchs before summoning a general council. A further
indication of their mind can be found in their continued reluctance
to approve of the addition of the *Filioque* to the Creed. As late as
10 June, the most advanced unionists among the Greeks admon-
ished the Roman Church 'not to do such a thing again'. Their
objection to the addition of the *Filioque* was not a mere isolated
prejudice; it was the expression of the Greek belief that what
affected the whole Church and its faith needed the action of the
whole Church, and that no part of the Church, however august,
should act alone.

Other pointers to the way in which the Greeks were thinking
can be found in the few contacts between them and the Pope
after the promulgation of the union. Eugenius wanted the election
of the new patriarch to take place immediately and in Florence and
hinted that he would consecrate him; the Greek prelates to whom
he was talking resisted the papal pressure, 'because we have a
custom that he should be elected in Constantinople by all our
eparchy and consecrated in our cathedral church' (*A.G.*, p. 471).
The Pope questioned the Greek discipline about divorce; he
received the answer that it was allowed only for good reasons. In
these cases and in others, such as the conferring of the sacrament of
Confirmation by priests, the Greeks were on the defensive to allow
no infringement of what they held to be their rights and customs.

When, therefore, they accepted the papal primacy 'without prejudice to all the privileges and rights' of the patriarchs of the East, they probably had in mind the retention not so much of the *status quo* as it had been, or as they vaguely imagined that it had been, in the past as the *status quo* as it was then (which they probably identified with the other), apart from the general right of appeal to Rome which they admitted, while they hoped that it would be used moderately. The concord reached by the Churches on the question that in Greek eyes was vastly more important, of the Procession of the Holy Spirit, was not dissimilar. It consisted in a mutual recognition of the orthodoxy of both the traditional Greek and Latin faiths that were expressed respectively by 'through' and 'from' but were substantially the same. Nevertheless, in the same breath as they agreed to unite with the Latins in respect of the Procession, the Greeks stipulated that they should not introduce the *Filioque* into their Creed nor change any of their customs (*A.G.*, pp. 432, 434)). Their idea was probably the same also as regards the primacy. They admitted the right of appeal and, apart from that, were set on making no other change in their traditional ways and customs, which were conveniently summarised as 'the privileges and rights of the patriarchs'.

The Latins may have had more precise ideas of what they meant by the phrase 'without prejudice to their privileges and rights'. In his speech to the Latin synod of 27 June 1439, Cardinal Cesarini referred to the Greek request 'that we should make some deliberation about the patriarchal Sees . . . as had been determined in the constitutions of the councils and, in the Lateran Council when Alexander [read: Innocent] III presided, he renewed the privileges of the patriarchal Sees'. It is noteworthy that the privileges are connected by Cesarini with the Council of the Lateran, and therefore it is not surprising that, when a few years later John of Torquemada wrote his commentary on the decree of union, he should have explained 'privileges' by reference to that council.

The patriarchs that the council of the Lateran had in view were Latin. The Patriarch of Constantinople was present in the council, having been appointed on the spot by the Pope who had quashed the elections of two other candidates come to vindicate their claims. The Patriarch of Jerusalem was also there in person and the Patriarch of Antioch by proxy. The Patriarch of Alexandria, though invited, did not come. In the eyes of Innocent III these Latins were the genuine holders of those ancient Sees and titles, in the line of succession from their Greek predecessors.

With reference to them, the relevant *capitulum* reads: 'Renewing the ancient privileges of the patriarchal Sees . . . we enact that after the Roman Church . . . the Constantinopolitan should hold the first place, the Alexandrine the second, the Antiochene the third, that of Jerusalem the fourth, to each its proper dignity being preserved; so that, after their prelates have received from the Roman Pontiff the pallium, which is the sign of the fulness of the pontifical office, and taken to him an oath of fidelity and obedience, they may lawfully bestow the pallium on their suffragans, receiving from them for themselves the canonical profession and for the Roman Church the promise of obedience. They may have the standard of the Lord's cross carried before them everywhere, except in the city of Rome and wherever the Supreme Pontiff or his legate with the insignia of his apostolic dignity is present. There shall be right of appeal to them in need in all the provinces subject to their jurisdiction, without prejudice to appeals made to the Holy See, which are always to have the preference'.[21]

The order of the patriarchs thus enumerated in the Council of the Lateran referred to the Latin patriarchs, understood as legitimate successors in the oriental Sees, and implicitly denied the legitimacy of any claims to possess those Sees made by Greeks. The repetition of the order, on the contrary, in the Council of Florence was a formal recognition of the Greek incumbents as legitimate patriarchs, even though there were Latins with the same titles and presumably the old pretensions. Nevertheless, it may be doubted whether the Fathers of Florence realised that they were doing anything more than merely repeating an old piece of legislation, and it can be taken as certain that they did not mean to make any change, although among the signatories of the definition of Florence there are to be read:' I, Blasio, Patriarch of Jerusalem signed', and 'I, Dorotheus, humble Metropolitan of Monembasia and procurator of the apostolic See of the most holy Patriarch of Jerusalem, my lord Joachim, agreed and signed'.

21 MANSI, 22, 989–992.

They clearly had not considered the implications when they repeated the *capitulum* of the Lateran Council.

Cesarini and the Latins probably had this same *capitulum* of the Lateran Council in mind when they included 'without prejudice to their privileges and rights' in the first draft of the decree of union. What else they thought of, especially when by chance the word 'all' was added and finally accepted by a reluctant Pope, there is no knowing, and the meaning they attached to the word 'rights' of the patriarchs mentioned in the decree (the Lateran spoke only of 'privileges') is equally mysterious. Torquemada in his commentary repeated the Lateran to explain 'privileges'. About 'rights' he wrote only ' "For let the Apostolic See so retain its own strength, that it does not lessen the rights it had granted others", says St. Gregory in c. *quanto* dist. lxiii; and in c. *de ecclesiasticis* xxv q. ii: 'Just as we defend our rights, so do we preserve to all the individual churches their rights" '.[22]

Torquemada might have referred also to the Profession of Faith made by Michael VIII Palaeologus in the Council of Lyons (1274) and repeated by him several times afterwards, for it contains a statement on patriarchal Churches. Cesarini certainly and the Latins were familiar with it, for they had drawn their *cedula* about Purgatory from it, and so probably had it in mind also when they debated about the relations between the Churches.

'Also the same Roman Church holds the supreme and full primacy and principality over the universal Catholic Church. . . . To which anyone can appeal who has suffered oppression in what belongs to the ecclesiastical forum and can have recourse to its judgement in all causes that regard ecclesiastical tribunals; and to the same all Churches are subject: to it their prelates give obedience and reverence. The fullness of power however, belongs to it in such a way that it admits to part of the care [of the Churches: cf. 2 Cor. xi, 28] the other Churches, many of which and especially the patriarchal ones the same Roman Church has honoured with diverse privileges, [The Greek translation has: 'in such a way that the same Roman Church has honoured with diverse privileges the other Churches, especially the patriarchal ones,'] on condition, however, that her venerated prerogative whether in general councils or in other matters be always inviolate.'[23]

[22] *Ioannes de Torquemada, O.P. Apparatus super decretum Florentinum Unionis Graecorum*, ed. E. CANDAL (Romae, 1942), p. 114.
[23] MANSI, 24, 72E–73A.

What Michael VIII accepted when he made his Profession of Faith Eugenius asserted even more clearly in the Bull, *Non mediocri dolore*, written to settle the question of precedence between cardinals and metropolitans. There he wrote: 'The Roman Church founded all patriarchal, archiepiscopal, episcopal and cathedral dignities and, as was lawful to it, it gave power generously to one, more generously to another and most generously to still another as it judged fit',[24] in the same way as branches spring from the trunk of a tree or streams of water from a source, some bigger, some smaller. For the Latin mind, therefore, the 'rights' of the patriarchs originated in a grant from Rome and depended for their continued existence and their degree on the will of the Pope. Eugenius agreed to retain those rights, whatever they were, but in any case of doubt it would naturally be the Holy See that would settle what those rights were and what was their extension.

[24] *Bullarum, diplomatum et privilegiorum sanctorum Romanorum Pontificum Taurinensis editio (Magnum Bullarium Romanum)* vol. V (Turin, 1860), p. 36. Cf. W. ULLMANN, *Eugenius IV, Cardinal Kemp, and Archbishop Chichele*, in *Medieval Studies Presented to Aubrey Gwynn, S.J.*, edd. J. A. WATT, J. B. MORRALL, F. X. MARTIN, O.S.A. (Dublin, 1961), pp. 349–58.

CHAPTER TWENTY-ONE

TWO PREJUDICES DISPELLED

It is a matter for wonder that the Council of Florence ever took place, for the papal policy ever since the Council of Lyons had been to refuse to hold a council with the Greeks, and it is a matter for even greater wonder that, when the council was held, the Latins never tried to impose the acceptance of their own rite on the Greeks as a condition of union, for at least since the time of Innocent III they had treated the Greek rite as inferior.

Whenever there had been a question of reunion, the Greeks had insisted on a general council as the necessary and only safe way. They held that the schism between the Churches originated in the Latin Church's acting arbitrarily and without consulting the rest; the cure could be only a common decision in a common council under the guidance of the Holy Spirit. For them, the Council of Lyons, summoned to unite the Churches, was no council at all: 'The Greeks present at Lyons had been delegated neither by the patriarchs who rule the Oriental Church nor by the people, but by the Emperor only,who, without trying to win their consent, wanted to effect union by force'.[1] But even the Emperor had not tried to achieve union without a council. When, in 1262, 1264 and 1267, he was offering the submission of himself and the Greek Church to the papacy as a means of averting the threat of invasion from Sicily, he had added that it should be effected through a general council. His error, or misfortune, lay in thinking that the Greek Church would co-operate in a council whose purpose was a pre-arranged union without previous discussion. Yet the council was held; Michael's delegates recited a profession of faith in his name and in that of his son, and a vague letter was read out purporting to come from the Greek Church. The Church, however, had rejected the project beforehand and it still refused to accept it when it was an accomplished fact, and no amount of pressure and persecution availed to make it change.

The Council of Lyons ranked for the Latin Church as an oecumenical council that had defined the Procession of the Holy

[1] Barlaam to Pope Benedict XII in 1339; *P.G.*, 151, 1333–4.

Spirit and united the Churches. It was a fact of history, that the Latins inevitably recalled whenever negotiations were restarted between East and West. It furnished them with a ready reply, that the Churches had been united and that all that was necessary for union was that the Greeks should implement what had already been arranged. That did not satisfy the Greeks who still pleaded for a general council that they could accept, as a necessary preliminary to union. The Greek from Calabria, Barlaam, who had come to Avignon as the messenger of the Emperor Andronicus in 1339, pressed for a council: 'That, most holy Father, is the only way in my opinion, by which union of the Churches can come about'.[2] The reply, courteous but firm, that he received was that it would be unseemly to debate truths already defined; if the Greeks had doubts about the Procession of the Holy Spirit, they could send a delegation of their learned men to the West for instruction, who on their return could enlighten the rest.

The proposal of a general council was put forward again some ten years later by the Emperor John Cantacuzenus, when his negotiations with Clement V for a crusade against the Turk inevitably brought up the question of union. If what the Emperor later wrote in the fourth book of his *Histories* is true in detail, Clement was not averse to a meeting at some town midway between Avignon and Constantinople. No council, however, took place, for the Pope was then involved in wars in Italy and died very shortly afterwards in 1352.[3] It should, however, be noted that at that precise period Constantinople was in the throes of the Palamite controversy and that, as with Cantacuzenus's protection Palamas emerged victorious, a wave of anti-Latinism swept over the Eastern Church. It was not the propitious moment for a common council, and it may be that the agreement to hold one was not quite as firm as Cantacuzenus thought in retrospect.

Less than twenty years later, there was again talk of a common council. It was the result of the short but successful crusade led by Amadeus of Savoy to check the Turkish threat to Constantinople, which also rescued the Greek Emperor John V from the Bulgars. Before the 'Green Knight' returned home, John V had promised to make his ecclesiastical submission in person to the Pope, and a synod, in the presence of the three oriental Patriarchs of Constantinople, Alexandria and Jerusalem, had met in Constantinople

[2] *P.G.*, 151, 1334C.   [3] *P.G.*, 154, 66–78.

to discuss union. The decision was not unfavourable, but the usual condition was included, that union should be effected by a general council with free discussion, which in Greek eyes made a triumph of the Eastern Church inevitable, since truth was on its side. On 6 November 1367, Pope Urban V welcomed such good will with twenty-three Bulls despatched to various eastern destinations, but not one of them said a word about a council. When, however, on 22 February 1370, he announced to the Greek world that John V had made a profession of Latin faith in Rome, he gave also the information that he had not permitted the convocation of a council, in order that settled doctrine 'may not be brought to the sifting of doubt and prying discussion, and that by useless debate we may not replace the old faith by a new'.[4]

The next Urban was the cause of the Latin Schism which precluded further projects for an East-West council. That Schism was ended by the Council of Constance, which deposed John XXIII, accepted the abdication of Gregory XII, deposed the unyielding Benedict XIII and elected Martin V. A small Greek delegation was present in Constance at Martin's election and witnessed his coronation. It gave him glowing accounts of Greek readiness for union and fired him to enthusiasm. He twice appointed a legate to lead a small Latin representation to Constantinople to give the Greeks the council they wanted and to receive their submission. Events made him less sanguine but hardly less keen. For the rest of his reign he used every opportunity to arrange a council in Italy, and at his death Eugenius IV and the Council of Basel vied with each other in promoting a council of union. The hesitation, indeed the refusal, that had characterised the popes of the previous century was completely gone. It had become no longer a question of whether there should be a common council, but of when and where it should be, with the Latins the chief instigators of the project, and a council such as the Greeks had always demanded, of full and free discussion on all the matters that divided the Churches. The result was the Council of Florence. If the Christians of the mid-thirteenth century had lived to see that day, they would have been lost in wonderment.

They would have marvelled no less in respect of the question of ecclesiastical rite. At the start of the Latin kingdom of Constantinople in 1204, Innocent III had made no secret of his disdain

[4] RAYNALDUS, ad annum 1370, III.

for the Greek rite. It is true that he did not have oriental sacraments repeated, but he wanted the oriental rite for the consecration of bishops and the ordination of priests supplemented by the anointings they lacked, thereby 'following not so much our rite as the divine command'.[5] and his sufferance of oriental Orders was by a 'kind of dissimulation'[6] He insisted that all future ordinations of priests and bishops, even of Greeks for Greeks, should be in the Latin rite and he would, no doubt, have liked to have seen the Greek rite completely superseded by the Latin. The Council of Lyons, however, left the Greek rite intact and did not impose even the recital of the *Filioque* in the Creed, though shortly afterwards Popes Innocent V and Nicholas III did impose it, in an endeavour to obtain from the East some concrete acknowledgement of the union of Lyons. That union was never achieved in practice, and so there is no means of knowing how the question of rites would have fared in a united Church of that time; probably not very well, if one may judge from indications offered by the action of later popes.

Urban V, for example, looked on the possession of Crete by the Venetians as an advantage because thereby 'ecclesiastical censures can more easily than is usual be put into execution by means of the secular arm', and he renewed for Crete Innocent III's directives that no Greek should be ordained except by a Latin or Greek Catholic bishop and added that those so ordained 'should celebrate Masses and other divine offices according to the rite that the aforesaid Roman Church observes'; any Greek monk or priest at all who declined to employ the Roman rite should no longer be allowed to hear confessions or to preach.[7] The same Pope granted to John V, after his profession of Catholic faith in Rome, the privilege of a portable altar, but it was to be used only by a Latin cleric and for services of the Latin rite. Urban's successor, Gregory XI, was even more strict. On 26 September 1374, he bade the Greek Maximus Lascaris Kalopheros, by then a convert of some nine years' standing and at that time Chancellor of the Patriarch of Constantinople and abbot of a Greek monastery, not only to profess the faith, but also to follow the rite, of the Roman Church.[8]

---

[5] *P.L.*, 215, 282.   [6] *P.L.*, 215, 1353.
[7] Bull dated 28 July, 1368; RAYNALDUS, ad annum 1368, XX.
[8] O. HALECKI, *Un Empereur de Byzance à Rome* (Warsaw, 1930), p. 294.

Then came the Schism of the West which, if it did much to modify Latin views on the legitimacy of a council with the Greeks, perhaps did little to make their rite more acceptable. Gregory Camblak, Archbishop of Kiev, had come to Constance with his Ruthenian priests in 1418 and advocated union of the Churches by means of a council. Reichental's comment, which probably reflected the view most prevalent among the Fathers at that time, seems to condemn the oriental rite. In his account he described their oriental Mass and ended: 'It was thought that a complete union would be brought about. But the council did not wish to allow that they should remain so all their lives'.

What the views were of Eugenius IV, who as Cardinal Condulmaro was present at Constance, cannot be said, but he is not likely to have been in advance of the times. A letter of his, as Pope, offers a hint but does not dissolve the doubt. Writing on 10 March 1435 to a certain Gregory, Archbishop of Moldo-Wallachia, the Pope reminded him that he had, as a convert from the Greek Church, 'expressly professed the rite of the Roman Church in all its articles' [of faith, for later the double Procession of the Holy Spirit is mentioned], and he encouraged him to win over and to receive with an absolution 'according to the form of the said Roman Church' as many orientals in Hungary as he could.[9] Rite in that context meant faith, but it possibly meant also rite in the narrower connotation, for the two were probably regarded as inseparable. There are plenty of examples of that loose use of the word 'rite' meaning primarily 'faith' and along with that also liturgical usage. Nevertheless the sense of 'faith' was uppermost, and as the Latins regarded the Greek faith as erroneous, so they looked on the rite as tainted also. There were several well-known converts to the Latin Church about that time. They all seem to have adopted the Latin rite, e.g. the three brothers Chrysoberges who became Dominicans. Maximus Chrysoloras had permission to use the Latin rite in a Greek translation and he was not the only one who was granted a like privilege.

The Council of Florence dealt with the question of rites, yet never mentioned the word. In the previous century, the popes had in practice made acceptance of the Latin rite synonymous with union. Florence distinguished between faith and liturgical rite, and effected union on the basis of identity of faith and diversity

---

[9] RAYNALDUS, ad annum 1435, XXVII.

of rites, without ever discussing the almost, for that time, revolutionary principle that it was sanctioning by its action. The statement about the Eucharist submitted by the Latins to the Greeks for their acceptance, which was later embodied in the final decree of union, granted the principle of equality of rite, when it declared that the sacrament was effectuated 'in leavened or unleavened bread' and that priests should employ the one or the other 'according to the custom of their Latin or Oriental Church'.

Isidore, Archbishop of Kiev and All Russia, and appointed Apostolic Legate to make the union a living reality among the orientals of northern Europe, in his message to them stressed that principle as the chief practical fruit of the union. The popes were faithful to it. Eugenius sent Andrew Chrysoberges from Rhodes to Cyprus to enquire into complaints that the Latins of the latter island were not honouring it and to insist that they should. Nicholas V, though he forbade Latins to adopt the Greek rite, did not deny the principle: 'For although the rites of the Oriental Church are praiseworthy, all the same it is not permitted to mix the rites of the Church, nor did the holy Council of Florence ever allow that',[10] and he authorised a Greek to retain his rite for marriage and burial, when, according to local custom, he had forfeited it for himself and his sons by marrying a Latin according to the Latin rite.[11] That silent revolution, effected at Florence, was admittedly no more than a return to the ancient discipline, but for that day it was surprising, and it has survived.

[10] *E.P.*, doc., 297.   [11] *E.P.*, doc., 303.

INDEX

Abrahamus Cretensis, 125–6, 142
Adimari, Cardinal, 95
Adrian, Pope, 269, 270
Agallianus, Theodore, 215, 218
Agatho, Pope, 269, 270, 271
Albergati, Nicholas, Cardinal, in Venice, 178, 197, 180, 237; president of Council, 185
Albert, King of Hungary, 73
Alberto de Crispis, 67
Alexander VIII, Pope, 129
Alexander V, anti-pope, 249
Alexius, King of Trebizond, 106, 108
Alfonso V of Aragon, I of Naples, 36, 42, 192, 197
Allatius, Leo, 79, 89, 128, 205, 212, 220–1
Aloysius of Perano, O.F.M., Bishop of Forlì, 6, 267
Altaemps, Duke of, 129
Amiroutzes, George, written *votum* for union 122, 161, 163, accepted axiom, 120, 256; wrote tractate? 204–12
Andrea da S. Croce, 27, 29, 30, 100, 243–4
Antoninus, St., 226, 227
Antonio da Massa, O.F.M., 233, 234–5
Antony, Metropolitan of Heraclea, 21, 115, 120, 159, 168
Aristotle, 79, 80, 105
Armenians, 40, 100
Arsenius, Metropolitan of Caesarea, 214, 220
Attendolo, Michele, 191
Augustine, St., 62, 271
Aurispa, Giovanni, 67
Avrami, Bishop of Susdal, 69, 72, **73**

Bajezid, Sultan, 3, 105
Bartholomew, Abbot, 195
Basel, Council of, 69, 97–9, 100; method of voting, 243; numbers present, 182; relations with Eugenius IV, 4, 35–7, 39, 40; relations with Greeks, 66–7, 181, 182; rival curial offices, 191
Beaupère, John, 97
Beccus, John, 215–8
Bedford, Duke of, 96
Bembo, Cardinal, 130
Benedict XIII, Pope, 289

U

Berardi, Giovanni, Bishop of Taranto, 195, 196
Bessarion, Metropolitan of Nicaea, Cardinal, 6, 8, 10, 13, 60, 66; 'Life', 45–54
—— spokesman of Greeks, 61, 69; accepts the axiom, 120, 256; active unionist, 62, 70, 100, 159, 162, 163, 274; on the addition, 204, 235; on the primacy, 266, 267–8, 273
—— *Oratio dogmatica*, 83, 91, 93, 256; relations with others, 21, 60, 72, 75, 76, 82
Boniface IX, Pope, 3, 250
Boucicaut, 3, 250
Boullotes, 33, 122
Branda da Castiglione, Cardinal, 95, 96
Busbecke, Augerius de, 127

Callistus III, Pope, 51, 76
Callistus, Metropolitan of Dristra, 159, 162
Camblak, Gregory, Archbishop of Kiev, 291
Cantareno, Giovanni, Latin Patriarch of Constantinople, 75
Caryyophilus, John Matthew, 79, 126, 127, 142, 210, 212
Casimir, King of Lithuania, 73, 75
Celestine, Pope, 211
Centurione, Prince of Achaia, 105
Cervini, Cardinal, 129
Cesarini, Giuliano, Cardinal, 4–7, 10, 17, 41, 179; 'Life', 95–103
—— relations with Eugenius IV, 42, 188; with Greeks, 60, 67, 274–5; speaker in Council, 17, 47, 50, 69, 136
Chalcedon, Council of, 280
Chalcocandylas, Laonicus, 227
Chaldeans of Cyprus united, 40
Charles VII, King of France, 181
Charles of Anjou, 254
Chrysoberges, Andrew, O.P., Archbishop of Rhodes, 6, 53, 149, 292; speaker in sessions, 47, 100
Chrysoloras, Manuel, 250, 291
Clement V, 288
Clement VIII, anti-pope, 3
Colocci, Angelo, 130
Colonna, Cardinal, 129
Comnene, Maria, 45, 106, 108

DATE